EXISTENTIALISM
From Dostoevsky to Sartre

WALTER KAUFMANN was Professor of Philosophy at Princeton University, where he taught after receiving his Ph.D. from Harvard in 1947 until his death in 1980. He held visiting appointments at many American and foreign universities, including Columbia, Cornell, Heidelberg, Jerusalem, and the Australian National University; and his books have been translated into Dutch, German, Italian, Japanese, and Spanish.

Kaufmann's *Religions in Four Dimensions: Existential and Aesthetic, Historical and Comparative* (1976) includes over 250 of his photographs, 185 of them in color. His *Existentialism, Religion, and Death* is a Meridian book.

EXISTENTIALISM
From Dostoevsky to Sartre

REVISED AND EXPANDED

EDITED, WITH AN INTRODUCTION,
PREFACES, AND NEW TRANSLATIONS

by

Walter Kaufmann

A MERIDIAN BOOK

To Felix

MERIDIAN
Published by the Penguin Group
Penguin Books USA Inc., 375 Hudson Street, New York, New York 10014, U.S.A.
Penguin Books Ltd, 27 Wrights Lane, London W8 5TZ, England
Penguin Books Australia Ltd, Ringwood, Victoria, Australia
Penguin Books Canada Ltd, 2801 John Street, Markham, Ontario, Canada L3R 1B4
Penguin Books (N.Z.) Ltd, 182-190 Wairau Road, Auckland 10, New Zealand

Penguin Books Ltd, Registered Offices: Harmondsworth, Middlesex, England

Published by Meridian, an imprint of New American Library, a division of Penguin
Books USA Inc.

 REGISTERED TRADEMARK—MARCA REGISTRADA

Permissions and Acknowledgments for Expanded Edition

KIERKEGAARD: "Dread and Freedom," reprinted from *The Concept of Dread*, by
Søren Kierkegaard, translated by Walter Lowrie. Copyright 1944, © 1957 by Princeton
University Press. Reprinted by permission of Princeton University Press.

"Authority," reprinted from *On Authority and Revelation: The Book on Adler, Or a
Cycle of Ethico-Religious Essays*, by Søren Kierkegaard, translated by Walter Lowrie.
Copyright 1955 by Princeton University Press. Reprinted by permission of Princeton
University Press.

"Truth is Subjectivity," reprinted by *Concluding Unscientific Postscript*, by Søren
Kierkegaard, translated by David F. Swenson and Walter Lowrie. Copyright 1941, ©
1969 by Princeton University Press. Reprinted by permission of Princeton University
Press and The American Scandinavian Foundation.

ORTEGA: "Man Has No Nature," reprinted from *History as a System And Other
Essays Toward a Philosophy of History*, by José Ortega y Gasset, translated by Helene
Weyl. Copyright 1941, © 1961 by W. W. Norton & Company, Inc. Reprinted by
permission of W. W. Norton & Company, Inc.

HEIDEGGER: "My Way to Phenomenology," reprinted from *On Time and Being*, by
Martin Heidegger, translated by Joan Stambaugh. Copyright © 1972 by Harper &
Row, Publishers, Inc. Reprinted by permission of Harper & Row Publishers, Inc.

"What is Metaphysics?" reprinted from *Existence and Being*, translated by R.F.C. Hull
and Alan Crick. First American edition published 1949 by Henry Regnery Company.
Reprinted by permission of Henry Regnery Company and Vision Press Limited.

SARTRE: "Marxism and Existentialism," reprinted from *Search for a Method*, by Jean-
Paul Sartre, translated by Hazel Barnes. Copyright © 1963 by Alfred A. Knopf, Inc.
Reprinted by permission of Alfred A. Knopf, Inc., and Methuen & Co. Ltd.

(The following page constitutes an extension of this copyright page.)

Library of Congress Cataloging-in-Publication Data

Existentialism : from Dostoevsky to Sartre / edited, with an
  introduction, prefaces, and new translations by Walter Kaufmann. —
  Rev. and expanded.
    p.   cm.
  ISBN 0-452-00930-8
  1. Existentialism. 2. Existentialism in literature.
I. Kaufmann, Walter Arnold.
B819.E87 1989
142′.78—dc19   88-39280
                                                                 CIP

First Printing/World Publishing Company, September, 1956
First Printing, Expanded Edition/New American Library, March, 1975

13 14 15 16 17 18 19 20 21

PRINTED IN THE UNITED STATES OF AMERICA

Contents

PREFACE TO THE EXPANDED EDITION   ix

PREFACE   x

ONE: KAUFMANN: Existentialism from
Dostoevsky to Sartre   11

TWO: DOSTOEVSKY: Notes from Underground   52

THREE: KIERKEGAARD: The First Existentialist   83

    1. *On His Mission*   85
    2. *On His Works*   87
    3. *On His Mode of Existence*   88
    4. *"That Individual"*   94
    5. *Dread and Freedom*   101
    6. *Authority*   105
    7. *"Truth is Subjectivity"*   121

FOUR: NIETZSCHE: "Live Dangerously"   121

    1. *"The Challenge of Every Great
    Philosophy"*   122
    2. *"The Gay Science"*   125
    3 *On Free Death*   128

4. *The Beginning of The Will to Power*   130
5. *From Ecce Homo*   132

FIVE: RILKE: The Notes of Malte Laurids
Brigge   134

SIX: KAKFA: Three Parables   142

1. *An Imperial Message*   144
2. *Before the Law*   145
3. *Couriers*   151

SEVEN: ORTEGA: "Man Has No Nature"   152

EIGHT: JASPERS: Existenzphilosophie   158

1. *On My Philosophy*   158
2. *Kierkegaard and Nietzsche*   185
3. *The Encompassing*   211

NINE: HEIDEGGER: The Quest for Being   233

1. *My Way to Phenomenology*   234
2. *What is Metaphysics?*   242
3. *The Way Back into the
Ground of Metaphysics*   265

TEN: SARTRE: Existentialism   280

1. *The Wall*   281
2. *Self-Deception*   299
3. *Portrait of the Antisemite*   329
4. *Existentialism is a Humanism*   345
5. *Marxism and Existentialism*   369

ELEVEN: CAMUS: The Myth of Sisyphus   375

NOTES   379
SOURCES AND ACKNOWLEDGMENTS   383

Preface to the Expanded Edition

All of the old selections are still here, and so is the introductory essay, except for some small revisions on page 42. But I have added many new selections. The only new author is *Ortega y Gasset*. This short chapter shows clearly how he stated some of Sartre's best-known ideas years before Sartre. His relation to Heidegger is discussed in the preface to the Ortega chapter.

The *Kierkegaard* chapter has been strengthened by the inclusion of three additional selections: "Dread and Freedom," "Authority," and "Truth is Subjectivity." The *Heidegger* chapter now contains two new essays, both complete: "My Way to Phenomenology," which is easier to read than anything else Heidegger has ever published and throws a great deal of light on him, and "What is Metaphysics?" which has long been acknowledged to be one of his most important publications.

Finally, the greatest event in the history of existentialism since the original edition of this book appeared was *Sartre's* embrace of Marxism, and a selection from his essay "Marxism and Existentialism," in which he defined his position, now concludes the Sartre chapter. In sum, there are seven new selections that should greatly add to the usefulness of this book.

W. K.

Preface

Some anthologies treat great literature and philosophy and as if they could be used to furnish a cultural supermarket where the reader shops around. Of course, it is the reader's right to browse, to skip, and not to read, whether a volume is by a single author or by ten. What matters is that a book should offer, when read straight through, more than the sum of the parts. The present volume is intended to tell a story, and the growing variations of some major themes, the echoes, and the contrasts ought to add not only to the enjoyment but also to the reader's understanding.

There are several new translations made especially for this book. Jaspers' essay "On My Philosophy" has been translated by Felix Kaufmann, and I myself have translated the material from Nietzsche, Rilke, and Heidegger.

I am deeply indebted to Princeton University for a year's leave of absence and to the Fulbright Commission for a research grant which enabled me, among other things, to listen to lectures by Jaspers and Heidegger and to talk with them and many of their colleagues and former students. To Heidegger I am also indebted for answering, orally and in writing, questions about his essay which is here offered in English for the first time.

My wife, Hazel Kaufmann, has given me invaluable aid and comfort.

W. K.

ONE

Kaufmann: Existentialism from Dostoevsky to Sartre

Existentialism is not a philosophy but a label for several widely different revolts against traditional philosophy. Most of the living "existentialists" have repudiated this label, and a bewildered outsider might well conclude that the only thing they have in common is a marked aversion for each other. To add to the confusion, many writers of the past have frequently been hailed as members of this movement, and it is extremely doubtful whether they would have appreciated the company to which they are consigned. In view of this, it might be argued that the label "existentialism" ought to be abandoned altogether.

Certainly, existentialism is not a school of thought nor reducible to any set of tenets. The three writers who appear invariably on every list of "existentialists"—Jaspers, Heidegger, and Sartre—are not in agreement on essentials. Such alleged precursors as Pascal and Kierkegaard differed from all three men by being dedicated Christians; and Pascal was a Catholic of sorts while Kierkegaard was a Protestant's Protestant. If, as is often done, Nietzsche and Dostoevsky are included in the fold, we must make room for an impassioned anti-Christian and an even more fanatical Greek-Orthodox Russian imperialist. By the time we consider adding Rilke, Kafka, and Camus, it becomes plain that one essential feature shared by all these men is their perfervid individualism.

The refusal to belong to any school of thought, the repudiation of the adequacy of any body of beliefs whatever, and especially of systems, and a marked dissatisfaction with traditional philosophy as superficial, academic, and remote from life—that is the heart of existentialism.

Existentialism is a timeless sensibility that can be discerned here and there in the past; but it is only in recent times that it has hardened into a sustained protest and preoccupation.

It may be best to begin with the story of existentialism before attempting further generalizations. An effort to tell this story with a positivist's penchant for particulars and a relentless effort to suppress one's individuality would only show that existentialism is completely uncongenial to the writer. This is not meant to be a defense of arbitrariness. A personal perspective may suggest one way of ordering diffuse materials, and be fruitful, if only by way of leading others to considered dissent.

I. DOSTOEVSKY

In some of the earliest philosophers, such as Pythagoras and Heraclitus and Empedocles, we sense a striking unity of life and thought; and after the generation of the Sophists, Socrates is said to have brought philosophy down to earth again. In the Socratic schools and in Stoicism a little later, philosophy is above all a way of life. Throughout the history of philosophy other, more or less similar, examples come to mind, most notably Spinoza. It is easy, and it was long fashionable, to overestimate the beautiful serenity of men like these, and it is well to recall the vitriolic barbs of Heraclitus, the inimitable sarcasm of Socrates, and the passions of Spinoza. Even so, it is an altogether new voice that we hear in Dostoevsky's *Notes from Underground*.

The pitch is new, the strained protest, the self-preoccupation. To note a lack of serenity would be ridiculous: poise does not even remain as a norm, not even as an element of contrast; it gives way to poses, masks—the drama of the mind that is sufficient to itself, yet conscious of its every weakness and determined to exploit it. What we perceive is an unheard-of song of songs on individuality: not classical, not Biblical, and not at all romantic. No, individuality is not retouched, idealized, or holy; it is wretched and revolting, and yet, for all its misery, the highest good.

The bias against science may remind us of romanticism;

but the *Notes from Underground* are deeply unromantic. Nothing could be further from that softening of the contours which distinguished all romantics from the first attack on classicism to Novalis, Keats, and Wordsworth. Romanticism is flight from the present, whether into the past, the future, or another world, dreams, or, most often, a vague fog. It is self-deception. Romanticism yearns for deliverance from the cross of the Here and Now: it is willing to face anything but the facts.

The atmosphere of Dostoevsky's *Notes* is not one of soft voices and dim lights: the voice could not be shriller, the light not more glaring. No prize, however great, can justify an ounce of self-deception or a small departure from the ugly facts. And yet this is not literary naturalism with its infatuation with material circumstances: it is man's inner life, his moods, anxieties, and his decisions, that are moved into the center until, as it were, no scenery at all remains. This book, published in 1864, is one of the most revolutionary and original works of world literature.

If we look for anything remotely similar in the long past of European literature, we do not find it in philosophy but, most nearly, in such Christian writers as Augustine and Pascal. Surely, the differences are far more striking even here than any similarity; but it is in Christianity, against the background of belief in original sin, that we first find this wallowing in man's depravity and this uncompromising concentration on the dark side of man's inner life.

In Rousseau's *Confessions*, too, his Calvinistic background has to be recalled; but he turned against it and denied original sin, affirmed the natural goodness of man, and blamed his depravity on society. Then he proceeded to explain how all depravity could be abolished in the good society, ruled by the general will. In Dostoevsky's *Notes from Underground* no good society can rid man of depravity: the book is among other things an inspired polemic against Rousseau and the whole tradition of social philosophy from Plato and Aristotle through Hobbes and Locke to Bentham, Hegel, and John Stuart Mill. The man whom Dostoevsky has created in this book holds out for what traditional Christianity has called depravity; but he believes neither in original sin nor in God, and for him man's self-will is not depravity: it is only perverse from the point of view of rationalists and others who value neat schemes above the rich texture of individuality.

Dostoevsky himself was a Christian, to be sure, and for that matter also a rabid anti-Semite, anti-Catholic, and anti-Western Russian nationalist. We have no right whatsoever to attribute to him the opinions of all of his most interesting characters. Unfortunately, most readers fail to distinguish between Dostoevsky's views and those of the Grand Inquisitor in Ivan's story in *The Brothers Karamazov*, though it is patent that this figure was inspired by the author's hatred of the Church of Rome; and many critics take for Dostoevsky's reasoned judgments the strange views of Kirilov, though he is mad. As a human being, Dostoevsky was as fascinating as any of his characters; but we must not ascribe to him, who after all believed in God, the outlook and ideas of his underground man.

I can see no reason for calling Dostoevsky an existentialist, but I do think that Part One of *Notes from Underground* is the best overture for existentialism ever written. With inimitable vigor and finesse the major themes are stated here that we can recognize when reading all the other so-called existentialists from Kierkegaard to Camus.

II. KIERKEGAARD

Kierkegaard was dead nine years when *Notes from Underground* was published first in 1864. He had not known of Dostoevsky, nor did Dostoevsky know of him. Nietzsche, on the other hand, read *Notes from Underground* in 1887 and was impressed as rarely in his life; and a year and a half later, toward the end of his career, he heard of Kierkegaard, too late to secure any of his books. Henceforth, the sequence of our major characters is clear. It is only at the beginning, faced with Kierkegaard and Dostoevsky, that we do better to reverse the strict chronology to start with Dostoevsky.

Kierkegaard confronts us as an individual while Dostoevsky offers us a world. Both are infinitely disturbing, but there is an overwhelming vastness about Dostoevsky and a strident narrowness about Kierkegaard. If one comes from Kierkegaard and plunges into Dostoevsky, one is lost like a man brought up in a small room who is suddenly placed in a sailboat in the middle of the ocean. Or you might even think that Dostoevsky had set out deliberately to make fun of Kierkegaard. Those, on the other hand, who listen to the *Notes from Underground* as to an overture, are well prepared when the curtain rises to hear Kierkegaard's account of how he first became a writer. Even his *Point of View for My Work as an Author* won't be altogether unfamiliar. It is as if Kierkegaard had stepped right out of Dostoevsky's pen.

The underground man pictures the ease of the "crystal palace" as a distant possibility and tells us that some individual would certainly rebel and try to wreck this utterly insufferable comfort. And Kierkegaard, not exiled to Siberia, as Dostoevsky was as a young man, but well-to-do in the clean, wholesome atmosphere of Copenhagen, sees how easy life is being made and resolves "to create difficulties everywhere."

If it is the besetting fault of Dostoevsky criticism that the views and arguments of some of his characters are ascribed, without justification, to the author, the characteristic flaw of the growing literature on Kierkegaard is that the author is forgotten altogether and his works are read impersonally as one might read those of Hegel. Nothing could be less in keeping with the author's own intentions. Hence it is well to begin a study of Kierkegaard with *The Point of View for My Work as an Author.*

How strange Kierkegaard is when he speaks of himself, and how similar to Dostoevsky's underground man—in contents, style, and sensibility! There is something novel about both which may be brought out by a brief contrast with Heinrich Heine. Heine's self-consciousness is almost proverbial and at one time embarrassed romantic readers; but the strain in Heine is due largely to the tension between reverie and reason. Kierkegaard's self-consciousness, like the underground man's, is far more embarrassing because it comes from his humiliating concern with the reactions and the judgments of the very public which he constantly professes to despise. That he was physically misshapen might have remained without effect on his style and thought; but, like the underground man, he was inwardly out of joint—so much so that Heine seems quite healthy by comparison. How fluent is Heine's prose, and how contorted Kierkegaard's! Their love of irony and even vitriol they shared; but Heine's world is relatively neat and clean-cut: even his melancholy seems pleasant compared to Kierkegaard's. They were contemporaries who died within a year, and yet Heine seems almost classical today, and Kierkegaard painfully modern.

Both concerned themselves with Hegel: Heine even knew him personally, while Kierkegaard, a little younger, heard only the diatribes of the old Schelling after Hegel's death. Heine came to part with Hegel because the philosopher was not liberal enough for him and too authoritarian. For Kierkegaard, Hegel was too rational and liberal. Heine cannot fairly be called a romantic because he steadfastly refused to give up the ideals of the Enlightenment and because he would not curb his piercing critical intelligence to spare a feeling. Kierkegaard escapes classification as a romantic because he, too, rejects the dim twilight of sentiment as well as any lovely synthesis of intellect and feeling, to insist on the absurdity of the beliefs which he accepts.

Dostoevsky is surely one of the giants of world literature; Kierkegaard, one of its greatest oddities: an occasionally brilliant but exasperating stylist, a frequently befuddled thinker, yet a writer who intrigues and fascinates by virtue of his individuality. His own suggestion for his epitaph is unsurpassable: "That Individual."

Kierkegaard not only *was* an individual but tried to introduce the individual into our thinking as a category. In the vast thicket of his unpruned prose it is not easy to discover his importance for philosophy. He was an aggressive thinker, and the main targets of his attacks are Hegel, of whom he lacked any thorough first-hand knowledge, and Christianity as it existed for approximately eighteen centuries, which seems at first glance to have no immediate bearing on philosophy. In fact, Kierkegaard was in revolt against the wisdom of the Greeks: it was the Greek heritage that he attacked both in philosophy and in Christianity.

Owing to the vast prestige of Greek philosophy, which in turn was influenced by a profound respect for mathematics, Western thought has made its calculations, as it were, without the individual. Where something of the sort is recognized at all today, it is customary to blame secularism and to preach a return either to the Middle Ages, as if the individual had been central then, or to Plato's belief in the eternal verities or values. Kierkegaard, however, was an anti-Plato no less than an anti-Hegel, and an anti-Thomas no less than an anti-Copernicus. He sweeps away the whole conception of a cosmos as a mere distraction. "And it came to pass after these things that God did tempt Abraham, and said unto him, Abraham: and he said, here I am. And he said, Take now thy son, thine only one, Isaac, whom thou lovest." This is for

Kierkegaard man's situation, *la condition humaine*, man's fate. The world has no part in it; it is no help. Here is man, and "one thing is needful": a decision.

Kierkegaard rejects belief in the eternal verities, as well as Plato's trust in reason as a kind of second sight. Ethics is for him not a matter of seeing the good but of making a decision. The crucial difference between an informed and un-informed, a reasoned and un-reasoned, a responsible and irresponsible decision, escapes Kierkegaard. Yet he is unquestionably right that reason cannot absolve us from the need for decisions, and he sees that Greeks and Christians and modern philosophy have tried to ignore this all-important fact. They have tried to escape the need for choices whether they sought refuge in attempts to contemplate what is eternal or in analysis of moral terms, whether they tried to prove their Weltanschauungen or tried to prove the superiority of Christianity or, perhaps, God's existence. Kierkegaard attacks the proud tradition of theology, ethics, and metaphysics as a kind of whistling in the dark, as self-deception, as an unrelenting effort to conceal crucial decisions that we have made and must make behind a web of wholly secondary, and at times invalid, demonstrations.

At least by implication, Kierkegaard contests the dualistic legacy of Plato and the popular conception of the soul or self as substance, comparable to the body. The self is essentially intangible and must be understood in terms of possibilities, dread, and decisions. When I behold my possibilities, I experience that dread which is "the dizziness of freedom," and my choice is made in fear and trembling.

These are motifs that remain central in all so-called existentialism: we recognize them in the non-denominational religiousness of Jaspers and in Sartre's atheism as well as in the mutually opposed theologies of Barth and Bultmann. Here lies Kierkegaard's importance for a vast segment of modern thought: he attacks received conceptions of Christianity, suggests a radical revision of the popular idea of the self, and focusses attention on decision.

He was a man in revolt, and even if one quite agrees that a revolt was called for, one may yet regret that he went much too far and that his followers have not seen fit to redress his excesses. Instead of offering a circumspect critique of reason, indicating what it can and cannot do, he tried a grand assault

Instead of questioning to what extent mathematics or the other sciences are valid models for philosophy, or ethics in particular, he had recourse to patently invalid arguments. Instead of asking whether Descartes' fine ideal that our reasoning should be clear and distinct, reinforced since by the tremendous progress of the sciences, might not eventually lead philosophers to concentrate on logic and trivialities to the neglect of large and certainly important areas, Kierkegaard rashly renounced clear and distinct thinking altogether.

Kierkegaard's central error is epitomized by his two epigrams: "The conclusions of passion are the only reliable ones" and "What our age lacks is not reflection but passion." This was not true in the 19th century, much less is it true today. Even those who share his violent distaste for desiccated writing should not find it difficult to see that his diagnosis is mistaken and that his prescription would be fatal. Reason alone, to be sure, cannot solve some of life's most central problems. Does it follow that passion *can,* or that reason ought to be abandoned altogether?

At this point Kierkegaard falls back into Plato's dichotomy of reason and belief, of mathematics and mere myth, as if, where mathematic certainty is unattainable, we must be satisfied with stories which cannot be questioned. (Plato's myths, of course, are beautiful—but never scrutinized or simply countered with a rival story which might make a different point with equal grace.) This spurious alternative—that where reason cannot offer certain knowledge it is altogether impotent—was made more fateful yet by its revaluation in Christianity. Plato had maintained on the whole that in the things that matter most reason is competent, while in Christianity the position gained adherents that those questions which our reason can decide are *eo ipso* not of ultimate importance while the most crucial statements must be above rational scrutiny. St. Thomas was one of those who opposed this position, but rational scrutiny was allowed by him—insofar as it was allowed at all—only against the background of the stake for heretics which he specifically affirmed. Kierkegaard, of course, was far closer to Luther: anti-philosophical and individualistic. A little more subtly, to be sure, he echoes Luther's famous dicta: "Whoever wants to be a Christian should tear the eyes out of his reason" and "You must part with reason and not know anything of it and even kill it; else one will not get into the kingdom of heaven" and "reason is a whore."

III. NIETZSCHE

Read superficially, as he usually has been read, Nietzsche may appear to be in the same tradition; but he is not. It is for this reason above all that his "attempt at a critique of Christianity" (that is the subtitle of Nietzsche's *Antichrist*) must neither be ignored, whether to shield the author or Christianity, nor dismissed as a barbarian protest against sympathy and virtue. To be sure, Nietzsche was, no less than Kierkegaard, an apostle of passion and a critic of hypocrisy, but he did not extol passion at the expense of reason, and he repudiated Christianity not because he considered it too rational but because he considered it the archenemy of reason; and his caustic critique of faith, both in the *Antichrist* and elsewhere, reads like a considered censure of Kierkegaard among others.

It is the differences between Nietzsche and Kierkegaard that strike us first; and in an over-all accounting, the differences would surely far outweigh the similarities which Karl Jaspers has catalogued so carefully. (See his lecture on the two men, below.) Jaspers assimilates Nietzsche to Kierkegaard and loses hold of that which mattered most to Nietzsche.

Before Nietzsche published *Zarathustra,* he wrote in *The Gay Science:* "What is good-heartedness, refinement, and genius to me, when the human being who has these virtues tolerates slack feelings in his faith and judgments . . . Among certain pious ones, I found a hatred of reason and appreciated it: at least they thus betrayed their bad intellectual conscience." In his *Zarathustra,* Nietzsche says: "Weariness that wants to reach the ultimate with one leap, with one fatal leap, a poor ignorant weariness that does not want to want any more: this created all gods and afterworlds. Believe me, my brothers: it was the body that despaired of the body . . ." And in his *Antichrist,* five years later, in his long critique of faith he writes: " 'Faith' means not *wanting* to know what is true." Every one of these barbs, which could be multiplied almost at will by anyone who knows his Nietzsche, is as applicable to Kierkegaard as to those Nietzsche had in mind when he wrote; perhaps even more so, seeing how persistently the Dane deceived himself. After all, Kierkegaard himself insisted that it was "the secret writing in my inmost parts which explains everything"; and when we read his books in these terms, his conception of three stages and the "teleological suspension of the ethical" are seen to be, in part, the desperate attempts of a misshapen man who was, as he reveals in other contexts, completely dominated by the figure of his father, to convince himself as well as a woman that the strange way in which he had broken his engagement with her had nothing at all to do with all-too-human motives. It would be absurd to claim that such a psychological analysis does justice to his work. Of course, it does not. The only reason for as much as mentioning these matters is that the desire not to know the truth was an important element in Kierkegaard's faith.

Sigmund Freud could not have said of Kierkegaard what, according to Ernest Jones, he often said of Nietzsche: "that he had a more penetrating knowledge of himself than any other man who ever lived or was ever likely to live."

Was Nietzsche an "existentialist"? When he first received attention, different facets of his thought were noted, and it was only in a defeated Germany after the first World War that Kierkegaard, who had made much of the "existential," became popular and Nietzsche was seen in a new light. Judged by our initial criteria, Nietzsche might well be called an existentialist. The refusal to belong to any school of thought, the repudiation of the adequacy of any body of beliefs whatever, opposition to philosophic systems, and a marked dissatisfaction with traditional philosophy as superficial, academic, and remote from life—all this is eminently characteristic of Nietzsche no less than of Kierkegaard, Jaspers, or Heidegger. Nor could it be argued that this conception of existentialism is generous to the point of being altogether amorphous and meaningless. Clearly, it excludes such relatively more traditional philosophers as, for example, Whitehead or even Russell, let alone the neo-Thomists; and although positivism and the analytic movement are also in revolt against traditional philosophy, the above description does not fit them.

Still, it is possible to be a little more specific about existentialism. There is yet another feature which all but determines the popular image of this movement. Consider the titles of three of Kierkegaard's major works: *Fear and Trembling, The Concept of Dread,* and *The Sickness unto Death* (which is despair). Death and dread are central in Heidegger's thought, too; death and failure are crucial in Jaspers';

and all of these phenomena are prominent in Sartre's work as well. It is entirely proper to consider the writings of these four men as the hard core of existentialism: Kierkegaard introduced the "existential"; Jaspers entitled one of his main works *Existenzerhellung* and another, smaller volume *Existenzphilosophie;* Heidegger's *Sein und Zeit* is widely taken for the *magnum opus* of this movement; and Sartre is the only major writer who admits he is an existentialist.

If we consider this striking preoccupation with failure, dread, and death one of the essential characteristics of existentialism, Nietzsche can no longer be included in this movement. The theme of suffering recurs often in his work, and he, too, concentrates attention on aspects of life which were often ignored in the nineteenth century; but he makes much less of dread and death than of man's cruelty, resentment, and hypocrisy—of the immorality that struts around masked as morality. It is not the sombre and depressed moods that he stresses most but quite another state of mind which appears even much less often in the literature of the past: a "Dionysian" joy and exultation that says Yes to life not in a mood of dogged resolution, which is prominent in later German existentialism, but with love and laughter.

If we broaden our definition of existentialism to include preoccupation with extreme states of mind generally, it fits Nietzsche, too, as well as Rilke, the Dionysian poet. Nevertheless, the difference between Nietzsche's *amor fati* and the German existentialists is quite considerable, though in many ways French existentialism is much closer to him. Nietzsche's wit, his praise of laughter, and his sparkling prose, now limpid, now like granite, could scarcely be more unlike the vast and solemn tomes of Jaspers or the twilight style of Heidegger. Nor does Kierkegaard with his more epic and self-conscious humor, writing—in the words of an admirer —"almost with tongue in cheek," equal the devastating and incisive style of Nietzsche.

In the story of existentialism, Nietzsche occupies a central place: Jaspers, Heidegger, and Sartre are unthinkable without him, and the conclusion of Camus' *The Myth of Sisyphus* sounds like a distant echo of Nietzsche. Camus has also written at length about Nietzsche; Nietzsche is the first name mentioned in Sartre's philosophic main work, *L'être et le néant;* Jaspers has written two whole books about him and discussed him in detail in several others; and Heidegger, in his later works, considers Nietzsche even more important than Jaspers ever did. As we shall see, however, Heidegger's and Jaspers' Nietzsche pictures tell at least as much about the German existentialists as about Nietzsche.

Existentialism suggests only a single facet of Nietzsche's multifarious influence, and to call him an existentialist means in all likelihood an insufficient appreciation of his full significance. To be sure, his name is linked legitimately with the names of Jaspers, Heidegger, and Sartre; but it is linked no less legitimately with the names of Nicolai Hartmann and Max Scheler, and with Spengler, and with Freud and Adler, and with Thomas Mann and Hermann Hesse, with Stefan George no less than with Rilke, and with Shaw and Gide as well as with Malraux. Almost every one of these writers saw something different in him.

Existentialism without Nietzsche would be almost like Thomism without Aristotle; but to call Nietzsche an existentialist is a little like calling Aristotle a Thomist.

IV. JASPERS

It is in the work of Jaspers that the seeds sown by Kierkegaard and Nietzsche first grew into existentialism or, as he prefers to say, *Existenzphilosophie*. One reason for his opposition to the label "existentialism" is that it suggests a school of thought, a doctrine among others, a particular position. Even of the term *Existenzphilosophie* he once said after using it: "The name is misleading insofar as it seems to restrict. Philosophy can never wish to be less than primordial, eternal philosophy itself." *Existenzphilosophie* is meant to be a protest against the betrayal of this primordial and eternal philosophy by the professors who teach philosophy at our modern universities.

Nietzsche was occasionally much more caustic than Jaspers about modern scholars; Kierkegaard was even more preoccupied with this theme and more vitriolic; and neither of them as much as approximated Schopenhauer's furor. In all three cases, however, this opposition was merely incidental to a specific positive purpose. Schopenhauer resented his own failure as a *Privatdozent* and the success of Fichte, Schelling, and particularly Hegel; and his positive intent was to obtain a hearing for his own philosophy which was developed in *The World as Will and Idea*. Kierkegaard's central purpose was to persuade modern men that the one thing needful was

to become a Christian, and he considered philosophy a dangerous distraction and believed that the professors taught a false
conception of Christianity. Nietzsche, too, had, Jaspers notwithstanding, a wealth of positive ideas, and his main
objection to the university professors was that, being state
employees, they were prone to shirk uncomfortable insights.
Philosophers in particular were, Nietzsche claimed, too often
motivated by the wish to justify the moral prejudices of
society. This fault, he felt, was not confined to university
professors but came close to being the original sin of philosophy; and his great revolt was aimed not at professors but
at Christianity and Platonism.

To Jaspers the differences between Kierkegaard and Nietzsche seem much less important than that which they have in
common. What mattered most to them, does not matter to
Jaspers: he dismisses Kierkegaard's "forced Christianity" no
less than Nietzsche's "forced anti-Christianity" as relatively
unimportant; he discounts Nietzsche's ideas as absurdities,
and he does not heed Kierkegaard's central opposition to
philosophy. All the many philosophers since Hegel and
Schelling, however, fare far worse: they are at best instructive
but lack human substance: "The *original philosophers* of the
age are *Kierkegaard* and *Nietzsche*." The crucial fact for
Jaspers is that their thinking was not academically inspired
but rooted in their *Existenz*.

For Jaspers any content is secondary, and in his essay "On
My Philosophy" he san say: "As the realization overcame me
that, at the time, there was no true philosophy at the universities, I thought that facing such a vacuum even he, who
was too weak to create his own philosophy, had the right to
hold forth about philosophy, to declare what it once was and
what it could be." His own philosophy came only later. The
initial impulse of Jaspers' *Existenzphilosophie* was not a
doctrine but a dissatisfaction with mere doctrines and the
conviction that genuine philosophizing must well up from a
man's individual existence and address itself to other individuals to help them to achieve true existence.

The negative aspect of this effort is at first glance clearer
than the positive development. For that matter, the negative
part alone would be sufficient to insure the author a considerable following outside the universities, and even among university professors outside the philosophy departments. In the
nineteen-fifties, as book after book from Jaspers' pen ap-

peared and found its audience—*Von der Wahrheit* (1947), with 1100 pages, came out in a first edition of 5000 copies— scarcely any seminar or course of lectures at a German university, not to speak of other countries, dealt with Jaspers. At the very same time, lectures and seminars on Nietzsche were almost as common as courses on Kant and the Greeks, and Heidegger was discussed everywhere. In part, to be sure, this was due to the large number of professorships held by Heidegger's former pupils. It was also due to the character of Jaspers' philosophy.

Traditional philosophers from Plato to Nietzsche offered a wealth of ideas and suggestions, theories and doctrines, constructions and analyses which can be expounded by a lecturer or studied and interpreted. Since the death of Hegel, this kind of exposition has come more and more to dominate most courses in philosophy. Consider an outstanding exponent of this approach: Kuno Fischer who taught philosophy at Heidelberg a generation before Jaspers started teaching there. His ten-volume history of modern philosophy is still famous, and the two volumes on Hegel, whom Fischer greatly admired, are no worse than the rest. Fischer paraphrases difficult texts, and when they become too difficult he quotes. Does he understand what he paraphrases? Sometimes. Does he force the reader to think, to share in a common enterprise with Hegel? Does he make us feel like exclaiming, as Hegel did at times, "Oh God! Why did you curse me to be a philosopher?" Certainly not. This is how Jaspers himself makes this point: "Kuno Fischer is outstanding both by virtue of his rational and clear reproductions, which remain useful, and by virtue of his utter innocence of philosophy itself which simply cannot be reproduced in this way." In the case of Plato most readers should see this immediately: any mere summary would be a travesty of Plato who wants above all to make his readers think, to make them thoughtful, to stir them up. Indeed, Plato might well have said, as Jesus did: "I am come to kindle a fire on the earth; and what would I rather than that it burnt already."

It was neither Hegel nor Plato who first brought this home to Jaspers, but Kierkegaard. *"Beim Referieren Kierkegaards merkte ich, dass er nicht referierbar ist."* What is *referieren*? One of the favorite pastimes of German professors and students: the word is hard to translate but means making a report on an author by way of offering a condensed paraphrase, a summary, an outline of his argument. Trying to do this with Kierkegaard, Jaspers discovered that it was impossible. Most American writers on Kierkegaard still have this discovery ahead of them.

Jaspers chose Kierkegaard as a model, but without accepting those of his ideas which are easily repeatable. He decided to become *unreferierbar*, too, or—to put it differently—he made up his mind to concentrate his efforts on a sustained attempt, indeed an epic effort, to kindle a fire.

Of his three-volume *Philosophie* which is, of all his many books, the one which he himself likes best, he says: any reader who is looking for a doctrine in it is bound to be disappointed; and a reader who wants to remain passive and inert inside is bound to feel empty and let down. "These readers must say that I really say nothing. What does not happen in their case is what I have called the beating of the other wing which is necessary if that which is said in the text (as the beating of one wing) is to achieve the fulfillment of its meaning and soar up."

Any content is a mere means to transcend all contents. No statement has been understood until it is seen to be an invitation to be dissatisfied with all statements. "Philosophy" is given up in favor of "philosophizing." "The only significant content of philosophizing, however, consists in the impulses, the inner constitution, the way of seeing and judging, the readiness to react by making choices, the immersion in historical presentness, which grow in us, recognize themselves, and feel confirmed on the way past all objective contents."

Being much more modest than Kierkegaard, Jaspers is not in the habit of comparing himself with Socrates; but at this point a comparison is called for. It may seem unfair in principle: worse than comparing a modern sculptor with Michelangelo, for Socrates was not only a philosopher's philosopher, but if ever there was a great human being, it was he. The contrast is meant only to crystallize three problems raised by Jaspers' effort.

First, Socrates stirred up the youth of Athens simply by being himself. It was, more than anything he said, his character and life that made them feel dissatisfied with their existence and the doctrines others offered. He was an incarnate challenge to their way of life and thinking, an exemplary personality, the embodiment of a new ethic.

Insofar as he engaged in philosophy he did not teach or

preach but relied on dialogue. The content was furnished by his partners who began by thinking they had knowledge, and his own function was mainly critical. He liberated others from confusions and a blind trust in untenable beliefs, and incidentally taught them a method.

Finally, Socrates never wrote a book. He relied exclusively on close personal contact in which dialogue and character could do their work together. Kierkegaard who, in a few years' time, wrote far more books, many pseudonymous, than most serious thinkers ever write, called himself a master of "indirect communication." There is an important sense in which Socrates was the master of *direct* communication *par excellence.*

Jaspers, on the other hand, entrusts his comparable effort to more than twenty books of which more than a dozen have appeared in the first ten years after World War II; and there are tomes of eleven hundred, nine hundred, and seven hundred pages, two of almost five hundred, and another three of approximately 350 pages. There is no volume of stories or plays, of memoirs or dialogues among them. The manner is quite unlike either Kierkegaard or Socrates: it is a huge monologue; as it were, a series of lectures. And Jaspers' trust in this form of communication continues unabated: his eleven-hundred page book came out as volume one, and before completing volume two he hopes to finish another almost equally ambitious project.

In view of this, the question of contents arises much more urgently than in the case of Socrates, or even Kierkegaard who kept experimenting with a wide variety of literary styles. What is the content of these many books, albeit a content which is not what ultimately matters to the author? Much of the time, Jaspers *referiert:* he reports what others have said, alternating between paraphrases and direct quotations. Then he passes judgment, by way of trying to induce dissatisfaction with the knowledge and the statements and the contents offered us.

After his report on the interpretation of dreams, for example, in the fourth, completely revised, edition of his *Allgemeine Psychopathologie,* Jaspers concludes: "All in all, it seems to me that in the principles of dream interpretation something right has been hit. My objection is less to the rightness (although the phantasies and frivolities in this area have been endless) than to the importance. After one has become acquainted with the principles and a few cases, one learns hardly anything further. It is a wonderful phenomenon, the dream, but after one's first enthusiasm for its investigation one must soon confess in disappointment: its yield for the knowledge of psychic life remains small after all." A psychoanalyst may feel that this is a little like saying: "Columbus discovered America; so what? In the last analysis his contribution to our knowledge of the universe was small." Piqued, he might even ask about the importance of Jaspers' bulky *Psychopathologie*. If this last question, however, were asked not in a spirit of sarcasm but with a genuine perplexity about the value of all such endeavors, Jaspers would not only admit that "its yield for the knowledge of psychic life remains small after all"; he would even say that this is one of his central points.

Later in the same book, another report on Freud concludes somewhat abruptly: "Especially the writings of some of his pupils are, owing to this simplicity, intolerably boring. One always knows in advance that in every work the same is said." Again, Freud's pupils might reply that few judgments could be more applicable to Jaspers himself. The same material is treated over and over again: three of his books contain a chapter with a relatively popular exposition of "the Encompassing"; the same judgments concerning Kant and Kierkegaard and all the great philosophers are repeated in book after book, while his main work on the great philosophers has not yet been completed; and for almost every point, view, or opinion one can choose a formulation from approximately half a dozen places in his writings, if not more, and sometimes the same formulations are repeated. More important by far, the central point is everywhere the same, with the insistence of Ecclesiastes who, however, confined himself to less than a dozen pages.

What seems endless repetition from the outside can be viewed from inside as relentless effort, as a tireless attempt to break down modern man's superstitious overconfidence in science or, no less, theology or, for that matter, also philosophers who pretend to furnish knowledge. In one of the rare passages in which he mentions Heidegger by name, Jaspers says, late in his *Psychopathologie*, referring to Heidegger's main work, *Sein und Zeit:* "Notwithstanding the value of his concrete exposition, I consider this attempt, in principle, the wrong way for *philosophy*. For it leads those who follow it not to philosophizing but to the knowledge of a total conception of man's being. This structure of thought does not become an aid for the historically concrete existence of the individual (by way of enhancing and confirming the reliable practice of his life) but becomes instead another veil which is the more fatal because it is precisely with sentences that come closest to Existence that real Existence is apt to be missed and to become unserious."

Heidegger's concern with man's concrete existence is congenial to Jaspers, but Heidegger's attempt in *Sein und Zeit* to offer knowledge seems doubly regrettable to Jaspers. As for Heidegger's later writings, Jaspers has long stopped as much as reading them. Heidegger, in turn, considers Jaspers' "philosophizing" and ceaseless "transcending" as an abdication before that which matters most; and he no longer reads the books of Jaspers. At one time, however, Heidegger sought Jaspers' company and they talked philosophy for days at a time; and some of Jaspers' admirers even believe that it was his three-volume *Philosophie* that induced Heidegger to give up the project of publishing the promised second half of *Sein und Zeit*. The approach of Heidegger's later works, however, with their open animus against logic and science, and their search, as Jaspers sees it, for an esoteric gnosis is even more distasteful to Jaspers than an overconfidence in scientific knowledge.

Jaspers' attitude, and indeed that of the other existentialists, too, toward one science in particular deserves special attention: psychology. It was with some justice that Nietzsche asked in the last chapter of his *Ecce Homo:* "Who among philosophers before me has been a psychologist?" And as we read the *Notes from Underground*, we might well ask: what novelist before Dostoevsky deserves to be called a psychologist? And confronted with Kierkegaard's treatment of original sin in *The Concept of Dread*, we ask again: what theologian before Kierkegaard was a psychologist? And might not Jaspers ask: who among philosophers before me has been a psychiatrist and a doctor of medicine? And Heidegger might well ask: who among philosophers before me has found it necessary to insist again and again that what he offered in his major work was *not* psychology. Sartre, finally, entitles an important chapter of his central philosophic work "Existential Psychoanalysis." Yet this is only half the story.

Nietzsche developed detailed psychologic theories which

were meant to be based, as far as possible, on solid evidence. What he wished to offer was science, and he frequently lamented the paucity of observations in this area, the lack of adequate physiological foundations, and the need for planned research. Living as a recluse, he had to base his ideas on self-observation and a few acquaintances and on his reading; but he did not make a virtue of necessity. In *Ecce Homo* he remarked, "my genius lies in my nostrils"; but he did not think that his nose was a broad enough base for the future of psychology.

In Germany Nietzsche's psychology has been neglected, on the whole, together with his interest in science. The only German book on *Nietzsches psychologische Errungenschaften* is by Klages, the characterologist whose militant irrationalism was repudiated even by the Nazis. In general one pretended that Nietzsche had gone through a "positivistic" phase before he returned to his true self by writing *Zarathustra*, and his psychology was relegated to this "middle period" by a consent of the ignorant, as it were. In fact, Nietzsche's impassioned psychologic interest reaches its climax precisely in his later work. What matters in the present context is that Jaspers and Heidegger, who have written a great deal about him, are not aware of this and that, decidedly, they do not follow Nietzsche's example. Rather they go back to Kierkegaard.

In Kierkegaard, too, we find a number of psychological insights, though their quantity has often been exaggerated, and they go hand in hand, as already remarked, with self-deception and, still more important, a profound resentment against science. It is interesting that his conception of the "existential" is developed above all in the *Concluding Unscientific Postscript*.

This bias against science is less interesting in Kierkegaard whose central problem was, as he himself said, "to become a Christian" than in German existentialism. It is very outspoken in Heidegger, much more subtle in Jaspers. There are many passages in Jaspers' writings where he strongly recommends a thorough study of at least one science; but his motivation is the very opposite of Nietzsche's who might well have said that a good background in psychology is indispensable for worthwhile work in ethics or aesthetics or some other branches of philosophy. What Jaspers wants us to discover is the limits of all science: only then shall we be ready for *Existenzphilosophie*.

Like many another German philosopher and above all

Heidegger, Jaspers almost seems to feel that "psychology" is a bad word: just as the reputation of a German thinker demands that the French do not understand him—witness what Gounod has done with Goethe's *Faust,* and Sartre with German philosophy—it would apparently impair his profundity if what he did were mere psychology. (Nietzsche was an exception in both respects and insisted that the French understood him much better than the Germans.) Looking back on his relatively early *Psychologie der Weltanschauungen,* Jaspers criticizes it, not in Nietzsche's spirit for being as yet insufficiently scientific—on the contrary: "It was hidden philosophy that here misunderstood itself as an objectively descriptive psychology." To be sure, his work had not been descriptive only but hortatory, too: his descriptions had been strongly colored by his valuations, and no sensitive reader could miss the author's earnest appeal that we repudiate some attitudes and model ourselves on others. What is so striking is that Jaspers is inclined to discount his often interesting analyses as really sub-philosophic, while he evidently sets store by his hortations or, as he himself prefers to say, his *Existenzerhellung* and *Apellieren:* the attempt to illuminate the reader about his condition (in the sense of *condition humaine*) and to appeal to him to face it with as much nobility as he can muster.

Something of the sort may also be found in Spinoza's *Ethics* or in Nietzsche, or in Socrates or Kant. Indeed, all the great philosophers said also, among other things, to use the words of Rilke: "You must change your life." Two things, however, set Jaspers apart from all the great philosophers from Socrates to Nietzsche.

First, the accent is reversed: they were chiefly preoccupied with highly theoretical analyses, and they set store by their success in these; and it was only indirectly that they challenged us to change our life. Second, the chief respect in which they challenged us to change was to become more analytical, reflective, critical—and few would have hesitated to say "rational."

Jaspers is far from being anti-rational; under no circumstances would he have us defy reason; but unlike the great philosophers of the past he insists that the rational sphere is subphilosophic and that philosophy begins only where reason fails us or, in Jaspers' phrase, has suffered shipwreck.

In one of the most fascinating books ever written by one philosopher about another, Jaspers adduces hundreds of quotations from Nietzsche, without distinguishing between what is early and what is late, between what Nietzsche himself published and what his sister fished out of his wastebasket; and Jaspers is never content until he has "*also* found the contradiction." With this amazing and assuredly unscientific method which defies the canons of philology and history, all of Nietzsche's definite ideas, theories, and arguments are easily dissolved and he is finally reduced to Jaspers' conception of him: "endless reflection, sounding out and questioning everything, digging without reaching a new foundation, except in new absurdities." In another passage, in another book, Jaspers also dismisses Nietzsche's conclusions wholesale as "a pile of absurdities and vacuities." The fact is, of course, that these conclusions are never presented or experienced as conclusions of an argument, of a development, of a concrete human being, but as so many quotations on file cards, which can be shuffled and juxtaposed at will.

If he considers Nietzsche's conclusions absurd and empty, why has Jaspers written two books about Nietzsche and referred to him at length in other books? Because the effect achieved by Jaspers' method is, as Jaspers sees it, quite invaluable: "Out of every position one may have adopted, i.e. out of every finitude, we are expelled; we are set *whirling*." Reason suffers shipwreck and is thus prepared for true philosophizing.

Jaspers' characterization of "all true philosophizing" is eminently applicable to the effect at which he aimed in his big book on *Nietzsche:* "It loosens us from the fetters of determinate thinking, not by abandoning such thinking but by pushing it to its limits. . . . The plunge from the rigidities which were deceptive after all turns into the ability to stay in suspense; what seemed abyss becomes the space of freedom: the seeming Nothing turns into that from which true Being speaks to us."

With its complete disregard for the dates of his myriad quotations or their context, with its studied failure to pay heed to the development of Nietzsche's thought either over the years or even in specific arguments, Jaspers' book, however stimulating and deeply disturbing, makes its subtitle a mockery: "Introduction to the Understanding of His Philosophizing." A far fairer estimate is found toward the end of Jaspers' essay on his own philosophy (included in this volume) where he says: "My *Nietzsche* was to be an introduction to that shaking up of thought from which *Existenzphilosophie* must spring."

Jaspers is surely far closer to Kierkegaard than to Nietzsche. In Jaspers' *Existenzphilosophie*, Kierkegaard's revolt against Hegelianism reaches its philosophic climax: Jaspers must be understood less as the heir of Nietzsche than as the antipode of Kuno Fischer.

The protest against Hegel's avowed aim "to raise philosophy to the level of a science" leads to a philosophizing which is personal to the point of repudiating all content in favor of an appeal to man's "inner constitution." The opposition to the Hegelian professors for whom philosophy was system and history of philosophy, and in both aspects a species of objective knowledge, leads to the tireless insistence that philosophic "truth is subjectivity," to cite the fateful paradox of Kierkegaard. The Hegelian principle that any judgment must be mediated and developed is abandoned, and judgments are offered abruptly and apparently dogmatically, but labelled as subjective: conviction and conscience are reinstated in their immediacy. "Communication" is made central as in Kierkegaard, but Jaspers' books, possibly even more than Kierkegaard's, have the appearance of a vast monologue or, to point up what is common to both men, a sermon. Jaspers says "communication" but means hortation, homily, appeal.

Of any real openness for another point of view, let alone a Hegelian immersion in it, there is scarcely a trace in Jaspers' work: whether he construes Nietzsche or censures Schelling, devoting a whole book to each, or attacks Bultmann, the existentialist theologian (the controversy has been published in another book), he always operates from a fixed base of moral integrity and passes sentence, moral sentence. In his revolt against the objectivity of Hegel's internal criticism, Jaspers offers strictures which remain completely external to the positions judged. Not satisfied with such external philosophic criticism (if that is not, in fact, a contradiction in terms), Jaspers usually begins or ends with an examination of his adversary's character: Nietzsche allegedly lacked a capacity for friendship; Schelling lacked a noble soul, and Jaspers doubts the substance of his first marriage; and the critique of Bultmann ends with a critical profile of "Bultmann's spiritual personality."

Jaspers says that truth begins *zu zweien*, in a situation where there are two human beings; he insists that I must con-

stantly doubt my own position; he speaks of a "loving fight";
and he writes and lectures about "the philosophic practice of
life." It may be urged as an *internal* criticism that in his practice we find little of all this: he does not consider other
points of view on the same level with his own; he does not
risk his position by exposing it to the perspective of another.
We do not witness a loving fight but the proceedings in a
court of law.

Like most skeptics, but unlike Nietzsche, Jaspers brings his
omnivorous doubt to a stop before the fortress of his moral
principles. It may be because he feels that Nietzsche's philosophizing was in fact quite different from his own that Jaspers
in his seventies has come to the conclusion that Kierkegaard
was really far greater than Nietzsche. Surely, Kierkegaard
envisaged his own mission as completely hortatory, called attention to the supra-rational, and urged us to soar above reason.

V. HEIDEGGER

Martin Heidegger has arrived at the opposite evaluation. In
his later writings he dismisses Kierkegaard as merely a religious writer, and he devotes more and more attention to the
works of Nietzsche whom he has come to consider one of the
very greatest philosophers of all time and, alas, the last great
metaphysician of the West. This conception, first developed at
length in a noteworthy essay on "Nietzsche's Word 'God is
Dead' " is, of course, diametrically opposed to Jaspers'; but
like Jaspers' it is supported by a great many quotations and
depends on a complete disregard for the context, both of the
quotations and of Nietzsche's over-all development and
thought.

It may seem that their historical interpretations are not
really important: after all, Bertrand Russell's philosophical
importance is quite independent of the many caricatures he
has drawn in his witty but unreliable *History of Western
Philosophy*. There are some important differences. First,
Jaspers and Heidegger are in this instance not, as Russell
often is, unfair to an opponent, but they deal with a man
whom they consider the greatest philosopher of his time and
more than that: a revolutionary who, as both men see it, has
changed the whole climate of modern thought, making it imperative for us today to begin our philosophic efforts in relation to him. Secondly, Jaspers maintains: "All knowledge is

interpretation. The procedure in understanding texts is a simile for all comprehension of Being." And Heidegger's philosophy has increasingly turned from an attempt to comprehend Being directly into a series of efforts to comprehend it by way of interpretations of selected texts. Under these circumstances, the deeply unscientific nature of Jaspers' and Heidegger's interpretations certainly deserves the utmost emphasis.

In their elaborate Nietzsche interpretations, Jaspers and Heidegger "demonstrate," with a tremendous show of learning, opposite conclusions. In his Nietzsche image each of them has drawn his own portrait as his rival sees him: in Heidegger's eyes, Jaspers is as inconclusive as his Nietzsche, philosophizing endlessly without ever evolving a philosophy; to Jaspers, in turn, it seems that Heidegger who began by using terms that look existential and who once spoke with an existential pathos is really a metaphysician like his Nietzsche. Yet each sees himself in a different light as offering a new beginning where Nietzsche left off: Jaspers with his *Existenzphilosophie,* Heidegger with his "overcoming of metaphysics."

Heidegger's and Jaspers' opposite evaluations of the relative stature of Nietzsche and Kierkegaard further illuminate the gulf that separates the two men who are generally lumped together, much against their will, as "existentialists." Heidegger disdains the openly hortatory tone—so much so that some of his readers fail to notice altogether that he, too, appeals to us to change our lives. (Heidegger's enthusiastic exhortations, immediately after Hitler came to power, that the students and professors at the German universities must now think in the service of the Nazi state—his inaugural address as Rektor at Freiburg has been printed—are a very noteworthy exception.) His flair for the most intricate terminology and what in *Sein und Zeit* looks almost like a subtle system has reminded many students of scholasticism and his originally Catholic background.

An early disciple and distinguished colleague, on the other hand, would sum up Heidegger's importance by asserting that he introduced Nietzsche into philosophy. Without Heidegger —that is the surely false suggestion—Nietzsche would still be considered a mere literary figure. To put the matter differently: by being so exceedingly difficult and "scholastic" Heidegger made discussion of death and despair and dread and care and other previously unacademic subjects quite respectable. He made it possible for professors to discuss with a good conscience matters previously considered literary, if that.

The question is how well Heidegger himself has dealt with these phenomena and others. His detractors see him as an obscurantist whose involved constructions with their multiple plays on words conceal a mixture of banalities and falsehoods. His admirers say that he has shown the temporality of man's existence, that he strikes new paths by raising the question of Being, and that he is the great anti-Cartesian who has overcome the fatal bifurcation of matter and mind and the isolation of the thinking self. His critics, in turn, retort that this last feat is common to most modern philosophers and that Heidegger, unlike some of the others, achieved it only by renouncing Descartes' rule that we must think as clearly and distinctly as the mathematicians. This, say his admirers, leads to positivism; what is wanted is a new way of thinking.

Heidegger himself, at least in his written work, tends to lump together followers and critics as having failed completely to understand *Sein und Zeit,* the early work on which his reputation largely rests. In 1949, a little more than twenty years after the publication of *Being and Time,* he writes: "Philosophy could hardly have given a clearer demonstration of the power of this oblivion of Being than it has furnished us by the somnambulistic assurance with which it has passed by the real and only question of *Being and Time.* What is at stake here is, therefore, not a series of misunderstandings of a book but our abandonment by Being." The same assurance speaks out of Heidegger's Letter "On Humanism," published in 1947: "It is widely supposed that the attempt made in *Being and Time* ended in a dead-end street"; for the book was subtitled "First Half," and the sequel was never published. "Let us not bother about this opinion," Heidegger continues. "Until today thought, which in *Being and Time* attempted a few steps, has not advanced at all beyond this treatise."

Since *Being and Time,* Heidegger has mostly published interpretations: first, a book on Kant, widely repudiated by Kant scholars; then interpretations of poems by Hölderlin, eventually collected in a volume; and in between an essay on Plato which pictures his "doctrine of truth" as a fateful innovation and as the beginning of that Western philosophical tradition which allegedly comes to an end in Nietzsche. Today we must attempt a new beginning with the help of a new understanding of the pre-Socratics. Even as Jaspers is trying to crown his life's work with a tome on the great philosophers, including Jesus and the Buddha among many others, Heidegger hopes to complete a major work on the pre-Socratics. Some of his reinterpretations have by now appeared in various places, notably a forty-eight page essay on Anaximander's one surviving sentence; but, at least so far, the classical philologists, including even those who yield to none in their respect for *Being and Time,* priding themselves on being friends and former pupils, are agreed that his interpretations are untenable. Even so, some who know their Kant are awed by the erudition of his classical interpretations; Nietzsche scholars find his Rilke essay stimulating and profound; and Rilke scholars bow before his Nietzsche exegesis.

What has provoked far more controversy than anything else he has written is the growing body of his self-interpretations. Most of his old pupils who felt close to him in the period of *Being and Time* insist, though for the most part not in print, that he did *not* mean what he now explains he meant. Some are altogether embarrassed by his later work and confine their admiration to *Being and Time* and such other relatively early essays as, for example, *What is Metaphysics?*

The differences between Heidegger and Schelling are unquestionably much more striking than the similarities, but these few parallels are of some interest. Above all, there are two Heideggers as once there were two Schellings: the early and the late one. In both cases the late philosophy has esoteric, if not mystic, touches and is supported by the most tremendous sense of a historic mission. Unlike Kant, Fichte, and Hegel who felt that it was given to them to bring to an end a long and remarkable development, Heidegger claims, as Schelling did, that he is making a new start and that with him a new age is beginning. Moreover, Heidegger's famous question "Why is there any being at all and not rather nothing?" (raised in 1929 in *What is Metaphysics?* and again in the longer *Introduction to Metaphysics*)—the question of which he conceded in 1949 that it might seem that "the metaphysician Leibniz" had asked it before—was repeatedly raised as a basic question by Schelling, as Jaspers points out at length in a late work on Schelling, published 1955.

One of the points on which Heidegger and Jaspers are agreed is that, since Sartre is an avowed existentialist, they do not care to be called by the same name. Even so their reasons are different. Jaspers' main reason, which would be decisive in itself, is that the word suggests a doctrine among others, shared by a group among other groups. Secondly, his moral censure of Schelling and Freud suggests that he does not approve of Sartre's "spiritual personality," and even less of that of the Paris existentialist as the popular image pictures him. Moreover, Sartre makes a great deal of his debt to Heidegger without acknowledging what he has learnt from Jaspers which would seem to be a great deal. Sartre even dismisses Jaspers in print as a professed Catholic, while in fact Jaspers is a Protestant who has developed into a non-denominational proponent of "Biblical religion."

Heidegger's reasons for insisting that he is not an existentialist are set forth in detail in his Letter "On Humanism" which was prompted indirectly by Sartre's famous lecture "Existentialism is a Humanism." (Sartre's lecture is included in the present volume, unabridged.) Heidegger says, in part: "Sartre formulates the basic principle of existentialism in these words: existence precedes essence. Here he uses the terms *existentia* and *essentia* in the old sense of metaphysics which says since Plato: the *essentia* precedes the *existentia*. Sartre reverses this sentence. But the reversal of a metaphysical sentence remains a metaphysical sentence. Being such a sentence, it remains, like all metaphysics, in the oblivion of the truth of Being." And Heidegger concludes: "The main principle of Sartre about the priority of *existentia* over *essentia* certainly justifies the name 'existentialism' as a title which is appropriate for this philosophy." By the same token, the label is inappropriate for Heidegger's philosophy which, as he emphasizes again and again in his later works, was from the outset concerned with Being.

Even in *Being and Time*, human existence (*das Dasein*) was discussed at length only as the mode of Being best knowable by us; and throughout the book Heidegger kept reminding even his first readers that his interest was not in man as such—not, as he put it repeatedly, anthropological. On the contrary, he called his effort even then "fundamental ontology"; and ontology, of course, is the study of Being, not of man's existence. Traditional ontology, however, did not get beyond the study of "beings as such" while Heidegger hoped to penetrate to Being itself. Originally, he tried to do this by way of an analysis of man's existence, which was timely, made him fashionable overnight, and gave thousands the impression that Heidegger had brought philosophy down to earth.

In his later writings, the very violence he does to language suggests to a new generation that he is trying to say something new and, to use one of Rilke's favorite words, *unsäglich:* something extreme and unsayable. Heidegger's preoccupation with the roots of words, which results in false etymologies and plays on words according to his critics, gives his followers the feeling that he is going to the roots while others remain at the surface. His critique of all traditional philosophy from Plato to Nietzsche, his insistence that all modern philosophic thinking is vitiated by Latin mistranslations of Greek words, and the demand that we must now recover the original experience of the earliest Greek thinkers, going back to the beginnings, communicates a sense of radicalism and occasionally even the excitement of an archaeological excavation.

As layer upon layer of misunderstanding is exposed, the reader feels that something glorious is about to come to view. Alas, it usually remains about to come to view. It is as if night had fallen when Heidegger himself is at last ready to translate the dicta of the pre-Socratics. The great discovery is made, but we cannot quite see it, not because his version looks like what we knew before—it does not—but because it is so very dark.

More often even Heidegger employs such phrases as "set out on the way" or "try to reach the point from which the question can one day be asked." No archaeologist, of course, can avoid this preliminary search for a good site. Heidegger, like Schliemann and Sir Arthur Evans, enlists the help of poets, which adds to the excitement and makes his later works, for all their frequent obscurity, no less unacademic compared to most philosophy than was *Being and Time*. His favorite poet, to be sure, is not Homer whose laughter rings through the ages as he relates the foibles of the gods, but Hölderlin, the dark poet whose splendid rhythms carry ordinary readers over vast abysses of obscurity. Some of his last verse, still of hymnic power, even bears the stamp of madness and was written after brief confinement in an asylum, before insanity destroyed his powers altogether.

Hölderlin's schizophrenia certainly does not disprove his competence as a guide for a philosopher. It is irrelevant from a logical point of view, and yet symptomatic. It underlines Heidegger's deliberate defiance of common sense and his recourse not merely to what is extraordinary but—and here we find a striking similarity with a great deal of modern fiction—to what is pathological.

No philosopher should be viewed only in the context of his time, against the background of contemporary art and literature; but to see him also, briefly, in this context is, no doubt, legitimate. So viewed, Heidegger belongs to the contemporary revolt against representation. Even as modern prose and painting are no longer satisfied with the representation of events or things, Heidegger feels that the time has come for philosophy to break with what he calls representational thinking. His partisans occasionally counter criticisms saying that they presuppose the competence of common sense or logic, and their voices show the scorn with which a critic of Picasso might be told that he is a mere Philistine.

What Heidegger proposes to put in the place of representational thinking he calls *das andenkende Denken,* a thinking that *recalls.* This translation has his own enthusiastic approval. We must try to remember and call back what is forgotten: Being, not beings; not mere objects but that of which we are a part. The method which he recommends is to recall what has been thought, instead of thoughtlessly assuming that we know it all or that in view of modern progress the beginnings have long been surpassed. On the contrary, our common sense is alienated from the source of our being, and we must enlist the aid of uncommon creations such as, for example, hymns by Hölderlin, or the later and obscure verses of Rilke (which he esteems less than Hölderlin's), or possibly a Sophoclean chorus.

To note that Heidegger's interpretations are unscientific might be said to beg the question. If Jaspers' interpretations are not tenable historically and philologically, that is a defect by his own explicit standards and can be held against him as an inescapable internal criticism; but Heidegger does not claim to be scientific—on the contrary. If Nietzsche's scorn of "the belly of Being" is applicable to some of Heidegger's later speculations, and his Being is "the shadow of God" and a post-Christian "after-world," there is at least one further image of Nietzsche's Zarathustra of which Heidegger reminds us—a characterization which helps to explain his wide appeal: "You, the bold seekers and tempters, and whoever embarks with cunning sails on terrible seas—you, drunk with riddles, glad of the twilight, whose soul flutes lure astray to every whirl-pool, because you do not want to grope along a thread with cowardly hand; and where you can *guess,* you hate to *deduce.*"

VI. SARTRE

It is mainly through the work of Jean-Paul Sartre that existentialism has come to the attention of a wide international audience. Even Heidegger's great prestige in Germany after the second World War is due, in no small part, to his tremendous impact on French thought. Nevertheless, Sartre is widely considered a mere *littérateur,* and in the nineteen hundred and fifties it has become much more fashionable to criticize him, or rather dismiss him, than to take him seriously, let alone to praise him. Oddly, it is widely urged against him that he is in some ways strikingly unacademic, as if academic existentialism were not a contradiction in terms.

Sartre's writings bear the stamp of his experience from the outset. In 1938 he lays down his experience of the thirties in *La Nausée.* No reader can fail to notice that it is his own experience, not mere cerebration. In 1939, on the eve of the War, he prints five stories, including "The Wall" and the long "Childhood of a Leader" which fuse existentialist motifs with an agonized awareness of the moral, existential issues of the period and a wealth of psychologic observations, rarely equalled since the *Notes from Underground.* The strictly philosophic writings of that period are still rather academic, being exercises in the phenomenology of Husserl, though it is characteristic that the subject of these exercises is emotion.

In the war, Sartre becomes a soldier fighting against Hitler, is captured, returns to Paris, and fights in the resistance. It was of the experience of these years that his philosophic *chef-d'oeuvre* was born, *L'être et le néant;* and Sartre's comments on commitment and decision, dread, and death are charged with life. It is often said that he accepted all these themes from Heidegger and that his thought is second-hand. Yet Heidegger's treatment of the same themes is, more often than not, abstract to the point of being neither "evident" in Husserl's sense nor even plausible: we are aware of the relations between words which have the same roots, but much less clear about the connections between the phenomena which he describes; the thought process seems determined by the words. In Sartre's work, too, there are many highly abstract pages, and at times he is misled by words and writes what is no longer meaningful. Yet many of his pages on the central themes of existentialism have the plausibility and contact with experience which are lacking in the similar analyses of Heidegger.

Sartre's attitude toward psychology differs strikingly from Heidegger's and Jaspers'. He has no fear of being taken for a man who writes psychology, and he does not consider it subphilosophical to base discussions of despair, decision, dread, and self-deception on experience. He does not upbraid Freud for presenting "brutalizing demands" (Jaspers), nor does he insist that his own discussion has nothing to do "with psychology or psychoanalysis" (Heidegger). Sartre attacks Freud on specific grounds. His attack is, rather characteristically, less than gracious. He writes as if it were a well-known fact that there are two schools of psychoanalysis, Freud's and Sartre's (he calls the latter "existential psychoanalysis"); and he contrasts them without emphasizing which came earlier in time. It has never been the forte of philosophers to acknowledge their debts.

Sartre is a philosopher in the French tradition which, more often than not, has produced men who stand at the borderline of philosophy and literature: Montaigne, Pascal, Voltaire, Rousseau, and even Bergson come to mind in this connection. As in most of these cases, it would be beside the point to speculate how much space he will receive in future histories of philosophy. Undoubtedly, he will be remembered, not least for his unprecedented versatility: he is much more interesting than most of his contemporaries whether he writes short stories or novels, essays or philosophy, or plays, or literary criticism.

In most of these respects as well as in temperament, Sartre is much closer to Nietzsche than to German existentialism. Not the least thing he shares with Nietzsche is the multiplicity of styles that gives expression to a new experience of life and a new vision of man, dazzling variety that is still one at heart. Sartre is no mere virtuoso: there is a common core in his multifarious writings.

Probably, the short story "The Wall" is the best introduction to the heart of Sartre's thought. Even as, despite its ending, it is above comparison with O. Henry, it is also, despite its style, far richer than the short stories of Hemingway. It is a classic treatment of the central existentialist motif of confrontation with death and contains important themes which can be found, too, in some of his other works; for example, in the two plays *Les mains sales* (translated as *Dirty Hands* or *Red Gloves*) and, more obviously, *Les morts sans sépulture* (*The Victors*). In these works man's highest value is integrity, and Sartre goes out of his way to point up its utter independence of social utility. Here another similarity to Nietzsche may be noted. "The value of a human being," Nietzsche said, "does not lie in his usefulness: for it would continue to exist even if there were nobody to whom he could be useful." The value of Nietzsche's man is highly complex, while Sartre's insistence on integrity may seem relatively simple. A closer comparison, however, shows that the features Nietzsche stressed are found in Sartre, too, if less explicitly: passion and its mastery, independence of convention, and that creative freedom which finds ultimate expression in being a law unto oneself.

Nowhere is Nietzsche's influence on Sartre clearer than in Sartre's play *The Flies*. The ethic put forward there is clearly not that of "Existentialism is a Humanism" but Nietzsche's, and the play abounds in echoes of Nietzsche. (For detailed proof see section 51 of my *Tragedy and Philosophy*.)

Sartre's debt to Heidegger has often been exaggerated, while his debt to Nietzsche, Ortega (see Chapter Seven), and Jaspers has been insufficiently appreciated. But as one reads Sartre one often has the feeling that he is writing from experience. Even where he borrows, which is often, he adapts, and he has lived with the problems he discusses. The chapter on "Self-Deception" (or "Bad Faith": *mauvaise foi*) is a sample of his more abstract and academic style; but here, too, we encounter lively illustrations, and the attempt to gain clarity about oneself seems to be deeply felt.

One of the central ideas in this chapter is encountered in Jaspers' writings long before Sartre's book appeared in 1943: the contrast of man's facticity and transcendence (for example, near the end of section VI of the lecture on "The Encompassing" which is included in this volume). Sartre is not as utterly unfair to Freud as Jaspers was when he wrote in 1931: "The self-reflection of the human being of integrity, which . . . had culminated in Kierkegaard and Nietzsche, has here degenerated into the uncovering of sexual desires and typical childhood experiences; it is the covering up of genuine, dangerous self-reflection by a mere rediscovery of already known types." Yet the very same theme, including even Jaspers' charge that psychoanalysis somehow implies that man should "return back to nature which no longer requires him to be human," is taken up in Sartre's analysis of self-deception. But what in Jaspers' writings sounds didactic, moralistic, and abstract, a solemn sermon quite remote from Freud's explicit statements, comes to life in Sartre's pages. Freud's attack on self-deception is quite apt to lead to self-deception on a different level: we face our repressions—and see ourselves as victims of "the censor" or our parents. Having read Sartre, we understand Jaspers and Heidegger better: it is as if he must have come first and their, more abstract, treatments later.

In fact, it was Nietzsche who came first to write of faith and self-deception, of the last man and the overman; and then Jaspers and Heidegger dealt with similar topics, writing like professors, expounding despair and death and the attempt to know oneself in terms of quaint big words and one-two-three, and even Roman three, Arabic two, small b. Sartre in his café, alas, sees the waiter "playing at being a waiter" and feels that he himself must play at being a professor of philosophy: he makes a point of knowing such professional philosophers as Heidegger, Husserl, and Hegel to whom he pays homage, and he even mentions Professor Scheler in connection with "the man of resentment" rather than referring to Nietzsche whom Scheler, of course, had read. The pity of it is that Sartre clothes his analysis in spurious dialectic: he speaks of "the nothing" like Heidegger, takes "in-itself" and "for-itself" from Hegel, and above all plays on the word "being" in a way that veils his meaning from most readers, while the few who recognize his systematic confusion of "am" and "am nothing but" are apt to feel that this invalidates his whole analysis—which it does not.

The *en-soi* (in-itself) is in Sartre's thought the being which rests in itself, the being of such things as tables. The *pour-soi* (for-itself) is that being which is aware of itself: man. Its structure is different from that of the *en-soi,* and the phenomenon of self-deception serves the author as a.clue: what must the *pour-soi* be like in order to make self-deception possible? The form of this question is reminiscent of both Kant and Heidegger; and it is at least questionable whether this transcendental mold does not do violence to Sartre's thoughts. Does he explain, for example, how it is possible for a man to deceive himself to the point of believing that he has done some specific thing which in fact he has not done? Does his account explain how one can persuade oneself that one has not done what in fact one has done? At the very least, however, Sartre argues in a manner which invites such questions: he thinks on a level where discussion is possible; his thought provokes discussion and is offered, as it were, as part of a discussion.

It may well be the most crucial flaw of German existentialism that, all protestations to the contrary notwithstanding, it is essentially a monologue. Either a language is constructed within which important criticisms are impossible, and questions not put in this language are dismissed as common sense, naive, positivistic, and in any case not philosophical, or the mode of utterance is homiletic. In either case it is oracular, and it is one of Sartre's greatest virtues that *his* style of thought is *not*.

What makes self-deception possible, according to Sartre, is that the *pour-soi* differs from the *en-soi* or, to be concrete: a man is not a homosexual, a waiter, or a coward in the same way in which he is six feet tall or blond. If it were merely a matter of one's being "not only" a waiter or a homosexual and of one's character not being exhausted by that fact—and some of Sartre's paradoxical assertions look as if this were his only point—it could be retorted that it is no less true that a man is not a six-footer and nothing else. The crux of the matter is suggested by such words as possibility, choice, and decision. If I am six feet tall, that is that. It is a fact no less than that the table is, say, two feet high. Being a coward or a waiter, however, is different: it depends on ever new decisions. I may say: I must leave now—or, I am that way—because I am a waiter, or a coward, as if being a waiter or a coward were a brute fact. Actually, this apparent statement of fact veils a decision. This theme is elaborated further and without forbidding terminology in Sartre's "Portrait of the Antisemite."

Here Sartre tries to show that a man is not an antisemite the way he is blond: he chooses to be an antisemite, says Sartre, because he is afraid of freedom, openness, and change and longs to be as solid as a thing. He wants an identity, he wants to be something in the manner in which a table is something, or a rock. At the outset, perhaps, he plays at being an antisemite; but when it has become second nature, the man has achieved nothing less than an escape from freedom: he has abdicated his humanity.

Sartre does not deduce his "portrait" from an *a priori*

philosophy: the observations which are here distilled into an essay are found four years before *L'être et le néant* in "The Childhood of a Leader" which he published in the same volume with "The Wall."

In the English-speaking world, Sartre's lecture on *Existentialism* is probably his best known work. This is rather unfortunate because it is after all only an occasional lecture which, though brilliant and vivid in places and unquestionably worthy of attention, bears the stamp of the moment. It contains unnecessary misstatements of fact as well as careless and untenable arguments and a definition of existentialism which has been repudiated by Jaspers and Heidegger, and ought to be repudiated by Sartre, too, because it is no less unfair to his own thought. By now it has become a commonplace that existentialism is the doctrine that existence precedes essence, and this phrase obstructs the understanding of this complex movement as well as of Sartre's philosophy. Even his explanation of the meaning of this definition invites hosts of criticisms, and the same is also true of his arguments, a little later in the lecture, for a somewhat Kantian ethic. Oddly perhaps, enough good things remain to warrant reading and re-reading.

The intention of this lecture was to offer a defense of Sartre's thought against some criticisms which appeared important to him at the time, in 1946. Ten years later, the objections to Sartre have become a little different, at least in the United States. They serve as a pretext for a rather cavalier treatment of his thought which is discounted, not examined. It is for this reason that a few irrelevant objections which stand in the way of serious criticism may be briefly noted and rebutted.

The first, most common, and least serious point is that he writes, or sometimes has written, in a café and deals rather too much with sex. An English reviewer remarked that his five short stories leave *Lady Chatterley's Lover* sleeping at the door-post, and an American publisher has placed this invitation on the cover of a paperback edition. In his philosophic main work, too, he deals with sex; and another American publisher has brought out a translation of some of this material ahead of the rest of the book. Sartre's treatment of sex, however, whether in fiction or philosophy, is designed to increase our understanding of important problems, never to arouse desire. As for the café, most philosophers today probably write in a den (which Sartre did not have when he returned from fighting Hitler; and his room was not heated while the café was); but Socrates pursued philosophy in the market place which is not feasible in a northern climate, the less if you want to write. For a philosopher with a keen concern with psychological observation, moreover, a café may be much better than a den.

Secondly, it is a wide-spread assumption in the United States that an avowed atheist is *eo ipso* no philosopher. This view is founded on the long association of philosophy and theology in American colleges and blinks the fact that for over a hundred and fifty years most important philosophers have been pantheists, atheists, or agnostics, and that in English philosophy God has played scarcely any part at all since Bishop Berkeley assigned a rather odd role to him early in the eighteenth century. The British philosophers, however, do not usually make a point of their disbelief, while Sartre does; and his un-British insistence on the relevance of ideas to life makes him doubly suspect. Therefore, it is well to keep in mind that perhaps the most compassionate and venerable of all mortals, the Buddha, also made a point of his lack of belief, and for essentially the same reason as Sartre.

The differences between the two men could scarcely be more striking, even though the Buddha stressed despair and suffering no less than the existentialists. It would be folly to paint Sartre in the image of the Buddha: he is not saintly but aggressively human; he does not preach disenchantment but commitment in the world; like Nietzsche, Sartre remains "faithful to the earth" and says, "Life begins on the other side of despair." Few men could be more unlike each other.

Nevertheless, the Buddha, too, opposed any reliance on the divine because he wanted men to realize their complete responsibility. His final, and perhaps most characteristic, words, according to tradition, were: "Work out your own salvation with diligence." And if the diligence is rather uncharacteristic of the existentialists, the Buddha's still more radical dictum with which the Dhammapada opens is nothing less than the quintessence of Sartre's thought: "All that we are is the result of what we have thought."

Few words in world literature equal the impact of this saying. All man's alibis are unacceptable: no gods are responsible for his condition; no original sin; no heredity and no environment; no race, no caste, no father, and no mother; no wrong-headed education, no governess, no teacher; not even an impulse or a disposition, a complex or a childhood trauma. Man is free; but his freedom does not look like the glorious liberty of the Enlightenment; it is no longer the gift of God. Once again, man stands alone in the universe, responsible for his condition, likely to remain in a lowly state, but free to reach above the stars.

Toward the end of *L'être et le néant* Sartre argues that it is man's basic wish to fuse his openness and freedom with the impermeability of things, to achieve a state of being in which the *en-soi* and *pour-soi* are synthesized. This ideal, says Sartre, one can call God, and "man is the being who wants to be God." The chapter ends: "But the idea of God is contradictory . . . man is a useless passion."

Man's situation, as Sartre sees it, is absurd and tragic; but does that rule out integrity, nobility, or valor, or the utmost effort? In its limitation to this one life, Sartre's image of the human situation differs radically from the Buddhist view in which life follows on life and salvation remains always possible. Sartre's world is closer to Shakespeare's. There are situations in which, whatever choice we make, we cannot escape guilt. This is Jaspers' view, too. Secular existentialism is a tragic world view without, however, being pessimistic. Even in guilt and failure man can retain his integrity and defy the world.

There remains a final objection which concerns not only Sartre but Heidegger and Jaspers, too: have they themselves retained their integrity in view of their political behavior? The very critics who would be the first to make a point of the vulgarity of the preceding charges have most frequently pressed this point. In the case of other philosophers it might be irrelevant to introduce their politics and morals; but Sartre has said, and Heidegger and Jaspers have said much the same: "Existentialism must be lived to be really sincere. To live as an existentialist means to be ready to pay for this view and not merely to lay it down in books."

The first point to note is that existentialism clearly does not entail one specific political program, and the fact that the three leading existentialists followed divergent paths during the Hitler years is not surprising in itself. And yet it does not follow that all three were equally in keeping with their writings. Heidegger, who in *Sein und Zeit* had spoken much of resolutely facing death, joined the Nazis after Hitler came to power and, as Rektor of his university, delivered an inaugural address which, fortunately for him, is not widely read. If, as he now says, he soon abandoned Nazism, it is the more remarkable that his resolve was kept so quiet that even today many remain unconvinced. Jaspers, with a Jewish wife, made the decision to keep quiet, but was ready once again in 1945 to speak of guilt and shipwreck, dread, and death. It is surely exceedingly polite to say: though their voices be the voices of Nietzsche and Kierkegaard, their lives are the lives of Kant and Hegel.

Sartre, back from the war, fought in the resistance. That is often forgotten today. But what is not forgotten is his more recent decision to make common cause with the Communist Party in France. In the United States, this is held against him more than anything else. His decision is utterly quixotic. Unlike Heidegger in 1933, Sartre derives no advantage from it whatsoever. Moreover, he himself insists that he is not a Communist, that he cannot accept the doctrines of the party, and that he knows that his head would soon fall if they should come to power. It is his impassioned opposition to the *status quo* and his conviction that the Communists, but not the socialists, are serious about overthrowing it that leads him to believe that he must for the present make a common front with them. Unconsciously he reminds us of a lesson we learnt from the Greeks, from Plato in particular: that philosophical profundity and political sense do not always go together; on the contrary. (John Locke illustrates the same point from the other side; so does John Stuart Mill.) Radicalism is sometimes eminently fruitful in philosophy, while political good sense is probably inseparable from moderation, compromise, and patience.

Existentialism has developed no political philosophy, and the so-called existentialists have made widely different political decisions. If we recalled Dostoevsky, Kierkegaard, and Nietzsche, the variety would increase even further, though perhaps no more than in the case of Thomists. Some have compromised themselves, and some have not. None of them can simply be dismissed on that score. And Sartre is unquestionably one of the most interesting thinkers of our time.

VII. A STORY WITH A MORAL

The movement we have followed through more than a hundred years is not confined to Kierkegaard and Dostoevsky's *Notes* and Nietzsche, Jaspers, Heidegger, and Sartre. There is Rilke whose later verse has left a deep impression on the thought of Heidegger, while his prose work, *The Notes of Malte Laurids Brigge,* was a formative influence on Sartre. And there is Kafka in whose major works and parables the absurdity of man's condition has found classical expression. The French existentialists are steeped in Kafka no less than in Dostoevsky. By the same token, it might be objected, Husserl ought to be included, seeing that he influenced both Heidegger and Sartre so profoundly. Husserl himself, however, was decidedly no existentialist even in the widest sense of that word, while Rilke and Kafka share some of the most characteristic features of this movement, as does Camus in whose *Myth of Sisyphus* a tragic world view is redeemed by Nietzsche's *amor fati.*

In the end, Rilke, Kafka, and Camus pose a question, seconded by Dostoevsky and by Sartre's plays and fiction: could it be that at least some part of what the existentialists attempt to do is best done in art and not philosophy? [It sometimes happens, though this is assuredly no rule, that at some given time and place one of the arts, perhaps a single man, towers above the rest and says more adequately what the others say less well. In Italy around the time of 1300 Dante was that man, and two hundred years later it was, if not Michelangelo, in any case sculpture and painting. In Dostoevsky's Russia it was the novel. In Denmark around 1850 it was a new and peculiar kind of prose: we think of Kierkegaard and Andersen. In Nietzsche's Germany there was no poet and no novelist to rival him.] It is conceivable that Rilke and Kafka, Sartre and Camus have in their imaginative works reached heights of which the so-called existentialist philosophers, including Sartre, not to speak of Camus' essays, have for all their efforts fallen short, if they have not altogether missed their footing in their bold attempts to scale the peaks and fallen into frequent error and confusion. Whether this is so or not, that is a crucial question which no student of this movement can avoid.

So far, no mention has been made of the religious existentialists, except for Kierkegaard whose influence on Jaspers, Heidegger, and Sartre makes him a key figure of this movement. What of Berdyaev, Buber, Bultmann, Tillich, or Marcel? Three things may be said to justify their omission here. First, religion has always been existentialist: it has always insisted that mere schools of thought and bodies of belief are not enough, that too much of our thinking is remote from that which truly matters, and that we must change our lives. It has always been preoccupied with suffering, death, and dread, with care, guilt, and despair. What is new is that this preoccupation has since Kierkegaard entered philosophy as well as poetry and fiction, severed from its earlier religious context.

Secondly, not one of the later religious existentialists has so far left a mark, like Kierkegaard, on literature or on philosophy. Many of them have been deeply influenced by those we have considered here: Bultmann by Heidegger, Marcel by Jaspers, Tillich above all by Schelling. They have availed themselves of a specifically modern language to remind us of what their diverse religions have always said.

Third: in an anthology they might, for all that, have been represented. This, however, is not a collection of flowers or a meadow on which we pick a blossom here and there. It is an attempt to tell a story and follow a path. The religious existentialists have not played an important part in our story: it can be told without referring to them. Those, on the other hand, who know the story will be better prepared for the religious existentialists, too.

Does our story have a moral? After all, the existentialists have no desire simply to divert us. The story is the story of a protest and a challenge. Kierkegaard would have you become a Christian; Nietzsche says: "Be a man and do not follow me —but yourself!" Heidegger tries to arouse us from the oblivion of Being. And all of them contrast inauthentic life and authentic life.

What is striking to a philosopher is that practically all English-speaking philosophy is included in the condemnation of inauthentic life: it is considered superficial and trivial. Nor is this merely a partisan view. When we have read Dostoevsky, Kierkegaard, and Nietzsche, Rilke, Kafka, Jaspers, Heidegger, Sartre, and Camus, and then look at the prose of English and American philosophers and at the problems *they* discuss, our first impression may well be that they managed the rare feat of being frivolous and dull at once. Dostoevsky, Kierkegaard, and Nietzsche, however, as well as Rilke and Kafka are dead; and except for Nietzsche they were not philosophers in any case. And when we compare the writings of our own philosophers with those of Jaspers,

Heidegger, and Sartre's philosophic efforts, the picture is changed.

It is one of the saddest features of our age that we are faced with an entirely unnecessary dichotomy: on the one hand there are those whose devotion to intellectual cleanliness and rigor is exemplary but who refuse to deal with anything but small, and often downright trivial, questions; in the other camp are men like Toynbee and some of the existentialists who deal with the big and interesting questions, but in such a manner that the positivists point to them as living proofs that any effort of this kind is doomed to failure. Aware of their opponents' errors, both sides go to ever greater extremes; the split widens; and the intelligent layman who is left in the middle will soon lose sight of both.

The existentialists have tried to bring philosophy down to earth again like Socrates; but the existentialist and the analytical philosopher are each only half a Socrates. The existentialist has taken up the passionate concern with questions that arise from life, the moral pathos, and the firm belief that, to be serious, a philosophy has to be lived. The analytical philosophers, on the other hand, insist—as Socrates did, too —that no moral pathos, no tradition, and no views, however elevated, justify unanalyzed ideas, murky arguments, or a touch of confusion. In Nietzsche—and more or less in every great philosopher before him, too—philosophy occurred in the tension between these two timeless tendencies, now inclining one way, now the other. Today this dual heritage has been developed in different camps, and between them they have made us aware of the pitfalls of traditional philosophy no less than of each other's faults. That the existentialists and analysts will get together is not likely. But if the feat of Socrates is really to be repeated and philosophy is to have a future outside the academies, there will have to be philosophers who think in the tension between analysis and existentialism.

TWO

Dostoevsky: NOTES FROM UNDERGROUND[1]

[*Preface:* Fyodor Mikhailovich Dostoevsky was born in Moscow in 1821. His *Notes from Underground* was first published in 1864 and followed in rapid succession by *Crime and Punishment, The Idiot, The Possessed,* and *The Brothers Karamazov.* When he died in 1881, he was a national hero.

In the Western world he became a major influence only after the first World War, but Nietzsche read *Notes from Underground* in 1887 and wrote: "I did not even know the name of Dostoevsky just a few weeks ago . . . An accidental reach of the arm in a bookstore brought to my attention *L'esprit souterrain,* a work just translated into French. . . . The instinct of kinship (or how should I name it?) spoke up immediately; my joy was extraordinary." The part here reprinted Nietzsche characterizes as "really a piece of music, very strange, very un-Germanic music" and goes on to speak of "a kind of self-derision of the γνῶϑι σαυτόν [know thyself]. Incidentally, these Greeks have a lot on their conscience: falsification was their true trade; the whole of European psychology is sick with Greek *superficiality;* and without that little bit of Judaism, etc., etc., etc."

The final point of this first enthusiastic reaction on a postcard to a friend requires comment. It was the Old Testament that Milton cited in *Areopagitica* when he argued against the Platonic conception of reason, and of virtue enforced by law and censorship, to propose instead that "reason is but choosing." What Milton demanded was freedom, choice, decision.

Kierkegaard's revolt against philosophy is similarly motivated: even where he thinks that he is arguing against Hegelianism he is often in rebellion against the whole Greek philosophic heritage, against the Greek image of man.

Dozens of other themes are sounded in these pages, too. Reading how the underground man "could not even become an insect," we think of Kafka's *Metamorphosis*. The analysis of resentment is developed by Nietzsche. Section VI anticipates the psychology of Sartre's "Portrait of the Antisemite." These are but a few examples.

Notes from Underground has two parts of which only the first is offered here. The second, which is longer, recites some incidents out of the narrator's earlier life. These incidents do not explain how he became the way he is, but illustrate his character and some of his observations in Part One. Like most of Dostoevsky's writings, Part Two is eminently worth reading, but it does not greatly add to the thought content of Part One. To cut up a work of fiction might be barbarous, but what is here reprinted is much less like fiction than, stylistically too, like Kierkegaard's reflections on himself (which follow) and like Rilke's *Notes of Malte Laurids Brigge* (offered later).

The final page of Part One has been omitted because it marks the transition to Part Two. Otherwise the text is uncut.]

UNDERGROUND

I

I am a sick man . . . I am a spiteful man. I am an unattractive man. I believe my liver is diseased. However, I know nothing at all about my disease, and do not know for certain what ails me. I don't consult a doctor for it, and never have, though I have a respect for medicine and doctors. Besides, I am extremely superstitious, sufficiently so to respect medicine, anyway (I am well-educated enough not to be superstitious, but I am superstitious). No, I refuse to consult a doctor from spite. That you probably will not understand. Well, I understand it, though. Of course, I can't explain who it is precisely that I am mortifying in this case by my spite: I am perfectly well aware that I cannot "pay out" the doctors by not consulting them; I know better than any one that by all this I am only injuring myself and no one else. But still, if I don't consult a doctor it is from spite. My liver is bad, well—let it get worse!

I have been going on like that for a long time—twenty years. Now I am forty. I used to be in the government service, but am no longer. I was a spiteful official. I was rude and took pleasure in being so. I did not take bribes, you see, so I was bound to find a recompense in that, at least. (A poor jest, but I will not scratch it out. I wrote it thinking it would sound very witty; but now that I have seen myself that I only wanted to show off in a despicable way, I will not scratch it out on purpose!)

When petitioners used to come for information to the table at which I sat, I used to grind my teeth at them, and felt intense enjoyment when I succeeded in making anybody unhappy. I almost always did succeed. For the most part they were all timid people—of course, they were petitioners. But of the uppish ones there was one officer in particular I could not endure. He simply would not be humble, and clanked his sword in a disgusting way. I carried on a feud with him for eighteen months over that sword. At last I got the better of him. He left off clanking it. That happened in my youth, though.

But do you know, gentlemen, what was the chief point about my spite? Why, the whole point, the real sting of it lay in the fact that continually, even in the moment of the acutest spleen, I was inwardly conscious with shame that I was not only not a spiteful but not even an embittered man, that I was simply scaring sparrows at random and amusing myself by it. I might foam at the mouth, but bring me a doll to play with, give me a cup of tea with sugar in it, and maybe I should be appeased. I might even be genuinely touched, though probably I should grind my teeth at myself afterwards and·lie awake at night with shame for months after. That was my way.

I was lying when I said just now that I was a spiteful official. I was lying from spite. I was simply amusing myself with the petitioners and with the officer, and in reality I never could become spiteful. I was conscious every moment in myself of many, very many elements absolutely opposite to that. I felt them positively swarming in me, these opposite elements. I knew that they had been swarming in me all my life and craving some outlet from me, but I would not let them, would not let them, purposely would not let them come out. They tormented me till I was ashamed: they drove me to convulsions and—sickened me, at last, how they sickened me! Now, are not you fancying, gentlemen, that I am expressing remorse for something now, that I am asking your forgiveness for something? I am sure you are fancying that . . . However, I assure you I do not care if you are. . . .

It was not only that I could not become spiteful, I did not know how to become anything: neither spiteful nor kind, neither a rascal nor an honest man, neither a hero nor an insect. Now, I am living out my life in my corner, taunting myself with the spiteful and useless consolation that an intelligent man cannot become anything seriously, and it is only the fool who becomes anything. Yes, a man in the nineteenth century must and morally ought to be pre-eminently a characterless creature; a man of character, an active man is pre-eminently a limited creature. That is my conviction of forty years. I am forty years old now, and you know forty years is a whole life-time; you know it is extreme old age. To live longer than forty years is bad manners, is vulgar, immoral. Who does live beyond forty? Answer that, sincerely and honestly. I will tell you who do: fools and worthless fellows. I tell all old men that to their face, all these venerabe old men, all these silver-haired and reverend seniors! I tell the whole world that to its face! I have a right to say so, for I shall go on living to sixty myself. To seventy! To eighty! . . . Stay, let me take breath. . . .

You imagine no doubt, gentlemen, that I want to amuse you. You are mistaken in that, too. I am by no means such a mirthful person as you imagine, or as you may imagine; however, irritated by all this babble (and I feel that you are irritated) you think fit to ask me who am I—then my answer is, I am a collegiate assessor. I was in the service that I might have something to eat (and solely for that reason), and when last year a distant relation left me six thousand roubles in his will I immediately retired from the service and settled down in my corner. I used to live in this corner before, but now I have settled down in it. My room is a wretched, horrid one in the outskirts of the town. My servant is an old country-woman, ill-natured from stupidity, and, moreover, there is always a nasty smell about her. I am told that the Petersburg climate is bad for me, and that with my small means it is very expensive to live in Petersburg. I know all that better than all these sage and experienced counsellors and monitors. . . . But I am remaining in Petersburg; I am not going away from Petersburg! I am not going away because . . . ech! Why, it is absolutely no matter whether I am going away or not going away.

But what can a decent man speak of with most pleasure? Answer: Of himself.

Well, so I will talk about myself.

II

I want now to tell you, gentlemen, whether you care to hear it or not, why I could not even become an insect. I tell you solemnly, that I have many times tried to become an insect. But I was not equal even to that. I swear, gentlemen, that to be too conscious is an illness—a real thoroughgoing illness. For man's everyday needs, it would have been quite enough to have the ordinary human consciousness, that is, half or a quarter of the amount which falls to the lot of a cultivated man of our unhappy nineteenth century, especially one who has the fatal ill-luck to inhabit Petersburg, the most theoretical and intentional town on the whole terrestrial globe. (There are intentional and unintentional towns.) It would have been quite enough, for instance, to have the consciousness by which all so-called direct persons and men of action live. I bet you think I am writing all this from affectation, to be witty at the expense of men of action; and what is more, that from ill-bred affectation, I am clanking a sword like my officer. But, gentlemen, whoever can pride himself on his diseases and even swagger over them?

Though, after all, every one does do that; people do pride themselves on their diseases, and I do, may be, more than any one. We will not dispute it; my contention was absurd. But yet I am firmly persuaded that a great deal of consciousness, every sort of consciousness, in fact, is a disease. I stick to that. Let us leave that, too, for a minute. Tell me this: why does it happen that at the very, yes, at the very moments when I am most capable of feeling every refinement of all that is "good and beautiful," as they used to say at one time, it would, as though of design, happen to me not only to feel but to do such ugly things, such that . . . Well, in short, actions that all, perhaps, commit; but which, as though purposely, occurred to me at the very time when I was most conscious that they ought not to be committed. The more conscious I was of goodness and of all that was "good and beautiful," the more deeply I sank into my mire and the more ready I was to sink in it altogether. But the chief point was that all this was, as it were, not accidental in me, but as though it were bound to be so. It was as though it were my most normal condition, and not in the least disease or depravity, so that at last all desire in me to struggle against this depravity passed. It ended by my almost believing (perhaps actually believing) that this was perhaps my normal condition. But at first, in the beginning, what agonies I endured in that struggle! I did not believe it was the same with other people, and all my life I hid this fact about myself as a secret. I was ashamed (even now, perhaps, I am ashamed): I got to the point of feeling a sort of secret abnormal, despicable enjoyment in returning home to my corner on some disgusting Petersburg night, acutely conscious that that day I had committed a loathsome action again, that what was done could never be undone, and secretly, inwardly gnawing, gnawing at myself for it, tearing and consuming myself till at last the bitterness turned into a sort of shameful accursed sweetness, and at last—into positive real enjoyment! Yes, into enjoyment, into enjoyment! I insist upon that. I have spoken of this because I keep wanting to know for a fact whether other people feel such enjoyment? I will explain; the enjoyment was just from the too intense consciousness of one's own degradation; it was from feeling oneself that one had reached the last barrier, that it was horrible, but that it could not be otherwise; that there was no escape for you; that you never could become a different man; that even if time and faith were still left you to change into something different you would most likely not wish to change; or if you did wish to, even then you would do nothing; because perhaps in reality there was nothing for you to change into.

And the worst of it was, and the root of it all, that it was all in accord with the normal fundamental laws of over-acute consciousness, and with the inertia that was the direct result of those laws, and that consequently one was not only unable to change but could do absolutely nothing. Thus it would follow, as the result of acute consciousness, that one is not to blame in being a scoundrel; as though that were any consolation to the scoundrel once he has come to realize that he actually is a scoundrel. But enough. . . . Ech, I have talked a lot of nonsense, but what have I explained? How is enjoyment in this to be explained? But I will explain it. I will get to the bottom of it! That is why I have taken up my pen. . . .

I, for instance, have a great deal of *amour propre*. I am as suspicious and prone to take offence as a humpback or a dwarf. But upon my word I sometimes have had moments when if I had happened to be slapped in the face I should, perhaps, have been positively glad of it. I say, in earnest, that I should probably have been able to discover even in that a peculiar sort of enjoyment—the enjoyment, of course, of despair; but in despair there are the most intense enjoyments, especially when one is very acutely conscious of the hopelessness of one's position. And when one is slapped in the face—why then the consciousness of being rubbed into a pulp would positively overwhelm one. The worst of it is, look at it which way one will, it still turns out that I was always the most to blame in everything. And what is most humiliating of all, to blame for no fault of my own but, so to say, through the laws of nature. In the first place, to blame because I am cleverer than any of the people surrounding me. (I have always considered myself cleverer than any of the people surrounding me, and sometimes, would you believe it, have been positively ashamed of it. At any rate, I have all my life, as it were, turned my eyes away and never could look people straight in the face.) To blame, finally, because even if I had had magnanimity, I should only have had more suffering from the sense of its uselessness. I should certainly have never been able to do anything from being magnanimous—neither to forgive, for my assailant would perhaps have slapped me from the laws of nature, and one cannot forgive the laws of nature; nor to forget, for even if it were owing to the laws of nature, it is insulting all the same. Finally, even if I had wanted to be anything but magnanimous, had desired on the contrary to revenge myself on my assailant, I could not have revenged myself on any one for anything because I should certainly never have made up my mind to do anything, even if I had been able to. Why should I not have made up my mind? About that in particular I want to say a few words.

III

With people who know how to revenge themselves and to stand up for themselves in general, how is it done? Why, when they are possessed, let us suppose, by the feeling of revenge, then for the time there is nothing else but that feeling left in their whole being. Such a gentleman simply dashes straight for his object like an infuriated bull with its horns down, and nothing but a wall will stop him. (By the way: facing the wall, such gentlemen—that is, the "direct" persons and men of action—are genuinely nonplussed. For them a wall is not an evasion, as for us people who think and consequently do nothing; it is not an excuse for turning aside, an excuse for which we are always very glad, though we scarcely believe in it ourselves, as a rule. No, they are nonplussed in all sincerity. The wall has for them something tranquillizing, morally soothing, final—maybe even something mysterious . . . but of the wall later.)

Well, such a direct person I regard as the real normal man, as his tender mother nature wished to see him when she graciously brought him into being on the earth. I envy such a man till I am green in the face. He is stupid. I am not disputing that, but perhaps the normal man should be stupid, how do you know? Perhaps it is very beautiful, in fact. And I am the more persuaded of that suspicion, if one can call it so, by the fact that if you take, for instance, the antithesis of the normal man, that is, the man of acute consciousness, who has come, of course, not out of the lap of nature but out of a retort (this is almost mysticism, gentlemen, but I suspect this, too), this retort-made man is sometimes so nonplussed in the presence of his antithesis that with all his exaggerated consciousness he genuinely thinks of himself as a mouse and not a man. It may be an acutely conscious mouse, yet it is a mouse, while the other is a man, and therefore, et cetera, et cetera. And the worst of it is, he himself, his very own self, looks on himself as a mouse; no one asks him to do so; and that is an important point. Now let us look at this mouse in action. Let us suppose, for instance, that it feels insulted, too (and it almost always does feel insulted), and wants to revenge itself, too. There may even be a greater accumulation of spite in it than in *l'homme de la nature et de la vérité*. The base and nasty desire to vent that spite on its assailant rankles perhaps even more nastily in it than in *l'homme de la nature et de la vérité*. For through his innate stupidity the latter looks upon his revenge as justice pure and simple; while in consequence of his acute consciousness the mouse does not believe in the justice of it. To come at last to the deed itself, to the very act of revenge. Apart from the one fundamental nastiness the luckless mouse succeeds in creating around it so many other nastinesses in the form of doubts and questions, adds to the one question so many unsettled questions that there inevitably works up around it a sort of fatal brew, a stinking mess, made up of its doubts, emotions, and of the contempt spat upon it by the direct men of action who stand solemnly about it as judges and arbitrators, laughing at it till their healthy sides ache. Of course the only thing left for it is to dismiss all that with a wave of its paw, and, with a smile of assumed contempt in which it does not even itself believe, creep ignominiously into its mouse-hole. There in its nasty, stinking, underground home our insulted, crushed and ridiculed mouse promptly becomes absorbed in cold, malignant and, above all, ever-lasting spite. For forty years together it will remember its injury down to the smallest, most ignominious details, and every time will add, of itself, details still more ignominious, spitefully teasing and tormenting itself with its own imagina-tion. It will itself be ashamed of its imaginings, but yet it will recall it all, it will go over and over every detail, it will invent unheard of things against itself, pretending that those things might happen, and will forgive nothing. Maybe it will begin to revenge itself, too, but, as it were, piecemeal, in trivial ways, from behind the stove, incognito, without be-lieving either in its own right to vengeance, or in the success of its revenge knowing that from all its efforts at revenge it will suffer a hundred times more than he on whom it revenges itself, while he, I daresay, will not even scratch himself. On its deathbed it will recall it all over again, with interest ac-cumulated over all the years and. . . .

But it is just in that cold, abominable half despair, half belief, in that conscious burying oneself alive for grief in the underworld for forty years, in that acutely recognized and yet partly doubtful hopelessness of one's position, in that hell of unsatisfied desires turned inward, in that fever of oscillations, of resolutions determined for ever and re-pented of again a minute later—that the savour of that strange enjoyment of which I have spoken lies. It is so sub-tle, so difficult of analysis, that persons who are a little lim-ited, or even simply persons of strong nerves, will not under-stand a single atom of it. "Possibly," you will add on your own account with a grin, "people will not understand it either who have never received a slap in the face," and in that way you will politely hint to me that I, too, perhaps, have had the experience of a slap in the face in my life, and so I speak as one who knows. I bet that you are thinking that. But set your minds at rest, gentlemen, I have not received a slap in the face, though it is absolutely a matter of indifference to me what you may think about it. Possibly, I even regret, myself, that I have given so few slaps in the face during my life. But enough . . . not another word on that subject of such extreme interest to you.

I will continue calmly concerning persons with strong nerves who do not understand a certain refinement of enjoyment. Though in certain circumstances these gentlemen bellow their loudest like bulls, though this, let us suppose, does them the greatest credit, yet, as I have said already, confronted with the impossible they subside at once. The impossible means the stone wall! What stone wall? Why, of course, the laws of nature, the deductions of natural science, mathematics. As soon as they prove to you, for instance, that you are descended from a monkey, then it is no use scowling, accept it for a fact. When they prove to you that in reality one drop of your own fat must be dearer to you than a hundred thousand of your fellow-creatures, and that this conclusion is the final solution of all so-called virtues and duties and all such prejudices and fancies, then you have just to accept it, there is no help for it, for twice two is a law of mathematics. Just try refuting it.

"Upon my word," they will shout at you, "it is no use protesting: it is a case of twice two makes four! Nature does not ask your permission, she has nothing to do with your wishes, and whether you like her laws or dislike them, you are bound to accept her as she is, and consequently all her conclusions. A wall, you see, is a wall . . . and so on, and so on."

Merciful Heavens! but what do I care for the laws of nature and arithmetic, when, for some reason, I dislike those laws and the fact that twice two makes four? Of course I cannot break through the wall by battering my head against it if I really have not the strength to knock it down, but I am not going to be reconciled to it simply, because it is a stone wall and I have not the strength.

As though such a stone wall really were a consolation, and really did contain some word of conciliation, simply because it is as true as twice two makes four. Oh, absurdity of absurdities! How much better it is to understand it all, to recognize it all, all the impossibilities and the stone wall; not to be reconciled to one of those impossibilities and stone walls if it disgusts you to be reconciled to it; by the way of the most inevitable, logical combinations to reach the most revolting conclusions on the everlasting theme, that even for the stone wall you are yourself somehow to blame, though again it is as clear as day you are not to blame in the least, and therefore grinding your teeth in silent impotence to sink into luxurious inertia, brooding on the fact that there is no one even for you to feel vindictive against, that you have not, and perhaps never will have, an object for your spite, that it is a sleight of hand, a bit of juggling, a card-sharper's trick, that it is simply a mess, no knowing what and no knowing who, but in spite of all these uncertainties and jugglings, still there is an ache in you, and the more you do not know, the worse the ache.

IV

"Ha, ha, ha! You will be finding enjoyment in toothache next," you cry, with a laugh.

"Well? Even in toothache there is enjoyment," I answer. I had toothache for a whole month and I know there is. In that case, of course, people are not spiteful in silence, but moan; but they are not candid moans, they are malignant moans, and the malignancy is the whole point. The enjoyment of the sufferer finds expression in those moans; if he did not feel enjoyment in them he would not moan. It is a good example, gentlemen, and I will develop it. Those moans express in the first place all the aimlessness of your pain, which is so humiliating to your consciousness; the whole legal system of nature on which you spit disdainfully, of course, but from which you suffer all the same while she does not. They express the consciousness that you have no enemy to punish, but that you have pain; the consciousness that in spite of all possible Vagenheims you are in complete slavery to your teeth; that if some one wishes it, your teeth will leave off aching, and if he does not, they will go on aching another three months; and that finally if you are still contumacious and still protest, all that is left you for your own gratification is to thrash yourself or beat your wall with your fist as hard as you can, and absolutely nothing more. Well, these mortal insults, these jeers on the part of some one unknown, end at last in an enjoyment which sometimes reaches the highest degree of voluptuousness. I ask you, gentlemen, listen sometimes to the moans of an educated man of the nineteenth century suffering from toothache, on the second or third day of the attack, when he is beginning to moan, not as he moaned on the first day, that is, not simply because he has toothache, not just as any coarse peasant, but as a man affected by progress and European civilization, a man who is "divorced from the soil and the national elements," as they express it now-a-days. His moans become nasty, disgustingly malignant, and go on for whole days and nights. And of course he knows himself that he is doing himself no sort of good with his moans; he knows better than any one that he is only lacerating and harassing himself and others for nothing; he knows that even the audience before whom he is making his efforts, and his whole family, listen to him with loathing, do not put a ha'porth of faith in him, and inwardly understand that he might moan differently, more simply, without trills and flourishes, and that he is only amusing himself like that from ill-humour, from malignancy. Well, in all these recognitions and disgraces it is that there lies a voluptuous pleasure. As though he would say: "I am worrying you, I am lacerating your hearts, I am keeping every one in the house awake. Well, stay awake then, you, too, feel every minute that I have toothache. I am not a hero to you now, as I tried to seem before, but simply a nasty person, an impostor. Well, so be it, then! I am very glad that you see through me. It is nasty for you to hear my despicable moans: well, let it be nasty; here I will let you have a nastier flourish in a minute. . . ." You do not understand even now, gentlemen? No, it seems our development and our consciousness must go further to understand all the intricacies of this pleasure. You laugh? Delighted. My jests, gentlemen, are of course in bad taste, jerky, involved, lacking self-confidence. But of course that is because I do not respect myself. Can a man of perception respect himself at all?

V

Come, can a man who attempts to find enjoyment in the very feeling of his own degradation possibly have a spark of respect for himself? I am not saying this now from any mawkish kind of remorse. And, indeed, I could never endure saying, "Forgive me, Papa, I won't do it again," not because I am incapable of saying that—on the contrary, perhaps just because I have been too capable of it, and in what a way, too! As though of design I used to get into trouble in cases when I was not to blame in any way. That was the nastiest part of it. At the same time I was genuinely touched and penitent, I used to shed tears and, of course, deceived myself, though I was not acting in the least and there was a sick feeling in my heart at the time. . . . For that one could not blame even the laws of nature, though the laws of nature have continually all my life offended me more than anything. It is loathsome to remember it all, but it was loathsome even then. Of course, a minute or so later I would realize wrathfully that it was all a lie, a revolting lie, an affected lie, that is, all this penitence, this emotion, these vows of reform. You will ask why did I worry myself with such antics: answer, because it was very dull to sit with one's hands folded, and so one began cutting capers. That is really it. Observe yourselves more carefully, gentlemen, then you will understand that it is so. I invented adventures for myself and made up a life, so as at least to live in some way. How many times it has happened to me—well, for instance, to take offence simply on purpose, for nothing; and one knows oneself, of course, that one is offended at nothing, that one is putting it on, but yet one brings oneself, at last to the point of being really offended. All my life I have had an impulse to play such pranks, so that in the end I could not control it in myself. Another time, twice, in fact, I tried hard to be in love. I suffered, too, gentlemen, I assure you. In the depth of my heart there was no faith in my suffering, only a faint stir of mockery, but yet I did suffer, and in the real, orthodox way; I was jealous, beside myself . . . and it was all from *ennui*, gentlemen, all from *ennui;* inertia overcame me. You know the direct, legitimate fruit of consciousness is inertia, that is, conscious sitting-with-the-hands-folded. I have referred to this already. I repeat, I repeat with emphasis: all "direct" persons and men of action are active just because they are stupid and limited. How explain that? I will tell you: in consequence of their limitation they take immediate and secondary causes for primary ones, and in that way persuade themselves more quickly and easily than other people do that they have found an infallible foundation for their activity, and their minds are at ease and you know that is the chief thing. To begin to act, you know, you must first have your mind completely at ease and no trace of doubt left in it. Why, how am I, for example to set my mind at rest? Where are the primary causes on which I am to build? Where are my foundations? Where am I to get them from? I exercise myself in reflection, and consequently with me every primary cause at once draws after itself another still more primary, and so on to infinity. That is just the essence of every sort of consciousness and reflection. It must be a case of the laws of nature again. What is the result of it in the end? Why, just the same. Remember I spoke just now of vengeance. (I am sure you did not take it in.) I said that a man revenges himself because he sees justice in it. Therefore he has found a primary cause, that is, justice. And so he is at rest on all sides, and consequently he carries out his revenge calmly and successfully, being persuaded that he is doing a just and honest thing. But I see no justice in it, I find no sort of virtue in it either, and consequently if I attempt to revenge myself, it is only out of spite. Spite, of course, might overcome everything, all my doubts, and so might serve quite successfully in place of a primary cause, precisely because it is not a cause. But what is to be done if I have not even spite (I began with that just now, you know). In consequence again of those accursed laws of consciousness, anger in me is subject to chemical disintegration. You look into it, the object flies off into air, your reasons evaporate, the criminal is not to be found, the wrong becomes not a wrong but a phantom, something like the toothache, for which no one is to blame, and consequently there is only the same outlet left again—that is, to beat the wall as hard as you can. So you give it up with a wave of the hand because you have not found a fundamental cause. And try letting yourself be carried away by your feelings, blindly, without reflection, without a primary cause, repelling consciousness at least for a time; hate or love, if only not to sit with your hands folded. The day after to-morrow, at the latest, you will begin despising yourself for having knowingly deceived yourself. Result: a soap-bubble and inertia. Oh, gentlemen, do you know, perhaps I consider myself an intelligent man, only because all my life I have been able neither to begin nor to finish anything. Granted I am a babbler, a harmless vexatious babbler, like all of us. But what is to be done if the direct and sole vocation of every intel-

ligent man is babble, that is, the intentional pouring of water
though a sieve?

VI

Oh, if I had done nothing simply from laziness! Heavens,
how I should have respected myself, then. I should have respected myself because I should at least have been capable
of being lazy; there would at least have been one quality, as
it were, positive in me, in which I could have believed myself. Question: What is he? Answer: A sluggard; how very
pleasant it would have been to hear that of oneself! It would
mean that I was positively defined, it would mean that there
was something to say about me. "Sluggard"—why, it is a
calling and vocation, it is a career. Do not jest, it is so. I
should then be a member of the best club by right, and
should find my occupation in continually respecting myself.
I knew a gentlemen who prided himself all his life on being
a connoisseur of Lafitte. He considered this as his positive
virtue, and never doubted himself. He died, not simply with
a tranquil, but with a triumphant, conscience, and he was
quite right, too. Then I should have chosen a career for
myself, I should have been a sluggard and a glutton, not a
simple one, but, for instance, one with sympathies for everything good and beautiful. How do you like that? I have
long had visions of it. That "good and beautiful" weighs
heavily on my mind at forty. But that is at forty; then—oh,
then it would have been different! I should have found for
myself a form of activity in keeping with it, to be precise,
drinking to the health of everything "good and beautiful."
I should have snatched at every opportunity to drop a tear
into my glass and then to drain it to all that is "good and
beautiful." I should then have turned everything into the
good and the beautiful; in the nastiest, unquestionable trash,
I should have sought out the good and the beautiful. I should
have exuded tears like a wet sponge. An artist, for instance,
paints a picture worthy of Gay. At once I drink to the health
of the artist who painted the picture worthy of Gay, because
I love all that is "good and beautiful." An author has written
As you will: at once I drink to the health of "any one you
will" because I love all that is "good and beautiful."

I should claim respect for doing so. I should persecute any
one who would not show me respect. I should live at ease, I

snould die with dignity, why, it is charming, perfectly charm·
ing! And what a good round belly I should have grown, what
a treble chin I should have established, what a ruby nose I
should have coloured for myself, so that every one would
have said, looking at me: "Here is an asset! Here is something real and solid!" And, say what you like, it is very
agreeable to hear such remarks about oneself in this negative
age.

VII

But these are all golden dreams. Oh, tell me, who was it
first announced, who was it first proclaimed, that man
only does nasty things because he does not know his own
interests; and that if he were enlightened, if his eyes were
opened to his real normal interests, man would at once cease
to do nasty things, would at once become good and noble
because, being enlightened and understanding his real advantage, he would see his own advantage in the good and
nothing else, and we all know that not one man can, consciously, act against his own interests, consequently, so to say,
through necessity, he would begin doing good? Oh, the babe!
Oh, the pure, innocent child! Why, in the first place, when in
all these thousands of years has there been a time when man
has acted only from his own interest? What is to be done
with the millions of facts that bear witness that men, *consciously*, that is fully understanding their real interests, have
left them in the background and have rushed headlong on
another path, to meet peril and danger, compelled to this
course by nobody and by nothing, but, as it were, simply
disliking the beaten track, and have obstinately, wilfully,
struck out another difficult, absurd way, seeking it almost in
the darkness. So, I suppose, this obstinacy and perversity were
pleasanter to them than any advantage. . . . Advantage!
What is advantage? And will you take it upon yourself to
define with perfect accuracy in what the advantage of man
consists? And what if it so happens that a man's advantage,
sometimes, not only may, but even must, consist in his desiring in certain cases what is harmful to himself and not
advantageous. And if so, if there can be such a case, the
whole principle falls into dust. What do you think—are
there such cases? You laugh; laugh away, gentlemen, but
only answer me: have man's advantages been reckoned up

with perfect certainty? Are there not some which not only have not been included but cannot possibly be included under any classification? You see, you gentlemen have, to the best of my knowledge, taken your whole register of human advantages from the averages of statistical figures and polit-ico-economical formulas. Your advantages are prosperity, wealth, freedom, peace—and so on, and so on. So that the man who should, for instance, go openly and knowingly in opposition to all that list would, to your thinking, and indeed mine, too, of course, be an obscurantist or an absolute mad-man: would not he? But, you know, this is what is surpris-ing: why does it so happen that all these statisticians, sages and lovers of humanity, when they reckon up human ad-vantages invariably leave out one? They don't even take it into their reckoning in the form in which it should be taken, and the whole reckoning depends upon that. It would be no great matter, they would simply have to take it, this ad-vantage, and add it to the list. But the trouble is, that this strange advantage does not fall under any classification and is not in place in any list. I have a friend for instance . . . Ech! gentlemen, but of course he is your friend, too; and indeed there is no one, no one, to whom he is not a friend! When he prepares for any undertaking this gentleman immediately explains to you, elegantly and clearly, exactly how he must act in accordance with the laws of reason and truth. What is more, he will talk to you with excitement and passion of the true normal interests of man; with irony he will upbraid the shortsighted fools who do not under-stand their own interests, nor the true significance of virtue; and, within a quarter of an hour, without any sudden outside provocation, but simply through something inside him which is stronger than all his interests, he will go off on quite a different tack—that is, act in direct opposition to what he has just been saying about himself, in opposition to the laws of reason, in opposition to his own advantage, in fact in opposition to everything . . . I warn you that my friend is a compound personality, and therefore it is difficult to blame him as an individual. The fact is, gentlemen, it seems there must really exist something that is dearer to al-most every man than his greatest advantages, or (not to be illogical) there is a most advantageous advantage (the very one omitted of which we spoke just now) which is more important and more advantageous than all other advantages, for the sake of which a man if necessary is ready to act in opposition to all laws; that is, in opposition to reason, honour, peace, prosperity—in fact, in opposition to all those excellent and useful things if only he can attain that fundamental, most advantageous advantage which is dearer to him than all. "Yes, but it's advantage all the same" you will retort. But excuse me, I'll make the point clear, and it is not a case of playing upon words. What matters is, that this advantage is remarkable from the very fact that it breaks down all our classifications, and continually shatters every system constructed by lovers of mankind for the benefit of mankind. In fact, it upsets everything. But before I mention this advantage to you, I want to compromise myself personally, and therefore I boldly declare that all these fine systems, all these theories for explaining to mankind their real normal interests, in order that inevitably striving to pursue these interests they may at once become good and noble—are, in my opinion, so far, mere logical exercises! Yes, logical exercises. Why, to maintain this theory of the regeneration of mankind by means of the pursuit of his own advantage is to my mind almost the same thing as . . . as to affirm, for instance, following Buckle, that through civilization mankind becomes softer, and consequently less bloodthirsty and less fitted for warfare. Logically it does seem to follow from his arguments. But man has such a predilection for systems and abstract deductions that he is ready to distort the truth intentionally, he is ready to deny the evidence of his senses only to justify his logic. I take this example because it is the most glaring instance of it. Only look about you: blood is being spilt in streams, and in the merriest way, as though it were champagne. Take the whole of the nineteenth century in which Buckle lived. Take Napoleon—the Great and also the present one. Take North America—the eternal union. Take the farce of Schleswig-Holstein. . . . And what is it that civilization softens in us? The only gain of civilization for mankind is the greater capacity for variety of sensations—and absolutely nothing more. And through the development of this many-sidedness man may come to find enjoyment in bloodshed. In fact, this has already happened to him. Have you noticed that it is the most civilized gentlemen who have been the subtlest slaughterers, to whom the Attilas and Stenka Razins could not hold a candle, and if they are not so conspicuous as the Attilas and Stenka Razins it is simply because they are so often met with, are so ordinary and have become so familiar to us. In any case civilization has made mankind if not more bloodthirsty, at least more vilely, more loathsomely bloodthirsty. In old days he saw justice in bloodshed and with his conscience at peace exterminated those he thought proper. Now we do think bloodshed abominable and yet we engage in this abomination, and with more energy than ever. Which is worse? Decide that for yourselves. They say that Cleopatra (excuse an instance from Roman history) was fond of sticking gold pins into her slave-girls' breasts and derived gratification from their screams and writhings. You will say that that was in the comparatively barbarous times; that these are barbarous times too, because also, comparatively speaking, pins are stuck in even now; that though man has now learned to see more clearly than in barbarous ages, he is still far from having learnt to act as reason and science would dictate. But yet you are fully convinced that he will be sure to learn when he gets rid of certain old bad habits, and when common sense and science have completely re-educated human nature and turned it in a normal direction. You are confident that then man will cease from *intentional* error and will, so to say, be compelled not to want to set his will against his normal interests. That is not all; then, you say, science itself will teach man (though to my mind it's a superfluous luxury) that he never has really had any caprice or will of his own, and that he himself is something of the nature of a piano-key or the stop of an organ, and that there are, besides, things called the laws of nature; so that everything he does is not done by his willing it, but is done of itself, by the laws of nature. Consequently we have only to discover these laws of nature, and man will no longer have to answer for his actions and life will become exceedingly easy for him. All human actions will then, of course, be tabulated according to these laws, mathematically, like tables of logarithms up to 108,000, and entered in an index; or, better still, there would be published certain edifying works of the nature of encyclopaedic lexicons, in which everything will be so clearly calculated and explained that there will be no more incidents or adventures in the world.

Then—this is all what you say—new economic relations will be established, all ready-made and worked out with mathematical exactitude, so that every possible question will vanish in the twinkling of an eye, simply because every possible answer to it will be provided. Then the "Palace of Crystal" will be built. Then . . . . In fact, those will be halcyon days. Of course there is no guaranteeing (this is my comment) that it will not be, for instance, frightfully dull then (for what will one have to do when everything will be calculated and tabulated), but on the other hand everything will be extraordinarily rational. Of course boredom may lead you to anything. It is boredom sets one sticking golden pins into people, but all that would not matter. What is bad (this is my comment again) is that I dare say people will be thankful for the gold pins then. Man is stupid, you know, phenomenally stupid; or rather he is not at all stupid, but he is so ungrateful that you could not find another like him in all creation. I, for instance, would not be in the least surprised if all of a sudden, *à propos* of nothing, in the midst of general prosperity a gentleman with an ignoble, or rather with a reactionary and ironical, countenance were to arise and, putting his arms akimbo, say to us all: "I say, gentlemen, hadn't we better kick over the whole show and scatter rationalism to the winds, simply to send these logarithms to the devil, and to enable us to live once more at our own sweet foolish will!" That again would not matter, but what is annoying is that he would be sure to find followers—such is the nature of man. And all that for the most foolish reason, which, one would think, was hardly worth mentioning: that is, that man everywhere and at all times, whoever he may be, has preferred to act as he chose and not in the least as his reason and advantage dictated. And one may choose what is contrary to one's own interests, and sometimes one *positively ought* (that is my idea). One's own free unfettered choice, one's own caprice, however wild it may be, one's own fancy worked up at times to frenzy—is that very "most advantageous advantage" which we have overlooked, which comes under no classification and against which all systems and theories are continually being shattered to atoms. And how do these wiseacres know that man wants a normal, a virtuous choice? What has made them conceive that man must want a rationally advantageous choice? What man wants is simply *independent* choice, whatever that independence may cost and wherever it may lead. And choice, of course, the devil only knows what choice.

VIII

"Ha! ha! ha! But you know there is no such thing as choice in reality, say what you like," you will interpose with a chuckle. "Science has succeeded in so far analysing man that we know already that choice and what is called freedom of will is nothing else than——"

Stay, gentlemen, I meant to begin with that myself. I confess, I was rather frightened. I was just going to say that the devil only knows what choice depends on, and that perhaps that was a very good thing, but I remembered the teaching of science . . . and pulled myself up. And here you have begun upon it. Indeed, if there really is some day discovered a formula for all our desires and caprices—that is, an explanation of what they depend upon, by what laws they arise, how they develop, what they are aiming at it one case and in another and so on, that is a real mathematical formula —then, most likely, man will at once cease to feel desire, indeed, he will be certain to. For who would want to choose by rule? Besides, he will at once be transformed from a human being into an organ-stop or something of the sort; for what is a man without desires, without freewill and without choice, if not a stop in an organ? What do you think? Let us reckon the chances—can such a thing happen or not?

"H'm!" you decide. "Our choice is usually mistaken from a false view of our advantage. We sometimes choose absolute nonsense because in our foolishness we see in that nonsense the easiest means for attaining a supposed advantage. but when all that is explained and worked out on paper (which is perfectly possible, for it is contemptible and senseless to suppose that some laws of nature man will never understand), then certainly so-called desires will no longer exist. For if a desire should come into conflict with reason we shall then reason and not desire, because it will be impossible retaining our reason to be *senseless* in our desires, and in that way knowingly act against reason and desire to injure ourselves. And as all choice and reasoning can be really calculated—because there will some day be discovered the laws of our so-called freewill—so, joking apart, there may one day be something like a table constructed of them, so that we really shall choose in accordance with it. If, for instance, some day they calculate and prove to me that I made a long nose at some one because I could not help making a long nose at him and that I had to do it in that particular way, what *freedom* is left me, especially if I am a learned man and have taken my degree somewhere? Then I should be able to calculate my whole life for thirty years beforehand. In short, if this could be arranged there would be nothing left for us to do; anyway, we should have to understand that. And, in fact, we ought unwearyingly to repeat to ourselves that at such and such a time and in such and such circumstances nature does not ask our leave; that we have got to take her as she is and not fashion her to suit our fancy, and if we really aspire to formulas and tables of rules, and well, even . . . to the chemical retort, there's no help for it, we must accept the retort too, or else it will be accepted without our consent. . . ."

Yes, but here I come to a stop! Gentlemen, you must excuse me for being over-philosophical: it's the result of forty years underground! Allow me to indulge my fancy. You see, gentlemen, reason is an excellent thing, there's no disputing that, but reason is nothing but reason and satisfies only the rational side of man's nature, while will is a manifestation of the whole life, that is, of the whole human life including reason and all the impulses. And although our life, in this manifestation of it, is often worthless, yet it is life and not simply extracting square roots. Here I, for instance, quite naturally want to live, in order to satisfy all my capacities for life, and not simply my capacity for reasoning, that is, not simply one twentieth of my capacity for life. What does reason know? Reason only knows what it has succeeded in learning (some things, perhaps, it will never learn; this is a poor comfort, but why not say so frankly?) and human nature acts as a whole, with everything that is in it, consciously or unconsciously, and, even if it goes wrong, it lives. I suspect, gentlemen, that you are looking at me with compassion; you tell me again that an enlightened and developed man, such, in short, as the future man will be, cannot consciously desire anything disadvantageous to himself, that that can be proved mathematically. I thoroughly agree, it can—by mathematics. But I repeat for the hundredth time, there is one case, one only, when man may consciously, purposely, desire what is injurious to himself, what is stupid, very stupid—simply in order to have the right to desire **for** himself even what is very stupid and not to be bound by an obligation to desire only what is sensible. Of course, this very stupid thing, this caprice of ours, may be in reality, gentlemen, more advantageous for us than anything else on earth, especially in certain cases. And in particular it may be more advantageous than any advantage even when it does us obvious harm, and contradicts the soundest conclusions of our reason concerning our advantage—for in any circumstances it preserves for us what is most precious and most important—that is, our personality, our individuality. Some, you see, maintain that this really is the most precious thing for mankind; choice can, of course, if it chooses, be in agreement with reason; and especially if this be not abused but kept within bounds. It is profitable and sometimes even praiseworthy. But very often, and even most often, choice is utterly and stubbornly opposed to reason . . . and . . . and . . . do you know that that, too, is profitable, sometimes even praiseworthy? Gentlemen, let us suppose that man is not stupid. (Indeed one cannot refuse to suppose that, if only from the one consideration, that, it man is stupid, then who is wise?) But if he is not stupid, he is monstrously ungrateful! Phenomenally ungrateful. In fact, I believe that the best definition of man is the ungrateful biped. But that is not all, that is not his worst defect; his worst defect is his perpetual moral obliquity, perpetual—from the days of the Flood to the Schleswig-Holstein period. Moral obliquity and consequently lack of good sense; for it has long been accepted that lack of good sense is due to no other cause than moral obliquity. Put it to the test and cast your eyes upon the history of mankind. What will you see? Is it a grand spectacle? Grand, if you like. Take the Colossus of Rhodes, for instance, that's worth something. With good reason Mr. Anaevsky testifies of it that some say that it is the work of man's hands, while others maintain that it has been created by nature herself. Is it many-coloured? May be it is many-coloured, too: if one takes the dress uniforms, military and civilian, of all peoples in all ages—that alone is worth something, and if you take the undress uniforms you will never get to the end of it; no historian would be equal to the job. Is it monotonous? May be it's monotonous too: it's fighting and fighting; they are fighting now, they fought first and they fought last—you will admit, that it is almost too monotonous. In short, one may say anything about the history of the world—anything that might enter the most disordered imagination. The only thing one can't say is that it's rational. The very word sticks in one's throat. And, indeed, this is the odd thing that is continually happening: there are continually turning up in life moral and rational persons, sages and lovers of humanity who make it their object to live all their lives as morally and rationally as possible, to be, so to speak, a light to their neighbours simply in order to show them that it is possible to live morally and rationally in this world. And yet we all know that those very people sooner or later have been false to themselves, playing some queer trick, often a most unseemly one. Now I ask you: what can be expected of man since he is a being endowed with such strange qualities? Shower upon him every earthly blessing, drown him in a sea of happiness, so that nothing but bubbles of bliss can be seen on the surface; give him economic prosperity, such that he should have nothing else to do but sleep, eat cakes and busy himself with the continuation of his species, and even then out of sheer ingratitude, sheer spite, man would play you some nasty trick. He would even risk his cakes and would deliberately desire the most fatal rubbish, the most uneconomical absurdity, simply to introduce into all this positive good sense his fatal fantastic element. It is just his fantastic dreams, his vulgar folly that he will desire to retain, simply in order to prove to himself—as though that were so necessary—that men still are men and not the keys of a piano, which the laws of nature threaten to control so completely that soon one will be able to desire nothing but by the calendar. And that is not all: even if man really were nothing but a piano-key, even if this were proved to him by natural science and mathematics, even then he would not become reasonable, but would purposely do something perverse out of simple ingratitude, simply to gain his point. And if he does not find means he will contrive destruction and chaos, will contrive sufferings of all sorts, only to gain his point! He will launch a curse upon the world, and as only man can curse (it is his privilege, the primary distinction between him and other animals), may be by his curse alone he will attain his object—that is, convince himself that he is a man and not a piano-key! If you say that all this, too, can be calculated and tabulated—chaos and darkness and curses, so that the mere possibility of calculating it all beforehand would stop it all, and reason would reassert itself, then man would purposely go mad in order to be rid of reason and gain his point! I believe in it, I answer for it, for the whole work of man really seems to consist in nothing but proving to himself every minute that he is a man and not a piano-key! It may be at the cost of his skin, it may be by cannibalism! And this being so, can one help being tempted to rejoice that it has not yet come off, and that desire still depends on something we don't know?

You will scream at me (that is, if you condescend to do so) that no one is touching my free will, that all they are concerned with is that my will should of itself, of its own free will, coincide with my own normal interests, with the laws of nature and arithmetic.

Good Heavens, gentlemen, what sort of free will is left when we come to tabulation and arithmetic, when it will all be a case of twice two make four? Twice two makes four without my will. As if free will meant that!

IX

Gentlemen, I am joking, and I know myself that my jokes are not brilliant, but you know one can't take everything as a joke. I am, perhaps, jesting against the grain. Gentlemen, I am tormented by questions; answer them for me. You, for instance, want to cure men of their old habits and reform their will in accordance with science and good sense. But how do you know, not only that it is possible, but also that it is *desirable*, to reform man in that way? And what leads you to the conclusion that man's inclinations *need* reforming? In short, how do you know that such a reformation will be a benefit to man? And to go to the root of the matter, why are you so positively convinced that not to act against his real normal interests guaranteed by the conclusions of reason and arithmetic is certainly always advantageous for man and must always be a law for mankind? So far, you know, this is only your supposition. It may be the law of logic, but not the law of humanity. You think, gentlemen, perhaps that I am mad? Allow me to defend myself. I agree that man is pre-eminently a creative animal, predestined to strive consciously for an object and to engage in engineering—that is, incessantly and eternally to make new roads, *wherever they may lead*. But the reason why he wants sometimes to go off at a tangent may just be that he is *predes-*

tined to make the road, and perhaps, too, that however stupid the "direct" practical man may be, the thought sometimes will occur to him that the road almost always does lead *somewhere*, and that the destination it leads to is less important than the process of making it, and that the chief thing is to save the well-conducted child from despising engineering, and so giving way to the fatal idleness, which, as we all know, is the mother of all the vices. Man likes to make roads and to create, that is a fact beyond dispute. But why has he such a passionate love for destruction and chaos also? Tell me that! But on that point I want to say a couple of words myself. May it not be that he loves chaos and destruction (there can be no disputing that he does sometimes love it) because he is instinctively afraid of attaining his object and completing the edifice he is constructing? Who knows, perhaps he only loves that edifice from a distance, and is by no means in love with it at close quarters; perhaps he only loves building it and does not want to live in it, but will leave it, when completed, for the use of *les animaux domestiques*— such as the ants, the sheep, and so on. Now the ants have quite a different taste. They have a marvellous edifice of that pattern which endures for ever—the ant-heap.

With the ant-heap the respectable race of ants began and with the ant-heap they will probably end, which does the greatest credit to their perseverance and good sense. But man is a frivolous and incongruous creature, and perhaps, like a chess player, loves the process of the game, not the end of it. And who knows (there is no saying with certainty), perhaps the only goal on earth to which mankind is striving lies in this incessant process of attaining, in other words, in life itself, and not in the thing to be attained, which must always be expressed as a formula, as positive as twice two makes four, and such positiveness is not life, gentlemen, but is the beginning of death. Anyway, man has always been afraid of this mathematical certainty, and I am afraid of it now. Granted that man does nothing but seek that mathematical certainty, he traverses oceans, sacrifices his life in the quest, but to succeed, really to find it, he dreads, I assure you. He feels that when he has found it there will be nothing for him to look for. When workmen have finished their work they do at least receive their pay, they go to the tavern, then they are taken to the police-station—and there is occupation for a week. But where can man go? Any-

way, one can observe a certain awkwardness about him when
he has attained such objects. He loves the process of attaining, but does not quite like to have attained, and that, of
course, is very absurd. In fact, man is a comical creature;
there seems to be a kind of jest in it all. But yet mathematical certainty is, after all, something insufferable. Twice two
makes four seems to me simply a piece of insolence. Twice
two makes four is a pert coxcomb who stands with arms
akimbo barring your path and spitting. I admit that twice
two makes four is an excellent thing, but if we are to give
everything its due, twice two makes five is sometimes a
very charming thing too.

And why are you so firmly, so triumphantly, convinced
that only the normal and the positive—in other words, only
what is conducive to welfare—is for the advantage of man?
Is not reason in error as regards advantage? Does not man,
perhaps, love something besides well-being? Perhaps he is
just as fond of suffering? Perhaps suffering is just as great
a benefit to him as well-being? Man is sometimes extraordinarily, passionately, in love with suffering, and that is a fact.
There is no need to appeal to universal history to prove
that; only ask yourself, if you are a man and have lived at
all. As far as my personal opinion is concerned, to care only
for well-being seems to me positively ill-bred. Whether it's
good or bad, it is sometimes very pleasant, too, to smash
things. I hold no brief for suffering nor for well-being either.
I am standing for . . . my caprice, and for its being
guaranteed to me when necessary. Suffering would be out of
place in vaudevilles, for instance; I know that. In the
"Palace of Crystal" it is unthinkable; suffering means doubt,
negation, and what would be the good of a "palace of crystal" if there could be any doubt about it? And yet I think
man will never renounce real suffering, that is, destruction
and chaos. Why, suffering is the sole origin of consciousness.
Though I did lay it down at the beginning that consciousness is the greatest misfortune for man, yet I know man
prizes it and would not give it up for any satisfaction. Consciousness, for instance, is infinitely superior to twice two
makes four. Once you have mathematical certainty there is
nothing left to do or to understand. There will be nothing
left but to bottle up your five senses and plunge into contemplation. While if you stick to consciousness, even though
the same result is attained, you can at least flog yourself at

times, and that will, at any rate, liven you up. Reactionary as it is, corporal punishment is better than nothing.

x

You believe in a palace of crystal that can never be destroyed—a palace at which one will not be able to put out one's tongue or make a long nose on the sly. And perhaps that is just why I am afraid of this edifice, that it is of crystal and can never be destroyed and that one cannot put one's tongue out at it even on the sly.

You see, if it were not a palace, but a hen-house, I might creep into it to avoid getting wet, and yet I would not call the hen-house a palace out of gratitude to it for keeping me dry. You laugh and say that in such circumstances a hen-house is as good as a mansion. Yes, I answer, if one had to live simply to keep out of the rain.

But what is to be done if I have taken it into my head that that is not the only object in life, and that if one must live one had better live in a mansion. That is my choice, my desire. You will only eradicate it when you have changed my preference. Well, do change it, allure me with something else, give me another ideal. But meanwhile I will not take a hen-house for a mansion. The palace of crystal may be an idle dream, it may be that it is inconsistent with the laws of nature and that I have invented it only through my own stupidity, through the old-fashioned irrational habits of my generation. But what does it matter to me that it is inconsisent? That makes no difference since it exists in my desires, or rather exists as long as my desires exist. Perhaps you are laughing again? Laugh away; I will put up with any mockery rather than pretend that I am satisfied when I am hungry. I know, anyway, that I will not be put off with a compromise, with a recurring zero, simply because it is consistent with the laws of nature and actually exists. I will not accept as the crown of my desires a block of buildings with tenements for the poor on a lease of a thousand years, and perhaps with a sign-board of a dentist hanging out. Destroy my desires, eradicate my ideals, show me something better, and I will follow you. You will say, perhaps, that it is not worth your trouble; but in that case I can give you the same answer. We are discussing things seriously; but if you won't deign to give me your attention, I will drop your acquaintance. I can retreat into my underground hole.

But while I am alive and have desires I would rather my hand were withered off than bring one brick to such a building! Don't remind me that I have just rejected the palace of crystal for the sole reason that one cannot put out one's tongue at it. I did not say because I am so fond of putting my tongue out. Perhaps the thing I resented was, that of all your edifices there has not been one at which one could not put out one's tongue. On the contrary, I would let my tongue be cut off out of gratitude if things could be so arranged that I should lose all desire to put it out. It is not my fault that things cannot be so arranged, and that one must be satisfied with model flats. Then why am I made with such desires? Can I have been constructed simply in order to come to the conclusion that all my construction is a cheat? Can this be my whole purpose? I do not believe it.

But do you know what: I am convinced that we underground folk ought to be kept on a curb. Though we may sit forty years underground without speaking, when we do come out into the light of day and break out we talk and talk and talk. . . .

XI

The long and the short of it is, gentlemen, that it is better to do nothing! Better conscious inertia! And so hurrah for underground! Though I have said that I envy the normal man to the last drop of my bile, yet I should not care to be in his place such as he is now (though I shall not cease envying him). No, no; anyway the underground life is more advantageous. There, at any rate, one can. . . . Oh, but even now I am lying! I am lying because I know myself that it is not underground that is better, but something different, quite different, for which I am thirsting, but which I cannot find! Damn underground!

I will tell you another thing that would be better, and that is, if I myself believed in anything of what I have just written. I swear to you, gentlemen, there is not one thing, not one word of what I have written that I really believe. That is, I believe it, perhaps, but at the same time I feel and suspect that I am lying like a cobbler.

"Then why have you written all this?" you will say to me. "I ought to put you underground for forty years without anything to do and then come to you in your cellar, to find out what stage you have reached! How can a man be left with nothing to do for forty years?"

"Isn't that shameful, isn't that humiliating?" you will say, perhaps, wagging your heads contemptuously. "You thirst for life and try to settle the problems of life by a logical tangle. And how persistent, how insolent are your sallies, and at the same time what a scare you are in! You talk nonsense and are pleased with it; you say impudent things and are in continual alarm and apologizing for them. You declare that you are afraid of nothing and at the same time try to ingratiate yourself in our good opinion. You declare that you are gnashing your teeth and at the same time you try to be witty so as to amuse us. You know that your witticisms are not witty, but you are evidently well satisfied with their literary value. You may, perhaps, have really suffered, but you have no respect for your own suffering. You may have sincerity, but you have no modesty; out of the pettiest vanity you expose your sincerity to publicity and ignominy. You doubtlessly mean to say something, but hide your last word through fear, because you have not the resolution to utter it, and only have a cowardly impudence. You boast of consciousness, but you are not sure of your ground, for though your mind works, yet your heart is darkened and corrupt, and you cannot have a full, genuine consciousness without a pure heart. And how intrusive you are, how you insist and grimace! Lies, lies, lies!"

Of course I have myself made up all the things you say. That, too, is from underground. I have been for forty years listening to you through a crack under the floor. I have invented them myself, there was nothing else I could invent. It is no wonder that I have learned it by heart and it has taken a literary form. . . .

But can you really be so credulous as to think that I will print all this and give it to you to read too? And another problem: why do I call you "gentlemen," why do I address you as though you really were my readers? Such confessions as I intend to make are never printed nor given to other people to read. Anyway, I am not strong-minded enough for that, and I don't see why I should be. But you see a fancy has occurred to me and I want to realize it at all costs. Let me explain.

Every man has reminiscences which he would not tell to

every one, but only to his friends. He has other matters in
his mind which he would not reveal even to his friends, but
only to himself, and that in secret. But there are other
things which a man is afraid to tell even to himself, and
every decent man has a number of such things stored away
in his mind. The more decent he is, the greater the number
of such things in his mind. Anyway, I have only lately determined to remember some of my early adventures. Till
now I have always avoided them, even with a certain un-
easiness. Now, when I am not only recalling them, but have
actually decided to write an account of them, I want to try
the experiment whether one can, even with oneself, be perfectly open and not take fright at the whole truth. I will
observe, in parenthesis, that Heine says that a true auto-
biography is almost an impossibility, and that man is bound
to lie about himself. He considers that Rousseau certainly
told lies about himself in his confessions, and even intentionally lied, out of vanity. I am convinced that Heine is
right; I quite understand how sometimes one may, out of
sheer vanity, attribute regular crimes to oneself, and indeed
I can very well conceive that kind of vanity. But Heine
judged of people who made their confessions to the public.
I write only for myself, and I wish to declare once and for
all that if I write as though I were addressing readers, that is
simply because it is easier for me to write in that form. It is
a form, an empty form—I shall never have readers. . . .

THREE

Kierkegaard: THE FIRST EXISTENTIALIST

[*Preface:* Søren Kierkegaard was born in Denmark in 1813 and died in 1855. Against the theoretical philosophy of Hegel and his predecessors he pitted a mode of reflection closer to the individual's concrete existence. He tried to live his thoughts—at times grotesquely, as he pictures his own efforts in *The Point of View* (below), but at other times, especially at the end of his life, with a complete and utter disregard for his temporal welfare. He died, having worn himself out with protests against the perversion of Christianity by Christian institutions and refusing the ministrations of his church. That he would have lived through the Hitler years like either of the leading German existentialists, is unthinkable. When fortune smiled at him, he dared a powerful paper that had praised his work, but which he detested as a scandal sheet, to pillory him. It did.

The first four selections develop Kierkegaard's conception of himself and provide some perspective for his work. The last three selections deal with three of the central themes of his thought.

"On his Mission" is from the *Concluding Unscientific Postscript*, pp. 164ff. The work was published over a pseudonym like many of his books, but in this case the author added his own name as editor. Ostensibly, then, the "I" here is not Kierkegaard himself. In this selection, three dots mark minor omissions; but in the following selections they are punctuation marks which the author sometimes used in place of dashes.

The selection "On his Works" is the "Conclusion" of Chapter I, Part II, in *The Point of View*, and sums up his discussion of his aesthetic works, the *Postscript*, and the religious works. The next selection picks up where the second one ended: it is the beginning of Chapter II. The final selection is from *"That Individual": Two "Notes" Concerning My Work as an Author*, which was published in 1859, posthumously, along with *The Point of View*. Of the first of the "two notes" only the introductory page and the final footnote have been omitted; from the second note only one paragraph has been used.

"Dread and Freedom" is excerpted from *The Concept of Dread*, one of Kierkegaard's most influential works. He subtitled it "A simple psychological deliberation oriented in the direction of the dogmatic problem of original sin" and published it over the pseudonym of Vigilius Haufniensis, June 17, 1844. The concept of dread, as understood by him, became central in the thought of Jaspers and, even more so, Heidegger. See especially *Being and Time* and *What is Metaphysics?*

"Authority" comes from *On Authority and Revelation: The Book on Adler, Or a Cycle of Ethico-Religious Essays*. Kierkegaard eventually decided not to publish this book because it so strongly attacked an individual: Magister Adler. Yet he clearly spoke his own mind in these very revealing and important pages, and he did publish, over his own name, the central discussion "Of the Difference Between a Genius and an Apostle," which is available together with *The Present Age* in Alexander Dru's translation, with an Introduction by Walter Kaufmann. But the selections on "Authority" come from Walter Lowrie's version of *On Authority and Revelation*, which provides a larger context. The first paragraph is from Kierkegaard's Preface. What follows comes from pp. 105-10, 116-18, 163, and 168f.

The last selection, "Truth is Subjectivity," is from *Concluding Unscientific Postscript* and should be considered against the background of the preceding selections—especially "On His Mission," which comes from the same book, and "Authority." The first part of this selection is from Kierkegaard's Preface, the second from pp. 25-31, the third from 178-82, and the last from 188-93. Kierkegaard's thesis raises many questions. Does he stick with the claims made in the first two sentences? Is the second sentence of the third paragraph, for example, consistent with these claims? Or does

Kierkegaard assume the objective truth of certain beliefs? The question he asks in the last paragraph of the first part raises the same problem. Why should he stake everything on his participation "in the happiness promised by Christianity" rather than the bliss promised by various other religions, unless he presupposes that the promises of Christianity, unlike those of other religions, are true?

In the second part he makes much of the fact that scholarship cannot firmly establish faith. Why does he ignore the no less obvious fact that it can, and often does, undermine faith? Does the section on "Authority" help us to understand him at this point?

In the third paragraph of the third part, the contrast of the passionate idolater with the Christian who "prays in a false spirit" is attractive. But is Kierkegaard's knowledge of what constitutes a false spirit objective or subjective? And are passion and the feeling of certainty a warrant of any kind of truth—even "subjective truth"? The contrast is posed in such terms that the reader may be ready to grant the ethico-religious superiority of those who are passionate and feel certain; but suppose it were posed in different terms, with a fanatic on one side and a person with more humility on the other. Is there nothing to be said in favor of those who are mindful of their fallibility precisely in matters of faith and morals?

Finally, it is psychologically true that absurd beliefs, being easily vulnerable by rational attack, tend to generate a great deal of passion. But is passionate faith of this sort to be sought and admired? If so, why stop at Christianity? Kierkegaard argues in *Concluding Unscientific Postscript*—having more of a sense of humor than most of his expositors—that nothing could be more absurd than Christianity. What of the belief that Hitler was God, or Father Divine, or some adolescent Hindu who claims to be God?

Some of Kierkegaard's motifs are clearly continuous with *Notes from Underground*. Some are taken up and developed by Jaspers and Heidegger. But Kierkegaard on faith should be compared with Sartre's "Portrait of the Antisemite."

1. On His Mission

It is now about four years ago that I got the notion of wanting to try my luck as an author. I remember it quite clearly; it was on a Sunday, yes, that's it, a Sunday afternoon. I was seated as usual, out-of-doors at the café in the Frederiksberg Garden . . . I had been a student for half a score of years. Although never lazy, all my activity nevertheless was like a glittering inactivity, a kind of occupation for which I still have a great partiality, and for which perhaps I even have a little genius. I read much, spent the remainder of the day idling and thinking, or thinking and idling, but that was all it came to . . .

So there I sat and smoked my cigar until I lapsed into thought. Among other thoughts I remember these: "You are going on," I said to myself, "to become an old man, without being anything, and without really undertaking to do anything. On the other hand, wherever you look about you, in literature and in life, you see the celebrated names and figures, the precious and much heralded men who are coming into prominence and are much talked about, the many benefactors of the age who know how to benefit mankind by making life easier and easier, some by railways, others by omnibuses and steamboats, others by the telegraph, others by easily apprehended compendiums and short recitals of everything worth knowing, and finally the true benefactors of the age who make spiritual existence in virtue of thought easier and easier, yet more and more significant. And what are you doing?" Here my soliloquy was interrupted, for my cigar was smoked out and a new one had to be lit. So I smoked again, and then suddenly this thought flashed through my mind: "You must do something, but inasmuch as with your limited capacities it will be impossible to make anything easier than it has become, you must, with the same humanitarian enthusiasm as the others, undertake to make something harder." This notion pleased me immensely, and at the same time it flattered me to think that I, like the rest of them, would be loved and esteemed by the whole community. For when all combine in every way to make everything easier, there remains only one possible danger, namely, that the ease becomes so great that it becomes altogether too great; then there is only one want left, though it is not yet a felt want, when people will want difficulty. Out of love for mankind, and out of despair at my embarrassing situation, seeing that I had accomplished nothing and was unable to make anything easier than it had already been made, and moved by a genuine interest in those who make everything easy, I conceived it as my task to create difficulties everywhere. . . .

So then I am striving towards the exalted goal of being hailed with acclamation—unless possibly I am derided, or maybe crucified; for it is quite certain that every man who shouts *bravo* shouts also *pereat,* if not crucify, and that even without being untrue to his character, since on the contrary he remains true to himself—*qua* shouter. But even though my effort be misunderstood, I am convinced nevertheless that it is just as noble as that of the others. When at a banquet, where the guests have already overeaten, one person is concerned about bringing on new courses, another about having a vomitive at hand, it is perfectly true that only the first has interpreted correctly the requirement of the guests, but I wonder whether the other might not also say that he is concerned about what the requirement might be.

2. On His Works

What does all this come to, when the reader puts together the points dwelt upon in the foregoing paragraphs? It means that this is a literary work in which the whole thought is the task of becoming a Christian. But it is a literary work which understood from the very first and consistently followed out the implication of the fact that the situation is Christendom—a reflective modification—and hence transformed into reflection all the relationships of Christianity. To become a Christian in Christendom means either to become what one is (the inwardness of reflection or to become inward through reflection), or it means that the first thing is to be disengaged from the toils of one's illusion, which again is a reflective modification. Here there is no room for vacillation or ambiguity of the sort one commonly experiences elsewhere when one does not know and cannot make out whether one is situated in paganism, whether the parson is a missionary in that sense, or whereabouts one is. Here one does not miss what is generally lacking, viz. a decisive categorical definition and a decisive expression for the situation: to preach Christianity . . . in Christendom. Everything is put in terms of reflection. The communication is qualified by reflection, hence it is indirect communication. The communicator is characterized by reflection, therefore he is negative—not one who says that he himself is a Christian in an extraordinary degree, or even lays claim to revelations (all of which answers to immediacy and direct communication); but, on the contrary, one who even affirms that he is not a Christian. That is to say, the communicator stands behind the other man, helping him negatively—for whether he actually succeeds in helping some one is another question. The problem itself is a problem of reflection: to become a Christian . . . when one is a Christian of a sort.

3. On His "Mode of Existence"

THE DIFFERENCE IN MY PERSONAL MODE OF EXISTENCE CORRESPONDING TO THE ESSENTIAL DIFFERENCE IN THE WORKS

In this age, and indeed for many ages past, people have quite lost sight of the fact that authorship is and ought to be a serious calling implying an appropriate mode of personal existence. They do not realize that the press in general, as an expression of the abstract and impersonal communication of ideas, and the daily press in particular, because of its formal indifference to the question whether what it reports is true or false, contributes enormously to the general demoralization, for the reason that the impersonal, which for the most part is irresponsible and incapable of repentance, is essentially demoralizing. They do not realize that anonymity, as the most absolute expression for the impersonal, the irresponsible, the unrepentant, is a fundamental source of the modern demoralization. On the other hand, they do not reflect that anonymity would be counteracted in the simplest possible way, and that a wholesome corrective would be furnished for the abstractness of printed communication, if people would but turn back again to antiquity and learn what it means to be a single individual man, neither more nor less—which surely even an author is too, neither more nor less. This is perfectly obvious. But in our age, which reckons as wisdom that which is truly the mystery of unrighteousness, viz. that one need not inquire about the communicator, but only about the communication, the objective only—in our age what is an author? An author is often merely an *x*, even when his name is signed, something quite impersonal, which addresses itself abstractly, by the aid of printing, to thousands and thousands, while remaining itself unseen and unknown, living a life as hidden, as anonymous, as it is possible for a life to be, in order, presumably, not to reveal the too obvious and striking contradiction between the prodigious means of communication employed and the fact that the author is only a single individual—perhaps also for fear of the control which in practical life must always be exercised over every one who wishes to teach others, to see whether his personal existence comports with his communication. But all this, which deserves the most serious attention on the part of one who would study the demoralization of the modern state—all this I cannot enter into more particularly here.

THE PERSONAL MODE OF EXISTENCE IN RELATION TO THE AESTHETIC WORKS

I come now to the first period of my authorship and my mode of existence. Here was a religious author, but one who began as an aesthetic author; and this first stage was one of incognito and deceit. Initiated as I was very early and very thoroughly into the secret that *Mundus vult decipi,* I was not in the position of being able to wish to follow such tactics. Quite the contrary. With me it was a question of deceiving inversely on the greatest possible scale, employing every bit of knowledge I had about men and their weaknesses and their stupidities, not to profit thereby, but to annihilate myself and weaken the impression I made. The secret of the deceit which suits the world which wants to be deceived consists partly in forming a coterie and all that goes with that, in joining one or another of those societies for mutual admiration, whose members support one another with tongue and pen in the pursuit of worldy advantage; and it consists partly in hiding oneself from the human crowd, never being seen, so as to produce a fantastic effect. So I had to do exactly the opposite. I had to exist in absolute isolation and guard my solitude, but at the same time take pains to be seen every hour of the day, living as it were upon the street, in company with Tom, Dick, and Harry, and in the most fortuitous situations. This is truth's way of deceiving, the everlastingly sure way of weakening, in a worldly sense, the impression one makes. It was, moreover, the way followed by men of a very different calibre from mine to make people take notice. Those reputable persons, the deceivers who want the communication to serve them instead of serving the communication, are on the look-out only to win repute for themselves. Those despised persons, the "witnesses for the truth," who deceive inversely, have ever been wont to suffer themselves to be set at naught in a worldly sense and be counted as nothing—in spite of the fact that they labour day and night, and suffer besides from having no support whatever in the illusion that the work they perform is their career and their "living."

So this had to be done, and it was done, not now and then, but every day. I am convinced that one-sixth of *Either/Or,* together with a bit of coterie, and then an author who was never to be seen—especially if this was carried on for a considerable time—must make a much more extraordinary effect. I, however, had made myself sure of being able to work as laboriously as I pleased and as the spirit prompted me, without having to fear that I might get too much renown. For in a certain sense I was working as laboriously in another direction—against myself. Only an author will be able to understand what a task it is to work *qua* author, i.e. with mind and pen, and yet be at the beck and call of everybody. Although this mode of existence enriched me immensely with observations of human life, it is a standard of conduct which would bring most men to despair. For it means the effort to dispel every illusion and to present the idea in all its purity—and verily, it is not truth that rules the world but illusions. Even if a literary achievement were more illustrious than any that has yet been seen—if only the author were to live as is here suggested, he would in a brief time have insured himself against worldly renown and the crowd's brutish adulation. For the crowd possesses no idealism, and hence no power of retaining impressions in spite of contrary appearances. It is always the victim of appearances. To be seen again and again, and to be seen in the most fortuitous situations, is enough to make the crowd forget its first impression of the man and become soon sick and tired of him. And, after all, to keep oneself perpetually in view does not consume a great deal of time, if only one employs one's time shrewdly (i.e. in a worldly sense insanely) and to the best effect, by going back and forth past the same spot, and that the most frequented spot in the city. Every one who husbands his reputation, in a worldly sense, will not return by the same way he went, even if it is the most convenient way. He will avoid being seen twice in so short a time, for fear people might suppose he had nothing to do, whereas if he sat in his room at home three-quarters of the

day and was idle, such a thought would never occur to anybody. On the other hand, an hour well spent, in a godly
sense, an hour lived for eternity and spent by going back and
forth among the common people . . . is not such a small
thing after all. And verily it is well pleasing to God that
the truth should be served in this way. His Spirit witnesseth
mightily with my spirit that it has the full consent of His
Divine Majesty. All the witnesses of the truth indicate their
approval, recognizing that one is disposed to serve the
truth, the idea, and not to betray the truth and profit by the
illusion. I experienced a real Christian satisfaction in ven-
turing to perform on Monday a little bit of that which one
weeps about on Sunday (when the parson prates about it
and weeps too) . . . and on Monday one is ready to laugh
about. I had real Christian satisfaction in the thought that, if
there were no other, there was definitely one man in Copenhagen whom every poor man could freely accost and converse with on the street; that, if there were no other, there
was one man who, whatever the society he more commonly
frequented, did not shun contact with the poor, but greeted
every maidservant he was acquainted with, every manservant,
every common labourer. I felt a real Christian satisfaction in
the fact that, if there were no other, there was one man who
(several years before existence set the race another lesson to
learn) made a practical effort on a small scale to learn the
lesson of loving one's neighbour and alas! got at the same
time a frightful insight into what an illusion Christendom
is, and (a little later, to be sure) an insight also into what
a situation the simpler classes suffered themselves to be seduced by paltry newspaper-writers, whose struggle or fight
for equality (since it is in the service of a lie) cannot lead
to any other result but to prompt the privileged classes in
self-defence to stand proudly aloof from the common man,
and to make the common man insolent in his forwardness.

The description of my personal existence cannot be carried out here in greater detail; but I am convinced that
seldom has any author employed so much cunning, intrigue,
and shrewdness to win honour and reputation in the world
with a view to deceiving it, as I displayed in order to deceive
it inversely in the interest of truth. On how great a scale
this was carried out I shall attempt to show by one single
instance, known to my friend Giødwad, the proof-reader of
Either/Or. I was so busy when I was reading the proofs of

Either/Or that it was impossible to spend the usual time sauntering back and forth on the street. I did not get through the work till late in the evening, and then I hastened to the theatre, where I remained literally only from five to ten minutes. And why did I do this? Because I feared the big book would create for me too great a reputation.[1] And why did I do this? Because I knew human nature, especially in Copenhagen. To be seen every night for five minutes by several hundred people sufficed to substantiate the opinion: He hasn't the least thing in the world to do; he is a mere idler.

Such was the existence I led by way of seconding my aesthetic work. Incidentally it involved a breach with all coteries. And I formed the polemical resolution to regard every eulogy as an attack, and every attack as a thing unworthy of notice. Such was my public mode of existence. I almost never made a visit, and at home the rule was strictly observed to receive no one except the poor who came to seek help. For I had no time to receive visitors at home, and any one who entered my home as a visitor might easily get a presentiment of a situation about which he should have no presentiment. Thus I existed. If Copenhagen ever has been of one opinion about anybody, I venture to say that it was of one opinion about me, that I was an idler, a dawdler, a *flâneur*, a frivolous bird, intelligent, perhaps brilliant, witty, etc. —but as for "seriousness," I lacked it utterly. I represented a worldly irony, *joie de vivre*, the subtlest form of pleasure-seeking—without a trace of "seriousness and positivity"; on the other hand, I was prodigiously witty and interesting.

When I look back upon that time, I am almost tempted to make some sort of apology to the people of importance and repute in the community. For true enough, I knew perfectly well what I was doing, yet from their standpoint they were right in finding fault with me, because by thus impairing my own prestige I contributed to the movement which was impairing power and renown in general—notwithstanding that I have always been conservative in this respect, and have found joy in paying to the eminent and distinguished the deference, awe, and admiration which are due to them. Yet my conservative disposition did not involve a desire to have this sort of distinction for myself. And just because the eminent and distinguished members of the community have shown me in so many ways not only sympathy but partiality, have sought in so many ways to draw me to their side (which certainly was honest and well-meant on their part)—just for this reason I feel impelled to make them an apology, although naturally I cannot regret what I have done, since I served my idea. People of distinction have always proved more consistent in their treatment of me than the simpler classes, who even from their own standpoint did not behave rightly, since they too (according to the foregoing account) attacked me . . . because I was not superior enough to hold myself aloof—which is very queer and ridiculous of the simpler classes.

This is the first period: by my personal mode of existence I endeavoured to support the pseudonyms, the aesthetic work as a whole. Melancholy, incurably melancholy as I was, suffering prodigious griefs in my inmost soul, having broken in desperation from the world and all that is of the world, strictly brought up from my very childhood in the apprehension that the truth must suffer and be mocked and derided, spending a definite time every day in prayer and devout meditation, and being myself personally a penitent—in short, being what I was, I found (I do not deny it) a certain sort of satisfaction in this life, in this inverse deception, a satisfaction in observing that the deception succeeded so extraordinarily, that the public and I were on the. most confidential terms, that I was quite in the fashion as the preacher of a gospel of worldliness, that though I was not in possession of the sort of distinction which can only be earned by an entirely different mode of life, yet in secret (and hence the more heartily loved) I was the darling of the public, regarded by every one as prodigiously interesting and witty. This satisfaction, which was my secret and which sometimes put me into an ecstasy, might have been a dangerous temptation. Not as though the world and such things could tempt me with their flattery and adulation. No, on that side I was safe. If I was to have been capsized, it would have to have been by this thought raised to a higher power, an obsession almost of ecstasy at the thought of how the deception was succeeding. This was an indescribable alleviation to a sense of resentment which smouldered in me from my childhood; because, long before I had seen it with my own eyes, I had been taught that falsehood, pettiness, and injustice ruled the world.—I often had to think of these words in *Either/Or:* "If ye but knew what it is ye laugh at"—if ye but knew with whom ye have to do, who this *flâneur* is!

4. "That Individual"

There is a view of life which conceives that where the crowd is, there also is the truth, and that in truth itself there is need of having the crowd on its side.[2] There is another view of life which conceives that wherever there is a crowd there is untruth, so that (to consider for a moment the extreme case), even if every individual, each for himself in private, were to be in possession of the truth, yet in case they were all to get together in a crowd—a crowd to which any sort of *decisive* significance is attributed, a voting, noisy, audible crowd—untruth would at once be in evidence.[3]

For a "crowd" is the untruth. In a godly sense it is true, eternally, Christianly, as St. Paul says, that "only one attains the goal"—which is not meant in a comparative sense, for comparison takes others into account. It means that every man can be that one, God helping him therein—but only one attains the goal. And again this means that every man should be chary about having to do with "the others," and essentially should talk only with God and with himself—for only one attains the goal. And again this means that man, or to be a man, is akin to deity.—In a worldly and temporal sense, it will be said by the man of bustle, sociability, and amicableness, "How unreasonable that only one attains the goal; for it is far more likely that many, by the strength of united effort, should attain the goal; and when we are many success is more certain and it is easier for each man severally." True enough, it is far more *likely;* and it is true also with respect to all earthly and material goods. If it is allowed to have its way, this becomes the only true point of view, for it does away with God and eternity and with man's kinship with deity. It does away with it or transforms it into a fable, and puts in its place the modern (or, we might rather say, the old pagan) notion that to be a man is to belong to a race endowed with reason, to belong to it as a specimen, so that the race or species is higher than the individual, which is to say that there are no more individuals but only specimens. But eternity which arches over and high above the temporal, tranquil as the starry vault at night, and

God in heaven who in the bliss of that sublime tranquillity holds in survey, without the least sense of dizziness at such a height, these countless multitudes of men and knows each single individual by name—He, the great Examiner, says that only one attains the goal. That means, every one can and every one should be this *one*—but only one attains the goal. Hence where there is a multitude, a crowd, or where decisive significance is attached to the fact that there is a multitude, *there* it is sure that no one is working, living, striving for the highest aim, but only for one or another earthly aim; since to work for the eternal decisive aim is possible only where there is one, and to be this one which all can be is to let God be the helper—the "crowd" is the untruth.

A crowd—not this crowd or that, the crowd now living or the crowd long deceased, a crowd of humble people or of superior people, of rich or of poor, etc.—a crowd in its very concept[4] is the untruth, by reason of the fact that it renders the individual completely impenitent and irresponsible, or at least weakens his sense of responsibility by reducing it to a fraction. Observe that there was not one single soldier that dared lay hands upon Caius Marius—this was an instance of truth. But given merely three or four women with the consciousness or the impression that they were a crowd, and with hope of a sort in the possibility that no one could say definitely who was doing it or who began it—then they had courage for it. What a falsehood! The falsehood first of all is the notion that the crowd does what in fact only the *individual* in the crowd does, though it be every *individual*. For "crowd" is an abstraction and has no hands: but each individual has ordinarily two hands, and so when an individual lays his two hands upon Caius Marius they are the two hands of the individual, certainly not those of his neighbour, and still less those of the . . . crowd which has no hands. In the next place, the falsehood is that the crowd had the "courage" for it, for no one of the individuals was ever so cowardly as the crowd always is. For every individual who flees for refuge into the crowd, and so flees in cowardice from being an individual (who had not the courage to lay his hands upon Caius Marius, nor even to admit that he had it not), such a man contributes his share of cowardliness to the cowardliness which we know as the "crowd."—Take the highest example, think of Christ—and the whole human race, all the men that ever were born or are to be born. But let the situation be one that challenges the individual, requiring each one for himself to be alone with Him in a solitary place and as an individual to step up to Him and spit upon Him—the man never was born and never will be born with courage or insolence enough to do such a thing. This is untruth.

The crowd is untruth. Hence none has more contempt for what it is to be a man than they who make it their profession to lead the crowd. Let some one approach a person of this sort, some individual—that is an affair far too small for his attention, and he proudly repels him. There must be hundreds at the least. And when there are thousands, he defers to the crowd, bowing and scraping to them. What untruth! No, when it is a question of a single individual man, then is the time to give expression to the truth by showing one's respect for what it is to be a man; and if perhaps it was, as it is cruelly said, a poor wretch of a man, then the thing to do is to invite him into the best room, and one who possesses several voices should use the kindest and most friendly. That is truth. If on the other hand there were an assemblage of thousands or more and the truth was to be decided by ballot, then this is what one should do (unless one were to prefer to utter silently the petition of the Lord's Prayer, "Deliver us from evil"): one should in godly fear give expression to the fact that the crowd, regarded as a judge over ethical and religious matters, is untruth, whereas it is eternally true that every man can be the *one*. This is truth.

The crowd is untruth. Therefore was Christ crucified, because, although He addressed himself to all, He would have no dealings with the crowd, because He would not permit the crowd to aid him in any way, because in this regard He repelled people absolutely, would not found a party, did not permit balloting, but would be what He is, the Truth, which relates itself to the individual.—And hence every one who truly would serve the truth is *eo ipso*, in one way or another, a martyr. If it were possible for a person in his mother's womb to make the decision to will to serve the truth truly, then, whatever his martyrdom turns out to be, he is *eo ipso* from his mother's womb a martyr. For it is not so great a trick to win the crowd. All that is needed is some talent, a certain dose of falsehood, and a little acquaintance with human passions. But no witness for the truth (Aл! and that is what every man should be, including you and me)— no witness for the truth dare become engaged with the crowd. The witness for the truth—who naturally has nothing to do with politics and must above everything else be most vigilantly on the watch not to be confounded with the politician—the God-fearing work of the witness to the truth is to engage himself if possible with all, but always individually, talking to every one severally on the streets and lanes . . . in order to disintegrate the crowd, or to talk even to the crowd, though not with the intent of educating the crowd as such, but rather with the hope that one or another individual might return from this assemblage and become a single individual. On the other hand the "crowd," when it is treated as an authority and its judgement regarded as the final judgement, is detested by the witness for the truth more heartily than a maiden of good morals detests the public dance-floor; and he who addresses the crowd as the supreme authority is regarded by him as the tool of the untruth. For (to repeat what I have said) that which in politcs or in similar fields may be justifiable, wholly or in part, becomes untruth when it is transferred to the intellectual, the spiritual, the religious fields. And one thing more I would say, perhaps with a cautiousness which is exaggerated. By "truth" I mean always "eternal truth." But politics, etc., have nothing to do with "eternal truth." A policy which in the proper sense of "eternal truth" were to make serious work of introducing "eternal truth" into real life would show itself in that very same second to be in the most eminent degree the most "impolitic" thing that can be imagined.

A crowd is untruth. And I could weep, or at least I could learn to long for eternity, at thinking of the misery of our age, in comparison even with the greatest misery of bygone ages, owing to the fact that the daily press with its anonymity makes the situation madder still with the help of the public, this abstraction which claims to be the judge in matters of "truth." For in reality assemblies which make this claim do not now take place. The fact that an anonymous author by the help of the press can day by day find occasion to say (even about intellectual, moral, and religious matters) whatever he pleases to say, and what perhaps he would be very far from having the courage to say as an individual; that every time he opens his mouth (or shall we say his abysmal gullet?) he at once is addressing thousands of thousands; that he can get ten thousand times ten thousand to repeat after him what he has said—and with all this nobody has any responsibility, so that it is not as in ancient times the relatively unrepentant crowd which possesses omnipotence, but the absolutely unrepentant thing, a nobody, an anonymity, who is the producer (*auctor*), and another anonymity, the public, sometimes even anonymous subscribers, and with all this, nobody, nobody! Good God! And yet our states call themselves Christian states! Let no one say that in this case it is possible for "truth" in its turn by the help of the press to get the better of lies and errors. O thou who speakest thus, dost thou venture to maintain that men regarded as a crowd are just as quick to seize upon truth which is not always palatable as upon falsehood which always is prepared delicately to give delight?—not to mention the fact that acceptance of the truth is made the more difficult by the necessity of admitting that one has been deceived! Or dost thou venture even to maintain that "truth" can just as quickly be understood as falsehood, which requires no preliminary knowledge, no schooling, no discipline, no abstinence, no self-denial, no honest concern about oneself, no patient labour?

Nay, truth—which abhors also this untruth of aspiring after broad dissemination as the one aim—is not nimble on its feet. In the first place it cannot work by means of the fantastical means of the press, which is the untruth; the communicator of the truth can only be a single individual. And again the communication of it can only be addressed to the individual; for the truth consists precisely in that conception of life which is expressed by the individual. The truth can neither be communicated nor be received except as it were under God's eyes, not without God's help, not without God's being involved as the middle term, He himself being the Truth. It can therefore only be communicated by and received by "the individual," which as a matter of fact can be every living man. The mark which distinguishes such a man is merely that of the truth, in contrast to the abstract, the fantastical, the impersonal, the crowd—the public which excludes God as the middle term (for the *personal* God cannot be a middle term in an *impersonal* relationship), and thereby excludes also the truth, for God is at once the Truth and the middle term which renders it intelligible.

And to honour every man, absolutely every man, is the truth, and this is what it is to fear God and love one's "neighbour." But from an ethico-religious point of view, to recognize the "crowd" as the court of last resort is to deny God, and it cannot exactly mean to love the "neighbour." And the "neighbour" is the absolutely true expression for human equality. In case every one were in truth to love his neighbour as himself, complete human equality would be attained. Every one who loves his neighbour in truth, expresses unconditionally human equality. Every one who, like me, admits that his effort is weak and imperfect, yet is aware that the task is to love one's neighbour, is also aware of what human equality is. But never have I read in Holy Scripture the commandment, Thou shalt love the crowd—and still less, Thou shalt recognize, ethico-religiously, in the crowd the supreme authority in matters of "truth." But the thing is simple enough: this thing of loving one's neighbour is self-denial; that of loving the crowd, or of pretending to love it, of making it the authority in matters of truth, is the way to material power, the way to temporal and earthly advantages of all sorts—at the same time it is the untruth, for a crowd is the untruth.

But he who acknowledges the truth of this view, which is seldom presented (for it often happens that a man thinks that the crowd is the untruth, but when it—the crowd—accepts his opinion *en masse,* everything is all right again), admits for himself that he is weak and impotent; for how could it be possible for an individual to make a stand against the crowd which possesses the power! And he could not wish to get the crowd on his side for the sake of ensuring that his view would prevail, the crowd, ethico-religiously regarded, being the untruth—that would be mocking himself. But although from the first this view involves an admission of weakness and impotence, and seems therefore far from inviting, and for this reason perhaps is so seldom heard, yet it has the good feature that it is even-handed, that it offends no one, not a single person, that it makes no invidious distinctions, not the least in the world. The crowd, in fact, is composed of individuals; it must therefore be in every man's power to become what he is, an individual. From becoming an individual no one, no one at all, is excluded, except he who excludes himself by becoming a crowd. To become a crowd, to collect a crowd about one, is on the contrary to affirm the distinctions of human life. The most well-meaning person who talks about these distinctions can easily offend an individual. But then it is not the crowd which possesses power, influence, repute, and mastery over men, but it is the invidious distinctions of human life which despotically ignore the single individual as the weak and impotent, which in a temporal and worldly interest ignore the eternal truth—the single individual.

* * *

"The individual" is the category through which, in a religious respect, this age, all history, the human race as a whole, must pass. And he who stood at Thermopylae was not so secure in his position as I who have stood in defence of this narrow defile, "the individual," with the intent at least of making people take notice of it. His duty was to prevent the hosts from pressing through the defile. If they pressed through, he was lost. My task is one which at least does not expose me to any such danger of being trampled underfoot, for my task was as a humble servant (yet, as I have said from the beginning and repeated again and again, "without authority") to provoke, if possible, to invite, to stir up the many to press through this defile of "the individual," through which, however, no one can pass except by becoming the individual—the contrary being a categorical impossibility. And yet, if I were to desire an inscription for my tombstone, I should desire none other than "That Individual"—if that is not now understood,[5] it surely will be. The pseudonyms in their time, when here at home all the talk was about system, always system, aimed a blow at the System[6] with the category of "the individual." Now one hardly hears the System any more mentioned[7]—not at least as the last word of fashion and as the requirement of the age. I marked the beginning of the literary production over my own name by the category of "the individual," and that remained as a stereotyped formula, showing that this thing of the individual is not a later invention of mine but my first thought. With the category of "the individual" is bound up any ethical importance I may have. If that category was right, if that category was in place, if I saw rightly at this point and understood rightly that it was my task (certainly not a pleasant nor a thankful one) to call attention to it, if that was the task given me to do, albeit with inward sufferings such as certainly are seldom experienced, and with outward sacrifices such as a man is not every day found willing to make—in that case I stand fast and my works with me.

5. Dread and Freedom

Innocence is ignorance. In his innocence man is not determined as spirit but is soulishly determined in immediate unity with his natural condition. Spirit is dreaming in man. This view is in perfect accord with that of the Bible, and by refusing to ascribe to man in the state of innocence a knowledge of the difference between good and evil it condemns all the notions of merit Catholicism has imagined.

In this state there is peace and repose; but at the same time there is something different, which is not dissension and strife, for there is nothing to strive with. What is it then? Nothing. But what effect does nothing produce? It begets dread. This is the profound secret of innocence, that at the same time it is dread. Dreamingly the spirit projects its own reality, but this reality is nothing, but this nothing constantly sees innocence outside of it.

Dread is a qualification of the dreaming spirit, and as such it has its place in psychology. When awake, the difference between myself and my other is posited; sleeping, it is suspended; dreaming, it is a nothing vaguely hinted at. The reality of the spirit constantly shows itself in a form which entices its possibility, but it is away as soon as one grasps after it, and it is a nothing which is able only to alarm. More it cannot do so long as it only shows itself. One almost never sees the concept dread dealt with in psychology, and I must therefore call attention to the fact that it is different from fear and similar concepts which refer to something definite, whereas dread is the reality of freedom as possibility anterior to possibility. One does not therefore find dread in the beast, precisely for the reason that by nature the beast is not qualified by spirit.

When we consider the dialectical determinants in dread, it appears that they have precisely the characteristic ambiguity of psychology. Dread is a *sympathetic antipathy and an antipathetic sympathy*. One easily sees, I think, that this is much more truly a psychological subject than is the concupiscence of which we have spoken. Language confirms this completely. One speaks of a sweet dread, a sweet feeling of apprehension, one speaks of a strange dread, a shrinking dread, etc.

The dread which is posited in innocence is, in the first place, not guilt; in the second place, it is not a heavy burden, not a suffering which cannot be brought into harmony with the felicity of innocence. If we observe children, we find this dread more definitely indicated as a seeking after adventure, a thirst for the prodigious, the mysterious. The fact that there are children in whom this is not found proves nothing, for neither in the beast does it exist, and the less spirit, the less dread. This dread belongs to the child so essentially that it cannot do without it; even though it alarms him, it captivates him nevertheless by its sweet feeling of apprehension. In all nations in which the childish character is preserved as the dreaming of the spirit this dread is found, and the deeper it is, the more profound is the nation. It is only a prosaic stupidity which thinks that this is a disorganization. Dread has here the same significance melancholy has at a far later point where freedom, after having passed through imperfect forms of its history, has to come to itself in a deeper sense.[8]

Just as the relation of dread to its object, to something which is nothing (language in this instance also is pregnant: it speaks of being in dread of nothing), is altogether ambiguous, so will the transition here from innocence to guilt be correspondingly so dialectical that, whatever it is, it evidently must be psychological, as it ought to be. The qualitative leap is outside of ambiguity, but he who through dread becomes guilty is innocent, for it was not he himself but dread, an alien power which laid hold of him, a power which he loved and yet dreaded—and yet he is guilty, he who after all loved it while he feared it. There is nothing in the world more ambiguous, and therefore this is the only psychological explanation, although (to repeat what I have said) it never occurs to it to want to be the explanation which explains the qualitative leap. Every theory about the prohibition tempting Adam or the seducer deceiving him has only for a superficial observation sufficient ambiguity, while it perverts ethics, introduces a quantitative determination, and would by the help of psychology pay man a compliment from which everyone who is ethically developed would beg to be excused, regarding it as a new and deeper seduction.

Everything turns upon dread coming into view. Man is a synthesis of the soulish and the bodily. But a synthesis is unthinkable if the two are not united in a third factor. This third factor is the spirit. In the state of innocence man is not merely an animal, for if at any time of his life he was merely an animal, he never would become a man. So then the spirit is present, but in a state of immediacy, a dreaming state. Forasmuch as it is present, it is in one way a hostile power, for it constantly disturbs the relation between soul and body, a relation which endures, and yet does not endure, inasmuch as it has endurance only by means of the spirit. On the other hand, it is a friendly power which has precisely the function of constituting the relationship. What then is man's relation to this ambiguous power? How is spirit related to itself and to its situation? It is related as dread. It cannot do away with itself, so long as itself is outside of itself. Neither can man sink down into the vegetative life, for he is determined as spirit. He cannot flee from dread, for he loves it; really he does not love it, for he flees from it. Innocence has now reached its apex. It is ignorance, but not an animal brutality, but an ignorance which is qualified by spirit, but which precisely is dread, because its ignorance is about nothing. Here there is no knowledge of good and evil, etc., but the whole reality of knowledge is projected in dread as the immense nothing of ignorance.

Innocence still *is*, but one word suffices, and with that ignorance is concentrated. Innocence of course cannot understand this word; but dread has as it were obtained its first prey; instead of nothing, innocence gets an enigmatic word. So when it is related in Genesis that God said to Adam, "Only of the tree of the knowledge of good and evil thou shalt not eat," it is a matter of course that Adam did not understand this word. For how could he have understood the difference between good and evil, seeing that this distinction was in fact consequent upon the enjoyment of the fruit?

When one assumes that the prohibition awakens the desire,

one posits a knowledge instead of ignorance; for Adam would have had to have a knowledge of freedom, since his desire was to use it. The explanation therefore anticipates what was subsequent. The prohibition alarms Adam [induces a state of dread] because the prohibition awakens in him the possibility of freedom. That which passed innocence by as the nothing of dread has now entered into him, and here again it is a nothing, the alarming possibility of *being able*. What it is he is able to do, of that he has no conception; to suppose that he had some conception is to presuppose, as commonly is done, what came later, the distinction between good and evil. There is only the possibility of being able, as a heightened expression of dread, because this in a more profound sense is and is not, because in a more profound sense he loves it and flees from it.

After the word of prohibition follows the word of judgment: "Thou shalt surely die." What it means to die, Adam of course cannot conceive; but if one assumes that these words were said to him, there is nothing to prevent his having a notion of the terrible. Indeed even the beast is able to understand the mimic expression and movement in the speaker's voice, without understanding the word. In case one lets the prohibition awaken desire, one may also let the word about punishment awaken a deterring conception. However, this confuses things. The terrible becomes in this instance merely dread; for Adam has not understood what was said, and here again we have only the ambiguity of dread. The infinite possibility of being able draws closer for the fact that this possibility indicates a possibility as its consequence.

Thus innocence is brought to its last extremity. It is in dread in relation to the prohibition and the punishment. It is not guilty, and yet it is in dread, as though it were lost.

Further than this psychology cannot go, but so far it can reach, and moreover it can verify this point again and again in its observation of human life. . . .

The possibility of freedom does not consist in being able to choose the good or the evil. Such thoughtlessness has as little support in the Scripture as in philosophy. Possibility means *I can*. In a logical system it is convenient enough to say that possibility passes over into actuality. In reality it is not so easy, and an intermediate determinant is necessary. This intermediate determinant is dread, which no more explains the qualitative leap than it justifies it ethically. Dread is not a

determinant of necessity, but neither is it of freedom; it is a
trammeled freedom, where freedom is not free in itself but
trammeled, not by necessity but in itself. If sin has come into
the world by necessity (which is a self-contradiction), then
there is no dread. If sin has come into the world by an act of
abstract *liberum arbitrium* (which no more existed at the beginning than it does at a later period of the world, for it is a
non-sense to thought), neither in this case is there dread. To
want to explain logically the entrance of sin into the world is
a stupidity which could only occur to people who are comically
anxious to get an explanation. . . .

One may liken dread to dizziness. He whose eye chances to
look down into the yawning abyss becomes dizzy. But the reason for it is just as much his eye as it is the precipice. For
suppose he had not looked down.

Thus dread is the dizziness of freedom which occurs when
the spirit would posit the synthesis, and freedom then gazes
down into its own possibility, grasping at finiteness to sustain
itself. In this dizziness freedom succumbs. Further than this
psychology cannot go and will not. That very instant everything is changed, and when freedom rises again it sees that it is
guilty. Between these two instants lies the leap, which no
science has explained or can explain. He who becomes guilty
in dread becomes as ambiguously guilty as it is possible to be.
Dread is a womanish debility in which freedom swoons. Psychologically speaking, the fall into sin always occurs in impotence. But dread is at the same time the most egoistic thing,
and no concrete expression of freedom is so egoistic as is the
possibility of every concretion. This again is the overwhelming
experience which determines the individual's ambiguous relation, both sympathetic and antipathetic. In dread there is the
egoistic infinity of possibility, which does not tempt like a
definite choice, but alarms (*ængster*) and fascinates with its
sweet anxiety (*Beængstelse*).

6. Authority

The misfortune of our age—in the political as well as in the
religious sphere, and in all things—is disobedience, unwilling-
ness to obey. And one deceives oneself and others by wishing

to make us imagine that it is doubt. No, it is insubordination: it is not doubt of religious truth but insubordination against religious authority which is the fault in our misfortune and the cause of it.

* * *

As a genius Paul can sustain no comparison with Plato or with Shakespeare, as an author of beautiful similes he ranks rather low, as stylist his is an obscure name, and as an upholsterer—well, I may admit that in this respect I don't know where to place him. One always does well to transform stupid seriousness into a jest—and then comes the really serious thing, the serious fact that Paul was an apostle, and as an apostle has no affinity either with Plato or Shakespeare or a stylist or an upholsterer, who are all of them (Plato as well as the upholsterer Hansen) beneath any comparison with him.

A *genius* and an *apostle* are qualitatively distinct, they are categories which belong each of them to their own qualitative spheres: that of *immanence* and that of *transcendence*. (1) The genius may well have something new to contribute, but this newness vanishes again in its gradual assimilation by the race, just as the distinction "genius" vanishes when one thinks of eternity. The apostle has paradoxically something new to contribute, the newness of which, precisely because it is paradoxical and not an anticipation of what may eventually be developed in the race, remains constant, just as an apostle remains an apostle to all eternity, and no immanence of eternity puts him essentially on the same plane with other men, since essentially he is paradoxically different. (2) The genius is what he is by reason of himself, i.e. by what he is in himself: an apostle is what he is by reason of his divine authority. (3) The genius has only immanent teleology: the apostle's position is that of absolute paradoxical teleology. . . .

Authority is the qualitatively decisive point. Or is there not, even within the relativity of human life, though it disappears in immanence, a difference between the king's command and the word of a poet or a thinker? And what difference is there except that the king's command has authority and therefore prohibits all critical and aesthetical impertinence with regard to form and content? On the other hand, the poet or the thinker, even within this relativity, has no authority, his saying is appraised purely aesthetically and philosophically by

appraising the content and form. But what is it that has fundamentally confused Christianity, unless it is that people have
at first in doubt become so nearly uncertain whether there is a
God that in rebellion against all authority they have forgotten
what authority is and the dialectic of it? A king is sensibly
present in such a way that one can sensibly convince oneself of
it, and, if it should be necessary, the king can quite sensibly
convince one that he exists. But God does not exist in such a
sense. Doubt has taken advantage of this to put God on the
same plane as all those who have no authority, geniuses, poets,
thinkers, whose utterances are appraised precisely by aesthetic
and philosophical criteria; and in case a thing is well said, then
the man is a genius, and in case a thing is unusually and
especially well said, then it is God who has said it!!!

By that trick God is really conjured away. What is he to do?
If God stops a man on the street, calls him by a revelation and
sends him out to the other men armed with divine authority—
then they say to him, "From whom art thou?" He answers,
"From God." But, lo, God cannot help his ambassador as a
king can who gives him an accompaniment of soldiers or
policemen, or his ring, or a letter in his handwriting which
everybody recognizes—in short, God cannot be at men's
service by providing them with a sensible certitude of the fact
that an apostle is an apostle—this too would be nonsense.
Even the miracle, if the apostle has this gift, gives no sensible
certitude, for the miracle is an object of faith. And moreover
it is nonsense to get *sensible* certitude that an apostle is an
apostle (the paradoxical determinant of a spiritual connection),
just as it is nonsense to get *sensible* certitude of the fact that
God exists, since God indeed is spirit. So then the apostle says
he is from God. The others answer, "Well then, let us see
whether the content of the doctrine is divine, for in that case
we will accept it along with the claim that it was revealed to
thee." In that way both God and the apostle are mocked. The
divine authority of the man thus called should be the surest
defense which secures the doctrine and keeps from it at the
majestic distance of the divine all impertinences; instead of
which the content and form of the doctrine must allow itself
to be criticized and sniffed at—before one is able in this way
to reach the conclusion that it was a revelation or no. And
meanwhile the apostle and God must presumably wait at the
door or in the porter's lodge until the case has been decided by

the wise men in the *bel étage*. The elect man should according
to God's ordinance assert his divine authority to chase away all
impertinent people who will not obey him but argue. And instead of obeying, men transform an apostle into an examinee
who comes as it were to the market place with a new doctrine.

What then is authority? Is authority the profundity of the
doctrine, its superiority, its cleverness? Not at all. If authority
thus predicated is merely profundity, raised to a higher power,
or reduplicated, then precisely there is no authority; for if a
pupil by his understanding of it appropriated the doctrine
totally and fully, there would in fact be no difference left between the teacher and the pupil. Authority, on the contrary,
is something which remains unchanged, which one cannot
acquire by having understood the doctrine in the fullest sense.
*Authority is a specific quality which comes from another place
and makes itself felt precisely when the content of the saying
or of the action is assumed to be indifferent.* Let us take an
example, as simple as possible, where nevertheless the situation
is plain. When the man who has the authority to say it says,
"Go!" and when he who has not authority says, "Go!"—then
indeed the saying "Go" along with its content is identical; appraised aesthetically, if you will, they are both equally well
said, but the authority makes the difference.

*   *   *

In case a son were to say, "I obey my father, not because
he is my father, but because he is a genius or because his commands are always profound and clever"—then this filial obedience is affected. The son accentuates something which is
entirely beside the point, he accentuates the cleverness and
profundity in a *command*, whereas a command is precisely
indifferent with regard to this qualification. The son is willing
to obey by virtue of his father's profundity and cleverness, and
by virtue of this it is precisely not possible to obey, for his
critical attitude with regard to the decision whether the command is profound and clever undermines obedience. And this
too is affectation when there is so much about accepting Christianity and believing in Christ on account of the profundity
of the doctrine. One accepts orthodoxy by accentuating something which is entirely beside the point. The whole of modern Speculation is therefore "affected" by reason of having
done away with *obedience* on the one hand and *authority* on

the other, and by then wanting to be orthodox. A clergyman who is entirely correct in his eloquence must speak thus in introducing a word of Christ: "This word was spoken by him to whom, according to his own statement all power hath been given in heaven and in earth. Now, thou, my hearer, must consider by thyself whether thou wilt bow to this authority or no, receive it and believe it or no. But if thou wilt not do so, then for heaven's sake do not go off and accept the word because it is clever and profound or wondrously beautiful, for this is blasphemy, it is wanting to treat God like an aesthetic critic. For so soon as the dominant note of authority, of the specific paradoxical authority, is heard, then this sort of appropriation, which otherwise is permissible and desirable, is a crime and a presumption."

But now how can an apostle prove that he has authority? Could he prove it physically, he would be no apostle. He has no other proof but his own assertion. And thus precisely it ought to be, for otherwise the believer would come into a direct relation to him, not into a paradoxical relationship. In the transitory situation of authority between man and man *qua* man the authority will ordinarily be recognized physically by means of force. An apostle has no other proof but his own assertion, and at the most by his willingness to suffer everything for the sake of the doctrine.

*   *   *

The experience of being shaken, of being deeply moved, the coming into being of subjectivity in the inwardness of emotion, the pious pagan and the pious Jew have in common with the Christian. Upon this common basis of more universal emotion the qualitative difference must be erected and make itself felt, for the more universal emotion has reference only to something abstract: to be moved by something higher, something eternal, by an idea. And one does not become a Christian by being moved by something indefinitely higher, and not every outpouring of religious emotion is a Christian outpouring. That is to say: emotion which is Christian is checked by the definition of concepts, and when emotion is transposed or expressed in words in order to be communicated, this transposition must occur constantly within the definition of the concepts. . . .

Love is falling in love, the primitivity of falling in love is the genesis of love. Love does not exist as something objective but comes into being every time a man loves, and it exists only in the lover; not only does it exist only *for* the lover but it exists only *in* the lover.

It is otherwise with every relation within the sphere of transcendence, and then again otherwise with the Christian concept of revelation. Christianity exists before any Christian exists, it must exist in order that one may become a Christian, it contains the determinant by which one may test whether one has become a Christian, it maintains its objective subsistence apart from all believers, while at the same time it is the inwardness of the believer. In short, here there is no identity between the subjective and the objective. Though Christianity comes into the heart of never so many believers, every believer is conscious that it has not arisen in his heart, is conscious that the objective determinant of Christianity is not a reminiscence, as love is of the fact of falling in love, is not an apparently objective something which nevertheless is subjective, like love which as an objective something is an illusion and loving is the reality. No, even if no one had perceived that God had revealed himself in a human form in Christ, he nevertheless has revealed himself. Hence it is that every contemporary (simply understood) has a responsibility if he does not perceive it.

7. "Truth is Subjectivity"

Our treatment of the problem does not raise the question of the truth of Christianity. It merely deals with the question of the individual's relationship to Christianity. It has nothing whatever to do with the systematic zeal of the personally indifferent individual to arrange the truths of Christianity in paragraphs; it deals with the concern of the infinitely interested individual for his own relationship to such a doctrine. To put it as simply as possible, using myself by way of illustration: I, Johannes Climacus, born in this city and now thirty years old, a common ordinary human being like most people, assume that there awaits me a highest good, an eternal happiness, in the same sense that such a good awaits a servant-girl or a professor. I have heard that Christianity proposes itself as a condition for the acquirement of this good, and now I ask how I may establish a proper relationship to this doctrine. "What extraordinary presumption," I seem to hear a thinker say, "what egotistical vanity to dare lay so much stress upon one's own petty self in this theocentric age, in the speculatively significant nineteenth century, which is entirely immersed in the great problems of universal history." I shudder at the reproof; and if I had not already hardened myself against a number of fearful things, I would no doubt slink quietly away, like a dog with his tail between his legs. But my conscience is quite clear in this matter; it is not I who have become so presumptuous of my own accord, but it is Christianity itself which compels me to ask the question in this manner. It puts quite an extraordinary emphasis upon my own petty self, and upon every other self however petty, in that it proposes to endow each self with an eternal happiness, provided a proper relationship is established.

Without having understood Christianity, since I merely present the problem, I have still understood enough to apprehend that it proposes to bestow an eternal happiness upon the individual man, thus presuming an infinite interest in his eternal happiness as *conditio sine qua non*; an interest by virtue of which the individual hates father and mother, and thus doubtless also snaps his fingers at speculative systems and outlines of universal history. Although I am only an outsider, I have at least understood so much, that the only unpardonable offense against the majesty of Christianity is for the individual to take his relationship to it for granted, treating it as a matter of course. However unassuming it may seem to permit oneself this kind of a relationship to Christianity, Christianity judges it as insolence. I must therefore respectfully decline the assistance of all the theocentric helpers and helpers' helpers, in so far as they propose to help me into Christianity on such a basis. Then I rather prefer to remain where I am, with my infinite interest, with the problem, with the possibility.

It is not entirely impossible that one who is infinitely interested in his eternal happiness may sometime come into possession of it. But it is surely quite impossible for one who has lost a sensibility for it (and this can scarcely be anything else than the infinite interest), ever to enjoy an eternal happiness. If the sense for it is once lost, it may perhaps be impossible to recover it. The foolish virgins had lost the infinite passion of expectation. And so their lamps were extinguished. Then came the cry: The bridegroom cometh. Thereupon they run to the market-place to buy new oil for themselves, hoping to begin all over again, letting bygones be bygones. And so it was, to be sure, everything was forgotten. The door was shut against them, and they were left outside; when they knocked for admittance, the bridegroom said: "I do not know you." This was no mere quip in which the bridegroom indulged, but the sober truth; for they had made themselves strangers, in the spiritual sense of the word, through having lost the infinite passion.

The objective problem consists of an inquiry into the truth of Christianity. The subjective problem concerns the relationship of the individual to Christianity. To put it quite simply: How may I, Johannes Climacus, participate in the happiness promised by Christianity? The problem concerns myself alone; partly because, if it is properly posed, it will concern everyone else in the same manner; and partly because all the others already have faith as something given, as a triviality of little value, or as a triviality which amounts to something only when tricked out with a few proofs. So that the posing of the problem cannot be regarded as presumption on my part, but only as a special kind of madness.

* * *

When Christianity is viewed from the standpoint of its historical documentation, it becomes necessary to secure an entirely trustworthy account of what the Christian doctrine really is. If the inquirer were infinitely interested in behalf of his relationship to the doctrine he would at once despair; for nothing is more readily evident than that the greatest attainable certainty with respect to anything historical is merely an *approximation*. And an approximation, when viewed as a basis for an eternal happiness, is wholly inadequate, since the incommensurability makes a result impossible. But the interest of the inquiring subject being merely historical (whether he also has an infinite interest in Christianity in his capacity as believer, in which case the whole enterprise might readily come to involve him in several contradictions, or whether he stands aloof, yet without any passionate negative decision *qua* unbeliever), he begins upon the tremendous task of research, adding new contributions of his own, and continuing thus until his seventieth year. Just two weeks before his death he looks forward to the publication of a new work, which it is hoped will throw light upon one entire side of the inquiry. Such an objective temper is an epigram, unless its antithesis be an epigram over it, over the restless concern of the infinitely interested subject, who surely needs to have such a question answered, related as it is to his eternal happiness. And in any case he will not upon any consideration dare to relinquish his interest until the last moment. . . .

One sometimes hears uneducated or half educated people, or conceited geniuses, speak with contempt of the labor of criticism devoted to ancient writings; one hears them foolishly deride the learned scholar's careful scrutiny of the most insignificant detail, which is precisely the glory of the scholar, namely, that he considers nothing insignificant that bears upon his science. No, philological scholarship is absolutely within its rights, and the present author yields to none in profound respect for that which science consecrates. But the scholarly critical theology makes no such clear and definite impression upon the mind; its entire procedure suffers from a certain conscious or unconscious ambiguity. It constantly seems as if this labor of criticism were suddenly about to yield a result for faith, issue in something relevant to faith. Here lies the difficulty. When a philologist prepares an edition of one of Cicero's writings, for example, and performs his task with great acumen, the scholarly apparatus held in beautiful subservience to the control of the spirit; when his ingenuity and his familiarity with the period, gained through formidable industry, combine with his instinct for discovery to overcome obstacles, preparing a clear way for the meaning through the obscure maze of the readings, and so forth—then it is quite safe to yield oneself in whole-hearted admiration. For when he has finished, nothing follows except the wholly admirable result that an ancient writing has now through his skill and competence received its most accurate possible form. But by no means that I should now base my eternal happiness on this work; for in relation to my eternal happiness, his astonishing acumen seems, I must admit, inadequate. Aye, I confess that my admiration for him would be not glad but despondent, if I thought he had any such thing in mind. But this is precisely how the learned theologian goes to work; when he has completed his task (and until then he keeps us in suspense, but holds this prospect before us) he draws the conclusion: *ergo*, now you can base your eternal happiness on these writings.

Anyone who posits inspiration, as a believer does, must consistently consider every critical deliberation, whether for or against, as a misdirection, a temptation for the spirit. . . .

I assume, accordingly, that the critics have succeeded in proving about the Bible everything that any learned theologian in his happiest moment has ever wished to prove about the Bible. These books and no others belong to the canon; they are authentic; they are integral; their authors are trustworthy—one may well say, that it is as if every letter were inspired. More than this it is impossible to say, for inspiration is an object of faith and subject to a qualitative dialectic; it is incapable of being reached by a quantitative approximation. Furthermore, there is not a trace of contradiction in the sacred writings. . . .

Well then, everything being assumed in order with respect to the Scriptures—what follows? Has anyone who previously did not have faith been brought a single step nearer to its acquisition? No, not a single step. Faith does not result simply from a scientific inquiry; it does not come directly at all. . . .

Here is the crux of the matter, and I come back to the case of the learned theology. For whose sake is it that the proof is sought? Faith does not need it; aye, it must even regard the proof as its enemy. But when faith begins to feel embarrassed and ashamed, like a young woman for whom her love is no longer sufficient, but who secretly feels ashamed of her lover and must therefore have it established that there is something remarkable about him—when faith thus begins to lose its passion, when faith begins to cease to be faith, then a proof becomes necessary so as to command respect from the side of unbelief.

*   *   *

When the question of truth is raised in an objective manner, reflection is directed objectively to the truth, as an object to which the knower is related. Reflection is not focussed upon the relationship, however, but upon the question of whether it is the truth to which the knower is related. If only the object to which he is related is the truth, the subject is accounted to be in the truth. When the question of the truth is raised subjectively, reflection is directed subjectively to the nature of the individual's relationship; if only the mode of this relationship is in the truth, the individual is in the truth even if he should happen to be thus related to what is not true. Let us take as an example the knowledge of God. Objectively, reflection is directed to the problem of whether this object is the true God; subjectively, reflection is directed to the question whether the individual is related to a something *in such a manner* that his relationship is in truth a God-relationship. On which side is the truth now to be found? Ah, may we not here resort to a mediation, and say: It is on neither side, but in the mediation of both? Excellently well said, provided we might have it explained how an existing individual manages to be in a state of mediation. For to be in a state of mediation is to be finished, while to exist is to become. Nor can an existing individual be in two places at the same time—he cannot be an identity of subject and object. When he is nearest to being in two places at the same time he is in passion; but passion is momentary, and passion is also the highest expression of subjectivity.

The existing individual who chooses to pursue the objective way enters upon the entire approximation-process by which it is proposed to bring God to light objectively. But this is in all eternity impossible, because God is a subject, and therefore exists only for subjectivity in inwardness. . . .

If one who lives in the midst of Christendom goes up to the house of God, the house of the true God, with the true conception of God in his knowledge, and prays, but prays in a false spirit; and one who lives in an idolatrous community prays with the entire passion of the infinite, although his eyes rest upon the image of an idol: where is there most truth? The one prays in truth to God though he worships an idol; the other prays falsely to the true God, and hence worships in fact an idol.

When one man investigates objectively the problem of immortality, and another embraces an uncertainty with the passion of the infinite: where is there most truth, and who has the greater certainty? The one has entered upon a never-ending approximation, for the certainty of immortality lies precisely in the subjectivity of the individual; the other is immortal, and fights for his immortality by struggling with the uncertainty. Let us consider Socrates. Nowadays everyone dabbles in a few proofs; some have several such proofs, others fewer. But Socrates! He puts the question objectively in a problematic manner: *if* there is an immortality. He must therefore be accounted a doubter in comparison with one of our modern thinkers with the three proofs? By no means. On this "if" he risks his entire life, he has the courage to meet death, and he has with the passion of the infinite so determined the pattern of his life that it must be found acceptable—*if* there is an immortality. Is any better proof capable of being given for the immortality of the soul? But those who have the three proofs do not at all determine their lives in conformity therewith; if there is an immortality it must feel disgust over their manner of life: can any better refutation be given of the three proofs? The bit of uncertainty that Socrates had, helped him because he himself contributed the passion of the infinite; the three proofs that the others have do not profit them at all, because they are dead to spirit and enthusiasm, and their three proofs, in lieu of proving anything else, prove just this. A young girl may enjoy all the sweetness of love on the basis of what is merely a weak hope that she is beloved, because she rests everything on this weak hope; but many a wedded matron more than once subjected to the strongest expressions of love, has in so far indeed had proofs, but strangely enough has not enjoyed *quod erat demonstrandum.* . . .

The objective accent falls on WHAT is said, the subjective accent on HOW it is said. This distinction holds even in the aesthetic realm, and receives definite expression in the principle that what is in itself true may in the mouth of such and such a person become untrue. In these times this distinction is particularly worthy of notice, for if we wish to express in a single sentence the difference between ancient times and our own, we should doubtless have to say: "In ancient times only an individual here and there knew the truth; now all know it, except that the inwardness of its appropriation stands in an inverse relationship to the extent of its dissemination. Aesthetically the contradiction that truth becomes untruth in this or that person's mouth, is best construed comically: In the ethico-religious sphere, accent is again on the "how." But this is not to be understood as referring to demeanor, expression, or the like; rather it refers to the relationship sustained by the existing individual, in his own existence, to the content of his utterance. Objectively the interest is focussed merely on the thought-content, subjectively on the inwardness. At its maximum this inward "how" is the passion of the infinite, and the passion of the infinite is the truth. But the passion of the infinite is precisely subjectivity, and thus subjectivity becomes the truth. . . .

When subjectivity is the truth, the conceptual determination of the truth must include an expression for the antithesis to objectivity, a memento of the fork in the road where the way swings off; this expression will at the same time serve as an indication of the tension of the subjective inwardness. Here is such a definition of truth: *An objective uncertainty held fast in an appropriation-process of the most passionate inwardness is the truth,* the highest truth attainable for an *existing* individual. At the point where the way swings off (and where this is cannot be specified objectively, since it is a matter of subjectivity), there objective knowledge is placed in abeyance. Thus the subject merely has, objectively, the uncertainty; but it is this which precisely increases the tension of that infinite passion which constitutes his inwardness. The truth is precisely the venture which chooses an objective uncertainty with the passion of the infinite. I contemplate the order of nature in the hope of finding God, and I see omnipotence and wisdom; but I also see much else that disturbs my mind and excites anxiety. The sum of all this is an objective uncertainty. But it is for this very reason that the inwardness becomes as intense as it is, for it embraces this objective uncertainty with the entire passion of the infinite. In the case of a mathematical proposition the objectivity is given, but for this reason the truth of such a proposition is also an indifferent truth.

But the above definition of truth is an equivalent expression for faith. Without risk there is no faith. Faith is precisely the contradiction between the infinite passion of the individual's inwardness and the objective uncertainty.

* * *

Without risk there is no faith, and the greater the risk the greater the faith; the more objective security the less inwardness (for inwardness is precisely subjectivity), and the less objective security the more profound the possible inwardness. When the paradox is paradoxical in itself, it repels the individual by virtue of its absurdity, and the corresponding passion of inwardness is faith. But subjectivity, inwardness, is the truth; for otherwise we have forgotten what the merit of the Socratic position is. But there can be no stronger expression for inwardness than when the retreat out of existence into the eternal by way of recollection is impossible; and when, with truth confronting the individual as a paradox, gripped in the anguish and pain of sin, facing the tremendous risk of the objective insecurity, the individual believes. But without risk no faith, not even the Socratic form of faith, much less the form of which we here speak.

When Socrates believed that there was a God, he held fast to the objective uncertainty with the whole passion of his inwardness, and it is precisely in this contradiction and in this risk, that faith is rooted. Now it is otherwise. Instead of the objective uncertainty, there is here a certainty, namely, that objectively it is absurd; and this absurdity, held fast in the passion of inwardness, is faith. The Socratic ignorance is as a witty jest in comparison with the earnestness of facing the absurd; and the Socratic existential inwardness is as Greek light-mindedness in comparison with the grave strenuosity of faith.

What now is the absurd? The absurd is—that the eternal truth has come into being in time, that God has come into being, has been born, has grown up, and so forth, precisely like any other individual human being, quite indistinguishable from other individuals. . . .

Suppose a man who wishes to acquire faith; let the comedy begin. He wishes to have faith, but he wishes also to safeguard himself by means of an objective inquiry and its approximation-process. What happens? With the help of the approximation-process the absurd becomes something different; it becomes probable, it becomes increasingly probable, it becomes extremely and emphatically probable. Now he is ready to believe it, and he ventures to claim for himself that he does not believe as shoemakers and tailors and simple folk believe, but only after long deliberation. Now he is ready to believe it; and lo, now it has become precisely impossible to believe it. Anything that is almost probable, or probable, or extremely and emphatically probable, is something he can almost know, or as good as know, or extremely and emphatically almost *know*—but it is impossible to *believe*. For the absurd is the object of faith, and the only object that can be believed. . . .

Suppose . . . Christianity is the absurd, held fast in the passion of the infinite. Suppose it refuses to be understood, and that the maximum of understanding which could come in question is to understand that it cannot be understood. Suppose it therefore accentuates existence so decisively that the individual becomes a sinner, Christianity the paradox, existence the period of decision. Suppose that speculation were a temptation, the most dubious of all. Suppose that the speculative philosopher is, not indeed the prodigal son, for so the anxious divinity would characterize only the offended individual whom he nevertheless continues to love, but is the naughty child who refuses to remain where existing individuals belong, namely, in the existential training school where one becomes mature only through inwardness in existing, but instead demands a place in the divine council chamber, constantly shouting that viewed eternally, divinely, theocentrically, there is no paradox. Suppose the speculative philosopher were the restless tenant, who though it is notorious that he is merely a tenant, in view of the abstract truth that all property is from the standpoint of the eternal and the divine, in common, insists on playing the owner, so that there is nothing else to do than to send for an officer to say to him what the policemen said to Geert Westphaler: "It hurts us to have to come on such an errand." . . .

If in olden times the fearful thing was that one might be offended, now the fearful thing is that there is nothing fearful any more, that in a trice, before the individual has time to look around, he becomes a philosopher who speculates over faith. And over what faith does he speculate? Is it over the faith that he has, and especially over whether he has it or not? Ah, no, such a subject is too trifling for an objective speculative philosopher. What he speculates about is the objective faith. The objective faith, what does that mean? It means a sum of doctrinal propositions. But suppose Christianity were nothing of the kind; suppose on the contrary it were inwardness, and hence also the paradox, so as to thrust the individual away objectively, in order to obtain significance for the existing individual in the inwardness of his existence, in order to place him as decisively as no judge can place an accused person, between time and eternity in time, between heaven and hell in the time of salvation. The objective faith—it is as if Christianity also had been promulgated as a little system, if not quite so good as the Hegelian; it is as if Christ—aye, I speak without offense—it is as if Christ were a professor, and as if the Apostles had formed a little scientific society. Verily, if it was once difficult to become a Christian, now I believe it becomes increasingly difficult year by year, because it has now become so easy that the only ambition which stirs any competition is that of becoming a speculative philosopher. And yet the speculative philosopher is perhaps at the farthest possible remove from Christianity, and it is perhaps far preferable to be an offended individual who nevertheless sustains a relation to Christianity than a speculative philosopher who assumes to have understood it. In so far there is hope that there will be some resemblance left between a Christian now and in the earliest days, so that it will again be regarded as folly for anyone to entertain the notion of becoming a Christian. In the earliest days the Christian was a fool in the eyes of the world, and to Jews and pagans alike it seemed folly for anyone to seek to become one. Now we are Christians as a matter of course, but if anyone desires to be a Christian with infinite passion he is judged to be a fool, just as it is always folly to put forth an infinite passionate exertion for the sake of becoming what one already is; as if a man were to sacrifice all his wealth to buy a jewel—which he already owned. Formerly a Christian was a fool in the eyes of the world, and now that all men are Christians he nevertheless becomes a fool—in the eyes of Christians.

FOUR

Nietzsche: "LIVE DANGEROUSLY"

[*Preface:* Friedrich Nietzsche was born in Germany in 1844 and died in 1900. Few thinkers of any age equal his influence. In England and in the United States it was long customary to associate him with the Nazis, which is rather like linking St. Francis with the Inquisition in which the order he had founded played a major role. Otherwise, to be sure, the two men have little in common. What is unique about Nietzsche's impact is not that the Nazis, who had no use at all for any of his books as a whole, brazenly used him, too, but that within a generation of his death he had profoundly influenced such men as Rilke, Hesse, Thomas Mann, Stefan George, Shaw, Gide, and Malraux—indeed the whole climate of German and French literature and thought. The existentialism of Jaspers, Heidegger, and Sartre is only one facet of this multifarious impact.

The purpose of the following selections is not to illustrate this multiplicity but rather to bring out that aspect of his thought which makes his inclusion in the story of existentialism imperative.

The initial selection is from the "untimely meditation" on *Schopenhauer as Educator* which was published when Nietzsche was 30 and still a professor of classical philology at Basel. Like some of the following selections, too, it was especially translated for this volume. The four items of the second selection come from *The Dawn*, section 173, and *The Gay Science*, sections 125, 283, and 290. The titles are

Nietzsche's own—also in the case of the immediately following chapter from his *Zarathustra*.

The Will to Power is a book composed by Nietzsche's
sister out of the notes he left, some still unutilized, some
long employed in the writing of his books. The preface is
one of several drafts for a major work he hoped to write. The
beginning of Book I, as it now stands, is literally only jot-
tings for a book he did not live to write. *Ecce Homo*, completed in 1888, was published only in 1908 after many of
the misconceptions which the author had tried frantically to
forestall had taken firm root.]

1. "The Challenge of Every Great Philosophy"

A traveler who had seen many countries and peoples and
several continents was asked what human traits he had found
everywhere; and he answered: men are inclined to laziness.
Some will feel that he might have said with greater justice:
they are all timorous. They hide behind customs and opinions. At bottom, every human being knows very well that he
is in this world just once, as something unique, and that no
accident, however strange, will throw together a second time
into a unity such a curious and diffuse plurality: he knows
it, but hides it like a bad conscience—why? From fear of
his neighbor who insists on convention and veils himself
with it. But what is it that compels the individual human
being to fear his neighbor, to think and act herd-fashion,
and not to be glad of himself? A sense of shame, perhaps,
in a few rare cases. In the vast majority it is the desire for
comfort, inertia—in short, that inclination to laziness of
which the traveler spoke. He is right: men are even lazier
than they are timorous, and what they fear most is the trou-
bles with which any unconditional honesty and nudity would
burden them. Only artists hate this slovenly life in borrowed
manners and loosely fitting opinions and unveil the secret,
everybody's bad conscience, the principle that every human
being is a unique wonder; they dare to show us the human
being as he is, down to the last muscle, himself and himself
alone—even more, that in this rigorous consistency of his
uniqueness he is beautiful and worth contemplating, as novel
and incredible as every work of nature, and by no means
dull. When a great thinker despises men, it is their laziness

that he despises: for it is on account of this that they have the appearance of factory products and seem indifferent and unworthy of companionship or instruction. The human being who does not wish to belong to the mass must merely cease being comfortable with himself; let him follow his conscience which shouts at him: "Be yourself! What you are at present doing, opining, and desiring, that is not really you." . . .

I care for a philosopher only to the extent that he is able to be an example. . . . Kant clung to the university, subjected himself to governments, remained within the appearance of religious faith, and endured colleagues and students: it is small wonder that his example produced in the main university professors and professors' philosophy. Schopenhauer has no consideration for the scholars' caste, stands apart, strives for independence of state and society—this is his example, his model, to begin with the most external features. . . . He was an out and out solitary; there was not one really congenial friend to comfort him—and between one and none there gapes, as always between something and nothing, an infinity. No one who has true friends can know what true solitude means, even if the whole world surrounding him should consist of adversaries. Alas, I can see that you do not know what it means to be alone. Wherever there have been powerful societies, governments, religions, or public opinions—in short, wherever there was any kind of tyranny, it has hated the lonely philosopher; for philosophy opens up a refuge for man where no tyranny can reach: the cave of inwardness, the labyrinth of the breast; and that annoys all tyrants. That is where the lonely hide; but there too they encounter their greatest danger. . . .

This was the first danger that overshadowed Schopenhauer's development: isolation. The second danger is to despair of truth. This danger confronts every thinker who begins from Kant's philosophy, assuming that he is a vigorous and whole human being in his suffering and aspiration and not merely a clacking thinking- or calculating-machine. . . . As soon as Kant would begin to exert a popular influence, we should find it reflected in the form of a gnawing and crumbling skepticism and relativism; and only among the most active and noble spirits, who have never been able to endure doubt, you would find in its place that upheaval and despair of all truth which Heinrich von Kleist, for example, experienced as an effect of Kant's philosophy. "Not long ago," he once writes in his moving manner, "I became acquainted with Kant's philosophy; and now I must tell you of a thought in it, inasmuch as I cannot fear that it will upset you as profoundly and painfully as me. We cannot decide whether that which we call truth is really truth or whether it merely appears that way to us. If the latter is right, then the truth we gather here comes to nothing after our death; and every aspiration to acquire a possession which will follow us even into the grave is futile. If the point of this idea does not penetrate your heart, do not smile at another human being who feels wounded by it in his holiest depths. My only, my highest aim has sunk, and I have none left." When will human beings again have the natural feelings of a Kleist? When will they learn again to measure the meaning of a philosophy by their "holiest depths"?

This, however, is necessary to estimate what, after Kant, Schopenhauer might mean to us. He can be the guide to lead us out of the cave of skeptical irritation or critical resignation up to the height of a tragic view, with the starry nocturnal sky stretching endlessly over us; and he was the first to lead himself this way. His greatness was that he confronted the image of life as a whole in order to interpret it as a whole, while the subtlest minds cannot be freed from the error that one can come closer to such an interpretation if one examines painstakingly the colors with which this image has been painted and the material underneath. . . .

The whole future of all the sciences is staked on an attempt to understand this canvas and these colors, but not the image. It could be said that only a man who has a firm grasp of the over-all picture of life and existence can use the individual sciences without harming himself; for without such a regulative total image they are strings that reach no end anywhere and merely make our lives still more confused and labyrinthine. In this, as I have said, lies Schopenhauer's greatness: that he pursues this image as Hamlet pursues the ghost, without permitting himself to be distracted, as the scholars do, and without letting himself be caught in the webs of a conceptual scholasticism, as happens to the unrestrained dialectician. The study of all quarter-philosophers is attractive only insofar as we see how they immediately make for those spots in the edifice of a great philosophy where the scholarly pro and con, and reflection, doubt, and contradiction are permitted; and thus they avoid the challenge of every great philosophy which, when taken as a whole, always says only: this is the image of all life, and from this learn the meaning of your life! And conversely: Read only your own life, and from this understand the hieroglyphs of universal life!

This is how Schopenhauer's philosophy, too, should always be interpreted first of all: individually, by the single human being alone for himself, to gain some insight into his own misery and need, into his own limitation . . . He teaches us to distinguish between real and apparent promotions of human happiness: how neither riches, nor honors, nor scholarship can raise the individual out of his discouragement over the worthlessness of his existence, and how the striving for these goals can receive meaning only from a high and transfiguring over-all aim: to gain power to help nature and to correct a little its follies and blunders. To begin with, for oneself; but eventually through oneself for all. That is, to be sure, an aspiration which leads us profoundly and heartily to resignation: for what, and how much, can after all be improved in the individual or in general? . . .

2. "The Gay Science"

The eulogists of work   Behind the glorification of "work" and the tireless talk of the "blessings of work" I find the same thought as behind the praise of impersonal activity for the public benefit: the fear of everything individual. At bottom, one now feels when confronted with work—and what is invariably meant is relentless industry from early till late— that such work is the best policy, that it keeps everybody in harness and powerfully obstructs the development of reason, of covetousness, of the desire for independence. For it uses up a tremendous amount of nervous energy and takes it away from reflection, brooding, dreaming, worry, love, and hatred; it always sets a small goal before one's eyes and permits easy and regular satisfactions. In that way a society in which the members continually work hard will have more security: and security is now adored as the supreme goddess. And now—horrors!—it is precisely the "worker" who has become dangerous. "Dangerous individuals are swarming all around." And behind them, the danger of dangers: the individual.

The Madman Have you not heard of that madman who lit a lantern in the bright morning hours, ran to the market place, and cried incessantly, "I seek God! I seek God!" As many of those who do not believe in God were standing around just then, he provoked much laughter. Why, did he get lost? said one. Did he lose his way like a child? said another. Or is he hiding? Is he afraid of us? Has he gone on a voyage? or emigrated? Thus they yelled and laughed. The madman jumped into their midst and pierced them with his glances.

"Whither is God" he cried. "I shall tell you. *We have killed him*—you and I. All of us are his murderers. But how have we done this? How were we able to drink up the sea? Who gave us the sponge to wipe away the entire horizon? What did we do when we unchained this earth from its sun? Whither is it moving now? Whither are we moving now? Away from all suns? Are we not plunging continually? Backward, sideward, forward, in all directions? Is there any up or down left? Are we not straying as through an infinite nothing? Do we not feel the breath of empty space? Has it not become colder? Is not night and more night coming on all the while? Must not lanterns be lit in the morning? Do we not hear anything yet of the noise of the grave-diggers who are burying God? Do we not smell anything yet of God's decomposition? Gods too decompose. God is dead. God remains dead. And we have killed him. How shall we, the murderers of all murderers, comfort ourselves? What was holiest and most powerful of all that the world has yet owned has bled to death under our knives. Who will wipe this blood off us? What water is there for us to clean ourselves? What festivals of atonement, what sacred games shall we have to invent? Is not the greatness of this deed too great for us? Must not we ourselves become gods simply to seem worthy of it? There has never been a greater deed; and whoever will be born after us—for the sake of this deed he will be part of a higher history than all history hitherto."

Here the madman fell silent and looked again at his listeners; and they too were silent and stared at him in astonishment. At last he threw his lantern on the ground, and it broke and went out. "I come too early," he said then; "my time has not come yet. This tremendous event is still on its way, still wandering—it has not yet reached the ears of man. Lightning and thunder require time, the light of the

stars requires time, deeds require time even after they are
done, before they can be seen and heard. This deed is still
more distant from them than the most distant stars—*and
yet they have done it themselves."*

It has been related further that on that same day the
madman entered divers churches and there sang his *requiem
aeternam deo.* Led out and called to account, he is said to
have replied each time, "What are these churches now if they
are not the tombs and sepulchers of God?"

Preparatory men I welcome all signs that a more manly,
a warlike, age is about to begin, an age which, above all,
will give honor to valor once again. For this age shall prepare the way for one yet higher, and it shall gather the
strength which this higher age will need one day—this age
which is to carry heroism into the pursuit of knowledge and
wage wars for the sake of thoughts and their consequences.
To this end we now need many preparatory valorous men
who cannot leap into being out of nothing—any more than
out of the sand and slime of our present civilization and
metropolitanism: men who are bent on seeking for that aspect in all things which must be *overcome;* men characterized by cheerfulness, patience, unpretentiousness, and contempt for all great vanities, as well as by magnanimity in
victory and forbearance regarding the small vanities of the
vanquished; men possessed of keen and free judgment
concerning all victors and the share of chance in every victory and every fame; men who have their own festivals,
their own weekdays, their own periods of mourning, who are
accustomed to command with assurance and are no less ready
to obey when necessary, in both cases equally proud and
serving their own cause; men who are in greater danger,
more fruitful, and happier! For, believe me, the secret of
the greatest fruitfulness and the greatest enjoyment of existence is: to *live dangerously!* Build your cities under Vesu-
vius! Send your ships into uncharted seas! Live at war with
your peers and yourselves! Be robbers and conquerors, as
long as you cannot be rulers and owners, you lovers of knowledge! Soon the age will be past when you could be satisfied
to live like shy deer, hidden in the woods! At long last the
pursuit of knowledge will reach out for its due: it will want to
rule and *own,* and you with it!

One thing is needful "Giving style" to one's character—

a great and rare art! It is exercised by those who see all the strengths and weaknesses of their own natures and then comprehend them in an artistic plan until everything appears as art and reason and even weakness delights the eye. Here a large mass of second nature has been added; there a piece of original nature has been removed: both by long practice and daily labor. Here the ugly which could not be removed is hidden; there it has been reinterpreted and made sublime. . . . It will be the strong and domineering natures who enjoy their finest gaiety in such compulsion, in such constraint and perfection under a law of their own; the passion of their tremendous will relents when confronted with stylized, conquered, and serving nature; even when they have to build palaces and lay out gardens, they demur at giving nature a free hand. Conversely, it is the weak characters without power over themselves who *hate* the constraint of style. . . . They become slaves as soon as they serve; they hate to serve. Such spirits—and they may be of the first rank—are always out to interpret themselves and their environment as *free* nature—wild, arbitrary, fantastic, disorderly, astonishing; and they will do well because only in this way do they please themselves. For one thing is needful: that a human being attain his satisfaction with himself—whether it be by this or by that poetry and art; only then is a human being at all tolerable to behold. Whoever is dissatisfied with himself is always ready to revenge himself therefor; we others will be his victims, if only by always having to stand his ugly sight. For the sight of the ugly makes men bad and gloomy.

3. On Free Death

Many die too late, and a few die too early. The doctrine still sounds strange: "Die at the right time!"

Die at the right time—thus teaches Zarathustra. Of course, how could those who never live at the right time die at the right time? Would that they had never been born! Thus I counsel the superfluous. But even the superfluous still make a fuss about their dying; and even the hollowest nut still wants to be cracked. Everybody considers dying important; but as yet death is no festival. As yet men have not learned how one hallows the most beautiful festivals.

I show you the death that consummates—a spur and a

promise to the survivors. He that consummates his life dies his death victoriously, surrounded by those who hope and promise. Thus should one learn to die; and there should be no festival where one dying thus does not hallow the oaths of the living.

To die thus is best; second to this, however, is to die fighting and to squander a great soul. But equally hateful to the fighter and the victor is your grinning death, which creeps up like a thief—and yet comes as the master.

My death I praise to you, the free death which comes to me because *I* want it. And when shall I want it? He who has a goal and an heir will want death at the right time for his goal and heir. And from reverence for his goal and heir he will hang no more dry wreaths in the sanctuary of life. Verily, I do not want to be like the ropemakers: they drag out their threads and always walk backwards.

Some become too old even for their truths and victories: a toothless mouth no longer has the right to every truth. And everybody who wants fame must take leave of honor betimes and practice the difficult art of leaving at the right time.

One must cease letting oneself be eaten when one tastes best: that is known to those who want to be loved long. There are sour apples, to be sure, whose lot requires that they wait till the last day of autumn: and they become ripe, yellow, and wrinkled all at once. In some, the heart grows old first; in others, the spirit. And some are old in their youth: but late youth preserves long youth.

For some, life turns out badly: a poisonous worm eats its way to their heart. Let them see to it that their dying turns out that much better. Some never become sweet; they rot already in the summer. It is cowardice that keeps them on their branch.

All-too-many live, and all-too-long they hang on their branches. Would that a storm came to shake all this worm-eaten rot from the tree!

Would that there came preachers of *quick* death! I would like them as the true storms and shakers of the trees of life. But I hear only slow death preached, and patience with everything "earthly".

Alas, do you preach patience with the earthly? It is the earthly that has too much patience with you, blasphemers!

Verily, that Hebrew died too early whom the preachers of slow death honor; and for many it has become a calamity that he died too early. As yet he knew only tears and the melancholy of the Hebrew, and hatred of the good and the just—the Hebrew Jesus: then the longing for death overcame him. Would that he had remained in the wilderness and far from the good and the just! Perhaps he would have learned to live and to love the earth—and laughter too.

Believe me, my brothers! He died too early; he himself would have recanted his teaching, had he reached my age. Noble enough was he to recant. But he was not yet mature. Immature is the love of the youth, and immature his hatred of man and earth. His mind and the wings of his spirit are still tied down and heavy.

But in the man there is more of the child than in the youth, and less melancholy: he knows better how to die and to live. Free to die and free in death, able to say a holy No when the time for Yes has passed: thus he knows how to die and to live.

That your dying be no blasphemy against man and earth, my friends, that I ask of the honey of your soul. In your dying, your spirit and virtue should still glow like a sunset around the earth: else your dying has turned out badly.

Thus I want to die myself that you, my friends, may love the earth more for my sake; and to earth I want to return that I may find rest in her who gave birth to me.

Verily, Zarathustra had a goal; he threw his ball: now you, my friends, are the heirs of my goal; to you I throw my golden ball. More than anything, I like to see you, my friends, throwing the golden ball. And so I still linger a little on the earth; forgive me for that.

Thus spoke Zarathustra.

4. The Beginning of "The Will to Power"

PREFACE

I   Of what is great one must either be silent or speak with greatness. With greatness—that means cynically and with innocence.

II   What I relate is the history of the next two centuries. I describe what is coming, what can no longer come differently: *the advent of nihilism.* . . . Our whole European culture is moving for some time now, with a tortured tension that is growing from decade to decade, as toward a catastrophe: restlessly, violently, headlong, like a river that wants to reach the end, that no longer reflects, that is afraid to reflect.

III He that speaks here has, conversely, done nothing so far but to reflect: as a philosopher and solitary by instinct who has found his advantage in standing aside, outside . . .

IV . . . Why has the advent of nihilism become necessary? Because the values we have had hitherto thus draw their final consequence; because nihilism represents the ultimate logical conclusion of our great values and ideals—because we must experience nihilism before we can find out what value these "values" really had.—We require, at some time, new values.

BOOK ONE: EUROPEAN NIHILISM

I Nihilism stands at the door: whence comes this uncanniest of all guests? Point of departure: it is an error to consider "social distress" or "physiological degeneration," or corruption of all things, as the cause of nihilism. Ours is the most honest and compassionate age. Distress, whether psychic, physical, or intellectual, need not at all produce nihilism (that is, the radical rejection of value, meaning, and desirability). Such distress always permits a variety of interpretations. Rather: it is in one particular interpretation, the Christian moral one, that nihilism is rooted.

II The end of Christianity—at the hands of its own morality (which cannot be replaced), which turns against the Christian God: the sense of truthfulness, highly developed by Christianity, is nauseated by the falseness and mendaciousness of all Christian interpretations of the world and of history; rebound from "God is the truth" to the fanatical faith "All is false"; an active Buddhism.

III Skepticism regarding morality is what is decisive. The end of the moral interpretation of the world, which no longer has any sanction after it has tried to escape into some beyond, leads to nihilism. "All lacks meaning." (The untenability of one interpretation of the world, upon which a tremendous amount of energy has been lavished, awakens the suspicion that all interpretations of the world are false.) . . .

IV Against this "meaninglessness" on the one hand, against our moral prejudices on the other: to what extent was all science and philosophy so far influenced by moral judgments? and will this not arouse the hostility of science?

or an anti-scientific mentality? . . . A critique of Christian morality is still lacking.

v . . . Since Copernicus man is rolling from the center toward x.

5. From "Ecce Homo"

In the end, nobody hears more out of things, including books, than he knows already. For that to which one lacks access from experience, one has no ears. Let us then imagine an extreme case: that a book speaks of all sorts of experiences which lie utterly beyond any possibility of frequent, or even rare, experiences—that it represents the first language for a new sequence of experiences. In that case, simply nothing is heard; and people have the acoustic illusion that where nothing is heard there *is* nothing.

This has been my usual experience and, if you will, the originality of my experience. Whoever thought that he had understood something of me had merely construed something out of me, after his own image. Not infrequently, it was an antithesis of me—for example, an "idealist"—and those who had understood nothing of me would deny that I should even be considered.

The word "overman," meant to designate a type that has turned out supremely well, by way of an antithesis to "modern" men, to "good" men, to Christians and other nihilists— a word which, coming from a Zarathustra, the annihilator of morality, becomes a very thoughtful word—has almost universally been understood with the greatest innocence in line with the very values whose antithesis has been embodied in the figure of Zarathustra: I mean, as an "idealistic" type of a higher kind of human being, half "saint," half "genius." Other scholarly oxen have suspected me of Darwinism in this connection. Even the "hero worship" of that great unconscious and involuntary counterfeiter, Carlyle, which I repudiate so maliciously, has been read into it.

* * *

In the end, why should I not give expression to my suspicion? Faced with a tremendous destiny, the Germans will once again make every attempt, in my case, too, to give birth to a mouse. So far, they have compromised themselves in relation to me; I doubt that in future they will do better. Oh,

how I wish to be a bad prophet this once!—My natural
readers and listeners are even now Russians, Scandinavians,
and Frenchmen. Will it always be that way?

In the history of knowledge the Germans are inscribed
with a series of ambiguous names: they have never produced
anything but "unconscious" counterfeiters. (Fichte, Schelling,
Schopenhauer, Hegel, Schleiermacher deserve this term no
less than Kant and Leibniz: all of them are mere Schleiermacher—veil-makers.) They shall never have the honor that
the first *honest* spirit in the history of the spirit—the spirit
in whom truth has come to sit in judgment over the counterfeiting of four thousand years—should be identified with the
German spirit. The "German spirit" is for *me* bad air: I find
it hard to breathe near this uncleanliness *in psychologicis*
which has become instinctive and betrays itself in the words
and mien of every German. They have never gone through a
seventeenth century of hard self-examination like the French:
men like La Rochefoucauld or Descartes are a hundred times
superior in honesty to the most eminent Germans. To this
day, they have had no psychologist. But psychology is almost
the measure for the *cleanliness* or *uncleanliness* of a race. . . .

What is called "deep" in Germany is precisely this instinctive uncleanliness in relation toward oneself of which I am
speaking: one does not *want* clarity about oneself.

I do not *want* "believers"; I think I am too sarcastic to
believe in myself; I never speak to masses.

I have a terrible fear that some day one will pronounce me
holy: one will guess why I bring out this book *before;* it
shall prevent that one raises the devil with me.

I do not want to be a saint, rather even a buffoon.—Perhaps
I am a buffoon.—Nevertheless—or rather, *not* nevertheless,
for to date nothing has been more mendacious than saints—
the truth speaks out of me.

FIVE

Rilke: THE NOTES OF MALTE LAURIDS BRIGGE

[*Preface:* Rainer Maria Rilke was born in Prague in 1875 and died in 1926. He is widely considered the greatest German poet since the death of Goethe. His poetry is usually, and plausibly, divided into two periods. The first of these culminated in the two volumes of *Neue Gedichte,* published in 1907 and 1908; the second, in *Duineser Elegien* and *Sonette an Orpheus,* both published in 1923. The late poems with their splendid rhythms, religious intensity, and wealth of obscurities have elicited a vast secondary literature, including attempts at detailed commentaries, while the many superb poems of the young Rilke, which are less obscure, are written about much less and neglected together with the poet's great prose work, *The Notes of Malte Laurids Brigge,* which appeared in 1910.

Speaking of prose, Nietzsche once remarked: "It will be said one day that Heine and I have been by far the first artists of the German language." At the very least, he was right insofar as Thomas Mann did say it. Rilke's *Malte* belongs in this select company, and his perhaps unexpected wit need not fear comparison with his great predecessors'.

The following selections, newly translated, are included here not merely because *Malte* influenced Sartre's *La Nausée,* or because Heidegger has written a long essay on a poem Rilke wrote into one copy of the book, but because so many existentialist motifs are sounded in this work: above all, the quest for authentic existence, the scorn of the inauthentic, the problem how to meet death, and the experience of time which brings us nearer death.]

This excellent *hôtel* is very old: even in King Clovis' times one died there in a few beds. Now one dies in 559 beds. Factory fashion, of course. In view of this enormous production rate, the individual death is not so well executed; but that is beside the point. It is the quantity that counts. Who, today, would still give anything for a well-executed death? No one. Even the rich, who could after all afford to die elaborately, are beginning to become negligent and indifferent; the wish to have a death of one's own is becoming rarer and rarer. A little while yet, and it will be as rare as a life of one's own. God, it's all there. One comes along, one finds a life, ready-made, one only has to put it on. One wants to go or is forced to go: well, no trouble at all: *voilà votre mort, monsieur.* One dies at random; one dies whatever death belongs to the disease one happens to have: for since one knows all diseases, one also knows that the different lethal conclusions belong to the diseases and not to the human beings; and the sick person, as it were, doesn't have anything to do.

In hospitals, where people die so agreeably and with so much gratitude toward doctors and nurses, one dies a death prepared by the institution: they like it that way. If, however, one dies at home, one chooses as a matter of course that polite death of the better circles with which, so to say, the funeral first class and the whole sequence of its touching customs begin. In front of such a house the poor stand and stare to their heart's content. Their death, of course, is trite, without all fuss. They are well satisfied if they find one that fits approximately. No matter if it is too big: one is always apt to grow a little more. But if it does not close over the chest or if it chokes, that is bad.

*   *   *

How wrong I was when I wrote my drama! Was I an ape and a fool that I required a third person to tell of the fate of two human beings who made things hard for each other? How readily I fell into this trap. And I certainly should have known that this third person who appears in every life and literature, this ghost of a third person who never existed, has no significance and must be denied. He is one of the pretexts of nature who is always intent on diverting men's attention from her deepest mysteries. He is the screen behind which a drama takes place. He is the noise at the entrance to the voiceless silence of a real conflict. Perhaps everybody has found it too difficult to speak of the two who matter; the third person, precisely because he is so unreal, represents an easy task; everybody knows how to cope with him. From the beginning of their dramas one can notice their impatience to get to the third person; they can hardly wait for him. As soon as he appears, all is well. But how dull things are if he is late; nothing can really happen without him: everything stands, freezes, waits.

* * *

Is it possible that, in spite of inventions and progress, in spite of culture, religion, and wisdom, one has remained at the surface of life? Is it possible that even this surface, which would at least have been something, has been covered with an incredibly dull material till it looks like salon furniture during the summer vacation? . . .

Is it possible that there are people who say "God" and suppose that this is something one can have in common?— Just look at two school children: one of them buys a knife, and his neighbor buys one just like it, on the very same day. And a week later they compare their two knives, and by now they are barely similar: so differently have they developed in different hands. (Sure, says the mother of one boy, if you always get everything to look used right away!) I see: Is it possible to believe that one can have a god without using him?

* * *

I am, of course, imagining things when I now claim that even then I felt that something had come into my life, straightaway into mine, with which I alone should have to go around—always, always. I see myself lying in my little crib, not sleeping, and somehow foreseeing vaguely that life would be this way: full of special things which are meant for *one* only and which are unutterable.

* * *

There is a creature that is completely harmless for your eyes: you scarcely notice it and forget it immediately. But as soon as, invisibly, it somehow gets into your ear, it develops there and, as it were, finally comes out of its cocoon; and there have been cases in which it penetrated to the brain and there spread devastation, somewhat like the pneumococci of the dog which enter through the nose.

This creature is the neighbor.

Well, since I have started traveling around by myself I have had innumerable neighbors: above and below, right and left, and sometimes all four kinds at once. I could simply write the history of my neighbors, and that would be a life's work. To be sure, it would really be the case history of the symptoms they caused in me; but this they have in common with all such creatures: they can only be inferred from the disturbances they create in certain tissues.

I have had unpredictable neighbors and very regular ones. I have sat there trying to discover the law of the first kind, for it was obvious that they too had a law. And when the punctual ones would stay out late one night, I would picture to myself what might have happened to them, and I would keep on my light and worry like a young wife. I have had neighbors who were hating just then, and neighbors who loved violently; and I have even had the experience how the one feeling changed into the other in the middle of the night —and then, of course, there could be no question of sleep. And one could observe quite generally that sleep is by no means as frequent as is commonly supposed. My two neighbors in St. Petersburg, for example, did not care much for sleep. One of them would stand there playing the violin; and I am sure that he was looking across to the over-awake houses which did not cease being lit up even in the most unlikely August nights. Of the other neighbor, on the right, I know that he was lying down; indeed, in my time he did not get up at all any more. He even had his eyes closed; but one could not claim that he was sleeping. He lay there and recited long poems, poems by Pushkin and Nekrassov, in the tone of voice in which children recite poems when they are told to. And in spite of the music of my neighbor on the left, it was this man with his poems who spun himself into a cocoon in my head; and God knows what would have

come out if the student who visited him from time to time
had not one day opened the wrong door. He told me the
story of his friend, and it turned out to be relatively soothing. At least it was a literal and unequivocal story of which
the worms of my conjectures perished.

This petty official next door had got the notion one Sunday that he wanted to solve a curious problem. He supposed
that he still had a long time to live—let us say, another
fifty years. His generosity toward himself put him into a
buoyant frame of mind. But now he wanted to outdo himself. It occurred to him that these years could be changed
into days, into hours, into minutes—indeed, if only one had
the endurance, into seconds; and he figured and figured and
attained a sum the like of which he had never seen. He felt
dizzy. He had to steady himself. Time is precious, he had
always heard; and now he was surprised that a man who
possessed such a lot of time should not be watched. How
easily he could be robbed! But then his good, almost gay,
mood returned: he put on his fur coat to look a little broader
and more impressive, and gave himself this whole fabulous
capital as a present, addressing himself with some condescension:

"Nikolai Kuzmich," he said benevolently and imagined
that he was also sitting on the horsehair sofa, without a fur
coat, thin and wretched; "I hope, Nikolai Kuzmich," he
said, "that your wealth won't go to your head. Remember
that this is not the most important thing: there are poor
people who are entirely respectable; there are even impoverished noblemen and daughters of generals who try to sell
things in the streets." And the benefactor went on adducing
several examples which were known all over the town.

The other Nikolai Kuzmich, the one on the horsehair sofa
who was receiving the present, did not yet look overjoyed at
all; it seemed likely that he would be reasonable. Indeed,
he did not change anything in his modest and regular way
of life, and he spent his Sundays trying to keep his accounts
in order. But soon, after only a few weeks, he noticed that
he was spending incredible amounts. I shall limit myself, he
thought. He got up earlier, washed himself less elaborately,
drank his tea standing up, ran to his office, and arrived far
too early. He saved a little time everywhere. But on Sunday
there were no savings to be found. Then he realized that
he had been cheated. I should not have changed my capital,

he said to himself. How long a year is! But this wretched small change, that is spent, one doesn't know how. And the afternoon became disagreeable as he sat there in his sofa corner waiting for the man in the fur coat from whom he wanted to ask back his time. He wanted to bolt the door and not permit the man to leave until he had produced it. "In bills," he wanted to say, "perhaps ten years each." Four tens and one five, and the rest he could keep in the devil's name. Yes, he was prepared to give him the rest, just to avoid any difficulties. Irritated, he sat there on his horse-hair sofa and waited, but the man did not come. And he, Nikolai Kuzmich, who had been easily able a few weeks ago to picture himself sitting there—now that he was really sitting there, he could not picture the other Nikolai Kuzmich, the one in the fur coat, the generous one. Heaven knows what had become of him; probably his frauds had been noticed and by now he was in prison somewhere. No doubt, this man had not ruined him alone. Such swindlers always work on a large scale.

It occurred to him that there must be some state institute, a kind of time bank, where he would be able to change at least some part of his shabby seconds. After all, they were genuine. He had never heard of such an institution, but in the address book one would certainly find something of the sort—under *T*, or perhaps it was called "Bank for Time"; it was easy to check under *B* too. Possibly the letter *I* had to be considered too, for it would presumably be an Imperial Institute, in view of its importance.

Later, Nikolai Kuzmich always insisted that on this Sunday afternoon he did not drink anything, though he felt, of course, depressed. So he was completely sober when the following events occurred, insofar as it is at all possible to say what happened. Perhaps he had dozed off a little in his corner, that might well be. This little nap relieved him a great deal at first. I have allowed myself to become involved in figures, he said to himself. Well, I really don't know anything about figures. But it is obvious that they must not be conceded too much importance; after all, they are no more than an official device, to keep things orderly. Has anybody ever seen one, except on paper? At a party, for example, one could not possibly meet a Seven or a Twenty-five. There they simply did not exist. And then there had been this little mix-up, merely owing to absentmindedness: time and money, as if those two could not be kept apart. Nikolai Kuzmich almost laughed. It was a good thing if one caught up with oneself like this, and in time, that was the important thing, in time. Now everything would become different. Time—that was a touchy affair, no doubt. But did it concern him alone? Did it not affect others in the same way which he had discovered, second by second, even if they did not know it?

Nikolai Kuzmich even felt some delight at the expense of the others: Let it—he just wanted to think, when something strange happened. He felt a draft past his face, past his ears, he felt it on his hands. He stood aghast. The window was shut tight. And as he was sitting there with wide open eyes in his dark room, he began to understand that what he felt now was time itself as it passed by. He literally recognized them, all these tiny seconds, one as tepid as the other, but fast, but fast. Heaven knows where they were rushing. That this had to happen to him of all people, when he considered any kind of wind a personal insult. Now he would be sitting there, and the draft would continue, his whole life long. He foresaw all the neuralgias he would get and was besides himself with rage. He jumped up, but his surprises were not over yet. Under his feet, too, there was something like a motion—not only one, several motions wavering in strange confusion. He froze with terror: could that be the earth? Certainly, this was the earth. After all, it moved. That had been mentioned in school, though it was passed over in a hurry, and later on they had tried to cover it up; it was not considered good taste to speak of it. But now that he had become sensitive, he could not help feeling this too. Whether other people felt it? Perhaps, but they did not show it. Probably, they did not mind it, these sailors. Nikolai Kuzmich, however, was unfortunately touchy precisely at this point: he even avoided trolley cars. He reeled around his room as if on deck, and had to hold on right and left. To make matters worse, he suddenly recalled something about the slanted axis of the earth. No, he could not stand all these motions. He felt wretched. Lie down and keep quiet, he had once read somewhere. And since then Nikolai Kuzmich had been lying.

He lay there with his eyes closed. And there were times, less stormy days, as it were, when things were quite tolerable. And then he had thought of the poems. You would hardly believe how much that helped. If you recite such a poem, slowly, with an even stress on the rhymes at the end of the line, there is, so to say, something stable on which you can fix your eyes—figuratively speaking, of course. How lucky he was to know all these poems. But he had always been especially interested in literature. He did not complain about his condition, the student who had known him for a long time assured me. Only, as time went on, he had developed an exaggerated admiration for those who, like the student, walked around and could stand the motion of the earth.

I remember this story so exactly because it soothed me no end. I may well say that I have never had another neighbor who was as agreeable as this Nikolai Kuzmich who, no doubt, would have admired me too.

*   *   *

We discover that we do not know our role; we look for a mirror; we want to remove our make-up and take off what is false and be real. But somewhere a piece of disguise that we forgot still sticks to us. A trace of exaggeration remains in our eyebrows; we do not notice that the corners of our mouth are bent. And so we walk around, a mockery and a mere half: neither having achieved being nor actors.

SIX

Kafka: THREE PARABLES

[*Preface:* Franz Kafka was born in Prague in 1883 and died in 1924. He published some short pieces, including *The Metamorphosis,* but did not finish or try to publish his two major works, *The Trial* and *The Castle.* In fact, he tried to destroy the manuscripts, and it was against his instructions that Max Brod published them after Kafka's death. Brod's arrangement of the various chapters has been challenged, and his interpretations in his postscripts and biography are, I think—and by no means only I—untenable; but everybody who admires Kafka is in Brod's debt.

Among the most important documents for the interpretation of *The Castle* are the following three parables. They are also excellent illustrations of Kafka's style: simple, seemingly artless prose that stirs intelligence and heart at once and transposes us into a Kafkaesque world. The translations are less than perfect—anyone who reads even a little German should try the original—but Kafka's world is there. (The last sentence of the second parable has been definitely mistranslated: *Die Lüge wird zur Weltordnung gemacht* means "The world-order is based upon a lie.")

Even in translation, these short parables satisfy, as perfectly as few works of world literature, the high standards defined in Nietzsche's epigram: "It is my ambition to say in ten sentences what everyone else says in a book—what everyone else does *not* say in a book." Although there are few writers to whom this dictum is less applicable than to Kierkegaard and Jaspers, there are critics who admire all four—probably because they are so frank about the absurdity of man's condition.

In the usual exegesis, Kafka's castle stands for God: the hero is remote from God, while the people in the village are nearer to God, and the problem is one of divine grace. At the beginning of the novel, however, we are told that the castle is the castle of Count Westwest, and after that the count no longer figures in the story. The German *"west"* means "decomposes." I suggest that in *The Castle* God is dead, and we are faced with a universe devoid of sense. The villagers are not close to God: in the words of Nietzsche's "madman" in *The Gay Science* (see above) "this tremendous event . . . has not yet reached the ears of men." They do not understand their situation. Thus the emperor has died in the first parable, and in the last parable there are no kings and the couriers shout messages that are meaningless. In one of Kafka's notebooks, finally—in number four—we find a one-page sketch from which I quote: "The old count, to be sure, was dead, and so the young one should have reigned; but it was not that way: there was a pause in history, and the deputation went into emptiness."

Kafka stands between Nietzsche and the existentialists: he pictures the world into which Heidegger's man, in *Sein und Zeit,* is "thrown," the godless world of Sartre, the "absurd" world of Camus.

The discussion of the parable about the "Law" in *The Trial* is no less important: it is Kafka's broadest hint about his method and his meaning. In his simple style, comparable to the Book of Genesis, he fashions stories which, like those of Genesis, invite a multitude of different interpretations; and he does not want to be reduced to one exclusive meaning. As we read and reread the beginning of *The Castle* and compare it with the variant beginning printed at the end of the book, it becomes quite clear that Kafka went out of his way to rule out any possibility of one exclusive exegesis. Ambiguity is of the essence of his art.

At the end of a half page on four variants of the old myth of Prometheus, Kafka writes in his third notebook: "The myth tries to explain the unexplainable. As it comes out of a ground of truth, it must end again in the unexplainable." It is for the sake of truthfulness that Kafka eschews reduction to a single explanation. The world that confronts us and our

life in it defy every attempt at a compelling exegesis: that
life lends itself to many different interpretations is of its
essence.

Kafka is no obscurantist or authoritarian: his intelligence
is bright and critical and clear, and in his major works no
less than in his "Letter to the Father" he points to the faults
and filth of those who command authority, and he does not
demand submission, let alone a *sacrificium intellectus*. Surely,
Kafka would have agreed that, although critical intelligence
is not sufficient to redeem humanity from misery, those who
renounce it are heading from the frying pan into the fire.]

1. An Imperial Message

The Emperor, so it runs, has sent a message to you, the humble subject, the insignificant shadow cowering in the re-
motest distance before the imperial sun; the Emperor from
his deathbed has sent a message to you alone. He has commanded the messenger to kneel down by the bed, and has
whispered the message to him; so much store did he lay on
it that he ordered the messenger to whisper it back into his
ear again. Then by a nod of the head he has confirmed that
it is right. Yes, before the assembled spectators of his death
—all the obstructing walls have been broken down, and on
the spacious and loftily-mounting open staircases stand in a
ring the great princes of the Empire—before all these he has
delivered his message. The messenger immediately sets out
on his journey; a powerful, an indefatigable man; now pushing with his right arm, now with his left, he cleaves a way
for himself through the throng; if he encounters resistance
he points to his breast, where the symbol of the sun glitters;
the way, too, is made easier for him than it would be for any
other man. But the multitudes are so vast; their numbers
have no end. If he could reach the open fields how fast he
would fly, and soon doubtless you would hear the welcome
hammering of his fists on your door. But instead how vainly
does he wear out his strength; still he is only making his
way through the chambers of the innermost palace; never
will he get to the end of them; and if he succeeded in that
nothing would be gained; he must fight his way next down
the stairs; and if he succeeded in that nothing would be
gained; the courts would still have to be crossed; and after

the courts the second outer palace; and once more stairs
and courts; and once more another palace; and so on for
thousands of years; and if at last he should burst through
the outermost gate—but never, never can that happen—the
imperial capital would lie before him, the center of the world,
crammed to bursting with its own refuse. Nobody could fight
his way through here, least of all one with a message from a
dead man.—But you sit at your window when evening falls
and dream it to yourself.

2. Before the Law

"Before the Law stands a doorkeeper on guard. To this
doorkeeper there comes a man from the country who begs
for admittance to the Law. But the doorkeeper says that he
cannot admit the man at the moment. The man, on reflection, asks if he will be allowed, then, to enter later. 'It is
possible,' answers the doorkeeper, 'but not at this moment.'
Since the door leading into the Law stands open as usual
and the doorkeeper steps to one side, the man bends down
to peer through the entrance. When the doorkeeper sees that,
he laughs and says: 'If you are so strongly tempted, try to
get in without my permission. But note that I am powerful.
And I am only the lowest doorkeeper. From hall to hall
keepers stand at every door, one more powerful than the
other. Even the third of these has an aspect that even I
cannot bear to look at.' These are difficulties which the man
from the country has not expected to meet; the Law, he
thinks, should be accessible to every man and at all times, but
when he looks more closely at the doorkeeper in his furred
robe, with his huge pointed nose and long, thin, Tartar
beard, he decides that he had better wait until he gets permission to enter. The doorkeeper gives him a stool and lets
him sit down at the side of the door. There he sits waiting
for days and years. He makes many attempts to be allowed
in and wearies the doorkeeper with his importunity. The
doorkeeper often engages him in brief conversation, asking him about his home and about other matters, but the
questions are put quite impersonally, as great men put
questions, and always conclude with the statement that the
man cannot be allowed to enter yet. The man, who has
equipped himself with many things for his journey, parts

with all he has, however valuable, in the hope of bribing the doorkeeper. The doorkeeper accepts it all, saying, however, as he takes each gift: 'I take this only to keep you from feeling that you have left something undone.' During all these long years the man watches the doorkeeper almost incessantly. He forgets about the other doorkeepers, and this one seems to him the only barrier between himself and the Law. In the first years he curses his evil fate aloud; later, as he grows old, he only mutters to himself. He grows childish, and since in his prolonged watch he has learned to know even the fleas in the doorkeeper's fur collar, he begs the very fleas to help him and to persuade the doorkeeper to change his mind. Finally his eyes grow dim and he does not know whether the world is really darkening around him or whether his eyes are only deceiving him. But in the darkness he can now perceive a radiance that streams immortally from the door of the Law. Now his life is drawing to a close. Before he dies, all that he has experienced during the whole time of his sojourn condenses in his mind into one question, which he has never yet put to the doorkeeper. He beckons the doorkeeper, since he can no longer raise his stiffening body. The doorkeeper has to bend far down to hear him, for the difference in size between them has increased very much to the man's disadvantage. 'What do you want to know now?' asks the doorkeeper, 'you are insatiable.' 'Everyone strives to attain the Law,' answers the man, 'how does it come about, then, that in all these years no one has come seeking admittance but me?' The doorkeeper perceives that the man is at the end of his strength and that his hearing is failing, so he bellows in his ear: 'No one but you could gain admittance through this door, since this door was intended only for you. I am now going to shut it.' "

"So the doorkeeper deluded the man," said K. immediately, strongly attracted by the story.

"Don't be too hasty," said the priest, "don't take over an opinion without testing it. I have told you the story in the very words of the scriptures. There's no mention of delusion in it."

"But it's clear enough," said K., "and your first interpretation of it was quite right. The doorkeeper gave the message of salvation to the man only when it could no longer help him."

"He was not asked the question any earlier," said the priest, "and you must consider, too, that he was only a door-keeper, and as such he fulfilled his duty."

"What makes you think he fulfilled his duty?" asked K. "He didn't fulfill it. His duty might have been to keep all strangers away, but this man, for whom the door was intended, should have been let in."

"You have not enough respect for the written word and you are altering the story," said the priest. "The story contains two important statements made by the doorkeeper about admission to the Law, one at the beginning, the other at the end. The first statement is: that he cannot admit the man at the moment, and the other is: that this door was intended only for the man. If there were a contradiction between the two, you would be right and the doorkeeper would have deluded the man. But there is no contradiction. The first statement, on the contrary, even implies the second. One could almost say that in suggesting to the man the possibility of future admittance the doorkeeper is exceeding his duty. At that moment his apparent duty is only to refuse admittance, and indeed many commentators are surprised that the suggestion should be made at all, since the door-keeper appears to be a precisian with a stern regard for duty. He does not once leave his post during these many years, and he does not shut the door until the very last minute; he is conscious of the importance of his office, for he says: 'I am powerful'; he is respectful to his superiors, for he says: 'I am only the lowest doorkeeper'; he is not garrulous, for during all these years he puts only what are called 'impersonal questions'; he is not to be bribed, for he says in accepting a gift: 'I take this only to keep you from feeling that you have left something undone'; where his duty is concerned he is to be moved neither by pity nor rage, for we are told that the man 'wearied the doorkeeper with his importunity'; and finally even his external appearance hints at a pedantic character, the large, pointed nose and the long, thin, black Tartar beard. Could one imagine a more faithful doorkeeper? Yet the doorkeeper has other elements in his character which are likely to advantage anyone seeking admittance and which make it comprehensible enough that he should somewhat exceed his duty in suggesting the possibility of future admittance. For it cannot be denied that he is a little simple-minded and consequently a little conceited. Take the statements he makes about his power and the power of the other doorkeepers and their dreadful aspect which even he cannot bear to see—I hold that these statements may be true enough, but that the way in which he brings them out shows that his perceptions are confused by simpleness of mind and conceit. The commentators note in this connection: 'The right perception of any matter and a misunderstanding of the same matter do not wholly exclude each other.' One must at any rate assume that such simpleness and conceit, however sparingly indicated, are likely to weaken his defense of the door; they are breaches in the character of the doorkeeper. To this must be added the fact that the doorkeeper seems to be a friendly creature by nature, he is by no means always on his official dignity. In the very first moments he allows himself the jest of inviting the man to enter in spite of the strictly maintained veto against entry; then he does not, for instance, send the man away, but gives him, as we are told, a stool and lets him sit down beside the door. The patience with which he endures the man's appeals during so many years, the brief conversations, the acceptance of the gifts, the politeness with which he allows the man to curse loudly in his presence the fate for which he himself is responsible—all this lets us deduce certain motions of sympathy. Not every doorkeeper would have acted thus. And finally, in answer to a gesture of the man's he stoops low down to give him the chance of putting a last question. Nothing but mild impatience—the doorkeeper knows that this is the end of it all—is discernible in the words: 'You are insatiable.' Some push this mode of interpretation even further and hold that these words express a kind of friendly admiration, though not without a hint of condescension. At any rate the figure of the doorkeeper can be said to come out very differently from what you fancied."

"You have studied the story more exactly and for a longer time than I have," said K. They were both silent for a little while. Then K. said: "So you think the man was not deluded?"

"Don't misunderstand me," said the priest, "I am only showing you the various opinions concerning that point. You must not pay too much attention to them. The scriptures are unalterable and the comments often enough merely express the commentator's bewilderment. In this case there even exists an interpretation which claims that the deluded person is really the doorkeeper."

"That's a far-fetched interpretation," said K. "On what is it based?"

"It is based," answered the priest, "on the simple-mindedness of the doorkeeper. The argument is that he does not know the Law from inside, but he knows only the way that leads to it, where he patrols up and down. His ideas of the interior are assumed to be childish, and it is supposed that he himself is afraid of the other guardians whom he holds up as bogies before the man. Indeed, he fears them more than the man does, since the man is determined to enter after hearing about the dreadful guardians of the interior, while the doorkeeper has no desire to enter, at least not so far as we are told. Others again say that he must have been in the interior already, since he is after all engaged in the service of the Law and can only have been appointed from inside. This is countered by arguing that he may have been appointed by a voice calling from the interior, and that anyhow he cannot have been far inside, since the aspect of the third doorkeeper is more than he can endure. Moreover, no indication is given that during all these years he ever made any remarks showing a knowledge of the interior except for the one remark about the doorkeepers. He may have been forbidden to do so, but there is no mention of that either. On these grounds the conclusion is reached that he knows nothing about the aspect and significance of the interior, so that he is in a state of delusion. But he is deceived also about his relation to the man from the country. For he is subject to the man and does not know it. He treats the man instead as his own subordinate, as can be recognized from many details that must still be fresh in your mind. But, according to this view of the story, it is just as clearly indicated that he is really subordinated to the man. In the first place, a bondsman is always subject to a free man. Now the man from the country is really free, he can go where he likes, it is only the Law that is closed to him, and access to the Law is forbidden him only by one individual, the doorkeeper. When he sits down on the stool by the side of the door and stays there for the rest of his life, he does it of his own free will; in the story there is no mention of any compulsion. But the doorkeeper is bound to his post by his very office, he does not dare strike out into the country, nor apparently may he go into the interior of the Law, even should he wish to. Besides, although he is in the service of the Law, his service is confined to this one entrance; that is to say, he serves only this man for whom alone the entrance is intended. On that ground too he is subject to the man. One must assume that for many years, for as long as it takes a man to grow up to the prime of life, his service was in a sense empty formality, since he had to wait for a man to come, that is to say, someone in the prime of life, and so had to wait a long time before the purpose of his service could be fulfilled, and, moreover, had to wait on the man's pleasure, for the man came of his own free will. But the termination of his service also depends on the man's term of life, so that to the very end he is subject to the man. And it is emphasized throughout that the doorkeeper apparently realizes nothing of all this. That is not in itself remarkable, since according to this interpretation the doorkeeper is deceived in a much more important issue, affecting his very office. At the end, for example, he says regarding the entrance to the Law: 'I am now going to shut it,' but at the beginning of the story we are told that the door leading into the Law stands always open, and if it stands open always, that is to say, at all times, without reference to the life or death of the man, then the doorkeeper is incapable of closing it. There is some difference of opinions about the motive behind the doorkeeper's statement, whether he said he was going to close the door merely for the sake of giving an answer, or to emphasize his devotion to duty, or to bring the man into a state of grief and regret in his last moments. But there is no lack of agreement that the doorkeeper will not be able to shut the door. Many indeed profess to find that he is subordinate to the man even in wisdom, towards the end, at least, for the man sees the radiance that issues from the door of the Law while the doorkeeper in his official position must stand with his back to the door, nor does he say anything to show that he has perceived the change."

"That is well argued," said K., after repeating to himself in a low voice several passages from the priest's exposition. "It is well argued, and I am inclined to agree that the doorkeeper is deluded. But that has not made me abandon my former opinion, since both conclusions are to some extent compatible. Whether the doorkeeper is clear-sighted or deluded does not dispose of the matter. I said the man is deluded. If the doorkeeper is clear-sighted, one might have doubts about that, but if the doorkeeper himself is deluded, then his delusion must of necessity be communicated to the man. That makes the doorkeeper not, indeed, a swindler, but a creature so simple-minded that he ought to be dismissed at once from his office. You mustn't forget that the doorkeeper's delusions do himself no harm but do infinite harm to the man."

"There are objections to that," said the priest. "Many aver that the story confers no right on anyone to pass judgment on the doorkeeper. Whatever he may seem to us, he is yet a servant of the Law; that is, he belongs to the Law and as such is set beyond human judgment. In that case one dare not believe that the doorkeeper is subordinate to the man. Bound as he is by his service, even at the door of the Law, he is incomparably freer than anyone at large in the world. The man is only seeking the Law, the doorkeeper is already attached to it. It is the Law that has placed him at his post; to doubt his integrity is to doubt the Law itself."

"I don't agree with that point of view," said K. shaking his head, "for if one accepts it, one must accept as true everything the doorkeeper says. But you yourself have sufficiently proved how impossible it is to do that."

"No," said the priest, "it is not necessary to accept everything as true, one must only accept it as necessary."

"A melancholy conclusion," said K. "It turns lying into a universal principle."

3. Couriers

They were offered the choice between becoming kings or the couriers of kings. The way children would, they all wanted to be couriers. Therefore there are only couriers who hurry about the world, shouting to each other—since there are no kings—messages that have become meaningless. They would like to put an end to this miserable life of theirs but they dare not because of their oaths of service.

SEVEN

Ortega: "MAN HAS NO NATURE"

[José Ortega y Gasset was born in 1883, like Jaspers, and died in 1955, exactly a hundred years after the death of Kierkegaard. He was a Spaniard, received his doctorate in philosophy in Madrid in 1904, and then studied for five years at German universities before he became professor of metaphysics at the University of Madrid. He also was active as a journalist, founded an important journal in 1923, became a member of parliament during the second Spanish republic and later civil governor of Madrid. When the Civil War broke out he went into exile in Argentina, then lived in Western Europe, and in 1948 returned to Madrid, where he lectured at the Institute of Humanities, of which he was a cofounder.

Ortega was a brilliant writer, and his style is occasionally so dazzling that it distracts attention from the content of his essays. Moreover, he often relied on metaphors rather than arguments and hence has been widely underestimated as a philosopher. His *The Revolt of the Masses* (1930) was an immense international success. It owed a great deal to Nietzsche, whom Ortega cited frequently throughout his works. The other major influence on his thought was that of Wilhelm Dilthey (1833-1911), who had made much of the distinction between the natural sciences and history.

The following selection comes from Ortega's *Historia como sistema* (1941), translated by H. Weyl, E. Clark, and W. Atkinson as *Toward a Philosophy of History* (1941). In the second edition, the title was changed to *History as a System* (1961). The similarity to Sartre's later ideas and formulations is striking. It is difficult to escape the impression that Ortega influenced Sartre, and as one reads more of Ortega, this impression deepens. Between the last two passages that follow, for example, there is a section that begins: "Yesterday I made the acquaintance of Hermione. She is a fascinating woman. . . ." This tone in presenting serious philosophical ideas surely brings to mind Sartre's manner.

The similarities between Ortega and Heidegger are more puzzling. Here the tone is strikingly different. Ortega's journalistic flair and fluency contrast sharply with Heidegger's professorial obscurities. Yet Ortega himself said in a two-page footnote of his essay on Goethe, in 1932: "There are scarcely one or two concepts in Heidegger that are not to be found also in my books, at times with a priority of thirteen years." Ortega referred specifically to his first book, *Meditations on Quixote*, which appeared in 1914 (American translation, 1961). Ortega insisted that he was scarcely indebted to Heidegger, which leaves open the question whether Heidegger owed anything to him. In 1927, when Heidegger's *Being and Time* appeared, none of Ortega's books had appeared in German, but Ernst Robert T. Curtius had written about him at length in *Die neue Rundschau* in 1924 and in *Europäische Revue* in 1926, comparing him to Max Scheler, who was Husserl's most original ex-disciple and Heidegger's friend and chief rival. The volume in which the first article appeared also carried contributions by Thomas Mann and Hermann Hesse, by Maxim Gorki, Arthur Schnitzler, Bernard Shaw, and other major figures. It is very likely that Heidegger knew of Ortega well before 1927. But the similarities need not all be due to direct influence. What Heidegger articulated in his scholastic manner was "in the air" in the twenties, and many parallels to Ortega can be accounted for by a common ancestry that includes above all Nietzsche and Dilthey.]

The stone is given its existence; it need not fight for being what it is—a stone in the field. Man has to be himself in spite of unfavorable circumstances; that means he has to make his own existence at every single moment. He is given the abstract possibility of existing, but not the reality. This he has to con-

quer hour after hour. Man must earn his life, not only eco-
nomically but metaphysically.

And all this for what reason? Obviously—but this is repeating the same thing in other words—because man's being and
nature's being do not fully coincide. Because man's being is
made of such strange stuff as to be partly akin to nature and
partly not, at once natural and extranatural, a kind of ontological centaur, half immersed in nature, half transcending it.
Dante would have likened him to a boat drawn up on the
beach with one end of its keel in the water and the other in the
sand. What is natural in him is realized by itself; it presents no
problem. That is precisely why man does not consider it his
true being. His extranatural part, on the other hand, is not
there from the outset and of itself; it is but an aspiration, a
project of life. And this we feel to be our true being; we call it
our personality, our self. Our extra- and antinatural portion,
however, must not be interpreted in terms of any of the older
spiritual philosophies. I am not interested now in the so-called
spirit (*Geist*), a pretty confused idea laden with speculative
wizardry.

If the reader reflects a little upon the meaning of the entity
he calls his life, he will find that it is the attempt to carry out a
definite program or project of existence. And his self—each
man's self—is nothing but this devised program. All we do we
do in the service of this program. Thus man begins by being
something that has no reality, neither corporeal nor spiritual;
he is a project as such, something which is not yet but aspires
to be. One may object that there can be no program without
somebody having it, without an idea, a mind, a soul, or whatever it is called. I cannot discuss this thoroughly because it
would mean embarking on a course of philosophy. But I will
say this: although the project of being a great financier has to
be conceived of in an idea, "being" the project is different
from holding the idea. In fact, I find no difficulty in thinking
this idea but I am very far from being this project.

Here we come upon the formidable and unparalleled character which makes man unique in the universe. We are dealing—and let the disquieting strangeness of the case be well
noted—with an entity whose being consists not in what it is
already, but in what it is not yet, a being that consists in not-
yet-being. Everything else in the world is what it is. An entity
whose mode of being consists in what it is already, whose

potentiality coincides at once with his reality, we call a "thing." Things are given their being ready-made.

*   *   *

At every moment of my life there open before me divers possibilities: I can do this or that. If I do this, I shall be A the moment after; if I do that, I shall be B. At the present moment the reader may stop reading me or may go on. And, however slight the importance of this article, according as he does the one or the other the reader will be A or will be B, will have made of himself an A or a B. Man is the entity that makes itself, an entity which traditional ontology only stumbled upon precisely as its course was drawing to a close, and which it in consequence gave up the attempt to understand: the *causa sui*. With this difference, that the *causa sui* had only to "exert itself" in being the *cause* of itself and not in determining what *self* it was going to cause. It had, to begin with, a *self* previously determined and invariable, consistent, for example, to infinity.

But man must not only make himself: the weightiest thing he has to do is to determine *what* he is going to be. He is *causa sui* to the second power. By a coincidence that is not casual, the doctrine of the living being, when it seeks in tradition for concepts that are still more or less valid, finds only those which the doctrine of the divine being tried to formulate. If the reader has resolved now to go on reading into the next moment, it will be, in the last instance, because doing this is what is most in accordance with the general program he has mapped out for his life, and hence with the man of determination he has resolved to be. This vital program is the *ego* of each individual, his choice out of divers possibilities of being which at every instant open before him.[1]

Concerning these possibilities of being the following remarks fall to be made:

1. That they likewise are not presented to me. I must find them for myself, either on my own or through the medium of those of my fellows with whom my life brings me in contact. I invent projects of being and of doing in the light of circumstance. This alone I come upon, this alone is given me: circumstance.[2] It is too often forgotten that man is impossible without imagination, without the capacity to invent for himself a conception of life, to "ideate" the character he is going to be.

Whether he be original or a plagiarist, man is the novelist of himself.[3]

2. That among these possibilities I must choose. Hence, I am free. But, be it well understood, I am free *by compulsion*, whether I wish to be or not. Freedom is not an activity pursued by an entity that, apart from and previous to such pursuit, is already possessed of a fixed being. To be free means to be lacking in constitutive identity, not to have subscribed to a determined being, to be able to be other than what one was, to be unable to install oneself once and for all in any given being. The only attribute of the fixed, stable being in the free being is this constitutive instability.

In order to speak, then, of man's being we must first elaborate a non-Eleatic concept of being, as others have elaborated a non-Euclidean geometry. The time has come for the seed sown by Heraclitus to bring forth its mighty harvest. . . .

Man invents for himself a program of life, a static form of being, that gives a satisfactory answer to the difficulties posed for him by circumstance. He essays this form of life, attempts to realize this imaginary character he has resolved to be. He embarks on the essay full of illusions and prosecutes the experiment with thoroughness. This means that he comes to *believe* deeply that this character is his real being. But meanwhile the experience has made apparent the shortcomings and limitations of the said program of life. It does not solve all the difficulties, and it creates new ones of its own. When first seen it was full face, with the light shining upon it: hence the illusions, the enthusiasm, the delights believed in store. With the back view its inadequacy is straightway revealed. Man thinks out another program of life. But this second program is drawn up in the light, not only of circumstance, but also of the first. One aims at avoiding in the new project the drawbacks of the old. In the second, therefore, the first is still active; it is preserved in order to be avoided. Inexorably man shrinks from being what he was. On the second project of being, the second thorough experiment, there follows a third, forged in the light of the second and the first, and so on. Man "goes on being" and "unbeing"—living. He goes on accumulating being—the past; he goes on making for himself a being through his dialectical series of experiments. This is a dialectic not of logical but precisely of historical reason—the *Realdialektik* dreamt of somewhere in his papers by Dilthey, the writer to whom we owe more than to anyone else concerning the idea of life, and who is, to my mind, the most important thinker of the second half of the nineteenth century.

In what does this dialectic that will not tolerate the facile anticipations of logical dialectic consist? This is what we have to find out on the basis of facts. We must know what is this series, what are its stages, and of what nature is the link between one and the next. Such a discovery is what would be called history were history to make this its objective, were it, that is to say, to convert itself into historical reason.

Here, then, awaiting our study, lies man's authentic "being" —stretching the whole length of his past. Man is what has happened to him, what he has done. Other things might have happened to him or have been done by him, but what did in fact happen to him and was done by him, this constitutes a relentless trajectory of experiences that he carries on his back as the vagabond his bundle of all he possesses. Man is a substantial emigrant on a pilgrimage of being, and it is accordingly meaningless to set limits to what he is capable of being. In this initial illimitableness of possibilities that characterizes one who has no nature there stands out only one fixed, pre-established, and given line by which he may chart his course, only one limit: the past. The experiments already made with life narrow man's future. If we do not know what he is going to be, we know what he is not going to be. Man lives in view of the past.

Man, in a word, has no nature; what he has is—history. Expressed differently: what nature is to things, history, *res gestae*, is to man.

EIGHT

Jaspers: EXISTENZPHILOSOPHIE

[*Preface:* The best introduction to Jaspers is his essay "On My Philosophy" which is here published in English for the first time, translated by Felix Kaufmann. Except for the postscript, the original version dates from 1941.

The discussions of Kierkegaard and Nietzsche and of "The Encompassing" are the first two lectures, also unabridged, from *Reason and Existenz,* translated by William Earle. The lectures were first given and published in 1935. Jaspers' interpretation of Kierkegaard and Nietzsche is discussed in Chapter One. I have taken the liberty of correcting an inaccurate translation of one Nietzsche quotation; another such quotation, which occurs under the heading "No Prophecy" near the end of section 2, may be compared with a more faithful rendering in the Nietzsche chapter above. In the immediately preceding paragraph ("Dancing") Mr. Earle, rather oddly, makes Kierkegaard and Nietzsche enemies of "seriousness." They were, however, not one whit less serious than Jaspers. What they opposed and derided was "gravity."]

1. On My Philosophy

I. THE COURSE OF MY DEVELOPMENT

On February 23, 1883 I was born in Oldenburg, a son of Karl Jaspers, the former sheriff and later bank director, and his wife Henriette, née Tantzen. I passed a well-guarded childhood in the company of my brothers and sisters, either in the country with my grandparents or at the seaside, sheltered by loved and revered parents, led by the authority of my father, brought up with a regard for truth and loyalty, for achievement and reliability, yet without church religion (except for the scanty formalities of the Protestant confession). I attended the high school of my home town, and from 1901 the University.

My path was not the normal one of professors of philosophy. I did not intend to become a doctor of philosophy by studying philosophy (I am in fact a doctor of medicine) nor did I, by any means, intend originally to qualify for a professorship by a dissertation on philosophy. To decide to become a philosopher seemed as foolish to me as to decide to become a poet. Since my schooldays, however, I was guided by philosophical questions. Philosophy seemed to me the supreme, even the sole, concern of man. Yet a certain awe kept me from making it my profession.

Instead I felt that I should look for my vocation in practical life. At first I chose the study of law with the intention of becoming an attorney. At the same time I attended classes in philosophy. That proved disappointing. The lectures offered nothing of what I sought in philosophy: neither the fundamental experiences of Being, nor guidance for inner action or self-improvement, but rather, questionable opinions making claim to scientific validity. The study of law left me unsatisfied, because I did not know the aspects of life which it serves. I perceived only the intricate mental juggling with fictions that did not interest me. What I sought was perception of reality. Concern with art and poetry were incomplete substitutes; so even was an enthusiastic journey to Italy to see *Roma aeterna*, to sense history and to gaze on beauty (1902). This aimless way of life came to an end after my third semester. I began the study of medicine, impelled by a desire for knowledge of facts and of man. This resolution to do disciplined work tied me to both laboratory and clinic for a long time to come. Ostensibly I was aiming at the practice of medicine; yet already with the secret thought of eventually pursuing an academic career at the university, though actually not in philosophy but in psychiatry or psychology. After some years (since 1909) I published my psychopathological researches. In 1913 I qualified as university lecturer in psychology.

Up until then my life had been a spiritual striving in what was, actually, politico-sociological space, untroubled by general happenings and without political consciousness, though with momentary forebodings of possible distant dangers. All intentness centered on my own private life, on the high moments of intimate communion with those closest to me. Contemplation of the works of the spirit, research, continual intercourse with things timeless, were the purpose and meaning of life's activities. Then in 1914 the World War caused the great breach in our European existence. The paradisiacal life before the World War, naive despite all its sublime spirituality, could never return: philosophy, with its seriousness, became more important than ever.

To a great extent my psychology had assumed the characteristics, without my being conscious of it, of what I subsequently called *Existenz Clarification*. This psychology was no longer merely an empirical statement of the facts and laws of events. It was an outline of the potentialities of the soul which holds a mirror up to man to show him what he can be, what he can achieve and how far he can go: such insights are meant as an appeal to freedom, to let me choose in my inner action what I really want. As the realization overcame me that, at the time, there was no true philosophy at the universities, I thought that facing such a vacuum even he, who was too weak to create his own philosophy, had the right to hold forth about philosophy, to declare what it once was and what it could be. Only then, approaching my fortieth birthday, I made philosophy my life's work.

II. MAKING TRADITION OUR OWN

We can ask primal questions, but we can never stand near the beginning. Our questions and answers are in part determined by the historical tradition in which we find ourselves. We apprehend truth from our own source within the historical tradition.

The content of our truth depends upon our appropriating the historical foundation. Our own power of generation lies in the rebirth of what has been handed down to us. If we do not wish to slip back, nothing must be forgotten; but if philosophizing is to be genuine our thoughts must arise from our own source. Hence all appropriation of tradition proceeds from the intentness of our own life. The more determinedly I exist, as myself, within the conditions of the time, the more clearly I shall hear the language of the past, the nearer I shall feel the glow of its life.

In what way the history of philosophy exists for us is a fundamental problem of our philosophizing which demands a concrete solution in each age. Philosophy is tested and characterized by the way in which it appropriates its history. It might seem to us that the truth of present-day philosophy manifests itself less in the formation of new fundamental concepts (as "borderline situation," "the Encompassing") than in the new sound it makes audible for us in old thoughts.

A merely theoretical contemplation of the history of philosophy is insufficient. If philosophy is practice, a demand to know the manner in which its history is to be studied is entailed: a theoretical attitude toward it becomes real only in the living appropriation of its contents from the texts. To apprehend thought with indifference prevents its appropriation. Knowledge that does not concern the knower comes between the content of knowledge and its resurrection; but in the assimilation of philosophy by later ages a lapse of thought is a constant feature. Concepts which were originally reality pass through history as pieces of learning or information. What was once life becomes a pile of dead husks of concepts and these in turn become the subject of an objective history of philosophy.

Everything depends therefore on encountering thought at its source. Such thought is the reality of man's being, which achieved consciousness and understanding of itself through it. Though one needs knowledge of the concepts that emerge in the history of philosophy, the purpose of such knowledge remains to gain entrance to the exalted living practice of these past thoughts. My own being can be judged by the depths I reach in making these historical origins my own. There is no palpable criterion for this in outward appearances. Such true thinking goes through history as a mystery which can reveal itself, however, to everyone with understanding, for this hidden thinking was once reality. Having been written down it can be rediscovered: at any time it can spark a new blaze.

The history of philosophy is not, like the history of the sciences, to be studied with the intellect alone. That which is receptive in us and that which impinges upon us from history is the reality of man's being, unfolding itself in thought.

A philosophical history of philosophy has the following characteristics:

1. *The real import of history is the Great, the Unique, the Irreplaceable* The great philosophers and the great works are standards for the selection of what is essential. Everything that we do in studying the history of philosophy ultimately serves their better understanding. All other questions are secondary, as, for instance, whether the Great is also the most effective, or whether, perhaps, precisely the misunderstanding of greatness has a wider public appeal because of its mediocrity and its lowered standard. How the quality of greatness appears to us, with constant transposition and questioning, in the totality of things, what we prefer and how we prefer it, that must prove its worth by our ability to see through the remainder, the widespread, the universally prevalent, in order to judge it fairly, and to appreciate it. What remains strange and incomprehensible to us is a limit to our own truth.

2. *Understanding of the ideas demands a thorough study of the texts* Philosophy can only be approached with the most concrete comprehension. A great philosopher demands unrelenting penetration into his texts. This necessitates both the realization of a whole philosophy in its entirety, and taking pains with every single sentence in order to become conscious of its every nuance. Comprehensive perception and accurate observation are the basis of our understanding.

3. *Understanding of philosophy demands a universal historical view* As a universal history of philosophy, the history of philosophy must become one great unity. Philosophizing, as it occurs in each historical age, involves the penetration, without limit, into the unity of the revelation of Being. This solitary, but vast, moment of a few millennia, emerging from three different sources (China, India, Occident), is real by virtue of a single internal connection. Though too immense to be envisaged as a pattern, it encompasses us nevertheless as a world. No one person can attain that concrete nearness everywhere. He can have his roots only in relatively few sublime works. The immensity of the Whole and the evocative tones of its unity are indispensable for achieving universal philosophic communication as well as for realizing the truth of each individual's concrete understanding.

4. *The philosopher's invisible realm of the spirit* The

philosopher lives, as it were, in a hidden, non-objective community to which every philosophizing person secretly longs to be admitted. Philosophy has no institutional reality and is not in competition with the church, the state, the real communities of the world. Any objectification, whether it be the formation of schools or sects, is the ruin of philosophy. For the freedom that can be attained in philosophizing cannot be handed down by the doctrine of an institution. Only as an individual can man become a philosopher. From becoming a philosopher he can derive no claims. He must not have the folly to wish to be recognized as a philosopher. Professorships in philosophy are instituted for free mediation of ideas by teaching, which does not preclude their being held by philosophers (Kant, Hegel, Schelling). But in philosophy's realm of the spirit there is no objective certainty and no confirmation. In the realm of the spirit, men become companions-in-thought through the millennia, become occasions for each other to find the way to truth from their own source, although they cannot present each other with ready-made truth. It is a self-development of individual in communication with individual. It is a development of the individual into community and from there to the plane of history, without breaking with contemporary life. It is the effort to live from and on behalf of the fundamenta, though these become audible to him who philosophizes, without objective certainty (as in religion), and only through indirect hints as possibilities in the totality of philosophy.

5. *The universal-historical view is a condition for the most decisive consciousness of one's own age* What can be experienced today becomes fully tangible only in the face of humanity's experiences—both those which can no longer be relived and those which become a living experience for the first time this very day. Only through being conscious can the contents of the past, transmuted into possibilities, become the fully real contents of the present. The life of truth in the realm of the spirit does not remove man from his world, but makes him effective for serving his historical present.

These fundamental views of history developed only slowly in me. I discovered that the study of past philosophers is of little use unless our own reality enters into it. Our reality alone allows the thinker's questions to become comprehensible. We can thereby read their works as if all philosophers were contemporaries.

The order in which the great stars of the philosophers' heaven rose for me is, perhaps, accidental. While I was still at school Spinoza was the first. Kant then became *the* philosopher for me and has remained so. In the voices of Plotinus, Nicholas of Cusa, Bruno, and Schelling I heard as truth the dreams of the metaphysicians. Kierkegaard located consciousness both of the Source, which is so indispensable today, and of our own historical situation. Nietzsche gained importance for me only late as the magnificent revelation of nihilism and the task of overcoming it (in my youth I had avoided him, repelled by the extremes, the rapture, and the diversity). Goethe contributed the atmosphere of *humanitas* and un-selfconsciousness. To breathe this atmosphere, to love with Goethe whatever is essential among the apparitions of the world, and like him to touch, with awe, the unveiled boundaries, was a blessing amid the unrest, and became a source of justice and reason. Hegel for a long time remained a well-nigh inexhaustible material for study, particularly for my teaching activity in seminars. The Greeks were always there; after the discipline of their coolness, I liked to turn to Augustine; however, despite the depth of his existential clarification displeasure with his rhetoric and with his lack of all scientific objectivity and with his ugly and violent emotions drove me back again to the Greeks. Only finally I occupied myself more thoroughly with Plato, who now seemed to me perhaps the greatest of all.

Among my deceased contemporaries I owe what I am able to think—those closest to me excepted—above all to the one and only Max Weber. He alone, through his being, showed me what human greatness can be. Nissl, the brain anatomist and psychiatrist, set an example for me, in the years I worked under him, of critical research and the purest scientific method.

Even in the history of philosophy we can witness the tremendous incisiveness of our age. Hegel is a consummation of two and a half millenia of thought. True, in his basic philosophic attitude, although not in his concrete positions, Plato is as alive today as ever, perhaps more than ever. Even now we can philosophize from Kant. In actuality, however, we cannot forget for one moment what has been brought about since by Kierkegaard and Nietzsche. We are so exposed that we constantly find ourselves facing nothingness. Our wounds are so deep that in our weak moments we wonder if we are not, in fact, dying from them.

At the present moment, the security of coherent philosophy, which existed from Parmenides to Hegel, is lost. This does not prevent us from philosophizing from the single foundation of man's being on which was based the thinking of those millennia in the Occident which are now, in some sense, concluded. To become aware of this foundation in yet another way, we are referred to India and China as the two other original paths of philosophic thought. Instead of slipping into nothingness at the disintegration of millennia we should like to feel unshakable ground beneath us. We should like to comprehend in one historical whole the only general phenomenon which may permit posterity to probe its substance more deeply than has ever been done. The alternative "nothing or everything" stands before our age as the question of man's spiritual destiny.

III. DRIVES TO THE BASIC QUESTIONS

Philosophy did not mean simply cognizance of the universe (that results from the sum total of the sciences in constant indetermination and transition), nor epistemology (which is a subject of logic), nor the knowledge of the systems and texts of the history of philosophy (such knowledge touches only the surface of thinking). Philosophy grew in me through my finding myself in the midst of life itself. Philosophical thought is *practical activity*, although a unique kind of activity.

Philosophic meditation is an accomplishment by which I attain Being and my own self, not impartial thinking which studies a subject with indifference. To be a mere onlooker were vain. Even scientific knowledge, if there is anything to it, is not a random observation of random objects; for the critical objectivity of significant knowledge is attained as a practice only philosophically in inner action.

Philosophy as practice does not mean its restriction to utility or applicability, that is, to what serves morality or produces serenity of soul. The process, in which knowledge is employed as a means of thinking out the possibilities that bear upon a finite objective, is a technical, not a philosophical, activity. Philosophizing is the activity of thought itself, by which the essence of man, in its entirety, is realized in the individual man. This activity originates from life in the depths where it touches Eternity inside Time, not at the surface where it moves in finite purposes, even though the depths appear to us only at the surface. It is for this reason that philosophical activity is fully real only at the summits of personal philosophizing, while objectivized philosophical thought is a preparation for, and a recollection of, it. At the summits the activity is the inner action by which I become myself; it is the revelation of Being; it is the activity of being oneself which yet simultaneously experiences itself as the passivity of being-given-to-oneself. The mystery of this boundary of philosophizing at which alone philosophy is real, is only circumscribed by the unrolling of thoughts in the philosophical work.

Since the basic questions of philosophy grow, as practical activity, from life, their form is at any given moment in keeping with the *historical* situation; but this situation is part of the continuity of tradition. The questions put earlier in history are still ours; in part identical with present ones, word for word, after thousands of years, in part more distant and strange, so that we make them our own only by translation. The basic questions were formulated by Kant with, I felt, moving simplicity: 1. What can I know? 2. What shall I do? 3. What may I hope? 4. What is man? Today these questions have been reborn for us in changed form and thus become comprehensible to us anew also in their origin. The transformation of these questions is due to our finding ourselves in the kind of life that our age produces:

1. *Science* has gained an ever-growing overwhelming importance; by its consequences it has become the fate of the world. Technically, it provides the basis for all human existence and compels the unpredictable transmutation of all conditions. Its contents cause wonder and ever greater wonder. Its inversions cause scientific superstitions and a desperate hatred of science. Science cannot be avoided. It extends further than in Kant's time; it is more radical than ever, both in the precision of its methods and in its consequences. The question "What can I know?" therefore becomes more concrete and at the same time more inexorable. Seen from our point of view Kant still knew too much (in wrongly taking his own transcendental philosophy for conclusive scientific knowledge instead of philosophical insights

to be accomplished in transcending) and too little (because the extraordinary mathematical, scientific and historial discoveries and possibilities of knowledge with their consequences were in great part still outside his horizon).

2. The community of masses of human beings has produced an order of life in regulated channels which connects individuals in a technically functioning organization, but not inwardly from the historicity of their souls. The emptiness caused by dissatisfaction with mere achievement and the helplessness that results when the channels of relation break down have brought forth a loneliness of soul such as never existed before, a loneliness that hides itself, that seeks relief in vain in the erotic or the irrational until it leads eventually to a deep comprehension of the importance of establishing *communication* between man and man.

Even when regulating his existence man feels as if the waves of events had drawn him beyond his depth in the turbulent ocean of history and as if he now had to find a foothold in the drifting whirlpool. What was firm and certain has nowhere remained the ultimate. Morality is no longer adequately founded on generally valid laws. The laws themselves are in need of a deeper foundation. The Kantian question "What shall I do?" is no longer sufficiently answered by the categorical imperative (though this imperative remains inevitably true), but has to be complemented by the foundation of every ethical act and knowledge in communication. For the truth of generally valid laws for my actions is conditioned by the kind of communication in which I act. "What shall I do?" presupposes "How is communication possible? How can I reach the depth of possible communication?"

3. We experience the limits of science as the limits of our ability to know and as limits of our realization of the world through knowledge and ability; the knowledge of science fails in the face of all ultimate questions. We experience limits of communication: something is lacking even when it succeeds. The failure of knowledge and the failure of communication cause a confusion in which Being and truth vanish. In vain a way out is sought either in obedience to rules and regulations or in thoughtlessness. The meaning of *truth* assumes another value. Truth is more than what we call truth (or rather correctness) in the sciences. We want to grasp truth itself; the way to it becomes a new, more urgent, more exciting task.

Our philosophizing can be subsumed thus within these three questions:

What can we know in the sciences?

How shall we realize the most profound communication?

How can truth become accessible to us?

The three fundamental drives for knowledge, for communication and for truth produce these questions. Through them we reach the path of searching. But the aims of this searching are man and Transcendence (or: the soul and the Deity). At them the fourth and fifth fundamental questions are aimed.

4. In the world *man* alone is the reality which is accessible to me. Here is presence, nearness, fullness, life. Man is the place at which and through which everything that is real exists for us at all. To fail to be human would mean to slip into nothingness. What man is and can become is a fundamental question for man.

Man, however, is not a self-sufficient separate entity, but is constituted by the things he makes his own. In every form of his being man is related to something other than himself: as a being to his world, as consciousness to objects, as spirit to the idea of whatever constitutes totality, as Existenz to Transcendence. Man always becomes man by devoting himself to this other. Only through his absorption in the world of Being, in the immeasurable space of objects, in ideas, in Transcendence, does he become real to himself. If he makes himself the immediate object of his efforts he is on his last and perilous path; for it is possible that in doing so he will lose the Being of the other and then no longer find anything in himself. If man wants to grasp himself directly, he ceases to understand himself, to know who he is and what he should do.

This confusion was intensified as a result of the process of education in the nineteenth century. The wealth of knowledge of everything that was produced a state in which it seemed that man could gain mastery over all Being without yet being anything himself. This happened because he no longer devoted himself to the thing as it was, but made it a function of his education. Where humanity founds itself only on itself, it is experienced again that it has no ground beneath it.

The question about humanity is pushed forward. It no longer suffices to ask beyond oneself with Kant "What may

I hope?" Man strives more decisively than ever for a certainty that he lacks, for the certainty that there is that which is eternal, that there is a Being through which alone he himself is. If the Deity is, then all hope is possible.

5. Hence the question "What is man?" must be complemented by the essential question whether and what Transcendence (Deity) is. The thesis becomes possible: Transcendence alone is the real Being. That the Deity is suffices. To be certain of that is the only thing that matters. Everything else follows from that. Man is not worth considering. In the Deity alone there is reality, truth, and the immutability of being itself. In the Deity there is peace, as well as the origin and aim of man who, by himself, is nothing, and what he is he is only in relation to the Deity.

But time and again it is seen: for us the Deity, if it exists, is only as it appears to us in the world, as it speaks to us in the language of man and the world. It exists for us only in the way in which it assumes concrete shape, which by human measure and thought always serves to hide it at the same time. Only in ways that man can grasp does the Deity appear.

Thus it is seen that it is wrong to play off against each other the question about man and the question about the Deity. Although in the world only man is reality for us that does not preclude that precisely the quest for man leads to Transcendence. That the Deity alone is truly reality does not preclude that this reality is accessible to us only in the world; as it were, as an image in the mirror of man, because something of the Deity must be in him for him to be able to respond to the Deity. Thus the theme of philosophy is oriented, in polar alternation, in two directions: *deum et animam scire cupio* [I desire knowledge of God and the soul].

In taking up again Kant's fundamental questions five questions arose: the question of science, of communication, of truth, of man, and of Transcendence. I shall now go a little further into the meaning of these questions, both into the impulses that lead to them and into the preliminaries of a philosophical answer:

1. *What is science?* —In my youth I sought philosophy as knowledge. The doctrines which I heard and read seemed to meet this claim. They reasoned, proved, refuted; they were analogous with all other knowledge; yet they aimed at the whole rather than at single subjects.

I soon found out that most philosophical and many scientific doctrines failed to yield certainty. My doubting did not become absolute and radical. It was not doubt in the style of Descartes; such doubt, which I encountered later, I did not entertain in reality, but only as a kind of game. Commencing at first with the sciences, my doubt questioned single assertions, each doubt being by way of an experiment.

It shook my faith in the representatives of science, though not in science itself, to discover that famous scientists propounded many things in their textbooks which they passed off as the results of scientific investigation although they were by no means proven. I perceived the endless babble, the supposed "knowledge". In school already I was astonished, rightly or wrongly, when the teachers' answers to objections remained unsatisfactory. The parson proved the existence of God from the failure of the stars to collide and paid no heed to the objection that the stars' great distance from each other makes the probability of a collision small, or that maybe there are collisions which we do not observe because they have not yet involved us. I observed the pathos of historians when they conclude a series of explications with the words "Now things necessarily had to happen in this way", while actually this statement was merely suggestive *ex post facto*, but not at all convincing in itself: alternatives seemed equally possible, and there was always the element of chance. As a physician and psychiatrist I saw the precarious foundation of so many statements and actions, and beheld the reign of imagined insights, e.g. the causation of all mental illnesses by brain processes (I called all this talk about the brain, as it was fashionable then, brain mythology; it was succeeded later by the mythology of psychoanalysis), and realized with horror how, in our expert opinions, we based ourselves on positions which were far from certain, because we had always to come to a conclusion even when we did not know, in order that science might provide a cover, however unproved, for decisions the state found necessary. I was surprised that so much of medical advice and the majority of prescriptions were based, not on rational knowledge, but merely on the patient's wish for treatment.

From these experiences the basic question emerged: What is science? What can it do? Where are its limits? It became clear that science, to deserve its name, must be cogent and universally valid. Self-discipline in making assertions is necessary above everything to maintain the sharpest criticism, the clearest consciousness of method, the knowledge in which way, for what reasons, and with what certainty, I know in each case. Neither skeptically to surrender everything, nor to seize something dogmatically as a conclusion in advance, but rather to retain the attitude of the researcher, accepting knowledge only on the way, with its' reasons, and relative to its viewpoints and methods, turned out to be far from easy. This attitude of mind is attainable only with an ever-active intellectual conscience. As a consequence of this procedure, it appeared that cogent validity does indeed exist and that it is a great privilege of man to be able to grasp it with clear judgment. It appeared, however, that such scientific knowledge is always particularized, that it does not embrace the totality of Being but only a specific subject, that it affords no aim to life, has no answer to the essential problems that move man, that it cannot even furnish a compelling insight into its own importance and significance. Man is reduced to a condition of perplexity by confusing the knowledge that he can prove with the convictions by which he lives.

If science, with its limitation to cogent and universally valid knowledge, can do so little, failing as it does in the essentials, in the eternal problems: why then science at all?

Firstly, there is an irrepressible urge to know the knowable, to view the facts as they are, to learn about the events that happen to us: for example, mental illnesses—how they manifest themselves in association with those that harbor them, or how mental illness might be connected with mental creativity. The force of the original quest for knowledge disappears in the grand anticipatory gestures of seeming total knowledge and increases in mastering what is concretely knowable.

Secondly, science has had tremendously far-reaching effects. The state of our whole world, especially for the last one hundred years, is conditioned by science and its technical consequences: the inner attitude of all humanity is determined by the way and content of its knowledge. I can grasp the fate of the world only if I can grasp science. There is a fundamental question: why, although there is rationalism and intellectualization wherever there are humans, has science emerged only in the Occident, taking former worlds off their hinges in its consequences and forcing humanity to obey it or perish? Only through science and face-to-face with science can I acquire an intensified consciousness of the historical situation, can I truly live in the spiritual situation of my time.

Thirdly, I have to turn to science in order to learn what it is, in all science, that impels and guides, without itself being cogent knowledge. The ideas that master infinity, the selection of what is essential, the comprehension of knowledge in the totality of the sciences—all this is not scientific insight, but reaches clear consciousness only through the pursuit of the sciences. Only by way of the sciences can I free myself from the bondage of a limited, dogmatic view of the world in order to arrive at the totality of the world and its reality.

The experience of the indispensability and compelling power of science caused me to regard throughout my life the following demands as valid for all philosophizing: there must be freedom for all sciences, so that there may be freedom from scientific superstition, i.e. from false absolutes and pseudo-knowledge. By freely espousing the sciences I become receptive to that which is beyond science but which can only become clear by way of it. Although I should pursue one science thoroughly, I should nevertheless turn to all the others as well; not in order to amass encyclopedic knowledge, but rather in order to become familiar with the fundamental possibilities, principles of knowledge, and the multiplicity of methods. The ultimate objective is to work out a methodology, which arises from the ground of a universal consciousness of Being and points up and illuminates Being.

Above all, the sciences are to be employed as a tool of philosophy. Philosophy is not to be ranged alongside them as merely another science. For even though it is linked to science and never occurs without it, philosophy is wholly different from science. Philosophy is the thinking by which I become aware of Being itself through inner action; or rather it is the thinking which prepares the ascent to Transcendence, remembers it, and in an exalted moment accomplishes the ascent itself as a thinking act of the whole human being.

2. *How is communication possible?* I do not know which impulse was stronger in me when I began to think: the original thirst for knowledge or the urge to communicate with man. Knowledge attains its full meaning only through the bond that unites men; however, the urge to achieve agreement with another human being was so hard to satisfy. I was shocked by the lack of understanding, paralyzed, as it

were, by every reconciliation in which what had gone before was not fully cleared up. Early in my life and then later again and again I was perplexed by people's rigid inaccessibility and their failure to listen to reasons, their disregard of facts, their indifference which prohibited discussion, their defensive attitude which kept you at a distance and at the decisive moment buried any possibility of a close approach, and finally their shamelessness, that bares its own soul without reserve, as though no one were present. When ready assent occurred I remained unsatisfied, because it was not based on true insight but on yielding to persuasion; because it was the consequence of friendly cooperation, not a meeting of two selves. True, I knew the glory of friendship (in common studies, in the cordial atmosphere of home or countryside). But then came the moments of strangeness, as if human beings lived in different worlds. Steadily the consciousness of loneliness grew upon me in my youth, yet nothing seemed more pernicious to me than loneliness, especially the loneliness in the midst of social intercourse that deceives itself in a multitude of friendships. No urge seemed stronger to me than that for communication with others. If the never-completed movement of communication succeeds with but a single human being, everything is achieved. It is a criterion of this success that there be a readiness to communicate with every human being encountered and that grief is felt whenever communication fails. Not merely an exchange of words, nor friendliness and sociability, but only the constant urge towards total revelation reaches the path of communication.

The painful stimulus that was philosophically decisive was the question how I was myself to blame for the insufficiency of communication. The insufficiency was indubitable fact. But the fault could not lie only with the others. I, too, am human like them. The same sources of inhibition of communication exist in me as in them. The inner action, by which I train myself, had to illumine my self-concealment, arbitrariness and obstinacy, and to compel me to strive towards a revelation that can never be completed. The philosophical insight became possible precisely through my own failure. We can only recognize that evil which is in ourselves. What we cannot *be* at all, we cannot *understand* either.

The philosophical mood arose from the experience of insufficiency in communication. Occupation with mere objects which does not lead somehow to communication seemed wrong to me. Solitary devotion to nature—this deep experience of the universe in the landscape and in the physical nearness to its shapes and elements, this source of strength for the soul—could seem like a wrong done to other human beings, if it became a means of avoiding them, and like a wrong done to myself, if it tempted me to a secluded self-sufficiency in nature. Solitude in nature can indeed be a wonderful source of *self-being;* but whoever remains solitary in nature is liable to impoverish his self-being and to lose it in the end. To be near to nature in the beautiful world around me therefore became questionable when it did not lead back to community with humanity and serve this community as background and as language. Subsequently the question "What do they mean for communication?" passed through my philosophizing with respect to all thought, all experience, and all subject-matters. Are they apt to promote communication or to impede it? Are they tempters to solitude or heralds of communication?

This led to the basic philosophical questions: How is communication possible? What forms of communication can be accomplished? What is their relation to each other? In what sense are solitude and the strength to be able to be alone sources of communication? The answers are given, especially in the second volume of my *Philosophy,* in terms of concrete representations—by psychological means—and their principles will be treated in my *Logic.*

The thesis of my philosophizing is: The individual cannot become human by himself. Self-being is only real in communication with another self-being. Alone, I sink into gloomy isolation—only in community with others can I be revealed in the act of mutual discovery. My own freedom can only exist if the other is also free. Isolated or self-isolating Being remains mere potentiality or disappears into nothingness. All institutions that maintain soothing contact between men under unexpressed conditions and within unadmitted limits are certainly indispensable for communal existence; but beyond that they are pernicious, because they veil the truth in the manifestation of human Existenz with illusory contentment.

3. *What is truth?* The limits of science and the urge toward communication both point to a truth that is more than a possession of the intellect.

The cogent correctness of the sciences is but a small part of truth. This correctness, in its universal validity, does not unite us completely as real human beings, but only as intellectual beings. It unites us in the object that is understood, in the particular, but not in the totality. Admittedly, men can be true friends through scientific research, by means of the ideas that are realized in this process, and the impulses towards Existenz that make their appearance in it. But the correctness of scientific knowledge unites all intellectual beings in their equality, as it were, as replaceable points, not, in its essence, as human beings.

To the intellect all else, in comparison with what is correct, counts only as feeling, subjectivity, instinct. In this division, apart from the bright world of the intellect, there is only the irrational, in which is lumped together, according to the point of view, what is despised or desired. The impulse which pursues real truth by thought springs from the dissatisfaction with what is merely correct. The division, spoken of previously, paralyzes this impulse; it causes man to oscillate between the dogmatism of the intellect that transcends its limits and, as it were, the rapture of the vital, the chance of the moment, life. The soul becomes impoverished in all the multiplicity of disparate experience. Then truth disappears from the field of vision and is replaced by a variety of opinions which are hung on the skeleton of a supposedly rational pattern. Truth is infinitely *more* than scientific correctness.

Communication, too, points to this *more*. Communication is the path to truth in all its forms. Thus the intellect finds clarity only in discussion. How man as an existent, as spirit, as Existenz, is or can be in communication—that is what allows all other truth to appear. The truth that makes itself felt at the boundary of science is the same that is felt in this movement of communication. The question arises what kind of truth it is.

We call the source of this truth the *Encompassing*, to distinguish it from the objective, the determinate, and particular forms in which beings confront us. This concept is by no means familiar and by no means self-evident. We may clarify the Encompassing philosophically, but we cannot know it objectively.

At this point the decision is made whether we can attain philosophizing or whether we fall back again at the boundary where the *leap to transcending thinking* must be made. If such words as feeling, instinct, heart, drives, and affections, which are suggestive of psychological analysis, are claimed as sources of truth, then we merely name the basis of our life, but it remains in darkness, causing us to slip down into supposedly comprehensible psychology, while actually everything depends on reaching the bright region of truly philosophical thought.

The methods of transcending are the bases of all philosophy. It is impossible to anticipate briefly what they accomplish. Perhaps a few words may *suggest,* even if not *explain,* what is meant.

Everything that becomes an *object* to me approaches me, as it were, from the dark background of Being. Every object is a determinate being (as *this* confronting me in a subject-object division), but never all Being. No being known as an object is *the* Being.

Does not the sum of all objects form the totality of Being? No. As the horizon encompasses all things in a landscape, so all objects are encompassed by that in which they are. As we move towards the horizon in the world of space without ever reaching it, because the horizon moves with us and re-establishes itself ever anew as the Encompassing at each moment, so objective research moves towards totalities at each moment which never become total and real Being, but must be passed through towards new vistas. Only if all horizons met in one closed whole, so that they formed a finite multiplicity, could we attain, by moving through all the horizons, the one closed Being. Being, however, is not closed for us and the horizons are not finite. On all sides we are impelled towards the Infinite.

We inquire after the Being which, with the manifestation of all encountered appearance in object and horizon, yet recedes itself. This Being we call the Encompassing. The Encompassing, then, is that which always makes its presence known, which does not appear itself, but from which everything comes to us.

With this fundamental philosophical thought we must think beyond all determinate beings to the Encompassing in which we are and to the Encompassing which we are ourselves. It is a thought turns us round, as it were, because it frees us from the shackles of determinate Being; yet the thought of the Encompassing is only a first approach. In its brevity it is still a purely formal concept. With further elaboration, modes of the Encompassing soon emerge (the Being of the Encompassing as such is world and Transcendence; the Being of the Encompassing that we are is an existent, consciousness in general, spirit, Existenz). Thus arises the task of clarifying all modes of the Encompassing. We become aware of truth in its total possibilities, its extent, its width and depth, only with the modes of the Encompassing.

The clarification of all the Encompassing derives its motive from our Reason and Existenz.

The impulses in which we open ourselves without limit, in which we want to give language to everything that is, embrace, as it were, all that is most strange and most distant, eking a relation with everything, denying communication to othing, these we call *reason*. This word, to be distinguished radically from *intellect*, meets the condition of truth as it can emerge from all modes of the Encompassing. Philosophical logic is the self-comprehension of reason.

Truth in this comprehensive sense, in which the truth of the intellect (and that of the sciences with it) is but an element, is founded in the *Existenz* that we can become. What matters is that our life is guided by something unconditional which can only spring from the *decision*. Decision makes Existenz real, forms life and changes it in inner action, which, through clarification, keeps us soaring upward. When it is founded on decision, love is no longer an unreliably moving passion, but the fulfillment to which alone real Being reveals itself.

What must be done in thinking of life is to be served by a philosophizing that discovers truth by retrospection and by anticipation. This philosophizing has no meaning unless a reality of the thinker complements the thought. This reality is not profession or application of a doctrine, but the practice of being human which propels itself forward in the echo of the thought. It is a movement, an upward soaring on two wings, as it were. Both wings, the thinking and the reality, must support the flight. Mere thinking would be an empty moving of possibilities, mere reality would remain a dull unconsciousness without self-comprehension, and therefore without unfolding.

This philosophizing emerged for me from psychology, which had to change and became Existenz Clarification. Existenz Clarification in its turn pointed to Philosophical World Orientation and to Metaphysics. Finally, the sense of this thinking is understands itself in a Philosophical Logic that considers not only the intellect and its products (judgment and conclusion), but discovers the foundation of truth, in its complete range, in the Encompassing. Being is not the sum of objects; rather objects extend, as it were, towards our intellect in the subject-object division, from the Encompassing of Being itself, which is beyond objective comprehension, but from which nevertheless all separate, determinate objective knowledge derives its limits and its meaning and from which it derives the mood that comes out of the totality in which it has significance.

4. *What is man?*   As a living being among others man is the subject of anthropology. In his inner aspect he is a subject for psychology, in his objective structures, that is in communal life, a subject for sociology. Man, in his empirical reality, can be a subject of research in many directions; but man is always more than he knows or can know about himself.

As something knowable man appears in his manifold empirical aspects. As a being that is known he is always divided up into whatever he will reveal himself to be according to the methods of research employed. He is never a unity and a whole, never man himself, once he has become the subject of knowledge.

If I want to reassure myself philosophically about being human I cannot, therefore, stop at the knowable aspects of empirical man in the world. Man, in a way, is everything (as Aristotle says about the soul). Becoming aware of man's being means becoming aware of Being in time as a whole. Man is the Encompassing that we are; yet even as the Encompassing, man is split. As I said before, we become aware of the Encompassing that we are in a number of ways: as an existent, as consciousness generally, as spirit, as Existenz. Man lives in his world as an existent. As thinking consciousness generally he is searchingly oriented towards objects. As spirit he shapes the idea of a whole in his world existence. As possible Existenz he is related to Transcendence through which he knows himself as given to himself in his freedom. How man achieves unity is a problem, infinite in time and insoluble; but it is nevertheless the path to his search. Man is less certain of himself than ever.

In philosophizing man is not a species of particular existent beside other existents, but he becomes clear to himself as something unique, something all-enclosing, something completely open, as the greatest potentiality and the greatest danger in the world, as being the exception of Being, as the communication of scattered Being, which in him reveals itself to itself.

5. *What is Transcendence?* Man is for us the most interesting being in the world.'We, as human beings ourselves, want to know what we are and can be; but a constant occupation with man causes surfeit. It seems as if, in that occupation, the essential was missed. For man cannot be comprehended on the basis of himself, and as we confront man's being there is disclosed the other through which he exists. For man as possible Existenz that is Transcendence but while man is in the world as a perceptive reality, Transcendence is, as if it were not there. Nor is it fathomable. Its being itself is doubtful. And yet all philosophizing is directed towards the goal of achieving certainty about Transcendence.

It may be objected that philosophy is mistakenly trying to achieve what only religion can achieve. In the cult religion offers the bodily presence, or at least experience, of Transcendence. It founds man on God's revelation. It points paths of faith in revealed reality, in mercy and salvation, and it gives guarantees. Philosophy can achieve none of that.

If philosophizing is a revolving round Transcendence, it must therefore have a relation to religion. The manner in which philosophy and religion react to each other is indeed an expression of their self-comprehension and of the depth of their realization. Historically we see this relation in the form of struggle, of subordination, of exclusion. A final and unchanging relation is not possible. Here a boundary shows itself. Where the problem is not merely grasped by insight but is actually solved, man has become narrow. When religion is excluded by philosophy or philosophy by religion; when one side asserts dominance over the other, by claiming to be the sole and most exalted authority, then man loses his openness to Being and his own potentiality in order to obtain a final closing of knowledge, but even this remains closed to him. He becomes, whether he limits himself to religion or to philosophy, dogmatic, fanatical and, finally, with failure, nihilistic. To remain truthful religion needs the conscience of philosophy. To retain a significant content philosophy needs the substance of religion; yet any formula, such as this, is too simple; for it obscures the fact that there is more than one original truth in man. All that is possible is to avoid mistaking one for the other. Philosophy, from its side, cannot wish to fight religion. It must acknowledge it, albeit as its polar opposite, yet related to it through this polarity. Religion must always interest it because philosophy is constantly stirred up, prodded, and addressed by it. Philosophy cannot wish to replace religion, compete with it, nor make propaganda on its own behalf against it. On the contrary: philosophy will have to affirm religion at least as the reality to which it, too, owes its existence. If religion were not the life of mankind, there would be no philosophy either.

Philosophy as such, however, cannot look for Transcendence in the guarantee of revelation, but must approach Being in the self-disclosures of the Encompassing that are present in man as man (not in the proofs of the intellect or in the insights which the intellect, as such, might obtain) and through the historicity of the language of Transcendence.

The question "What is Transcendence?" is not answered, therefore, by a knowledge of Transcendence. The answer comes indirectly by a clarification of the incompleteness of the world, the imperfectibility of man, the impossibility of a permanently valid world order, the universal failure—bearing in mind at the same time that there is not nothing, but that in nature, history, and human existence, the magnificent is as real as the terrible. The decisive alternative in all philosophizing is whether my thinking leads me to the point where I am certain that the "from outside" of Transcendence is the source of the "from inside", or whether I remain in Immanence with the negative certainty that there is no outside that is the basis and goal of everything—the world as well as what I am myself.

No proof of God succeeds in philosophy if it attempts to provide compelling knowledge; but it is possible for "proofs" of God to succeed as ways of transcending thought. Rational thinking can transcend the categories of all that is thinkable to the point where opposites coincide; it can go beyond them in the individual category, e.g. that of sufficient cause or purpose—to the, in fact, untenable thought of a last cause and a final purpose. In that way, the necessity of seeking is understood in the baselessness of our merely factual existence and our soul is kept open to the Origin. The representation of the fragmentation of Being and the radical contradictoriness present in every form demonstrates that nothing we can know endures through itself.

Part of the externality of Transcendence is its unknowability; its internality is the code message of all things. In view of the fact that the limit and the basis of all things can be made tangible, it is possible to perceive everywhere the thread of light which connects them with Transcendence. Even though Transcendence is thus immanent, it is so only in an unlimited ambiguity and cannot be grasped with any finality. Philosophizing merely establishes the general right to trust in that which seems to speak to me as the light of Transcendence.

How I understand this language, however, is based on what I really am myself. What I am myself is based on my original relations to Transcendence: in defiance and in surrender, in falling away and in soaring up, in obedience to the law of day and in the passion of night. When I philosophize I clarify and remember and prepare how, through these relations, I can experience Eternity in Time. The experience itself cannot be forced and cannot be proved: it is the fulfilled historicity of my Existenz.

Philosophy can further demonstrate the consequences that appear when the interpretation of Being wishes to restrict itself to pure immanence. It can lift the veils that threaten at all times to wrap man in untruth. It accomplishes this with unprovable propositions of the intellect, with supposed knowledge of the world as a whole, and with results seemingly scientific. But in doing away with pseudo-knowledge philosophy does not establish a positive knowledge of Transcendence comparable to scientific knowledge.

Philosophy can clarify our conscience; it can show how we experience the demand of a universal law that we recognize as inevitable. At the boundary it can show the real failure even of obedience to this law, and cause the individual to feel anew the demand for unconditional obedience which addresses him in his historicity—though without universality or universal validity; and here again philosophy can show the boundary and the failure in Time.

On all paths it is essential to reach the Source where in highest consciousness the demand becomes audible in the world which, in spite of failing to be realized in the world, yet produces the true Being through obedience to it.

Philosophy can clarify that such a Source is possible; yet what the Source is and what it speaks it cannot anticipate. For reality is historical and awaits every individual that arises anew in this world. Everything that philosophy says in substance and remembers in history remains relative, in so far as it is utterable, and has to be translated and appropriated in order to become a path to one's own original comprehension of the Unconditional.

In thinking along these lines, philosophy employs a twofold presupposition that is objectively unprovable but accomplishable in practice. First, man is autonomous in the face of all the authorities of the world: the individual, reared by authority, at the end of the process of his maturation decides in his immediacy and responsibility before Transcendence what is unconditionally true. Second, man is a datum of Transcendence: to obey Transcendence in that unconditional decision leads man to his own Being.

How I can succeed in reading the code message in the fulness of beings, in existing concretely in my relations with Transcendence, in gaining my own Being in historically formed obedience to Transcendence, all this is conjoined to the fundamental question how the One is in the many, what it is, and how I can become certain of the One.

IV. MY WORKS

Three times thus far I have attempted a systematic work: my *General Psychopathology* (1913), my *Psychology of Weltanschauungen* (1919), and my *Philosophy* (1932).

In my *Psychopathology* I did not present everything on the basis of a theory and did not order my findings on the basis of a total view of the matter; rather I developed methods of research to demonstrate what is consequent to each method. The system was in effect a systematization of methods. The purpose of my work was: liberation from dogmatic pseudo-knowledge, the strengthening of the open vision of research by a clear consciousness of their methods and their limitations. To know what I know, that is by no means a matter of course in scientific practice.

In my *Psychology of Weltanschauungen* I tried to present systematically the sum total of the human possibilities of faith, world views, and attitudes. It was an exuberant, youthful work, the contents of which I acknowledge as mine to this day, but the form of which was inadequate. I meant to let pass before me in pure contemplation whatever came, and yet, in fact, I traced the single truth of man's Being that was, to me, the given one, conceived it as a synthesis of polarities and everywhere demonstrated the stream of lapses, voids, inversions. It was hidden philosophy that here misunderstood itself as objectively descriptive psychology.

In my *Philosophy* my systematic approach arose from the three methods of transcending. In World Orientation, by means of a compelling Transcendence, I came to a consciousness of the apparency of all existents (Volume I). Transcending from this basis I make myself aware by means of Existenz Clarification of what I myself actually am and can be (Volume II). From both presuppositions transcending toward Transcendence becomes clear in Metaphysics. I pursue the paths of thought along which Being itself presents itself to me (Volume III).

In contradistinction to the two previous works, my *Philosophy* is formed throughout with conscious discipline. It was no longer simple to present; for the transcending that occurs in the act of accomplishment had to be developed anew each time as a calm breath of thought. Thus every chapter is unified by a single pervading movement. The chapters can only be understood as a whole in this movement of the idea, but each chapter can be understood by itself.

The content of the *Philosophy*, however, does not lie in its systematic basic ideas, but in that which happens through it. As my *Psychopathology* was not objective in its systematization, but methodological, so my later philosophizing is not ontological but incursive: it does not know what is, but it clarifies the Encompassing. What is important lies in the special contents and expositions.

Around these three major works are grouped some minor writings. A series of psychiatric publications in journals belong to my *Psychopathology;* the essay *Strindberg and Van Gogh* belongs to my *Psychology of Weltanschauungen.* Then followed years of respite and concentration of my thinking, before my *Philosophy*, to which the *Spiritual Situation of the Time* [published in English translation under the title *Man in the Modern Age*] belongs, appeared.

Since then I see my task contained in two projects which seem to me as if they will be the concluding work of my life. I have been working on both of these continually for many years. I call them *Philosophical Logic* and *Universal History of Philosophy*. With my *Philosophical Logic* I seek to make a contribution to the logical self-consciousness of this age that belongs as much to our newly-awakened philosophizing as did Hegel's logic to Idealism or inductive logic (that of John Stuart Mill, for example) to the positivist age. Here the systematic basic thoughts themselves become the essential content. In my *Universal History of Philosophy* I aim to present historically known philosophizing, without chronological order, as the one great phenomenon, always coherent in itself, of the revelation of Being in humanity; how from its roots (in China, India, Greece) it developed in great cycles, constantly conditioned by sociological circumstances and psychological events, in relation to science and religion, echoing art and poetry, how it strives towards a single, great, organized unity of opposites, which, at the boundaries, fail to yield solutions in Time, and, in failing, bring to awareness the truth of Transcendent Being.

These works do not yet exist. Parts of my *Logic* have been communicated in lectures that I gave in Groningen (*Vernunft und Existenz*, Groningen 1935 [Engl. transl. by William Earle, *Reason and Existenz*, Noonday Press, New York 1955]) and in Frankfurt (*Existenzphilosophie*, Berlin 1938). Of my historical studies works on *Nietzsche* (Berlin, 1936) and *Descartes* (Berlin, 1937) have been published. My *Nietzsche* was to be an introduction to the shaking up of thought from which Existenz philosophy must spring. In my *Descartes* I wanted to present historically typically modern errors at their root, viz. mistaking speculative thought for rationally cogent insight and the disaster of the inversion of modern science, which appeared, when this science began to flourish and has remained side by side with it ever since.

Logic and history of philosophy are complementary. One can hardly be grasped without the other. Work on the one therefore benefits work on the other. What is being developed there, as the world of thought, is demonstrated here as the reality of thought.

My philosophizing has ever stood against *System* as a totality in which Being and truth lie clearly before one's eyes and find their presentation in a book. But at the same time I was *systematic* in my thought from the beginning, in so far as I looked for order, continuity, and relation of my thoughts to each other. *System* wrongly tries to seize Being; the systematic approach aims methodically at securing the availability for the further course of philosophy of whatever means have been developed. The will against the System does not exclude the systematic approach; in fact, without this approach that will would lead to chaos. To develop the systematic approach as an "organon of reason" in a Logic, that seems to me to be the most important task of today.

V. EPILOGUE

What I planned in 1941 has only been accomplished in part. The years that followed, with their dangers and their hygienically uncongenial circumstances, sapped my ability to work and finally made work impossible. After 1945 the problems of the day supervened. The philosophical work remained in the background.

Since then the first volume of my *Philosophical Logic* has appeared under the title *Of Truth*. It is the fourth attempt at a systematic outline.

In addition a completely rewritten edition of my *General Psychopathology* appeared. Though my fundamental approach is the same, it has become a new book.

The series of smaller writings of the last years are attempts to make available to wider circles, in a shorter form, some of the material that escapes attention in my more extensive works.

2. Kierkegaard and Nietzsche

I. HISTORICAL REFLECTIONS; THE CONTEMPORARY SITUATION

The rational is not thinkable without its other, the non-rational, and it never appears in reality without it. The only question is, in what form the other appears, how it remains in spite of all, and how it is to be grasped.

It is appropriate for philosophizing to strive to absorb the non-rational and counter-rational, to form it through reason, to change it into a form of reason, indeed, finally to show it as identical with reason; all Being should become law and order.

But both the defiant will and honest mind turn against

this. They recognize and assert the unconquerable non-rational.

For knowing, this non-rational is found in the opacity of the here and now; in matter, it is what is only enveloped but never consumed by rational form; it is in actual empirical existence which is just as it is and not otherwise, which is subsumed under just those regularities we experience and not others; it is in the contents of faith for religious revelation. All philosophizing which would like to dissolve Being into pure rationality retains in spite of itself the non-rational; this may be reduced to a residue of indifferent matter, some primordial fact, an impulse, or an accident.

The will utilizes these possibilities in knowledge to its own advantage. A battle arises for and against reason. Opposed to pure, transparent reason's drive toward rest within the conceivable, stands a drive to destroy reason, not only to indicate its limits, but to enslave it. We want to subordinate ourselves to an inconceivable supersensible, which however appears in the world through human utterances and makes demands. We wish to subordinate ourselves to the natural character of impulses and passions, to the immediacy of what is now present. These drives are now translated by the philosophy which adheres to them into a knowledge of the non-rational: philosophy expresses its falling into the non-rational, the counter-rational, and the super-rational as a knowledge about them. Yet, even in the most radical defiance of reason, there remains a minimum of rationality.

To show how the many-fold distinction between reason and non-reason appears at the bases of all thinking would require an analysis of the history of philosophy out of its own actual principles. Let us recall a few selected points.

To the Greeks this problem of Being was already present in myth. The clarity of the Greek gods was surrounded by the sublime incomprehensibility of Fate, limiting their knowledge and power.

Most of the philosophers touched incidentally, although in important ways, upon what was inaccessible to reason.

Socrates listened to the forbidding voice of the uncomprehended daimon. Plato recognized madness, which if pathological is less than reason, but if divinely begotten, more; only through madness can poets, lovers, and philosophers come to a vision of Being. To be sure, according to Aristotle.

in human affairs, happiness was the result of rational deliberation, but not totally; happiness could appear without and even opposed to deliberation. For Aristotle, there were men, the *alogoi*, who had a better principle than deliberative reason; their affairs succeeded without and even counter to reason.

These examples stand alongside the general form of Greek thought, which opposed appearance to Being (Parmenides), the void to things (Democritus), non-being to genuine Being (Plato), and matter to form (Aristotle).

In Christianity, the opposition between reason and non-reason developed as struggle between reason and faith within each man; what was inaccessible to reason was no longer regarded simply as other than reason, but was a revelation of something higher. In the observations of the world, the non-rational was no longer mere chance, or blind chaos, or some astonishing principle surpassing reason, but was taken comprehensively as Providence. All the fundamental ideas of a rationally unintelligible faith could only be expressed in irrational antinomies. Every rational, literal interpretation of faith became a heresy.

In the succeeding centuries, on the other hand, Descartes and his followers attempted a radical grounding of reason upon itself alone—at least in the philosophical excogitation of Being which the individual accomplished by himself. Although Descartes left society, state, and church intact, the attitude of the Enlightenment arose as a consequence; with what I validly think and can empirically investigate, I can achieve the right organization of the world. Rational thought, in the sense of presuppositionless universality, is a sufficient basis for human life in general. From the beginning, however, a counter-movement worked against this philosophy of reason, whether it be called rationalism or empiricism. This counter-movement was led by men who, although in complete possession of rationality themselves, at the same time saw its limits: that other which was important before any reason, which made reason possible, and restrained it. Over against Descartes, stands Pascal; over against Descartes, Hobbes, and Grotius, stands Vico; over against Locke, Leibnitz, and Spinoza, stands Bayle.

The philosophy of the seventeenth and eighteenth centuries seems to work itself out in these great antitheses. But the thinkers were irreconcilable, and their ideas were mutually exclusive.

In contrast to this world of thought, the philosophers of German idealism made an astonishing attempt to create a reconciliation, seeing in reason more than reason itself. German philosophy in its great period went beyond all previous possibilities and developed a concept of reason which was historically independent. In Kant, a new beginning was created. This concept of reason got lost in the fantastic construction of Hegel but broke through again in Fichte and Schelling.

When one looks over the thought of centuries, the same thing always seems to happen: in whatever form this Other to reason appears, in the course of rational understanding it is either changed back into reason, or sometimes it is recognized as a limit in its place; but then in its consequences it is circumscribed and delimited by reason itself, or sometimes it is seen and developed as the source of a new and better reason.

It is as though at the bottom of this thought, even in all its unrest, there always lay the quiet of a reason which was never wholly and radically questioned. All awareness of Being grounded itself finally in reason or in God. All questioning was circumscribed by unquestioned assumptions; or else there were merely individual and historically inefficacious pioneers who never achieved a thorough understanding of themselves. The counter-movements against rationality were like a distant thunder announcing storms which could be released, but which were not yet.

Thus the great history of Western philosophy from Parmenides and Heraclitus through Hegel can be seen as a thorough-going and completed unity. Its great forms are even today preserved in the tradition, and are rediscovered as the true salvation from the destruction of philosophy. For a century we have seen individual philosophers become objects of special studies, and have seen restorations of their doctrines. We know the totality of past teachings in the sense of "doctrines" perhaps better than any of the earlier great philosophers. But the consciousness of a change into mere knowing about doctrines and about history, of separation from life itself and from actually believed truth, has made us question the ultimate sense of this tradition, great as it is and despite all the satisfaction it has provided and provides today. We question whether the truth of philosophizing has been grasped or even if it can be grasped in this tradition.

Quietly, something enormous has happened in the reality of Western man: a destruction of all authority, a radical disillusionment in an overconfident reason, and a dissolution of bonds have made anything, absolutely anything, seem possible. Work with the old words can appear as a mere veil which hid the preparing powers of chaos from our anxious eyes. This work seemed to have no other power than that of a long continued deception. The passionate revivifying of these words and doctrines, though done with good intentions, appears as without real effect, an impotent call to hold fast. Philosophizing to be authentic must grow out of our new reality, and there take its stand.

II. KIERKEGAARD AND NIETZSCHE

The contemporary philosophical situation is determined by the fact that two philosophers, Kierkegaard and Nietzsche, who did not count in their times and, for a long time, remained without influence in the history of philosophy, have continually grown in significance. Philosophers after Hegel have increasingly returned to face them, and they stand today unquestioned as the authentically great thinkers of their age. Both their influence and the opposition to them prove it. Why then can these philosophers no longer be ignored, in our time?

In the situation of philosophizing, as well as in the real life of men, Kierkegaard and Nietzsche appear as the expression of destinies, destinies which nobody noticed then, with the exception of some ephemeral and immediately forgotten presentiments, but which they themselves already comprehended.

As to what this destiny really is, the question remains open even today. It is not answered by any comparison of the two thinkers, but it is clarified and made more urgent. This comparison is all the more important since there could have been no influence of one upon the other, and because their very differences make their common features so much more impressive. Their affinity is so compelling, from the whole course of their lives down to the individual details of their thought, that their nature seems to have been elicited by the necessities of the spiritual situation of their times. With them a shock occurred to Western philosophizing whose final meaning can not yet be estimated.

Common to both of them is a type of thought and humanity which was indissolubly connected with a moment of this epoch, and so understood by them. We shall, therefore, discuss their affinity: first, in their thought; second, in their actual thinking Existenz; and third, in the way in which they understood themselves.

1. What is common to their thought: the questioning of reason

Their thinking created a new atmosphere. They passed beyond all of the limits then regarded as obvious. It is as if they no longer shrank back from anything in thought. Everything permanent was as if consumed in a dizzying suction: with Kierkegaard by an otherworldly Christianity which is like Nothingness and shows itself only in negation (the absurd, martyrdom) and in negative resolution; with Nietzsche, a vacuum out of which, with despairing violence, a new reality was to be born (the eternal return, and the corresponding dogmatics of Nietzsche).

Both questioned reason from the depths of Existenz. Never on such a high level of thought had there been such a thorough-going and radical opposition to mere reason. This questioning is never simply hostility to reason; rather both sought to appropriate limitlessly all modes of rationality. It was no philosophy of feeling, for both pushed unremittingly toward the concept for expression. It is certainly not dogmatic scepticism; rather their whole thought strove toward the genuine truth.

In a magnificent way, penetrating a whole life with the earnestness of philosophizing, they brought forth not some doctrines, not any basic position, not some picture of the world, but rather a new total intellectual attitude for men. This attitude was in the medium of infinite reflection, a reflection which is conscious of being unable to attain any real ground by itself. No single thing characterizes their nature; no fixed doctrine or requirement is to be drawn out of them as something independent and permanent.

Suspicion of scientific men   Out of the consciousness of

their truth, both suspect truth in the naive form of scientific knowledge. They do not doubt the methodological correctness of scientific insight. But Kierkegaard was astonished at the learned professors; they live for the most part with science and die with the idea that it will continue, and would like to live longer that they might, in a line of direct progress, always understand more and more. They do not experience the maturity of that critical point where everything turns upside down, where one understands more and more that there is something which one cannot understand. Kierkegaard thought the most frightful way to live was to bewitch the whole world through one's discoveries and cleverness—to explain the whole of nature and not understand oneself. Nietzsche is inexhaustible in destructive analyses of types of scholars, who have no genuine sense of their own activity, who can not be themselves, and who, with their ultimately futile knowledge, aspire to grasp Being itself.

Against the system   The questioning of every self-enclosed rationality which tries to make the whole truth communicable made both radical opponents of the "system," that is, the form which philosophy had had for centuries and which had achieved its final polish in German idealism. The system is for them a detour from reality and is, therefore, lies and deception. Kierkegaard granted that empirical existence could be a system for God, but never for an existing spirit; system corresponds with what is closed and settled, but existence is precisely the contrary. The philosopher of systems is, as a man, like someone who builds a castle, but lives next door in a shanty. Such a fantastical being does not himself live within what he thinks; but the thought of a man must be the house in which he lives or it will become perverted. The basic question of philosophy, what it itself is, and what science is, is posed in a new and unavoidable form. Nietzsche wanted to doubt better than Descartes, and saw in Hegel's miscarried attempt to make reason evolve nothing but Gothic heaven-storming. The will-to-system is for him a lack of honesty.

Being as interpretation   What authentic knowing is, was expressed by both in the same way. It is, for them, nothing but interpretation. They also understood their own thought as interpretation.

Interpretation, however, reaches no end. Existence, for Nietzsche, is capable of infinite interpretation. What has happened and what was done, is for Kierkegaard always capable of being understood in a new way. As it is interpreted anew, it becomes a new reality which yet is hidden; temporal life can therefore never be correctly understood by men; no man can absolutely penetrate through his own consciousness.

Both apply the image of interpretation to knowledge of Being, but in such a fashion that Being is as if deciphered in the interpretation of the interpretation. Nietzsche wanted to uncover the basic text, *homo natura,* from its overpaintings and read it in its reality. Kierkegaard gave his own writings no other meaning than that they should read again the original text of individual, human existential relations.

Masks With this basic idea is connected the fact that both, the most open and candid of thinkers, had a misleading aptitude for concealment and masks. For them masks necessarily belong to the truth. Indirect communication becomes for them the sole way of communicating genuine truth; indirect communication, as expression, is appropriate to the ambiguity of genuine truth in temporal existence, in which process it must be grasped through sources in every Existenz.

Being itself Both, in their thinking, push toward that basis which would be Being itself in man. In opposition to the philosophy which from Parmenides through Descartes to Hegel said, Thought is Being, Kierkegaard asserted the proposition, as you believe, so are you: Faith is Being. Nietzsche saw the Will to Power. But Faith and Will to Power are mere *signa,* which do not directly connote what is meant but are themselves capable of endless explication.

Honesty With both there is a decisive drive toward honesty. This word for them both is the expression of the ultimate virtue to which they subject themselves. It remains for them the minimum of the absolute which is still possible although everything else becomes involved in a bewildering questioning. It becomes for them also the dizzying demand for a veracity which, however, brings even itself into question, and which is the opposite of that violence which would like to grasp the truth in a literal and barbaric certitude.

Their readers   One can question whether in general anything is said in such thought. In fact, both Kierkegaard and Nietzsche were aware that the comprehension of their thought was not possible to the man who only thinks. It is important who it is that understands.

They turn to the individuals who must bring with them and bring forth from themselves what can only be said indirectly. The epigram of Lichtenberg applies to Kierkegaard, and he himself cites it: such works are like mirrors; if an ape peeks in, no apostle will look out. Nietzsche says one must have earned for oneself the distinction necessary to understand him. He held it impossible to teach the truth where the mode of thought is based. Both seek the reader who belongs to them.

2. *Their thinking Existenz in its actual setting: the age*

Such thinking is grounded in the Existenz of Kierkegaard and Nietzsche insofar as it belonged to their age in a distinctive way. That no single idea, no system, no requirement is decisive for them follows from the fact that neither thinker expressed his epoch at its peak, that they constructed no world, nor any image of a passing world. They did not feel themselves to be a positive expression of their times; they rather expressed what it was negatively through their very being: an age absolutely rejected by them and seen through in its ruin. Their problem appeared to be to experience this epoch to the end in their own natures, to be it completely in order to overcome it. This happened at first involuntarily, but then consciously through the fact that they were not representatives of their epoch, but needling and scandalous' *exceptions*. Let us look at this a little closer.

Their problem   Both had become aware of their *problem* by the end of their youth, even if unclearly. A decision which gripped the entire man, which sometimes was silent and no longer conscious, but which would return to force itself upon them, pushed them into a radical loneliness. Although without position, marriage, without any effective role in existence, they nevertheless appear as the great realists, who had an authentic feeling for the depths of reality.

Perception of substantial change in essence of men They touched this reality in their fundamental experience of their epoch as ruins; looking back over centuries, back to the beginnings in Greek antiquity, they felt the end of this whole history. At the crucial point, they called attention to this moment, without wanting to survey the meaning and course of history as a whole.

Men have tried to understand this epoch in economic, technological, historico-political, and sociological terms. Kierkegaard and Nietzsche, on the other hand, thought they saw a change in the very substance of man.

Kierkegaard looked upon the whole of Christianity as it is today as upon an enormous deception in which God is held to be a fool. Such Christianity has nothing to do with that of the New Testament. There are only two ways: either to maintain the deception through tricks and conceal the real conditions, and then everything comes to nothing; or honestly to confess the misery that in truth, today, not one single individual is born who can pass for a Christian in the sense of the New Testament. Not one of us is a Christian, but rather we live in a pious softening of Christianity. The confession will show if there is anything true left in this honesty, if it has the approval of Providence. If not, then everything must again be broken so that in this horror individuals can arise again who can support the Christianity of the New Testament.

Nietzsche expressed the historical situation of the epoch in one phrase: God is dead.

Thus, common to both, is an historical judgment on the very substance of their times. They saw before them Nothingness; both knew the substance of what had been lost, but neither willed Nothingness. If Kierkegaard presupposed the truth, or the possibility of the truth of Christianity, and Nietzsche, on the other hand, found in atheism not simply a loss but rather the greatest opportunity—still, what is common to both is a will toward the substance of Being, toward the nobility and value of man. They had no political program for reform, no program at all; they directed their attention to no single detail, but rather wanted to effect something through their thought which they foresaw in no clear detail. For Nietzsche, this indeterminateness was his "larger politics" at long range; for Kierkegaard, it was becoming

Christian in the new way of indifference to all worldly being. Both in their relation to their epoch were possessed by the question of what will become of man.

Modernity overcome They are modernity itself in a somersaulting form. They ran it to the ground, and overcame it by living it through to the end. We can see how both experienced the distress of the epoch, not passively, but suicidally through totally doing what most only half did: first of all, in their endless reflection; and then, in opposition to this, in their drive toward the basic; and finally, in the way in which, as they sank into the bottomless, they grasped hold upon the Transcendent.

(A) *Unlimited reflection* The age of reflection has, since Fichte, been characterized as reasoning without restraint, as the dissolving of all authority, as the surrender of content which gives to thinking its measure, purpose, and meaning, so that from now on, without hindrance and as an indifferent play of the intellect, it can fill the world with noise and dust.

Kierkegaard and Nietzsche did not oppose reflection in order to annihilate it, but rather in order to overcome it by limitlessly engaging in it and mastering it. Man cannot sink back into an unreflective immediacy without losing himself; but he can go this way to the end, not destroying reflection, but rather coming to the basis in himself in the medium of reflection.

Their "infinite reflection" has, therefore, a twofold character. It can lead to a complete ruin just as well as it can become the condition of authentic Existenz. Both express this, perhaps Kierkegaard is the clearer of the two:

Reflection cannot exhaust or stop itself. It is faithless, since it hinders every decision. It is never finished and, in the end, can become "dialectical twaddle"; in this respect, he called it the poison of reflection. But that it is possible, indeed necessary, lies grounded in the endless ambiguity of all existence and action for us: anything can mean something else for reflection. This situation makes possible on one side a sophistry of existence, enables the Existenz-less esthete to profit, who merely wants to savor everything as an interesting novelty. Even if he should take the most decisive step still he always holds before himself the possibility of reinterpreting everything, so that, in one blow, it is all changed. But on the other hand, this situation can be truly grasped by the knowledge that insofar as we are honest we live in a "sea of reflection where no one can call to another, where all buoys are dialectical."

Without infinite reflection we should fall into the quiet of the settled and established which, as something permanent in the world, would become absolute; that is, we should become superstitious. An atmosphere of bondage arises with such a settlement. Infinite reflection, therefore, is, precisely through its endlessly active dialectic, the condition of freedom. It breaks out of every prison of the finite. Only in its medium is there any possibility of an infinite passion arising out of immediate feeling which, because it is unquestioning, is still unfree. In infinite passion the immediate feeling, which is held fast and genuinely true throughout the questioning, is grasped as free.

But in order to prevent this freedom from becoming nothing through vacuous reflection, in order for it to fulfill itself, infinite reflection must strand itself. Then, for the first time, does it issue out of something real, or exhaust itself in the decision of faith and resolution. As untrue as the arbitrary and forced arrest of reflection is, so true is that basis by which reflection is mastered in the encounter of Existenz. Here Existenz is given to itself for the first time, so that it becomes master of infinite reflection through totally surrendering to it.

Reflection, which can just as well dissolve into nothing as become the condition of Existenz, is described as such and in the same way by both Kierkegaard and Nietzsche. Out of it, they have imparted an almost immeasurable wealth of thought in their works. This thinking, according to its own meaning, is possibility: it can indicate and prepare the way for the shipwreck, but cannot accomplish it.

Thus, in their thinking about the possibilities of man, both thinkers were aware of what they themselves were not in their thought. The awareness of possibilities, in analogy to poetry, is not a false, but rather a questioning and awakening reflection. Possibility is the form in which I permit myself to know about what I am not yet, and a preparation for being it.

Kierkegaard called his method most frequently, "an experimental psychology"; Nietzsche called his thought, "seductive."

Thus they left what they themselves were and what they ultimately thought concealed to the point of unrecognizability and, in its appearance, sunk into the incomprehensible. Kierkegaard's pseudonym writes: "The something which I am . . . is precisely a nothing." It gave him a high satisfaction to hold his "Existenz at that critical zero . . . between something and nothing, a mere perhaps." And Nietzsche willingly called himself a "philosopher of the dangerous perhaps."

Reflection is for both pre-eminently self-reflection. For them, the way to truth is through understanding oneself. But they both experienced how one's own substance can disappear this way, how the free, creative self-understanding can be replaced by a slavish rotation about one's own empirical existence. Kierkegaard knew the horror "of everything disappearing before a sick brooding over the tale of one's own miserable self." He sought for the way "between this devouring of oneself in observations as though one were the only man who had ever been, and the sorry comfort of a universal human shipwreck." He knew the "unhappy relativity in everything, the unending question about what I am." Nietzsche expressed it:

> *Among a hundred mirrors*
> *before yourself false . . .*
> *strangled in your own net*
> *Self-knower!*
> *Self-executioner!*
> *crammed between two nothings,*
> *a question mark . . .*

(B) *Drive toward the basic* The age which could no longer find its way amidst the multiplicity of its reflections and rationalizing words pushed out of reflection toward bases. Kierkegaard and Nietzsche here too seem to be forerunners. Later generations sought the basic in general in articulateness, in the esthetic charm of the immediately striking, in a general simplification, in unreflective experience, in the existence of the things closest to us. To them, Kierkegaard and Nietzsche seem useful; for both lived consciously with a passionate love for the sources of human communicability.

They were creative in language to the degree that their works belong to the peaks of the literatures of their countries; and they knew it. They were creative in the thrilling way which made them among the most widely read authors, even though the content was of the same weight and their genuine comprehension of the same difficulty as that of any of the great philosophers. But both also knew the tendency of the verbal to become autonomous, and they despised the literary world.

Both were moved by music to the point of intoxication; but both warned of its seduction, and along with Plato and Augustine belonged to those who suspected it existentially.

Everywhere they created formulas of striking simplicity. But both were full of concern before that simplicity which, in order to give some deceptive support to the weak and mediocre, offered flat, spiritless simplifications in place of the genuine simplicity which was the result of the most complicated personal development, which, like Being itself, never had a single rational meaning. They warned, as no thinker before had, against taking their words too simply, words which seemed to stand there apodictically.

In fact, they went by the most radical way to the basic, but in such a fashion that the dialectical movement never stopped. Their seriousness was absorbed neither into an illusion of the dogmatic fixedness of some supposed basis, nor into the purposes of language, esthetic charm, and simplicity.

(C) *Arrest in Transcendence* Both pursued a path which, for them, could not end short of a transcendental stop, for their reflections were not, like the usual reflections of modernity, stopped by the obvious limits of vital needs and interests. They, for whom it was a question of all or nothing, dared limitlessness. But this they could do only because from the very beginning onwards they were rooted in what was at the same time hidden from them: both, in their youth, spoke of an *unknown God*. Kierkegaard, even when twenty-five years old, wrote: "In spite of the fact that I am very far from understanding myself, I have . . . revered the unknown God." And Nietzsche at twenty years of age created his first unforgettable poem, "To the Unknown God":

> *I would know Thee, Unknown,*
> *Thou who grips deep in my soul,*
> *wandering through my life like a storm,*
> *Thou inconceivable, my kin!*
> *I would know Thee, even serve Thee.*

Never in their limitless reflection could they remain within the finite, conceivable, and therefore trivial; but just as little could they hold to reflection itself. Precisely because he had been thoroughly penetrated by reflection, Kierkegaard thought: "The religious understanding of myself has deserted me; I feel like an insect with which children are playing, so pitilessly does existence handle me." In his terrible loneliness, understood by and really bound to absolutely no one, he called to God: "God in heaven, if there were not some most inward center in a man where all this could be forgotten, who could hold out?"

Nietzsche was always conscious of moving on the sea of the infinite, of having given up land once and for all. He knew that, perhaps, neither Dante nor Spinoza knew his loneliness; somehow, they had God for company. But Nietzsche, empty in his loneliness, without men and without the ancient God, envisaged Zarathustra and meditated upon the eternal return, thoughts which left him as horrified as happy. He lived continually like someone mortally wounded. He suffered his problems. His thought is a self-arousal: "If I only had the courage to think all that I know." But, in this limitless reflecting, a deeply satisfying content was revealed which was in fact transcendent.

Thus both leaped toward Transcendence, but to a form of transcendence where practically no one could follow. Kierkegaard leaped to a Christianity which was conceived as an absurd paradox, as decision for utter world negation and martyrdom. Nietzsche leaped to the eternal return and supermen.

Thus the ideas, which were for Nietzsche himself the very deepest, can look empty to us; Kierkegaard's faith can look like a sinister alienation. If one takes the symbols of Nietzsche's religion literally, there is no longer any transcendental content in their will toward immanence: aside from the eternal cycle of things, there is the will of power, the affirmation of Being, the pleasure which "wills deep, deep eternity." Only with circumspection and by taking pains does a more essential content emerge. With Kierkegaard, who revivified the profound formulas of theology, it can seem like the peculiar art of perhaps a nonbeliever, forcing himself to believe.

The similarity of their thought is ever so much more striking precisely because of their apparent differences: the

Christian belief of the one, and the atheism emphasized by the other. In an epoch of reflection, where what had really passed away seemed still to endure, but which actually lived in an absence of faith—rejecting faith and forcing oneself to believe belong together. The godless can appear to be a believer; the believer can appear as godless; both stand in the same dialectic.

What they brought forth in their existential thinking would not have been possible without a complete possession of tradition. Both were brought up with a classical education. Both were nurtured in Christian piety. Their tendencies are unthinkable without Christian origins. If they passionately opposed the stream of this tradition in the form which it had come to assume through the centuries, they also found an historical and, for them, indestructible arrest in these origins. They bound themselves to a basis which fulfilled their own belief: Kierkegaard to a Christianity of the New Testament as he understood it, and Nietzsche to a pre-Socratic Hellenism.

But nowhere is there any final stop for them, neither in finitude, nor in an explicitly grasped basis, nor in a determinately grasped Transcendence, nor in an historical tradition. It is as though their very being, experiencing the abandonment of the age to the end, shattered and, in the shattering itself, manifested a truth which otherwise would never have come to expression. If they won an unheard-of mastery over their own selves, they also were condemned to a worldless loneliness; they were as though pushed out.

Their being as exceptions They were exceptions in every sense. Physically, their development was in retard of their character. Their faces disconcert one because of their relative unobtrusiveness. They do not impress one as types of human greatness. It is as if they both lacked something in sheer vitality. Or as though they were eternally young spirits, wandering through the world, without reality because without any real connection with the world.

Those who knew them felt attracted in an enigmatic way by their presence, as though elevated for a moment to a higher mode of being; but no one really loved them.

In the circumstances of their lives, one finds astonishing and alien features. They have been called simply insane. They would be in fact objects for a psychiatric analysis, if that were not to the prejudice of the singular height of their thought and the nobility of their natures. Indeed, then they would first come to light. But any typical diagnosis or classification would certainly fail.

They cannot be classed under any earlier type (poet, philosopher, prophet, savior, genius). With them, a new form of human reality appears in history. They are, so to speak, representative destinies, sacrifices whose way out of the world leads to experiences for others. They are by the total staking of their whole natures like modern martyrs, which, however, they precisely denied being. Through their character as exceptions, they solved their problem.

Both are irreplaceable, as having dared to be shipwrecked. We orient ourselves by them. Through them we have intimations of something we could never have perceived without such sacrifices, of something that seems essential which even today we cannot adequately grasp. It is as if the Truth itself spoke, bringing an unrest into the depths of our consciousness of being.

Even in the external circumstances of their lives we find astonishing similarities. Both came to a sudden end in their forties. Shortly before, without knowledge of their approaching end, they both made public and passionate attacks: Kierkegaard on church Christianity and on dishonesty, Nietzsche on Christendom itself.

Both made literary reputations in their first publications; but then their new books followed unceasingly, and they had to print what they wrote at their own expense.

They also both had the fate of finding a response which however was without understanding. They were merely sensations in an age when nothing opposed them. The beauty and sparkle of language, the literary and poetic qualities, the aggressiveness of their matter all misled readers from their genuine intentions. Both, toward the end, were almost idolized by those with whom they had the least in common. The age that wanted to surpass itself could, so to speak, wear itself out in ideas casually selected out of them.

The modern world has nourished itself on them precisely in its negligence. Out of their reflection, instead of remaining in the seriousness of endless reflection, it made an instrument for sophistry in irresponsible talk. Their words, like their whole lives, were savored for their great esthetic charm. They dissolved what remained of connections among men, not to lead to the bases of true seriousness, but in order to prepare a free path for caprice. Thus their influence became utterly destructive, contrary to the meaning of their thought and being.

3. *The ways in which they understood themselves: against interchangeability*

Their problem became clearer to them from their youth onward through a continually accompanying reflection. Both of them, at the end and in retrospect, gave us an indication of how they understood themselves through a total interpretation of their work. This interpretation remained convincing to the extent that we, today, in fact understand them as they wished to be understood. All their thought takes on a new sense beyond what is immediately comprehensible in it. This picture itself is inseparable from their work, for the fashion in which they understood themselves is not an accidental addition, but an essential feature of their total thought.

One of the motives in common for the comprehensive expression of their self-understanding is the will not to be mistaken for someone else. This was, they said, one of their deepest concerns, and out of it not only were they always seeking new forms of communication, but also they directly announced the total meaning as it appeared to them at the end. They always worked by all possible means to prepare a correct understanding of their work through the ambiguity of what they said.

Their self-consciousness They both had a clear perception of their epoch, seeing what was going on before them down to the smallest detail with a certitude that was overmastering: it was the end of a mode of life that had hung together for centuries. But they also perceived that no one else saw it, that they had an awareness of their epoch which no one else yet had, but which presently others, and finally all, would have. Thus they necessarily passed into an unprecedented intensity of *self-consciousness*. Their Existenz was in a very special state of affairs. It was not just a simple spiritual superiority which they must have noticed —Kierkegaard over everybody who encountered him, Nietzsche over most—but rather something monstrous which they made themselves into: unique, solitary world-historical destinies.

Their consciousness of failure, of exceptionality, of loneliness But this well-grounded self-consciousness, momentarily expressed and then suppressed again, is always with Kierkegaard moderated through the humility of his Christian attitude and, with both, is tempered by the psychological knowledge of their human failure. The astonishing thing with them again is that the precise mode of their failure is itself the condition of their distinctive greatness. For this greatness is not absolute greatness, but something that uniquely belongs to the situation of the epoch.

It is noteworthy how they both came to the same metaphors for this side of their natures. Nietzsche compared himself to the "scratchings which an unknown power makes on paper, in order to test a new pen." The positive value of his illness is his standing problem. Kierkegaard thought he indeed "would be erased by God's mighty hand, extinguished as an unsuccessful experiment." He felt like a sardine squashed against the sides of a can. The idea came to him that, "in every generation there are two or three who are sacrificed for the others, who discover in frightful suffering what others shall profit by." He felt like an "interjection in speaking, without influence upon the sentence," like a "letter which is printed upside down in the line." He compared himself with the paper notes in the financial crises of 1813, the year in which he was born. "There is something in me which might have been great, but due to the unfavorable market, I'm only worth a little."

Both were conscious of being exceptions. Kierkegaard developed a theory of the exception, through which he understood himself: he loved the universal, the human in men, but as something other, something denied to him. Nietzsche knew himself to be an exception, spoke "in favor of the exception, so long as it never wants to become the rule." He required of the philosopher "that he take care of the rule, since he is the exception."

Thus the last thing either wished was to become exemplary. Kierkegaard looked upon himself as "a sort of trial man." "In the human sense no one can imitate me. . . . I am a man as he could become in a crisis, an experimental rabbit, so to speak, for existence." Nietzsche turned away those who would follow him: "Follow not me, but you!"

This exceptionality, which was as excruciating to them as it was the unique requirement of their problem, they characterized—and here again they agree—as pure mentality, as though they were deprived of any authentic life. Kierkegaard said that he was "in almost every physical respect deprived of the conditions for being a whole man." He had never lived except as mind. He had never been a man: at very most, child and youth. He lacked "the animal side of humanity." His melancholy carried him almost to the "edge of imbecility" and was "something that he could conceal as long as he was independent, but made him useless for any service where he could not himself determine everything." Nietzsche experienced his own pure mentality as "through excess of light, through his radiance, condemned to be, not to love." He expressed it convulsively in the "Nightsong" of Zarathustra: "Light I am; ah! would that I were Night! . . . I live in my own light. . . ."

A terrible loneliness, bound up with their exceptionality, was common to both. Kierkegaard knew that he could have no friends. Nietzsche suffered his own growing loneliness in full consciousness to the limit where he felt he could endure it no longer. Again, the same image comes to both: Nietzsche compared himself to a fir tree on the heights overlooking an abyss: "Lonely! Who dares to be a guest here? Perhaps a bird of prey, gloating in the hair of the branches. . . ." And Kierkegaard: "Like a lonely fir tree, egotistically isolated, looking toward something higher, I stand there, throwing no shadow, only the wood dove building its nest in my branches."

Providence and chance In great contrast to the abandonment, failure, and contingency of their existence was the growing consciousness in the course of their lives of the meaning, sense, and necessity of all that happened to them.

Kierkegaard called it Providence. He recognized the divine in it: "That everything that happens, is said, goes on, and so forth, is portentous: the factual continually changes itself to mean something far higher." The factual for him is not something to abstract oneself from, but rather something to be penetrated until God himself gives the meaning. Even what he himself did became clear only later. It was "the extra which I do not owe to myself but to Providence.

It shows itself continually in such a fashion that even what I do out of the greatest possible conviction, afterwards I understand far better."

Nietzsche called it chance. And he was concerned to use chance. For him "sublime chance" ruled existence. "The man of highest spirituality and power feels himself grown for every chance, but also inside a snowfall of contingencies." But this contingency increasingly took on for Nietzsche a remarkable meaning: "What you call chance—you yourself are that which befalls and astonishes you." Throughout his life, he found intimations of how chance events which were of the greatest importance to him carried a secret meaning, and in the end he wrote: "There is no more chance."

Dancing At the limits of life's possibilities came not any heavy seriousness, but rather a complete lightness as the expression of their knowledge, and both used the image of the dance. In the last decade of his life Nietzsche, in ever-changing forms, used the dance as a metaphor for his thought, where it is original. And Kierkegaard said, "I have trained myself . . . always to be able to dance in the service of thought. . . . My life begins as soon as a difficulty shows up. Then dancing is easy. The thought of death is a nimble dancer. Everybody is too serious for me." Nietzsche saw his archenemy in the "spirit of seriousness" —in morals, science, purposefulness, etc. But to conquer seriousness meant not to reject it for the thoughtlessness of arbitrary caprice, but rather to pass through the most serious to an authentic soaring, the triumph of which is the free dance.

No prophecy The knowledge that they were exceptions prevented either from stepping forth as prophets. To be sure, they seem like those prophets who speak to us out of inaccessible depths but who speak in a contemporary way. Kierkegaard compared himself to a bird which foretells rain: "When in a generation, a thunderstorm begins to threaten, individuals like me appear." They are prophets who must conceal themselves as prophets. They were aware of their problem in a continual return from the extremities of their demands to a rejection of any idea which would make them models or ways of life. Kierkegaard repeated innumerable times that he was not an authority, or a prophet, apostle, or reformer, nor did he have the authority of position. His problem was to awaken men. He had a certain police talent, to be a spy in the service of the divinity. He uncovered, but he did not assert what should be done. Nietzsche wanted to "awaken the highest suspicion against himself," explaining that "to the humanity of a teacher belongs the duty of warning his students against himself." What he wanted he let Zarathustra say who left his disciples with: "Go away from me, and turn yourselves against me." And, even in *Ecce Homo*, Nietzsche says: "And finally, there is nothing in me of the founder of a religion. . . . I want no believers. . . . I have a terrible anxiety that some day, they will speak reverently of me. I will not be a saint, rather a Punch. Maybe I am Punch."

The deed There is in both a confusing polarity between the appearance of an absolute and definite demand and, at the same time, shyness, withdrawal, the appearance of not betting anything. The Seductive, the Perhaps, the Possible is the manner of their discourse; an unreadiness to be a leader was their own attitude. But both lived in secret longing to bring salvation if they could, and if it could be done in human honesty. Accordingly, both toward the end of their lives became daring, desperate, and then, in utter calm, rose to public attack. From then on, the reticence of merely envisaging possibilities was given up for a will to act. Both made a similar attack: Kierkegaard attacked the Christianity of the church; Nietzsche attacked Christendom as such. Both acted with sudden force and merciless resolution. Both attacks were purely negative actions: deeds from truthfulness, not for the construction of a world.

III. MEANING OF THE PHILOSOPHICAL SITUATION PRODUCED BY KIERKEGAARD AND NIETZSCHE

The significance of Kierkegaard and Nietzsche first becomes clear through what followed in consequence. The effect of both is immeasurably great, even greater in general thinking than in technical philosophy, but it is always ambiguous. What Kierkegaard really meant is clear neither in theology, nor in philosophy. Modern Protestant theology in Germany, when it is genuine, seems to stand under either a direct or indirect influence of Kierkegaard. But Kierkegaard with regard to practical consequences of his thought wrote in May, 1855, a pamphlet with the motto, "But at midnight there is a cry" (Matthew 25:6), where he says: "By ceasing to take part in the official worship of God as it now is . . . thou hast one guilt less, . . . thou dost not participate in treating God as a fool, calling it the Christianity of the New Testament, which it is not."

1. *Ambiguity of both*

In modern philosophy several decisive themes have been developed through Kierkegaard. The most essential basic categories of contemporary philosophizing, at least in Germany, go back to Kierkegaard—Kierkegaard whose whole thought however appeared to dissolve all previous systematic philosophy, to reject speculation, and who, when he recognized philosophy, said at most: "Philosophy can pay attention to but cannot nourish us."

It might be that theology, like philosophy, when it follows Kierkegaard is masking something essential in order to use his ideas and formulas for its own totally different purposes.

It might be that within theology there is an unbelief which employs the refined Kierkegaardian intellectual techniques of dialectical paradox to set forth a kind of creed which can be understood, and which believes itself the genuine Christian faith.

It might be that philosophizing in the fashion of Kierkegaard secretly nourishes itself on the substance of Christianity, which it ignores in words.

The significance of Nietzsche is no clearer. His effect in Germany was like that of no other philosopher. But it seems as though every attitude, every world-view, every conviction claims him as authority. It might be that none of us really knows what this thought includes and does.

2. *Their disordering influence*

The problem, therefore, for everyone who allows Kierkegaard and Nietzsche to influence him, is to become honest about how he really comes to terms with them, what they are to him, what he can make out of them.

Their common effect, to enchant and then to disillusion, to seize and then leave one standing unsatisfied as though one's hands and heart were left empty—such is only a clear expression of their own intention: that everything depends upon what their reader by his own inner action makes out of their communication, where there is no specific content as in the special sciences, works of art, philosophical systems, or some accepted prophecy. They deny every satisfaction.

3. *The problem of philosophizing in relation to both*

In fact, they are exceptions and not models for followers. Whenever anyone has tried to imitate Kierkegaard or Nietzsche, if only in style, he has become ridiculous. What they did themselves at moments approaches the limit where the sublime passes into the ridiculous. What they did was only possible once. To be sure, everything great is unique, and can never be repeated identically. But there is something essentially different in our relation to this uniqueness: and this whether we live through them, and, by making them our own, revive them, or see them through the distance of an orientation which changes us but makes them more remote.

They abandon us without giving us any final goals and without posing any definite problems. Through them, each one can only become what he himself is. What their consequences are is not yet decided even today. The question is: how those of us shall live who are not exceptions but who are seeking our inner way in the light of these exceptions.

We are in that cultural situation where the application of this knowledge already contains the kernel of dishonesty. It is as though through them we were forced out of a certain thoughtlessness, which without them would have remained even in the study of great philosophers. We can no longer tranquilly proceed in the continuity of a traditional, intellectual education. For through Kierkegaard and Nietzsche a mode of existential experience has become effective, whose consequences on all sides have not yet come to light. They posed a question which is not yet clear but which one can feel; this question is still open. Through them we have become aware that for us there is no longer any self-evident foundation. There is no longer any secure background for our thought.

For the individual working with them, there are two equally great dangers: really to encounter them and not to take them seriously at all. Unavoidably, one's attitude toward them is ambivalent. Neither constructed a world, and both seemed to have destroyed everything; yet both were positive spirits. We must achieve a distinctively new relation to the creative thinker if we are really to approach them otherwise than we would any great man.

4. *The question: What now?*

With respect to our epoch and the thought of Kierkegaard and Nietzsche, if we pose the question, what now? then Kierkegaard points in the direction of an absurd Christianity before which the world sinks away, and Nietzsche points to the distance, the indeterminate, which does not appear to be a substance out of which we can live. Nobody has accepted their answers; they are not ours. It is for us to see what will become of us through ourselves as we look upon them. This is, however, in no way to sketch out or establish anything in advance.

Thus we would err if we thought we could deduce what must now happen from a world-historical survey of the development of the human spirit. We do not stand outside like a god who can survey the whole at a glance. For us, the present cannot be replaced by some supposed world history out of which our situation and problems would emerge. And this lecture has no intention of surveying the whole, but rather of making the present situation perceptible by reflecting upon the past. Nobody knows where man and his thinking are going. Since existence, man, and his world are not at an end, a completed philosophy is as little possible as an anticipation of the whole. We men have plans with finite ends, but something else always comes out which no one willed. In the same way, philosophizing is an act which works upon the inwardness of man, but whose final meaning he cannot know. Thus the contemporary problem is not to be deduced from some a priori whole; rather it is to be brought to consciousness out of a basis which is now experienced and out of a content still unclearly willed. Philosophy as thought is always a consciousness of Being which is complete for this moment, but which knows it has no final permanence in its form of expression.

5. *The problem we have abstracted from the situation: Reason and Existenz*

Instead of some supposed total view of the actual and cultural situation, rather we philosophize in consciousness of a situation which again leads to the final limits and bases of the human reality. Today, no one can completely and clearly develop the intellectual problems that grow out of such a situation. We live, so to speak, in a seething cauldron of possibilities, continually threatened by confusion, but always ready in spite of everything to rise up again. In philosophizing, we must always be ready, out of the present questioning, to elicit those ideas which bring forth what is real to us: that is, our humanity. These ideas are possible when the horizon remains unlimited, the realities clear, and the real questions manifest. Out of such problems which force themselves upon thought, I have selected one for the next three lectures. The ancient philosophical problem, which appears in the relation of the rational to the non-rational, must be seen in a new light through an appropriation of the tradition with our eyes upon Kierkegaard and Nietzsche.

We formulate this fundamental problem as that of reason and Existenz. This abbreviated formula signifies no antithesis: rather a connection which at the same time points beyond itself.

The words "reason" and "Existenz" are chosen because for us they express in the most penetrating and pure form the problem of the clarification of the dark, the grasping of the bases out of which we live, presupposing no transparency, but demanding the maximum of rationality.

The word "reason" has here its Kantian scope, clarity and truth. The word "Existenz" through Kierkegaard has taken on a sense through which we look into infinite depths at what defies all determinate knowledge. The word is not to be taken in its worn-out sense as one of the many synonyms for "being"; it either means nothing, or is to be taken with its Kierkegaardian claims.

What we shall undertake in the next three lectures may seem to move around other themes. But in common, they shall strive to grasp in the form of logically conceived questions the meaning of what is closest to life. Philosophy. wherever it is successful, consists of those unique ideas in which logical abstractness and the actual present become, so to speak, identical. The basic drives of living philosophy can express themselves truly only in purely formal thought. There are intellectual operations which through comprehension and cooperation can bring about an inner act of the entire man: the bringing forth of oneself out of possibilities in thought so as to apprehend Being in empirical existence.

If my lectures do not come even close to satisfying these

high demands, it is still essential that the ideal of one's concerns be recognized. One can take courage to try to do that which passes beyond his strength from the fact that it is a human problem, and man is that creature which poses problems beyond his powers. And also from this, that whoever even once thought he heard softly the authentic philosophic note can never tire of trying to communicate it.

3. The Encompassing

INTRODUCTION: THE MEANING OF PHILOSOPHICAL LOGIC

One possible way of philosophizing is the movement of philosophical logic in those acts of thought which formally represent the various modes of Being. Since we shall make an initial investigation of this possibility in the three middle lectures, here we shall ignore all concrete philosophizing, that is, the development of particular physical, existential, or metaphysical subjects. Rather we shall be concerned with the horizons and forms within which philosophical contents can be established without deception—horizons which became visible when our humanity was pushed to its very limits by Kierkegaard and Nietzsche.

1. *The question of the Encompassing*

In order to see most clearly into what is true and real, into what is no longer fastened to any particular thing or colored by any particular atmosphere, we must push into the widest range of the possible. And then we experience the following: everything that is an object for us, even though it be the greatest, is still always within another, is not yet all. Wherever we arrive, the horizon which includes the attained itself goes further and forces us to give up any final rest. We can secure no standpoint from which a closed whole of Being would be surveyable, nor any sequence of standpoints through whose totality Being would be given even indirectly.

We always live and think within a horizon. But the very fact that it is a horizon indicates something further which again surrounds the given horizon. From this situation arises the question about the Encompassing. The Encompassing is not a horizon within which every determinate mode of Being and truth emerges for us, but rather that within which every particular horizon is enclosed as in something absolutely comprehensive which is no longer visible as a horizon at all.

2. *The two modes of the Encompassing*

The Encompassing appears and disappears for us in two opposed perspectives: either as Being itself, in and through which we are—or else as the Encompassing which we ourselves are, and in which every mode of Being appears to us. The latter would be as the medium or condition under which all Being appears as Being for us. In neither case is the Encompassing the sum of some provisional kinds of being, a part of whose contents we know, but rather it is the whole as the most extreme, self-supporting ground of Being, whether it is Being in itself, or Being as it is for us.

All of our natural knowledge and dealings with things lies between these final and no longer conditioned bases of encompassing Being. The Encompassing never appears as an object in experience, nor as an explicit theme of thinking, and therefore might seem to be empty. But precisely here is where the possibility for our deepest insight into Being arises, whereas all other knowledge about Being is merely knowledge of particular, individual being.

Knowledge of the many always leads to distraction. One runs into the infinite unless one arbitrarily sets a limit by some unquestioned purpose or contingent interest. And in that case, precisely at these limits, one always runs into bewildering difficulties. Knowledge about the Encompassing would put all the knowable as a whole under such conditions.

3. *Historical reflections on this basic philosophical question*

To seek this Being itself beyond the endlessness of the particular and partial was the first, and is always the new way, of philosophizing. This is what Aristotle meant when he said, "And indeed the question which was raised of old and is raised now and always, and is ever the subject of doubt is, what is Being" (*Metaphysics, 1028b*). Schelling, too, held it to be "the oldest and most correct explanation of what philosophy is . . . that it is the science of Being. But to find what Being is, that is, true Being—that is the difficulty: *hoc opus, hic labor est*" (II, 3, 76). That from the beginning of philosophy up to the present this question continually recurs might arouse confidence in the abiding, fundamental meaning of philosophy throughout its almost endless multiplicities of appearance.

The first difficulty is to understand the question correctly. And the correct understanding of the question shows itself in the answer, shows itself in the degree to which we can appropriate the truth and reject the falsity of historically given questions and answers in their basic and connected meaning. But such a task, in the light of the enormous projects and catastrophes of philosophy, can be accomplished neither through a collection of ideas, nor through forcibly limiting it to some supposedly basic feature to which everything is to be added. We must presuppose a philosophic attitude whose passion for the truth, in a continuing attempt to grasp one's own Existenz, achieves awareness of an unlimited range by continued questioning. In such an unlimited range, the simplicity of the origin may finally be given truly.

Of the two approaches to Being as the Encompassing, the most usual and most natural way for every beginning philosophy is toward Being in itself, conceived as Nature, World, or God. However, we shall approach it from the other, and since Kant unavoidable, way; we shall search into the Encompassing which we are. Although we know, or at least take into account, the fact that the Encompassing which we are is in no wise Being itself, still this can be seen in critical purity only after we have gone to the end of the path opened up by Kant.

I. THE ENCOMPASSING WHICH WE ARE: EMPIRICAL EXISTENCE, CONSCIOUSNESS AS SUCH, SPIRIT

Whether we call the Encompassing which we are our empirical existence, consciousness as such, or spirit, in no case can it be grasped as though it were something in the world which appeared before us. Rather it is that in which all other things appear to us. In general, we do not appropriately cognize it as an object; rather we become aware of it as a limit. This is confirmed when we abandon the determinate, clear—because objective—knowledge which is directed to particular things distinguishable from other things. We should like, so to speak, to stand outside ourselves in order to look and see what we are; but in this supposed looking we are and always remain enclosed within that at which we are looking.

Let us consider for a moment some beginnings from which, by repeated questioning, the Encompassing can be conceived. I am, first of all, an empirical existent. Empirical existence means the actual taken comprehensively, which immediately shows itself to empirical consciousness in the particularities of matter, living body, and soul, but which, as such particularities, is no longer the Encompassing of empirical existence. Everything which is empirically actual for me must in some sense be actual as a part of my being, as, for example, in the continually perceptible presence of my body as it is touched, altered, or as it is perceiving.

Empirical existence, as the overpowering Other which determines me, is the world. The Encompassing of empirical existence which I am when made into an object also becomes something alien like the world. As soon as our empirical existence becomes an object for investigation, we become absorbed into the being of the world which is that incomprehensible Other, Nature. In this fashion we are apprehended only as one sort of being among others, not yet as properly human. Knowledge of the Encompassing of empirical existence with which we are united removes from particular sciences the claim of grasping us as a whole.

Although I can never comprehend my empirical existence as an Encompassing, but only particular empirical forms like matter, life, and soul which I can never reduce back to a single principle, still I stand in the continuous presence of this embracing empirical reality. But even if we know the body, life, the soul, and consciousness merely as they become objectively accessible to us, even here we can, so to speak, see through them all back to that Encompassing of empirical existence with which we are one and which becomes only particularized in every physical, biological, and psychological object, but which, as such, is no longer the Encompassing. Thus the empirical awareness which I have as a living actuality is, as such, not constitutive by itself of that Encompassing which I am as an empirical existent.

The second mode of the Encompassing which I am is consciousness as such. Only what appears to our consciousness as experienceable, as an object, has being for us. What does not appear to consciousness, what can in no wise touch our cognition, is as good as nothing for us. Hence, everything which exists for us must take on that form in which it can be thought or experienced by consciousness. It must in some fashion appear in the form of an object; it must become present through some temporal act of consciousness; it must become articulated and thereby communicable through its thinkability. That all being for us must appear in those forms under which it can enter into consciousness is what imprisons us in the Encompassing of thinkability. But we can make clear its limits and, with this consciousness of limits, become open to the possibility of the Other which we do not know. Consciousness has two meanings however: (i) we are conscious as living existents and, as such, are not yet or no longer encompassing. This consciousness is carried by life itself, the unconscious ground of what we consciously experience. As living existents which we are *in* an absolute Encompassing of empirical existence, we become possible objects of empirical investigation for ourselves. We find ourselves divided into groups of races and into those always particular individualities into which this form of reality divides itself. However, we are not only countless single consciousnesses, which are more or less similar to one another; we are also therein (ii) consciousness as such. Through such consciousness we think we can refer to Being, not only in similar ways of perception and feeling, but in an identical way. Contrasting with empirical consciousness, this is the other sense of consciousness which we are as Encompassing. There is a leap between the multiplicity of subjective consciousness and the universal validity of that true consciousness which can only be *one*. As the consciousness of living beings, we are split into the multiplicity of endless particular realities, imprisoned in the narrowness of the individual and not encompassing. As consciousness in general, we participate in an inactuality, the universally valid truth, and, as such consciousness, are an infinite Encompassing. As a conscious living actuality, we are always a mere kind, even a unique individual enclosed within its own individuality. But we participate in the Encompassing through the possibility of knowledge and through the possibility of common knowledge of Being in every form in which it appears to consciousness. And, indeed, we participate, not only in the validity of the knowable, but also in a universally recognized, formal lawfulness in willing, action, and feeling. So defined, truth is timeless, and our temporal actuality is a more or less complete actualization of this timeless permanence.

216 JASPERS

This sharp separation, however, between the actuality of living consciousness in its temporal process and the inactuality of consciousness in general, as the site of the timeless meaning of the one common truth, is not absolute. Rather it is an abstraction which can be transcended through the clarification of the Encompassing. The actual existence of this timeless meaning insofar as it is something produced, something temporal, which grasps and moves itself, is a new sense of the Encompassing, and this is called spirit.

Spirit is the third mode of the Encompassing which we are. Out of the origins of its being, spirit is the totality of intelligible thought, action, and feeling—a totality which is not a closed object for knowledge but remains Idea. Although spirit is necessarily oriented to the truth of consciousness as such, as well as to the actuality of its Other (Nature as known and used), yet in both directions it is moved by Ideas which bring everything into clarity and connection. Spirit is the comprehensive reality of activity which is actualized by itself and by what it encounters in a world which is always given yet always being changed. It is the process of fusing and reconstructing all totalities in a present which is never finished yet always fulfilled. It is always on its way toward a possible completion of empirical existence where universality, the whole, and every particular would all be members of a totality. Out of a continuously actual and continuously fragmenting whole, it pushes forward, creating again and again out of its contemporary origins its own possible reality. Since it pushes toward the whole, spirit would preserve, enhance, and relate everything to everything else, exclude nothing, and give to everything its place and limits.

Spirit, in contrast to the abstraction of timeless consciousness as such, is again a temporal process, and as such it is comparable to empirical existence. But, as distinguished from this latter, it moves by a reflexivity of knowledge instead of by some merely biologico-psychological process. Understood from within and not capable of being investigated as a natural object, spirit is always directed toward the universality of consciousness as such. Thus it is a grasping of itself, a working upon itself through denial and approval. It produces itself by struggling with itself.

As mere empirical existence and as spirit, we are an encompassing reality. But as empirical existence, we are unconsciously bound to our ultimate bases in matter, life, and the psyche. When we understand ourselves as objects in this horizon, we see ourselves in an infinite, and only from the outside. We become split from one another, and only as thus split are we objects of scientific investigation (as matter, living beings, psyches). But as spirit we are consciously related to everything which is comprehensible to us. We transform the world and ourselves into the intelligible, which encloses totalities. As objects in this mode of the Encompassing, we know ourselves from within as the one, unique, all-embracing reality which is wholly spirit and only spirit.

The distinctions of empirical existence, consciousness as such, and spirit do not imply separable facts. Rather they represent three starting points through which we can come to feel that comprehensive Being which we are and in which all Being and everything scientifically investigable appears.

These three modes taken individually are not yet the Encompassing as we represent it. Consciousness as such, the location of universally valid truth, is in itself nothing independent. On one side, it points to its basis in empirical existence. On the other it points to spirit, the power it must let itself be dominated by if it would attain meaning and totality. In itself, consciousness as such is an unreal articulation of the Encompassing. Through it, the Encompassing is differentiated into those modes according to one of which the Encompassing can become individuated and knowable as empirical natural processes, and, according to the other of which it is understandable, a self-transparent, totalizing reality or Freedom. Empirical existence and spirit produce forms of reality; consciousness as such is the form in which we envisage the Encompassing as the condition of the universally valid and communicable.

II. THE ENCOMPASSING AS BEING ITSELF; WORLD AND TRANSCENDENCE

We pass beyond the Encompassing which we are (empirical existence, consciousness as such, and spirit) when we ask whether this whole is Being itself.

If Being itself is that in which everything that is for us must become present, then it might be thought that this appearance-for-us is in fact all Being. Thus Nietzsche, who conceived all Being as interpretation and our being as interpretative, wanted to reject any further being as an illusory otherworld. But the question does not stop with the limits of our knowledge of things, nor in the inwardness of the limiting consciousness of the Encompassing which we are. Rather this Encompassing which I am and know as empirical existence, consciousness as such, and spirit, is not conceivable in itself but refers beyond itself. The Encompassing which we are is not Being itself, but rather the genuine appearance in the Encompassing of Being itself.

This Being itself which we feel as indicated at the limits, and which therefore is the last thing we reach through questioning from our situation, is in itself the first. It is not made by us, is not interpretation, and is not an object. Rather it itself brings forth our questioning and permits it no rest.

The Encompassing which we are has one of its limits in fact. Even though we create the form of everything that we know, since it must appear to us in those modes according to which it can become an object, yet knowledge can not create the least particle of dust in its empirical existence. In the same way, Being itself is that which shows an immeasurable number of appearances to inquiry, but it itself always recedes and only manifests itself indirectly as that determinate empirical existence we encounter in the progress of our experiences and in the regularity of processes in all their particularity. We call it the World.

The Encompassing which we are has its other limit in the question through which it is. Being itself is the Transcendence which shows itself to no investigative experience, not even indirectly. It is that which as the absolute Encompassing just as certainly "is" as it remains unseen and unknown.

III. EXISTENZ, ANIMATION AND GROUND OF ALL MODES OF THE ENCOMPASSING

Any philosopher who is not lost in the perspective of the conceptual but wishes to push toward genuine Being feels a deep dissatisfaction looking at all the hitherto mentioned modes of the Encompassing. He knows too little in the vast superfluity of apparently immeasurable multiplicities toward which he is directed. He can not find Being itself in all the dimensions of an Encompassing so conceived. He is liberated into a vastness where Being becomes void. The Transcendent seems to be merely an unknowable which makes no difference, and the spirit comes to seem like a sublime whole, but one in which each individual in his deepest inwardness almost seems to have disappeared.

The central point of philosophizing is first reached in the awareness of potential Existenz.

Existenz is the Encompassing, not in the sense of the vastness of a horizon of all horizons, but rather in the sense of a fundamental origin, the condition of selfhood without which all the vastness of Being becomes a desert. Existenz, although never itself becoming an object or form, carries the meaning of every mode of the Encompassing.

While mere empirical existence, consciousness as such, and spirit all appear in the world and become scientifically investigable realities, Existenz is the object of no science. In spite of which, we find here the very axis about which everything in the world turns if it is to have any genuine meaning for us.

At first Existenz seems to be a new narrowing, for it is always merely one among others. It might appear as though the spaciousness of the Encompassing had been contracted into the uniqueness of the individual self which, in contrast to the reality of encompassing spirit, looks like the emptiness of a point. But this contracted point lodged, so to speak, in the body of empirical existence, in this particular consciousness, and in this spirit, is, in fact, the sole possible revelation of the depths of Being as historicity. In all modes of the Encompassing, the self can become genuinely certain of itself only as Existenz.

If we first contrast Existenz with consciousness as such, it becomes the hidden ground in me to which Transcendence is first revealed. The Encompassing which we are exists only in relation to something other than itself. Thus, as I am conscious only insofar as I have something else as an objective being before me by which I then am determined and with which I am concerned, so also I am Existenz only as I know Transcendence as the power through which I genuinely am myself. The Other is either the being which is in the world for consciousness as such, or it is Transcendence for Existenz. This twofold Other first becomes clear through the inwardness of Existenz. Without Existenz the meaning of Transcendence is lost. It remains only something indifferent and not to be known, something supposed to be at the bottom of things, something excogitated, or, perhaps for our animal consciousness, something weird or terrifying plunging it into superstition and anxiety, a subject to be investigated psychologically and removed through a rational insight into the factual by consciousness as such. Only through Existenz can Transcendence become present without superstition, as the genuine reality which to itself never disappears.

Further, Existenz is like the counterpart to spirit. Spirit is the will to become *whole;* potential Existenz is the will to be authentic. Spirit is intelligible throughout, coming to itself in the whole; but Existenz is the unintelligible, standing by and against other Existenzen, breaking up every whole and never reaching any real totality. For spirit, a final transparency would be the origin of Being; Existenz on the other hand remains in all clarity of spirit as the irremediably dark origin. Spirit lets everything disappear and vanish into universality and totality. The individual as spirit is not himself but, so to speak, the unity of contingent individuals and of the necessary universal. Existenz, however, is irreducibly in another; it is the absolutely firm, the irreplaceable, and therefore, as against all mere empirical existence, consciousness as such, and spirit, it is authentic being before Transcendence to which alone it surrenders itself without reservation.

Spirit wants to grasp the individual either as an example of a universal or as a part of a whole. On the other hand, Existenz, as the possibility of decision derivable from no universal validity, is an origin in time, is the individual as historicity. It is the apprehension of timelessness through temporality, not through universal concepts.

Spirit is historical by representing itself in retrospect as a transparent totality. Existenz is historical as eternity in time, as the absolute historicity of its concrete empirical existence in a spiritual opacity which is never removed. But Existenz is not merely this incompletion and perversity in all temporal existence, which, as such, must always expand and change into some spiritual totality, but rather temporal existence thoroughly and authentically penetrated: the paradox of the unity of temporality and eternity.

Spirit in its immediacy is the *potential Idea,* whose universality unfolds into full clarity. Existenz in its immediacy, on the other hand, is its historicity in relation to Transcendence, i.e., the irremovable immediacy of its faith.

The faith of spirit is the life of the universal Idea, where *Thought is Being* ultimately is valid. The faith of Existenz, however, is the Absolute in Existenz itself on which everything for it rests, in which spirit, consciousness as such, and empirical existence are all bound together and decided, where for the first time there is both impulse and goal; here Kierkegaard's proposition, "Faith is Being," applies.

When Existenz understands itself, it is not like my understanding of another, nor the sort of understanding whose contents can be abstracted from the person understanding, nor a sort of looking at; rather it is an origin which itself first arises in its own self-clarification. It is not like sharing in something else, but is at once the understanding and the being of what is understood. It is not understanding through universals, but moves above such understanding in the medium of spirit to become an understanding without any generalization in the absolute present, in deed, in love, and in every form of absolute consciousness. It is the difference between the love of another, which I understand but yet never really understand, and my own love, which I understand because I am that love. Or, in other words, the difference between understanding other things by empathy as process or experience, and understanding myself as unique since I know myself before Transcendence.

When we compare Existenz with consciousness as such, spirit, or any other mode of the Encompassing, the same thing appears: without Existenz everything seems empty, hollowed out, without ground, fake, because everything has turned into endless masks, mere possibilities, or mere empirical existence.

IV. REASON: THE BOND BETWEEN THE VARIOUS MODES OF THE ENCOMPASSING

We have seen as modes of the Encompassing:

a) Being as the Other, which was either World (empirical existence which can be investigated in a universally valid way) or Transcendence (as Being in itself).

b) The Being of the Encompassing which we are, which was either our empirical existence (the still indeterminate, comprehensive actuality), or consciousness as such (the site of all objective and intelligible validities for us), or spirit (the single whole of coherent movement of consciousness as it is activated by Ideas).

But for the source from which all these modes of the Encompassing receive animation and for which they speak, we touched upon Existenz, the dark ground of selfhood, the concealment out of which I come to encounter myself and for which Transcendence first becomes real.

Inextricably bound to Existenz is something else which concerns the connection of all these modes of the Encompassing. This is no new whole, but rather a continuing demand and movement. It is not a mode through which the Encompassing appears, but rather the *bond* which unites all modes of the Encompassing; it is called reason.

There is a question as to what "reason" means in the history of philosophy, how it comprehended itself, what it meant for Kierkegaard and Nietzsche, what they meant when they both trusted and mistrusted it. The clarification of the modes of the Encompassing must go into the ambiguity of what has passed for reason.

If reason means clear, objective thinking, the transformation of the opaque into the transparent, then it is nothing more than the Encompassing of consciousness as such. So considered, it would be better to call it, in accordance with the tradition of German idealism, understanding [Verstand].

If reason means the way to *totalities*, the life of the Idea, then it is the Encompassing of *spirit*.

But if reason means the pre-eminence of thought in all modes of the Encompassing, then more is included than mere thinking. It is then what goes beyond all limits, the omnipresent demand of thought, that not only grasps what is universally valid and is an *ens rationis* in the sense of being a law or principle of order of some process, but also brings to light the Other, stands before the absolutely counter-rational, touching it and bringing it, too, into being. Reason, through the pre-eminence of thought, can bring all the modes of the Encompassing to light by continually transcending limits, without itself being an Encompassing like them. It is, so to speak, like the final authentic Encompassing which continually must withdraw and remain inconceivable except in those modes of the Encompassing in which it moves.

Reason of itself is no source; but, as it is an encompassing bond, it is like a source in which all sources first come to light. It is the unrest which permits acquiescence in nothing;

it forces a break with the immediacy of the unconscious in every mode of the Encompassing which we are. It pushes on continually. But it is also that which can effect the great peace, not the peace of a self-confident rational whole, but that of Being itself opened up to us through reason.

Reason is the inextinguishable impulse to philosophize with whose destruction reason itself is destroyed. This impulse is to achieve reason, to restore reason; it is that reason which always rises clearer from all the deviations and narrowings of so-called "reason" and which can acknowledge the justice of objections to reason and set their limits.

Reason should not get caught within any mode of the Encompassing: not in empirical existence to favor a will-to-exist which in its very narrowness asserts itself purposively yet blindly; nor in consciousness as such in favor of endless validities which are indifferent to us; nor in spirit in favor of a self-enclosed, harmonious totality which can be contemplated but not lived.

Reason is always too little when it is enclosed within final and determinate forms, and it is always too much when it appears as a self-sufficient substitute.

With the rational attitude I desire unlimited clarity; I try to know scientifically, to grasp the empirically real and the compelling validities of the thinkable; but at the same time, I live with an awareness of the limits of scientific penetrability and of clarity in general; however, I push forward from all sources in all modes of the Encompassing toward a universal unfolding of them in thought and reject above all thoughtlessness.

But reason itself is no timeless permanence; it is neither a quiet realm of truth (such as the contents of scientific cognition whose validity does not change although their attainment is an endless and restless movement); nor is it Being itself. Neither is it the mere moment of some chance thought. Rather it is the binding, recollecting, and progressive power whose contents are always derived from its own limits and which passes beyond every one of these limits, expressing perpetual dissatisfaction. It appears in all forms of the modes of the Encompassing yet seems to be nothing itself, a bond which does not rest upon itself but always on something else out of which reason produces both what it itself is and what it can be.

Reason drives toward unity, but it is not satisfied either

with the one level of knowable accuracies for consciousness as such, or with the great effective unities of spirit. It goes along just as well with Existenz where the latter breaks through these unities, and so reason is again present in order to bring Existenzen separated by an abyss of absolute distance together into communication.

Its essence seems to be the universal, that which pushes toward law and order or is identical with it. But it remains a possibility in Existenz even when these fail. Reason is itself still the only thing by and for which the chaos of the negative in its passion for Night preserves its mode of potential Existenz, a reason which otherwise would be surrendered to what is absolutely alien at these extreme limits.

V. REASON AND EXISTENZ

The great poles of our being, which encounter one another in every mode of the Encompassing, are thus reason and Existenz. They are inseparable. Each disappears with the disappearance of the other. Reason should not surrender to Existenz to produce an isolating defiance which resists communication in despair. Existenz should not surrender to reason in favor of a transparency which is substituted for substantial reality.

Existenz only becomes clear through reason; reason only has content through Existenz.

There is an impulse in reason to move out of the immobility and endless triviality of the merely correct into a living bond through the totality of the ideas of the spirit, and out of these toward Existenz as that which supports and first gives authentic being to the spirit.

Reason is oriented toward its Other, toward the content of the Existenz which supports it, which clarifies itself in reason, and which gives decisive impulses to reason. Reason without content would be mere understanding, without any basis as reason. And, as the concepts of the understanding are empty without intuition, so reason is hollow without Existenz. Reason is not itself as mere understanding, but only in the acts of potential Existenz.

But Existenz is also oriented toward an Other. It is related to Transcendence through which it first becomes an independent cause in the world; for Existenz did not create itself. Without Transcendence, Existenz becomes a sterile, loveless, and demonic defiance. Existenz, oriented to reason through whose clarity it first experiences unrest and the appeal of Transcendence, under the needling questioning of reason first comes into its own authentic movement. Without reason, Existenz is inactive, sleeping, and as though not there.

Thus reason and Existenz are not two opposed powers which struggle with one another for victory. Each exists only through the other. They mutually develop one another and find through one another clarity and reality.

Although they never combine into an ultimate whole, every genuine accomplishment is whole only through them.

Reason without Existenz even in the richest possible field finally passes into an indifferent thinking, a merely intellectual movement of consciousness as such, or into a dialectic of the spirit. And as it slips away into intellectual universality without the binding root of its historicity, it ceases to be reason.

Irrational Existenz which rests upon feeling, experiencing, unquestioned impulse, instinct, or whim, ends up as blind violence, and therewith falls under the empirical laws which govern these actual forces. Without historicity, lost in the mere particularities of contingent empirical existence in a self-assertion unrelated to Transcendence, it ceases to be Existenz.

Each without the other loses the genuine continuity of Being and, therefore, the reliability which, although it can not be calculated, is nevertheless appropriate to genuine reason and Existenz. They separate themselves from one another only to become violent powers lacking any communication. In isolation they no longer mean what they should; only formulas without either basis or purpose remain, in a narrowing sphere or empirical existence. There, through a veil of justifications which are no longer true and no longer believed, they are simply the means of expression for mutually destructive empirical existents.

But there is rest nowhere in temporal existence. Rather there is always movement issuing forth from the ultimate substantial ground—movement in the tension between the individual and the universal, between the actual and the total range of the possible, between the unquestionable immediacy of existential faith and the infinite movement of reason.

VI. REFLECTIONS ON THE SIGNIFICANCE OF THE FORM OF THIS BASIC IDEA

After this survey of how we think of the modes of the Encompassing which we are and which Being itself is, and the polarity of reason and Existenz, let us now reflect on what such ideas, formally considered, can and can not mean—ideas whose development has given rise to whole philosophies.

Our knowledge of objects in the world has the form of relating them to one another and deriving them from one another. What appears to us is understood by understanding its relation to something else. But where, in philosophizing, we are concerned with the Encompassing, it is clear that we are dealing with something which can not be understood like some object in the world; more especially, we find that the modes of the Encompassing can not be derived from some particular which appears in them. For example: if we call the Encompassing thought, we can not derive thought itself from anything which can be thought of. Or if the Encompassing is our consciousness, it can not be derived from anything which appears to this consciousness. Or if it is the Whole, it can not be derived from any individual, be it ever so comprehensive. Or if it is empirical existence, then as such it can never be derived from any determinate, objectively known empirical thing. If it is reason, then we can not derive it from the non-rational. Or if it is Existenz, it can not be derived from any mode of the Encompassing, let alone one of its contents. In short, our being can never be derived from anything which appears to us; I myself can never be understood through anything which I encounter.

Just as little can Being in itself be derived from any being which we know. If we call it Being, it can never be derived from the multiplicity of beings. If it is Being in itself, it can never be derived from appearance. If it is Transcendence, we find we can never derive the absolute from the objective, actual, or empirically existent. There always arises in thinking man that which passes beyond everything of which he thinks.

In philosophy there has also been a contrary tendency to deduce from Being as such, as the Encompassing was regarded, the particular things we objectively know—to deduce the whole world, ourselves included, from a philosophically cognized origin, just as we grasp things in the world through their causes. This is again always a radical error which destroys philosophizing itself. For the Encompassing can never be known as a particular something from which other things can be deduced. Every object of thought, be it ever so comprehensive, every conceived whole, every objectively conceived Encompassing, remains as an object merely an individual, for it has other objects outside it and also stands over against us. The Encompassing itself, whether it be the Encompassing which we are or Being in itself, escapes from every determinate objectivity. Insofar as we are that Encompassing, it can only be illuminated; insofar as it is thought of as Being in itself, it is apprehended by inquiry into its infinite appearance; insofar as it speaks as Transcendence it is heard by absolute, historical Existenz.

Therefore, since the Encompassing is in no form known in itself, we can not deduce from it the being which appears to us. That could only occur if the Encompassing were previously known in itself. These false derivations proceed as though they had already cognitively mastered Being itself.

These deductions from one principle, perhaps in the form of a deduction of all categories of the thinkable and of whatever we can encounter in the world, are always merely relative derivations of individual groups in their connections. An exhaustive deduction has never succeeded and never can succeed. The attempt, however, has the value of sharpening our awareness of our limits.

Deductions of actual occurrences from theories of some fundamental reality construct models, but they never succeed in grasping anything except limited realities, mere aspects of empirical existence. They prove themselves to be functions of an endlessly progressive knowing; but they are never what in intention they might well like to be: cognition of the real in itself.

The deduction of the whole world including ourselves from Transcendence (by emanation, evolution, causality, etc.) is imaginary. The idea of creation is the expression of a primal secret, of an inconceivability, the subversion of the question through an uncaused cause.

However the Encompassing is conceived, the idea seems for a moment to achieve stability when it appears as an object for scientific research. This actually occurs in all modes

of the Encompassing. The error lies in trying to secure as a
content for knowledge what is true only as a limit for consciousness and a demand of the self.

The Encompassing in the form of empirical existence, consciousness as such, or spirit becomes an apparent object for
anthropology, psychology, sociology, and the humanistic sciences. These sciences investigate human phenomena in the
world, but in such a fashion that what they grasp is precisely
not the encompassing reality of this kind of being, a reality
which is always present to it even though unrecognized. No
history or sociology of religion has arrived in what they call
religion at that which was the Existenz itself of men. They
can only consider religion according to its factual character,
observe how it emerges into observable reality with a leap
which is incomprehensible. All these sciences push toward
something which is precisely what they can never reach.
They have the fascination of being concerned with something
genuinely relevant, but they deceive if they suppose they
can grasp Being itself through an immanence which deduces
and establishes things. These universal sciences, therefore,
can not consolidate themselves. All their demarcations are
only relative. Individually, they have the form of cutting
across all other sciences. But they never seem to reach their
own proper basis, since the encompassing which they have
before their eyes is no longer the Encompassing. Their magic
is deceptive, but it can become fruitful if there should ensue
a sense of the modest, relative, and open character of our
knowledge of our own appearance in the world.

Both reason and Existenz have a mode of thinking which
awakens them and pushes them toward clarity; to reason belongs philosophical logic, and to Existenz, the clarification of
Existenz.

However, if logic pretends to be a universal science of consciousness as such, it loses its philosophical truth and slips
into a deceptive science of the Whole. In these magnificent
doctrines of categories which unfold themselves out of a single principle, the whole of the Encompassing as the totality
of Being itself in its form, the thought of God before creation
would be penetrated and reproduced. But these investigations have truth only within an open philosophical logic as
an orientation toward the formal possibilities of thought in
its many directions which can only be added together, and
which are valid for objective appearance; but they are end-

less and they lack any thoroughly controlling principle which is supposed to produce them. As the elucidation of reason by itself, logic is philosophy and no longer a supposedly objective cognition of the Whole.

The clarification of Existenz does not cognize Existenz, but makes an appeal to its potentialities. However, as "existentialism," it pretends to be discourse about a known object; and precisely because it should perceive its limits and seek to clarify the absolute ground, it only wanders deeper into error, trying to subsume appearances in the world cognitively and judgmentally under its concepts.

Thus the authentic idea of the Encompassing disappears with every attempt to establish, isolate, and absolutize it. An Encompassing which has become objective is no longer the true Encompassing.

The idea of the Encompassing is rather, so to speak, a subverting idea which removes from us all the natural objectivity of our usual thought. In the world, we are concerned with things, contents, objects, but we never question in all this what we have, think, or will. We assert truths, but do not ask what truth itself is. We have to do with questions about the world, but do not ask about the questioner. Dominated by what is important in action or injury, as by something which is attainable and knowable, we never reach the limits from which this whole world of action, possession, and inquiry would become questionable. On the other hand, the idea of the Encompassing requires of us a recognition of the limits of all that exists for us by giving up the usual cognition of objects. Since it sets limits to objective cognition, it frees the real man and all being which he touches from a supposed identity with its knowability, or fixed knownness. Such thinking vitally encompasses the dead being of the known.

This is a simple thought, but philosophically one of infinitely rich consequences. First, it concerns the thinker himself. I am not authentically myself if I am merely what I know myself to be (in all modes of the schemata of the Ego and their determinations). Whenever I objectify myself, I am myself more than this object, namely, I am that being which can thus objectify itself. All characterizations of my being concern me only insofar as I am turned into an object; but, in such an object, I recognize only one side of myself, or myself in one particular aspect, but not myself. If I understand myself exclusively as an empirical existent, as a living natural being, since I have then objectified myself and conceived myself only insofar as I am an object, I have, at the same time, lost myself and substituted what I understand myself to be for what I can be.

To the being of the Encompassing belongs a self-awareness which sees itself just as much as empirical existence and life, as it achieves a critical limiting awareness of itself as consciousness as such and spirit; but it only becomes fully aware of itself, without the impoverishment which comes from absolutizing some limited aspect and the consequent extinction of its potentialities, as reason and Existenz.

Now if I were to soar beyond and conceive myself to be authentic Being itself, i.e., regard myself as Transcendence over and above mere empirical existence, consciousness, or spirit, I should again lose myself in false self-divinization, and cease to be possible Existenz and its actualization.

That *I am* over against all cognizable empirical existence in the world and, at the same time, am posited in my self-created freedom through Transcendence—to affirm such as the position of man in temporal existence is the task on his small path from which he is constantly tempted to deviate, both in his thinking about himself, and in the actual deeds which are connected therewith.

Secondly, the idea concerns absolutely all known being. I know this Other, just as with myself, only as it appears to me and not as it is in itself. No known being is Being itself. Every time I let Being itself slip into known being, Transcendence disappears and I become dark to myself.

In spite of these continual deviations, we must think about the Encompassing in order to make it really present, at first even in a false specificity, but then, by passing through the whole process of these modes of thinking the Encompassing, we can transcend them and push to their source which is no longer an object.

VII. PHILOSOPHICAL RESULT

The purpose and therefore the meaning of a philosophical idea is not the cognition of an object, but rather an alteration of our consciousness of Being and of our inner attitude toward things.

Understanding the meaning of the Encompassing has the significance of creating a possibility. The philosopher therein says to himself: preserve the open space of the Encompassing! Do not lose yourself in what is merely known! Do not let yourself become separated from Transcendence!

In thinking about temporal existence, one must continually run through the circuit of the modes of the Encompassing. We can remain static in none of its modes. Each demands the others. The loss of one mode lets all the others become false. The philosopher seeks to omit none.

The modes are related to one another. Their tension is not a battle where each seeks to annihilate the others, but rather a mutual enlivening and intensification. Hence the polarity of reason and Existenz must be prevented from being a mutual exclusion; rather, instead of each turning away from the other in hostility, each should grow through mutual questioning.

The relation between the two is not that of flat reciprocity but goes up and down. One can not expect that the higher will be automatically produced by the lower, or that with the lower as a condition, the higher can be depended upon to arise. For the higher has its own proper cause. The higher gives limits and order of rank to the lower without being able, however, to generate it. One should never forget the relation of every mode of the Encompassing to every other and the direction of this relation.

So far, every mode of the Encompassing appears in the light of reason as something relatively dark, and thus there is an external similarity among them in terms of more or less reason. An awareness of this requires that the philosopher not substitute mere vitality for Existenz, or Nature for Transcendence.

The open space of such philosophizing becomes a danger unless one keeps in steady consciousness one's potential Existenz: there is a danger that one may see oneself as lost through abstract thinking on the whole range of things. Genuine thinking about the Encompassing, however, is reflected back from the total range of revealed directions ever so much more decisively onto the concrete historicity of my own present. Now for the first time it is possible to be in the present without disappearing into the restrictions of the unthinking, the blind, and the unrelated. Now also it is possible to grasp the whole spaciousness of Being without losing oneself in the void of the mere universal of the understanding, in the meaningless facticity of empirical existence, or in some empty beyond. For the determinateness of the historical depths is bound up with the openness of unlimited ranges of Being, and the truth of one's own bases with their relation to the ungrounded openness of Being, Existenz with reason. The more unrestrictedly I penetrate by thought into the depths, the truer my love becomes in its historical present. Hölderlin said: "Who has thought about the deepest, loves what is most alive."

Man can seek the path of his truth in unfanatical absoluteness, in a decisiveness which remains open.

NINE

Martin Heidegger: THE QUEST FOR BEING

[*Preface:* Martin Heidegger was born in 1889. His major work, *Sein und Zeit,* appeared in 1927, and the many later printings retain the pagination of the original edition which is also cited in the following essay. Heidegger sometimes cites it as "S. u. Z." (equivalent to *B. & T.,* for *Being and Time*), even as Kant's *Kritik der reinen Vernunft* is often cited as "K. d. r. V."

In 1929 Heidegger published a seventeen-page lecture, *What is Metaphysics?* to which a nine-page postscript was added in 1943. Both have appeared in English, together with three other short pieces and editorial material almost twice the length of the texts (400 pp. in all), under the title *Existence and Being.* "What is Metaphysics" is reprinted here, unabridged, in translation. Next to *Being and Time* this essay is widely acknowledged to be the most important work Heidegger published before World War II. And it is interesting and revealing that he himself has returned to it again and again.

In 1949, Heidegger added a fifteen-page introduction to the fifth printing of his lecture. This introduction is a self-contained essay with a title of its own, "The Way Back into the Ground of Metaphysics," and Heidegger attached the utmost importance to it. He himself selected it for inclusion in the present volume.

The essay, not previously available in English, was translated for this purpose, and Heidegger answered questions, orally and in writing, about the translation of key terms and particularly difficult passages. My rendering of *Sein* as *Being*, of *Seiendes* as *beings*, of *vorstellendes Denken* as *representational thinking*, and of *andenkendes Denken* as *a thinking that recalls*, to give only a few examples, had his full approval; but he did not go over the entire text.

Every attempt was made to make the English version smooth and yet faithful, and the reader should keep in mind that Heidegger's difficulty is almost legendary, and that like Aristotle and Hegel before him, and like Faulkner in our time, he often deliberately defies the idiomatic vernacular, although at other times he appeals to it. Moreover, the "weight" of a word is scarcely less important to him than its meaning. The reader who is not put off by what at first seems strange but reads the essay through should, even at first reading, understand a good deal.

"My Way to Phenomenology," reprinted unabridged in Joan Stambaugh's translation, is a late essay of exceptional interest. It is autobiographical, not at all difficult to read, and throws a great deal of light on Heidegger.]

1. My Way to Phenomenology

My academic studies began in the winter of 1909-10 in theology at the University of Freiburg. But the chief work for the study in theology still left enough time for philosophy which belonged to the curriculum anyhow. Thus both volumes of Husserl's *Logical Investigations* lay on my desk in the theological seminary ever since my first semester there. These volumes belonged to the university library. The date due could be easily renewed again and again. The work was obviously of little interest to the students. But how did it get into this environment so foreign to it?

I had learned from many references in philosophical periodicals that Husserl's thought was determined by Franz Brentano. Ever since 1907, Brentano's dissertation "On the manifold meaning of being since Aristotle" (1862) had been the chief help and guide of my first awkward attempts to penetrate into philosophy. The following question concerned me in a quite vague manner: If being is predicated in manifold meanings, then what is its leading fundamental meaning? What does Being mean? In the last year of my stay at the *Gymnasium*, I stumbled upon the book of Carl Braig, then professor for dogmatics at Freiburg University: "On Being. Outline of Ontology." It had been published in 1896 at the time when he was an associate professor at Freiburg's theological faculty. The larger sections of the work give extensive text passages from Aristotle, Thomas of Aquinas and Suarez, always at the end, and in addition the etymology for fundamental ontological concepts.

From Husserl's *Logical Investigations*, I expected a decisive aid in the questions stimulated by Brentano's dissertation. Yet my efforts were in vain because I was not searching in the right way. I realized this only very much later. Still, I remained so fascinated by Husserl's work that I read in it again and again in the years to follow without gaining sufficient insight into what fascinated me. The spell emanating from the work extended to the outer appearance of the sentence structure and the title page. On that title page I encountered the name of the publisher Max Niemeyer. This encounter is before my eyes as vividly today as then. His name was connected with that of "Phenomenology," then foreign to me, which appears in the subtitle of the second volume. My understanding of the term "phenomenology" was just as limited and vacillating as my knowledge in those years of the publisher Max Niemeyer and his work. Why and how both names—Niemeyer Publishing House and Phenomenology—belong together would soon become clearer.

After four semesters I gave up my theological studies and dedicated myself entirely to philosophy. I still attended theological lectures in the years following 1911, Carl Braig's lecture course on dogmatics. My interest in speculative theology led me to do this, above all the penetrating kind of thinking which this teacher concretely demonstrated in every lecture hour. On a few walks when I was allowed to accompany him, I first heard of Schelling's and Hegel's significance for speculative theology as distinguished from the dogmatic system of Scholasticism. Thus the tension between ontology and speculative theology as the structure of metaphysics entered the field of my search.

Yet at times this realm faded to the background compared with that which Heinrich Rickert treated in his seminars: the two writings of his pupil Emil Lask who was killed as a simple soldier on the Galician front in 1915. Rickert dedicated the third fully revised edition of his work *The Object of Knowledge, Introduction to Transcendental Philosophy*, which was published the same year, "to my dear friend." The dedication was supposed to testify to the teacher's benefit derived from this pupil. Both of Emil Lask's writings—*The Logic of Philosophy and the Doctrine of Categories, A Study of the Dominant Realm of Logical Form* (1911) and *The Doctrine of Judgment* (1912)—themselves showed clearly enough the influence of Husserl's *Logical Investigations*.

These circumstances forced me to delve into Husserl's work anew. However, my repeated beginning also remained unsatisfactory, because I couldn't get over a main difficulty. It concerned the simple question how thinking's manner of procedure which called itself "phenomenology" was to be carried out. What worried me about this question came from the ambiguity which Husserl's work showed at first glance.

The first volume of the work, published in 1900, brings the refutation of psychologism in logic by showing that the doctrine of thought and knowledge cannot be based on psychology. In contrast, the second volume, which was published the following year and was three times as long, contains the description of the acts of consciousness essential for the constitution of knowledge. So it is a psychology after all. What else is section 9 of the fifth investigation concerning "The Meaning of Brentano's Delimitation of 'psychical phenomena' "? Accordingly, Husserl falls back with his phenomenological description of the phenomena of consciousness into the position of psychologism which he had just refuted. But if such a gross error cannot be attributed to Husserl's work, then what is the phenomenological description of the acts of consciousness? Wherein does what is peculiar to phenomenology consist if it is neither logic nor psychology? Does a quite new discipline of philosophy appear here, even one with its own rank and precedence?

I could not disentangle these questions. I remained without knowing what to do or where to go. I could hardly even formulate the questions with the clarity in which they are expressed here.

The year 1913 brought an answer. The *Yearbook for Philosophy and Phenomenological Investigation* which Husserl edited began to be published by the publisher Max Niemeyer. The first volume begins with Husserl's treatise *Ideas*.

"Pure phenomenology" is the "fundamental science" of philosophy which is characterized by that phenomenology. "Pure" means: "transcendental phenomenology." However, the "subjectivity" of the knowing, acting and valuing subject is posited as "transcendental." Both terms, "subjectivity" and transcendental," show that "phenomenology" consciously and decidedly moved into the tradition of modern philosophy but in such a way that "transcendental subjectivity" attains a more original and universal determination through phenomenology. Phenomenology retained "experiences of consciousness" as its thematic realm, but now in the systematically planned and secured investigation of the structure of acts of experience together with the investigation of the objects experienced in those acts with regard to their objectivity.

In this universal project for a phenomenological philosophy, the *Logical Investigations*, too—which had so to speak remained philosophically neutral—could be assigned their systematic place. They were published in the same year (1913) in a second edition by the same publisher. Most of the investigations had in the meantime undergone "profound revisions." The sixth investigation, "the most important with regard to phenomenology" (preface to the second edition) was, however, withheld. But the essay "Philosophy as Exact Science" (1910-11) which Husserl contributed to the first volume of the new journal *Logos* also only now acquired a sufficient basis for its programmatical theses through the *Ideas*.

In virtue of these publications, Niemeyer's work attained the foremost rank of philosophical publishers. At that time the rather obvious idea was current that with "phenomenology" a new school had arisen in European philosophy. Who could have denied the correctness of this statement?

But such historical calculation did not comprehend what had happened in virtue of "phenomenology," that is, already with the *Logical Investigations*. This remained unspoken, and can hardly even be rightly expressed today. Husserl's own programmatical explanations and methodological presentations rather strengthened the misunderstanding that through "phenomenology" a beginning of philosophy was claimed which denied all previous thinking.

Even after the *Ideas* was published, I was still captivated by the never-ceasing spell of the *Logical Investigations.* That magic brought about anew an unrest unaware of its own reason, although it made one suspect that it came from the inability to attain the act of philosophical thinking called "phenomenology" simply by reading the philosophical literature.

My perplexity decreased slowly, my confusion dissolved laboriously, only after I met Husserl personally in his workshop.

Husserl came to Freiburg in 1916 as Heinrich Rickert's successor. Rickert had taken over Windelband's chair in Heidelberg. Husserl's teaching took place in the form of a step-by-step training in phenomenological "seeing" which at the same time demanded that one relinquish the untested use of philosophical knowledge. But it also demanded that one give up introducing the authority of the great thinkers into the conversation. However, the clearer it became to me that the increasing familiarity with phenomenological seeing was fruitful for the interpretation of Aristotle's writing, the less I could separate myself from Aristotle and the other Greek thinkers. Of course I could not immediately see what decisive consequences my renewed occupation with Aristotle was to have.

As I myself practiced phenomenological seeing, teaching and learning in Husserl's proximity after 1919 and at the same time tried out a transformed understanding of Aristotle in a seminar, my interest leaned anew toward the *Logical Investigations,* above all the sixth investigation in the first edition. The distinction which is worked out there between sensuous and categorial intuition revealed itself to me in its scope for the determination of the "manifold meaning of being."

For this reason we—friends and pupils—begged the master again and again to republish the sixth investigation which was then difficult to obtain. True to his dedication to the cause of phenomenology, the publisher Niemeyer published the last chapter of the *Logical Investigations* again in 1922. Husserl notes in the preface: "As things stand, I had to give in to the wishes of the friends of this work and decide to make its last chapter available again in its old form." With the phrase "the friends of this work," Husserl also wanted to say that he himself could not quite get close to the *Logical Investigations* after the publication of the *Ideas.* At the new place of his academic activity, the passion and effort of his thought turned toward the systematic development of the plan presented in the *Ideas* more than ever. Thus Husserl could write in the preface mentioned to the sixth investigation: "My teaching activity in Freiburg, too, furthered the direction of my interest toward general problems and the system."

Thus Husserl watched me in a generous fashion, but at the bottom in disagreement, as I worked on the *Logical Investigations* every week in special seminars with advanced students in addition to my lectures and regular seminars. Especially the preparation for this work was fruitful for me. There I learned one thing—at first rather led by surmise than guided by founded insight: What occurs for the phenomenology of the acts of consciousness as the self-manifestation of phenomena is thought more originally by Aristotle and in all Greek thinking and existence as *aletheia*, as the unconcealedness of what-is present, its being revealed, its showing itself. That which phenomenological investigations rediscovered as the supporting attitude of thought proves to be the fundamental trait of Greek thinking, if not indeed of philosophy as such.

The more decisively this insight became clear to me, the more pressing the question became: Whence and how is it determined what must be experienced as "the things themselves" in accordance with the principle of phenomenology? Is it consciousness and its objectivity or is it the Being of beings in its unconcealedness and concealment?

Thus I was brought to the path of the question of Being, illumined by the phenomenological attitude, again made uneasy in a different way than previously by the questions prompted by Brentano's dissertation. But the path of questioning became longer than I suspected. It demanded many stops, detours and wrong paths. What the first lectures in Freiburg and then in Marburg attempted shows the path only indirectly.

"Professor Heidegger—you have got to publish something now. Do you have a manuscript?" With these words the dean of the philosophical faculty in Marburg came into my study one day in the winter semester of 1925-26. "Certainly," I answered. Then the dean said: "But it must be printed quickly." The faculty proposed me *unico loco* as Nicolai Hartmann's successor for the chief philosophical chair. Meanwhile, the ministry in Berlin had rejected the proposal with the explanation that I had not published anything in the last ten years.

Now I had to submit my closely protected work to the

public. On account of Husserl's intervention, the publishing house Max Niemeyer was ready to print immediately the first fifteen proof sheets of the work which was to appear in Husserl's *Jahrbuch*. Two copies of the finished page proofs were sent to the ministry by the faculty right away. But after some time, they were returned to the faculty with the remark: "Inadequate." In February of the following year (1927), the complete text of *Being and Time* was published in the eighth volume of the *Jahrbuch* and as a separate publication. After that the ministry reversed its negative judgment half a year later and made the offer for the chair.

On the occasion of the strange publication of *Being and Time*, I came first into direct relationship with the publishing house Max Niemeyer. What was a mere name on the title page of Husserl's fascinating work during the first semester of my academic studies became evident now and in the future in all the thoroughness and reliability, generosity and simplicity, of publication work.

In the summer of 1928, during my last semester in Marburg, the *Festschrift* for Husserl's seventieth birthday was in preparation. At the beginning of this semester Max Scheler died unexpectedly. He was one of the co-editors of Husserl's *Jahrbuch* where he published his great investigation *Formalism in Ethics and Material Ethics of Value* in the first and second volume (1916). Along with Husserl's *Ideas,* it must count as the most significant contribution to the *Jahrbuch*. Through its far-reaching effects, it placed the scope and effectiveness of the Niemeyer publishing house in a new light.

The *Festschrift* for Edmund Husserl appeared punctually for his birthday as a supplement to the *Jahrbuch*. I had the honor of presenting it to the celebrated teacher within a circle of his pupils and friends on April 8, 1929.

During the following decade all more extensive publications were withheld until the publishing house Niemeyer dared to print my interpretation of Hölderlin's hymn "As on a Holiday" in 1941 without giving the year of publication. I had given this lecture in May of the same year as a public guest lecture at the university of Leipzig. The owner of the publishing house, Mr. Hermann Niemeyer, had come from Halle to hear this lecture. Afterward we discussed the publication.

When I decided twelve years later to publish earlier lecture series, I chose the Niemeyer publishing house for this purpose.

It no longer bore the designation "Halle a.d. Saale." Following great losses and manifold difficulties, and visited by hard personal suffering, the present owner had re-established the firm in Tübingen.

"Halle a.d. Saale"—in the same city, the former *Privat-dozent* Edmund Husserl taught during the '90's of the last century at that university. Later in Freiburg, he often told the story of how the *Logical Investigations* came to be. He never forgot to remember the Max Niemeyer publishing house with gratitude and admiration, the house which took upon itself the venture of publishing, at the turn of the century, an extensive work of a little-known instructor who went his own new ways and thus had to estrange contemporary philosophy, which ignored the work for years after its appearance, until Wilhelm Dilthey recognized its significance. The publishing house could not know at that time that his name would remain tied to that of phenomenology in the future, that phenomenology would soon determine the spirit of the age in the most various realms—mostly in a tacit manner.

And today? The age of phenomenological philosophy seems to be over. It is already taken as something past which is only recorded historically along with other schools of philosophy. But in what is most its own phenomenology is not a school. It is the possibility of thinking, at times changing and only thus persisting, of corresponding to the claim of what is to be thought. If phenomenology is thus experienced and retained, it can disappear as a designation in favor of the matter of thinking whose manifestness remains a mystery.

Supplement 1969

In the sense of the last sentence, one can already read in *Being and Time* (1927) pp. 62-63: "its (phenomenology's) essential character does not consist in being *actual* as a philosophical school. Higher than actuality stands *possibility*. The comprehension of phenomenology consists solely in grasping it as possibility."

2. What is Metaphysics?

"What is metaphysics?" The question leads one to expect a discussion about metaphysics. Such is not our intention. Instead, we shall discuss a definite metaphysical question, thus, as it will appear, landing ourselves straight into metaphysics. Only in this way can we make it really possible for metaphysics to speak for itself.

Our project begins with the presentation of a metaphysical question, then goes on to its development and ends with its answer.

THE PRESENTATION OF A METAPHYSICAL QUESTION

Seen from the point of view of sound common sense, Philosophy, according to Hegel, is the "world stood on its head." Hence the peculiar nature of our task calls for some preliminary definition. This arises out of the dual nature of metaphysical questioning.

Firstly, every metaphysical question always covers the whole range of metaphysical problems. In every case it is itself the whole. Secondly, every metaphysical question can only be put in such a way that the questioner as such is by his very questioning involved in the question.

From this we derive the following pointer: metaphysical questioning has to be put as a whole and has always to be based on the essential situation of existence, which puts the question. We question here and now, on our own account. Our existence—a community of scientists, teachers and students—is ruled by science. What essential things are happening to us in the foundations of our existence, now that science has become our passion?

The fields of the sciences lie far apart. Their methodologies are fundamentally different. This disrupted multiplicity of disciplines is today only held together by the technical organisation of the Universities and their faculties, and maintained as a unit of meaning by the practical aims of those faculties. As against this, however, the root of the sciences in their essential ground has atrophied.

And yet—insofar as we follow their most specific intentions —in all the sciences we are related to what-is. Precisely from the point of view of the sciences no field takes precedence over another, neither Nature over History nor vice versa. No one methodology is superior to another. Mathematical knowledge is no stricter than philological or historical knowledge. It has merely the characteristic of "exactness," which is not to be identified with strictness. To demand exactitude of history would be to offend against the idea of the kind of strictness that pertains to the humanistic sciences. The world-relationship which runs through all the sciences as such constrains them to seek what-is *in itself,* with a view to rendering it, according to its quiddity (*Wasgehalt*) and its modality (*Seinsart*), an object of investigation and basic definition. What the sciences accomplish, ideally speaking, is an approximation to the essential nature of all things.

This distinct world-relationship to what-is in itself is sustained and guided by a freely chosen attitude on the part of our human existence. It is true that the pre-scientific and extra-scientific activities of man also relate to what-is. But the distinction of science lies in the fact that, in an altogether specific manner, it and it alone explicitly allows the object itself the first and last word. In this objectivity of questioning, definition and proof there is a certain limited submission to what-is, so that this may reveal itself. This submissive attitude taken up by scientific theory becomes the basis of a possibility: the possibility of science acquiring a leadership of its own, albeit limited, in the whole field of human existence. The world-relationship of science and the attitude of man responsible for it can, of course, only be fully understood when we see and understand what is going on in the world-relationship so maintained. Man—one entity (*Seiendes*) among others— "pursues" science. In this "pursuit" what is happening is nothing less than the irruption of a particular entity called "Man" into the whole of what-is, in such a way that in and through this irruption what-is manifests itself *as* and *how* it is. The manner in which the revelatory irruption occurs is the chief thing that helps what-is to become what it is.

This triple process of world-relationship, attitude, and irruption—a radical unity—introduces something of the inspiring simplicity and intensity of *Da-sein* into scientfic existence. If we now explicitly take possession of scientific *Da-sein* as clarified by us, we must necessarily say:

That to which the world-relationship refers is what-is—and nothing else.

That by which every attitude is moulded is what-is—and nothing more.

That with which scientific exposition effects its "irruption" is what-is—and beyond that, nothing.

But is it not remarkable that precisely at that point where scientific man makes sure of his surest possession he should speak of something else? What is to be investigated is what-is—and nothing else; only what-is—and nothing more; simply and solely what-is—and beyond that, nothing.

But what about this "nothing"? Is it only an accident that we speak like that quite naturally? Is it only a manner of speaking—and nothing more?

But why worry about this Nothing? "Nothing" is absolutely rejected by science and abandoned as null and void (*das Nichtige*). But if we abandon Nothing in this way are we not, by that act, really admitting it? Can we, though, speak of an admission when we admit Nothing? But perhaps this sort of cross-talk is already degenerating into an empty wrangling about words.

Science, on the other hand, has to assert its soberness and seriousness afresh and declare that it is concerned solely with what-is. Nothing—how can it be for science anything other than a horror and a phantasm? If science is right then one thing stands firm: science wishes to know nothing of Nothing. Such is after all the strictly scientific approach to Nothing. We know it by wishing to know nothing of Nothing.

Science wishes to know nothing of Nothing. Even so the fact remains that at the very point where science tries to put its own essence in words it invokes the aid of Nothing. It has recourse to the very thing it rejects. What sort of schizophrenia is this?

A consideration of our momentary existence as one ruled by science has landed us in the thick of an argument. In the course of this argument a question has already presented itself. The question only requires putting specifically: What about Nothing?

THE DEVELOPMENT OF THE QUESTION

The development of our enquiry into Nothing is bound to lead us to a position where either the answer will prove possible or the impossibility of an answer will become evident. "Nothing" is admitted. Science, by adopting an attitude of superior indifference, abandons it as that which "is not."

All the same we shall endeavour to enquire into Nothing. What is Nothing? Even the initial approach to this question shows us something out of the ordinary. So questioning, we postulate Nothing as something that somehow or other "is"— as an entity (*Seiendes*). But it is nothing of the sort. The question as to the what and wherefore of Nothing turns the thing questioned into its opposite. The question deprives itself of its own object.

Accordingly, every answer to this question is impossible from the start. For it necessarily moves in the form that Nothing "is" this, that or the other. Question and answer are equally nonsensical in themselves where Nothing is concerned.

Hence even the rejection by science is superfluous. The commonly cited basic rule of all thinking—the proposition that contradiction must be avoided—and common "logic" rule out the question. For thinking, which is essentially always thinking about something, would, in thinking of Nothing, be forced to act against its own nature.

Because we continually meet with failure as soon as we try to turn Nothing into a subject, our enquiry into Nothing is already at an end—always assuming, of course, that in this enquiry "logic" is the highest court of appeal, that reason is the means and thinking the way to an original comprehension of Nothing and its possible revelation.

But, it may be asked, can the law of "logic" be assailed? Is not reason indeed the master in this enquiry into Nothing? It is in fact only with reason's help that we can define Nothing in the first place and postulate it as a problem—though a problem that consumes only itself. For Nothing is the negation (*Verneinung*) of the totality of what-is: that which is absolutely not. But at this point we bring Nothing into the higher category of the Negative (*Nichthaftes*) and therefore of what is negated. But according to the overriding and unassailable teachings of "logic" negation is a specific act of reason. How,

then, in our enquiry into Nothing and into the very possibility
of holding such an enquiry can we dismiss reason? Yet is it so
sure just what we are postulating? Does the Not (*das Nicht*),
the state of being negated (*die Verneintheit*) and hence negation itself (*Verneinung*), in fact represent that higher category
under which Nothing takes its place as a special kind of thing
negated? Does Nothing "exist" only because the Not, i.e.
negation exists? Or is it the other way about? Does negation
and the Not exist only because Nothing exists? This has not
been decided—indeed, it has not even been explicitly asked.
We assert: "Nothing" is more original than the Not and
negation.

If this thesis is correct then the very possibility of negation
as an act of reason, and consequently reason itself, are somehow dependent on Nothing. How, then, can reason attempt
to decide this issue? May not the apparent nonsensicality of
the question and answer where Nothing is concerned only rest,
perhaps, on the blind obstinacy of the roving intellect?

If, however, we refuse to be led astray by the formal impossibility of an enquiry into Nothing and still continue to
enquire in the face of it, we must at least satisfy what remains
the fundamental pre-requisite for the full pursuit of any enquiry. If Nothing as such is still to be enquired into, it follows
that it must be "given" in advance. We must be able to
encounter it.

Where shall we seek Nothing? Where shall we find Nothing?
In order to find something must we not know beforehand that
it is there? Indeed we must! First and foremost we can only
look if we have pre-supposed the presence of a thing to be
looked for. But here the thing we are looking for is Nothing.
Is there after all a seeking without pre-supposition, a seeking
complemented by a pure finding?

However that may be, we do know "Nothing" if only as a
term we bandy about every day. This ordinary hackneyed
Nothing, so completely taken for granted and rolling off our
tongue so casually—we can even give an off-hand "definition"
of it:

Nothing is the complete negation of the totality of what-is.

Does not this characteristic of Nothing point, after all, in
the direction from which alone it may meet us?

The totality of what-is must be given beforehand so as to

succumb as such to the negation from which Nothing is then bound to emerge.

But, even apart from the questionableness of this relationship between negation and Nothing, how are we, as finite beings, to render the whole of what-is in its totality accessible *in itself*—let alone to ourselves? We can, at a pinch, think of the whole of what-is as an "idea" and then negate what we have thus imagined in our thoughts and "think" it negated. In this way we arrive at the formal concept of an imaginary Nothing, but never Nothing itself. But Nothing is nothing, and between the imaginary and the "authentic" (*eigentlich*) Nothing no difference can obtain, if Nothing represents complete lack of differentiation. But the "authentic" Nothing—is this not once again that latent and nonsensical idea of a Nothing that "is"? Once again and for the last time rational objections have tried to hold up our search, whose legitimacy can only be attested by a searching experience of Nothing.

As certainly as we shall never comprehend absolutely the totality of what-is, it is equally certain that we find ourselves placed in the midst of what-is and that this is somehow revealed in totality. Ultimately there is an essential difference between comprehending the totality of what-is and finding ourselves in the midst of what-is-in-totality. The former is absolutely impossible. The latter is going on in existence all the time.

Naturally enough it looks as if, in our everyday activities, we were always holding on to this or that actuality (*Seiendes*), as if we were lost in this or that region of what-is. However fragmentary the daily round may appear it still maintains what-is, in however shadowy a fashion, within the unity of a "whole." Even when, or rather, precisely when we are not absorbed in things or in our own selves, this "wholeness" comes over us—for example, in real boredom. Real boredom is still far off when this book or that play, this activity or that stretch of idleness merely bores us. Real boredom comes when "one is bored." This profound boredom, drifting hither and thither in the abysses of existence like a mute fog, draws all things, all men and oneself along with them, together in a queer kind of indifference. This boredom reveals what-is in totality.

There is another possibility of such revelation, and this is in the joy we feel in the presence of the being—not merely the person—of someone we love.

Because of these moods in which, as we say, we "are" this or that (i.e. bored, happy, etc.) we find ourselves (*befinden uns*) in the midst of what-is-in-totality, wholly pervaded by it. The affective state in which we find ourselves not only discloses, according to the mood we are in, what-is in totality, but this disclosure is at the same time far from being a mere chance occurrence and is the ground-phenomenon of our *Da-sein*.

Our "feelings," as we call them, are not just the fleeting concomitant of our mental or volitional behaviour, nor are they simply the cause and occasion of such behaviour, nor yet a state that is merely "there" and in which we come to some kind of understanding with ourselves.

Yet, at the very moment when our moods thus bring us face to face with what-is-in-totality they hide the Nothing we are seeking. We are now less than ever of the opinion that mere negation of what-is-in-totality as revealed by these moods of ours can in fact lead us to Nothing. This could only happen in the first place in a mood so peculiarly revelatory in its import as to reveal Nothing itself.

Does there ever occur in human existence a mood of this kind, through which we are brought face to face with Nothing itself?

This may and actually does occur, albeit rather seldom and for moments only, in the key-mood of dread (*Angst*). By "dread" we do not mean "anxiety" (*Aengstlichkeit*), which is common enough and is akin to nervousness (*Furchtsamkeit*) —a mood that comes over us only too easily. Dread differs absolutely from fear (*Furcht*). We are always *afraid* of this or that definite thing, which threatens us in this or that definite way. "Fear of" is generally "fear about" something. Since fear has this characteristic limitation—"of" and "about"—the man who is afraid, the nervous man, is always bound by the thing he is afraid of or by the state in which he finds himself. In his efforts to save himself from this "something" he becomes uncertain in relation to other things; in fact, he "loses his bearings" generally.

In dread no such confusion can occur. It would be truer to say that dread is pervaded by a peculiar kind of peace. And although dread is always "dread of," it is not dread of this or that. "Dread of" is always a dreadful feeling "about"—

but not about this or that. The indefiniteness of *what* we dread is not just lack of definition: it represents the essential impossibility of defining the "what." The indefiniteness is brought out in an illustration familiar to everybody.

In dread, as we say, "one feels something uncanny."[1] What is this "something" (*es*) and this "one"? We are unable to say what gives "one" that uncanny feeling. "One" just feels it generally (*im Ganzen*). All things, and we with them, sink into a sort of indifference. But not in the sense that everything simply disappears; rather, in the very act of drawing away from us everything turns towards us. This withdrawal of what-is-in-totality, which then crowds round us in dread, this is what oppresses us. There is nothing to hold on to. The only thing that remains and overwhelms us whilst what-is slips away, is this "nothing."

Dread reveals Nothing.

In dread we are "in suspense" (*wir schweben*). Or, to put it more precisely, dread holds us in suspense because it makes what-is-in-totality slip away from us. Hence we too, as existents in the midst of what-is, slip away from ourselves along with it. For this reason it is not "you" or "I" that has the uncanny feeling, but "one." In the trepidation of this suspense where there is nothing to hold on to, pure *Da-sein* is all that remains.

Dread strikes us dumb. Because what-is-in-totality slips away and thus forces Nothing to the fore, all affirmation (lit. "Is"-saying: *"Ist"-Sagen*) fails in the face of it. The fact that when we are caught in the uncanniness of dread we often try to break the empty silence by words spoken at random, only proves the presence of Nothing. We ourselves confirm that dread reveals Nothing—when we have got over our dread. In the lucid vision which supervenes while yet the experience is fresh in our memory we must needs say that what we were afraid of was "actually" (*eigentlich*: also "authentic") Nothing. And indeed Nothing itself, Nothing as such, was there.

With this key-mood of dread, therefore, we have reached that event in our *Da-sein* which reveals Nothing, and which must therefore be the starting-point of our enquiry.

What about Nothing?

THE ANSWER TO THE QUESTION

The answer which alone is important for our purpose has already been found if we take care to ensure that we really do keep to the problem of Nothing. This necessitates changing man into his *Da-sein*—a change always occasioned in us by dread—so that we may apprehend Nothing as and how it reveals itself in dread. At the same time we have finally to dismiss those characteristics of Nothing which have not emerged as a result of our enquiry.

"Nothing" is revealed in dread, but not as something that "is." Neither can it be taken as an object. Dread is not an apprehension of Nothing. All the same, Nothing is revealed in and through dread, yet not, again, in the sense that Nothing appears as if detached and apart from what-is-in-totality when we have that "uncanny" feeling. We would say rather: in dread Nothing functions as if *at one with* what-is-in-totality. What do we mean by "at one with"?

In dread what-is-in-totality becomes untenable (*hinfällig*). How? What-is is not annihilated (*vernichtet*) by dread, so as to leave Nothing over. How could it, seeing that dread finds itself completely powerless in face of what-is-in-totality! What rather happens is that Nothing shows itself as essentially belonging to what-is while this is slipping away in totality.

In dread there is no annihilation of the whole of what-is in itself; but equally we cannot negate what-is-in-totality in order to reach Nothing. Apart from the fact that the explicitness of a negative statement is foreign to the nature of dread as such, we would always come too late with any such negation intended to demonstrate Nothing. For Nothing is anterior to it. As we said, Nothing is "at one with" what-is as this slips away in totality.

In dread there is a retreat from something, though it is not so much a flight as a spell-bound (*gebannt*) peace. This "retreat from" has its source in Nothing. The latter does not attract: its nature is to repel. This "repelling from itself" is essentially an "expelling into": a conscious gradual relegation to the vanishing what-is-in-totality (*das entgleitenlassende Verweisen auf das versinkende Seiende im Ganzen*). And this total relegation to the vanishing what-is-in-totality—such being the form in which Nothing crowds round us in dread—is the essence of Nothing: nihilation.[2] Nihilation is neither an annihilation (*Vernichtung*) of what-is, nor does it spring from negation (*Verneinung*). Nihilation cannot be reckoned in terms of annihilation or negation at all. Nothing "nihilates" (*nichtet*) of itself.

Nihilation is not a fortuitous event; but, understood as the relegation to the vanishing what-is-in-totality, it reveals the latter in all its till now undisclosed strangeness as the pure "Other"—contrasted with Nothing.

Only in the clear night of dread's Nothingness is what-is as such revealed in all its original overtness (*Offenheit*): that it "is" and is not Nothing. This verbal appendix "and not Nothing" is, however, not an *a posteriori* explanation but an *a priori* which alone makes possible any revelation of what-is. The essence of Nothing as original nihilation lies in this: that it alone brings *Da-sein* face to face with what-is as such.

Only on the basis of the original manifestness of Nothing can our human *Da-sein* advance towards and enter into what-is. But insofar as *Da-sein* naturally relates to what-is, as that which it is not and which itself is, Da-sein *qua Da-sein* always proceeds from Nothing as manifest.[3]

Da-sein means *being projected into* Nothing (*Hineingehaltenheit in das Nichts*).

Projecting into Nothing, *Da-sein* is already beyond what-is-in-totality. This "being beyond" (*Hinaussein*) what-is we call Transcendence. Were *Da-sein* not, in its essential basis, transcendent, that is to say, were it not projected from the start into Nothing, it could never relate to what-is, hence could have no self-relationship.

Without the original manifest character of Nothing there is no self-hood and no freedom.

Here we have the answer to our question about Nothing. Nothing is neither an object nor anything that "is" at all. Nothing occurs neither by itself nor "apart from" what-is, as a sort of adjunct. Nothing is that which makes the revelation of what-is as such possible for our human existence. Nothing not merely provides the conceptual opposite of what-is but is also an original part of essence (*Wesen*). It is in the Being (*Sein*) of what-is that the nihilation of Nothing (*das Nichten des Nichts*) occurs.

But now we must voice a suspicion which has been withheld far too long already. If it is only through "projecting into

Nothing" that our *Da-sein* relates to what-is, in other words, has any existence, and if Nothing is only made manifest originally in dread, should we not have to be in a continual suspense of dread in order to exist at all? Have we not, however, ourselves admitted that this original dread is a rare thing? But above all, we all exist and are related to actualities which we ourselves are not and which we ourselves are—without this dread. Is not this dread, therefore, an arbitrary invention and the Nothing attributed to it an exaggeration?

Yet what do we mean when we say that this original dread only occurs in rare moments? Nothing but this: that as far as we are concerned and, indeed, generally speaking, Nothing is always distorted out of its original state. By what? By the fact that in one way or another we completely lose ourselves in what-is. The more we turn to what-is in our dealings the less we allow it to slip away, and the more we turn aside from Nothing. But all the more certainly do we thrust ourselves into the open superficies of existence.

And yet this perpetual if ambiguous aversion from Nothing accords, within certain limits, with the essential meaning of Nothing. It—Nothing in the sense of nihilation—relegates us to what-is. Nothing "nihilates" unceasingly, without our really knowing what is happening—at least, not with our everyday knowledge.

What could provide more telling evidence of the perpetual, far-reaching and yet ever-dissimulated overtness of Nothing in our existence, than negation? This is supposed to belong to the very nature of human thought. But negation cannot by any stretch of imagination produce the Not out of itself as a means of distinguishing and contrasting given things, thrusting this Not between them, as it were. How indeed could negation produce the Not out of itself, seeing that it can only negate when something is there to be negated? But how can a thing that is or ought to be negated be seen as something negative (*nichthaft*) unless all thinking as such is on the look-out for the Not? But the Not can only manifest itself when its source—the nihilation of Nothing and hence Nothing itself—is drawn out of concealment. The Not does not come into being through negation, but negation is based on the Not, which derives from the nihilation of Nothing. Nor is negation only a mode of nihilating behaviour, i.e. behaviour based *a priori* on the nihilation of Nothing.

Herewith we have proved the above thesis in all essentials: Nothing is the source of negation, not the other way about. If this breaks the sovereignty of reason in the field of enquiry into Nothing and Being, then the fate of the rule of "logic" in philosophy is also decided. The very idea of "logic" disintegrates in the vortex of a more original questioning.

However often and however variously negation—whether explicit or not—permeates all thinking, it cannot *of itself* be a completely valid witness to the manifestation of Nothing as an essential part of *Da-sein*. For negation cannot be cited either as the sole or even the chief mode of nihilation, with which, because of the nihilation of Nothing, *Da-sein* is saturated. More abysmal than the mere propriety of rational negation is the harshness of opposition and the violence of loathing. More responsible the pain of refusal and the mercilessness of an interdict. More oppressive the bitterness of renunciation.

These possible modes of nihilating behaviour, through which our *Da-sein* endures, even if it does not master, the fact of our being thrown upon the world[4] are not modes of negation merely. That does not prevent them from expressing themselves in and through negation. Indeed, it is only then that the empty expanse of negation is really revealed. The permeation of *Da-sein* by nihilating modes of behavior points to the perpetual, ever-dissimulated manifestness of Nothing, which only dread reveals in all its originality. Here, of course, we have the reason why original dread is generally repressed in *Da-sein*. Dread is there, but sleeping. All *Da-sein* quivers with its breathing: the pulsation is slightest in beings that are timorous, and is imperceptible in the "Yea, yea!" and "Nay, nay!" of busy people; it is readiest in the reserved, and surest of all in the courageous. But this last pulsation only occurs for the sake of that for which it expends itself, so as to safeguard the supreme greatness of *Da-sein*.

The dread felt by the courageous cannot be contrasted with the joy or even the comfortable enjoyment of a peaceable life. It stands—on the hither side of all such contrasts—in secret union with the serenity and gentleness of creative longing.

Original dread can be awakened in *Da-sein* at any time. It need not be awakened by any unusual occurrence. Its action corresponds in depth to the shallowness of its possible cause. It is always on the brink, yet only seldom does it take the leap and drag us with it into the state of suspense.

Because our *Da-sein* projects into Nothing on this basis of hidden dread, man becomes the "stand-in" (*Platzhalter*) for Nothing. So finite are we that we cannot, of our own resolution and will, bring ourselves originally face to face with Nothing. So bottomlessly does finalisation (*Verendlichung*) dig into existence that our freedom's peculiar and profoundest finality fails.

This projection into Nothing on the basis of hidden dread is the overcoming of what-is-in-totality: Transcendence.

Our enquiry into Nothing will, we said, lead us straight to metaphysics. The name "metaphysics" derives from the Greek τὰ μετὰ τὰ φυσικὰ. This quaint title was later interpreted as characterising the sort of enquiry which goes μετὰ—trans, beyond—what-is as such.

Metaphysics is an enquiry over and above what-is, with a view to winning it back again as such and in totality for our understanding.

In our quest for Nothing there is similar "going beyond" what-is, conceived as what-is-in-totality. It therefore turns out to be a "metaphysical" question. We said in the beginning that such questioning had a double characteristic: every metaphysical question at once embraces the whole of metaphysics, and in every question the being (*Da-sein*) that questions is himself caught up in the question.

To what extent does the question about Nothing span and pervade the whole of metaphysics?

Since ancient times metaphysics has expressed itself on the subject of Nothing in the highly ambiguous proposition: *ex nihilo nihil fit*—nothing comes from nothing. Even though the proposition as argued never made Nothing itself the real problem, it nevertheless brought out very explicitly, from the prevailing notions about Nothing, the over-riding fundamental concept of what-is.

Classical metaphysics conceives Nothing as signifying Not-being (*Nichtseiendes*), that is to say, unformed matter which is powerless to form itself into "being"[5] and cannot therefore present an appearance (εἶδος). What has "being" is the self-creating product (*Gebilde*) which presents itself as such in an image (*Bild*), i.e. something seen (*Anblick*). The origin, law and limits of this ontological concept are discussed as little as Nothing itself.

Christian dogma, on the other hand, denies the truth of the

proposition *ex nihilo nihil fit* and gives a twist to the meaning of Nothing, so that it now comes to mean the absolute absence of all "being"[6] outside God: *ex nihilo fit—ens creatum*: the created being is made out of nothing. "Nothing" is now the conceptual opposite of what truly and authentically (*eigentlich*) "is"; it becomes the *summum ens*, God as *ens increatum*. Here, too, the interpretation of Nothing points to the fundamental concept of what-is. Metaphysical discussion of what-is, however, moves on the same plane as the enquiry into Nothing. In both cases the questions concerning Being (*Sein*) and Nothing as such remain unasked. Hence we need not be worried by the difficulty that if God creates "out of nothing" he above all must be able to relate himself to Nothing. But if God is God he cannot know Nothing, assuming that the "Absolute" excludes from itself all nullity (*Nichtigkeit*).

This crude historical reminder shows Nothing as the conceptual opposite of what truly and authentically "is," i.e. as the negation of it. But once Nothing is somehow made a problem this contrast not only undergoes clearer definition but also arouses the true and authentic metaphysical question regarding the Being of what-is. Nothing ceases to be the vague opposite of what-is: it now reveals itself as integral to the Being of what-is.

"Pure Being and pure Nothing are thus one and the same." This proposition of Hegel's ("The Science of Logic," I, WW III, p. 74) is correct. Being and Nothing hang together, but not because the two things—from the point of view of the Hegelian concept of thought—are one in their indefiniteness and immediateness, but because Being itself is finite in essence and is only revealed in the Transcendence of *Da-sein* as projected into Nothing.

If indeed the question of Being as such is the all-embracing question of metaphysics, then the question of Nothing proves to be such as to span the whole metaphysical field. But at the same time the question of Nothing pervades the whole of metaphysics only because it forces us to face the problem of the origin of negation, that is to say, forces a decision about the legitimacy of the rule of "logic" in metaphysics.

The old proposition *ex nihilo nihil fit* will then acquire a different meaning, and one appropriate to the problem of Being itself, so as to run: *ex nihilo omne ens qua ens fit*: every being, so far as it is a being, is made out of nothing. Only in the

Nothingness of *Da-sein* can what-is-in-totality—and this in accordance with its peculiar possiblities, i.e. in a finite manner—come to itself. To what extent, then, has the enquiry into Nothing, if indeed it be a metaphysical one, included our own questing *Da-sein*?

Our *Da-sein* as experienced here and now is, we said, ruled by science. If our *Da-sein,* so ruled, is put into this question concerning Nothing, then it follows that it must itself have been put in question by this question.

The simplicity and intensity of scientific *Da-sein* consist in this: that it relates in a special manner to what-is and to this alone. Science would like to abandon Nothing with a superior gesture. But now, in this question of Nothing, it becomes evident that scientific *Da-sein* is only possible when projected into Nothing at the outset. Science can only come to terms with itself when it does not abandon Nothing. The alleged soberness and superiority of science becomes ridiculous if it fails to take Nothing seriously. Only because Nothing is obvious can science turn what-is into an object of investigation. Only when science proceeds from metaphysics can it conquer its essential task ever afresh, which consists not in the accumulation and classification of knowledge but in the perpetual discovery of the whole realm of truth, whether of Nature or of History.

Only because Nothing is revealed in the very basis of our *Da-sein* is it possible for the utter strangeness of what-is to dawn on us. Only when the strangeness of what-is forces itself upon us does it awaken and invite our wonder. Only because of wonder, that is to say, the revelation of Nothing, does the "Why?" spring to our lips. Only because this "Why?" is possible as such can we seek for reasons and proofs in a definite way. Only because we can ask and prove are we fated to become enquirers in this life.

The enquiry into Nothing puts us, the enquirers, ourselves in question. It is a metaphysical one.

Man's *Da-sein* can only relate to what-is by projecting into Nothing. Going beyond what-is is of the essence of *Da-sein*. But this "going beyond" is metaphysics itself. That is why metaphysics belongs to the nature of man. It is neither a department of scholastic philosophy nor a field of chance ideas. Metaphysics is the ground-phenomenon of *Da-sein*. It is *Da-sein* itself. Because the truth of metaphysics is so unfathomable there is always the lurking danger of profoundest error. Hence no scientific discipline can hope to equal the seriousness of metaphysics. Philosophy can never be measured with the yard-stick of the idea of science.

Once the question we have developed as to the nature of Nothing is really asked by and among our own selves, then we are not bringing in metaphysics from the outside. Nor are we simply "transporting" ourselves into it. It is completely out of our power to transport ourselves into metaphysics because, in so far as we exist, we are already there. φύσει γὰρ, ὦ φίλει, ἔνεστί τις φιλοσοφία τῇ τον ἀνδρὸς διανίᾳ (Plato: Phaedrus 279a). While man exists there will be philosophising of some sort. Philosophy, as we call it, is the setting in motion of metaphysics; and in metaphysics philosophy comes to itself and sets about its explicit tasks. Philosophy is only set in motion by leaping with all its being, as only it can, into the ground-possibilities of being as a whole. For this leap the following things are of crucial importance: firstly, leaving room for what-is-in-totality; secondly, letting oneself go into Nothing, that is to say, freeing oneself from the idols we all have and to which we are wont to go cringing; lastly, letting this "suspense" range where it will, so that it may continually swing back again to the ground-question of metaphysics, which is wrested from Nothing itself:

Why is there any Being at all—why not far rather Nothing?

POSTSCRIPT

Metaphysics is the word before which, however abstract and near to thinking it be, most of us flee as from one smitten with the plague. Hegel (1770-1831), Works XVII, p. 400.

The question "What is Metaphysics?" remains a question. For those who persevere with this question the following postscript is more of a foreword. The question "What is Metaphysics?" asks a question that goes beyond metaphysics. It arises from a way of thinking which has already entered into the overcoming of metaphysics. It is of the essence of such transitions that they are, within certain limits, compelled to speak the language of that which they help to overcome. The particular circumstances in which our enquiry into the nature of metaphysics is held should not lead us to the erroneous opinion that this question is bound to make the sciences its starting-point. Modern science, with its completely different ways of conceiving and establishing what-is, has penetrated to that basic feature of truth according to which everything that "is" is characterised by the will to will, as the prototype of which—"the will to power"—all appearance began. "Will," conceived as the basic feature of the "is-ness" (*Seiendheit*) of what-is, is the equation of what-is with the Real, in such a way that the reality of the Real becomes invested with the sovereign power to effect a general objectivisation. Modern science neither serves the purpose originally entrusted to it, nor does it seek truth in itself. As a method of objectivising what-is by calculation it is a condition, imposed by the will to will, through which the will to will secures its own sovereignty. But because all objectivisation of what-is ends in the provision and safeguarding of what-is and thus provides itself with the possibility of further advance, the objectivisation gets stuck in what-is and regards this as nothing less than Being (*Sein*). Every relationship to what-is thus bears witness to a knowledge of Being, but at the same time to its own inability by and of itself to authenticate the truth of this knowledge. This truth is merely the truth about what-is. Metaphysics is the history of this truth. It tells us what what-is is by conceptualising the "is-ness" of what-is. In the is-ness of what-is metaphysics thinks the thought of Being, but without being able to reflect on the truth of Being with its particular mode of thought. Metaphysics moves everywhere in the realm of the truth of Being, which truth remains the unknown and unfathomable ground. But supposing that not merely what-is comes from Being but that, in a manner still more original, Being itself reposes in its truth and that the truth of Being is a function of the Being of truth, then we must necessarily ask what metaphysics is in its own ground. Such a question must think metaphysically and, at the same time, think in terms of the ground of metaphysics, i.e. no longer metaphysically. All such questions must remain equivocal in an essential sense.

Any attempt to follow the train of thought of the preceding lecture is bound, therefore, to meet with obstacles. That is good. It will make our questioning more genuine. All questions that do justice to the subject are themselves bridges to their own answering. Essential answers are always but the last step in our questioning. The last step, however, cannot be taken without the long series of first and next steps. The essential answer gathers its motive power from the inwardness (*Inständigkeit*) of the asking and is only the beginning of a responsibility where the asking arises with renewed originality. Hence even the most genuine question is never stilled by the answer found.

The obstacles to following the thought of the lecture are of two kinds. The first arise from the enigmas which lurk in this region of thought. The others come from the inability and often the reluctance to think. In the region of cerebral enquiry even fleeting intimations can sometimes help, although real help only comes from those that have been carefully thought out. Gross errors may also bear fruit, flung out, perhaps, in the heat of blind controversy. Only, reflection must take everything back again in the calm mood of patient meditation.

The chief misgivings and misconceptions to which the lecture gives rise may be grouped under three heads. It is said that:

1. The lecture makes "Nothing" the sole subject of metaphysics. But since Nothing is simply the nugatory (*das Nichtige*), this kind of thinking leads to the idea that everything is nothing, so that it is not worth while either to live or to die. A "Philosophy of Nothing" is the last word in "Nihilism."

2. The lecture raises an isolated and, what is more, a morbid mood, namely dread, to the status of the one key-mood. But since dread is the psychic state of nervous people and cowards, this kind of thinking devalues the stout-hearted attitude of the courageous. A "Philosophy of Dread" paralyses the will to act.

3. The lecture declares itself against "logic." But since reason contains the criteria for all calculation and classification, this kind of thinking delivers all judgements regarding the truth up to a chance mood. A "Philosophy of Pure Feeling" imperils "exact" thinking and the certainty of action.

The right attitude to these propositions will emerge from a renewed consideration of the lecture. It may show whether Nothing, which governs the whole nature of dread, can be exhausted by an empty negation of what-is, or whether that which never and nowhere "is" discloses itself as that which differs from everything that "is," i.e. what we call "Being." No matter where and however deeply science investigates what-is it will never find Being. All it encounters, always, is what-is, because its explanatory purpose makes it insist at the outset on what-is. But Being is not an existing quality of what-is, nor, unlike what-is, can Being be conceived and established objectively. This, the purely "Other" than everything that "is," is that-which-is-not (*das Nicht-Seinde*). Yet this "Nothing" functions as Being. It would be premature to stop thinking at this point and adopt the facile explanation that Nothing is merely the nugatory, equating it with the non-existent (*das Wesenlose*). Instead of giving way to such precipitate and empty ingenuity and abandoning Nothing in all its mysterious multiplicity of meanings, we should rather equip ourselves and make ready for one thing only: to experience in Nothing the vastness of that which gives every being the warrant to be. That is Being itself. Without Being, whose unfathomable and unmanifest essence is vouchsafed us by Nothing in essential dread, everything that "is" would remain in Beinglessness (*Sein-losigkeit*). But this too, in its turn, is not a nugatory Nothing, assuming that it is of the truth of Being that Being may be without what-is, but never what-is without Being.

An experience of Being as sometimes "other" than everything that "is" comes to us in dread, provided that we do not, from dread of dread, i.e. in sheer timidity, shut our ears to the soundless voice which attunes us to the horrors of the abyss. Naturally if, in this matter of essential dread, we depart at will from the train of thought of the lecture; if we detach dread conceived as the mood occasioned by that voice from its relationship to Nothing, then dread is left over as an isolated "feeling" which we can analyse and contrast with other feelings in the well-known assortment of psychological stock-types. Using the simple distinction between "upper" and "lower" as a clue we can then group the various "moods" into classes: those which are exalting and those which are lowering. But this zealous quest for "types" and "counter-types" of "feelings," for the varieties and sub-varieties of these "types," will never get us anywhere. It will always be impossible for the anthropological study of man to follow the mental track of the lecture, since the latter, though paying attention to the voice of Being, thinks beyond it into the attunement occasioned by this voice—an attunement which takes possession of the essential man so that he may come to experience Being in Nothing.

Readiness for dread is to say "Yes!" to the inwardness of

things, to fulfil the highest demand which alone touches man to the quick. Man alone of all beings, when addressed by the voice of Being, experiences the marvel of all marvels: that what-is *is*. Therefore the being that is called in its very essence to the truth of Being is always attuned in an essential sense. The clear courage for essential dread guarantees that most mysterious of all possibilities: the experience of Being. For hard by essential dread, in the terror of the abyss, there dwells awe (*Scheu*). Awe clears and enfolds that region of human being within which man endures, as at home, in the enduring.

Dread of dread, on the other hand, may stray so far as to mistake the simple relationships obtaining in the essence of dread. What would all courage avail did it not find continual hold in the experience of essential dread? To the degree that we degrade this essential dread and the relationship cleared within it for Man to Being, we demean the essence of courage. Courage can endure Nothing: it knows, in the abyss of terror, the all-but untrodden region of Being, that "clearing" whence everything that "is" returns into *what* it is and is able to be. Our lecture neither puts forward a "Philosophy of Dread" nor seeks to give the false impression of being an "heroic" philosophy. Its sole thought is that thing which has dawned on Western thinking from the beginning as the one thing that has to be thought—Being. But Being is not a product of thinking. It is more likely that essential thinking is an occurrence of Being.

For this reason the scarcely formulated question now forces itself on us as to whether this kind of thinking conforms to the law of its truth when it only follows the thinking whose forms and rules constitute "logic." Why do we put this word in inverted commas? In order to indicate that "logic" is only *one* exposition of the nature of thinking, and one which, as its name shows, is based on the experience of Being as attained in Greek thought. The animus against "logic"—the logical degeneration of which can be seen in "logistics," derives from the knowledge of that thinking which has its source not in the observation of the objectivity of what-is, but in the experience of the truth of Being. "Exact" thinking is never the strictest thinking, if the essence of strictness lies in the strenuousness with which knowledge keeps in touch with the essential features of what-is. "Exact" thinking merely binds itself to the calculation of what-is and ministers to this alone.

All calculation makes the calculable "come out" in the sum

so as to use the sum for the next count. Nothing counts for calculation save what can be calculated. Any particular thing is only what it "adds up to," and any count ensures the further progress of the counting. This process is continually using up numbers and is itself a continual self-consumption. The "coming out" of the calculation with the help of what-is counts as the explanation of the latter's Being. Calculation uses everything that "is" as units of computation, in advance, and, in the computation, uses up its stock of units. This consumption of what-is reveals the consuming nature of calculation. Only because number can be multiplied indefinitely—and this regardless of whether it goes in the direction of the great or the small—is it possible for the consuming nature of calculation to hide behind its "products" and give calculative thought the appearance of "productivity"—whereas it is of the prime essence of calculation, and not merely in its results, to assert what-is only in the form of something that can be arranged and used up. Calculative thought places itself under compulsion to master everything in the logical terms of its procedure. It has no notion that in calculation everything calculable is already a whole before it starts working out its sums and products, a whole whose unity naturally belongs to the incalculable which, with its mystery, ever eludes the clutches of calculation. That which, however, is always and everywhere closed at the outset to the demands of calculation and, despite that, is always closer to man in its enigmatic unknowableness than anything that "is," than anything he may arrange and plan, this can sometimes put the essential man in touch with a thinking whose truth no "logic" can grasp. The thinking whose thoughts not only do not calculate but are absolutely determined by what is "other" than what-is, might be called essential thinking. Instead of counting *on* what-is *with* what-is, it expends itself in Being for the truth of Being. This thinking answers to the demands of Being in that man surrenders his historical being to the simple, sole necessity whose constraints do not so much necessitate as create the need (*Not*) which is consummated in the freedom of sacrifice. The need is: to preserve the truth of Being no matter what may happen to man and everything that "is." Freed from all constraint, because born of the abyss of freedom, this sacrifice is the expense of our human being for the preservation of the truth of Being in respect of what-is. In sacrifice there is expressed that hidden *thanking* which alone does homage to the grace wherewith Being has endowed the nature of man, in order that he may take over in his relationship to Being the guardianship of Being. Original thanking is the echo of Being's favour wherein it clears a space for itself and causes the unique occurrence: that what-is is. This echo is man's answer to the Word of the soundless voice of Being. The speechless answer of his thanking through sacrifice is the source of the human word, which is the prime cause of language as the enunciation of the Word in words. Were there not an occasional thanking in the heart of historical man he could never attain the thinking—assuming that there must be thinking (*Denken*) in all doubt (*Bedenken*) and memory (*Andenken*)—which originally thinks the thought of Being. But how else could humanity attain to original thanking unless Being's favour preserved for man, through his open relationship to this favour, the splendid poverty in which the freedom of sacrifice hides its own treasure? Sacrifice is a valediction to everything that "is" on the road to the preservation of the favour of Being. Sacrifice can be made ready and can be served by doing and working in the midst of what-is, but never consummated there. Its consummation comes from the inwardness out of which historical man by his actions—essential thinking is also an act—dedicates the *Da-sein* he has won for himself to the preservation of the dignity of Being. This inwardness is the calm that allows nothing to assail man's hidden readiness for the valedictory nature of all sacrifice. Sacrifice is rooted in the nature of the event through which Being claims man for the truth of Being. Therefore it is that sacrifice brooks no calculation, for calculation always miscalculates sacrifice in terms of the expedient and the inexpedient, no matter whether the aims are set high or low. Such calculation distorts the nature of sacrifice. The search for a purpose dulls the clarity of the awe, the spirit of sacrifice ready prepared for dread, which takes upon itself kinship with the imperishable.

The thought of Being seeks no hold in what-is. Essential thinking looks to the slow signs of the incalculable and sees in this the unforeseeable coming of the ineluctable. Such thinking is mindful of the truth of Being and thus helps the Being of truth to make a place for itself in man's history. This help effects no results because it has no need of effect. Essential thinking helps as the simple inwardness of existence, insofar as this inwardness, although unable to exercise such thinking or only having theoretical knowledge of it, kindles its own kind.

Obedient to the voice of Being, thought seeks the Word through which the truth of Being may be expressed. Only when the language of historical man is born of the Word does it ring true. But if it does ring true, then the testimony of the soundless voice of hidden springs lures it ever on. The thought of Being guards the Word and fulfils its function in such guardianship, namely care for the use of language. Out of long-guarded speechlessness and the careful clarification of the field thus cleared, comes the utterance of the thinker. Of like origin is the naming of the poet. But since like is only like insofar as difference allows, and since poetry and thinking are most purely alike in their care of the word, the two things are at the same time at opposite poles in their essence. The thinker utters Being. The poet names what is holy.

We may know something about the relations between philosophy and poetry, but we know nothing of the dialogue between poet and thinker, who "dwell near to one another on mountains farthest apart."[7]

One of the essential theatres of speechlessness is dread in the sense of the terror into which the abyss of Nothing plunges us. Nothing, conceived as the pure "Other" than what-is, is the veil of Being. In Being all that comes to pass in what-is is perfected from everlasting.

The last poem of the last poet of the dawn-period of Greece —Sophocles' "Oedipus in Colonos"—closes with words that hark back far beyond our ken to the hidden history of these people and marks their entry into the unknown truth of Being:

ἀλλ' ἀποπαύετε μηδ' ἐπὶ πλείω
θρῆνον ἐγείρετε.
πάντων γὰρ ἔχει τάδε κῦρος.

But cease now, and nevermore
Lift up the lament:
For all this is determined.

3. The Way Back into the Ground of Metaphysics

Descartes, writing to Picot, who translated the *Principia Philosophiae* into French, observed: "Thus the whole of philosophy is like a tree: the roots are metaphysics, the trunk is physics, and the branches that issue from the trunk are all the other sciences . . ." (*Opp. ed. Ad. et Ta.* IX, 14)

Sticking to this image, we ask: In what soil do the roots of the tree of philosophy have their hold? Out of what ground do the roots—and through them the whole tree—receive their nourishing juices and strength? What element, concealed in the ground, enters and lives in the roots that support and nourish the tree? What is the basis and element of metaphysics? What is metaphysics, viewed from its ground? What is metaphysics itself, at bottom?

Metaphysics thinks about beings as beings. Wherever the question is asked what beings are, beings as such are in sight. Metaphysical representation owes this sight to the light of Being. The light itself, i.e., that which such thinking experiences as light, does not come within the range of metaphysical thinking; for metaphysics always represents beings only as beings. Within this perspective, metaphysical thinking does, of course, inquire about the being which is the source and originator of this light. But the light itself is considered sufficiently illuminated as soon as we recognize that we look through it whenever we look at beings.

In whatever manner beings are interpreted—whether as spirit, after the fashion of spiritualism; or as matter and force, after the fashion of materialism; or as becoming and life, or idea, will, substance, subject, or *energeia;* or as the eternal recurrence of the same events—every time, beings as beings appear in the light of Being. Wherever metaphysics represents beings. Being has entered into the light. Being has arrived in a state of unconcealedness ('Αλήθεια). But whether and how Being itself involves such unconcealedness, whether and how it manifests itself in, and as, metaphysics, remains obscure. Being in its revelatory essence, i. e. in its truth, is not recalled. Nevertheless, when metaphysics gives answers to its question concerning beings as such, metaphysics speaks out of the unnoticed revealedness of Being.

The truth of Being may thus be called the ground in which metaphysics, as the root of the tree of philosophy, is kept and from which it is nourished.

Because metaphysics inquires about beings as beings, it remains concerned with beings and does not devote itself to Being as Being. As the root of the tree, it sends all nourishment and all strength into the trunk and its branches. The root branches out in the soil to enable the tree to grow out of the ground and thus to leave it. The tree of philosophy grows out of the soil in which metaphysics is rooted. The ground is the element in which the root of the tree lives, but the growth of the tree is never able to absorb this soil in such a way that it disappears in the tree as part of the tree. Instead, the roots, down to the subtlest tendrils, lose themselves in the soil. The ground is ground for the roots, and in the ground the roots forget themselves for the sake of the tree. The roots still belong to the tree even when they abandon themselves, after a fashion, to the element of the soil. They squander themselves and their element on the tree. As roots, they do not devote themselves to the soil—at least not as if it were their life to grow only into this element and to spread out in it. Presumably, the element would not be the same element either if the roots did not live in it.

Metaphysics, insofar as it always represents only beings as beings, does not recall Being itself. Philosophy does not concentrate on its ground. It always leaves its ground—leaves it by means of metaphysics. And yet it never escapes its ground.

Insofar as a thinker sets out to experience the ground of metaphysics, insofar as he attempts to recall the truth of Being itself instead of merely representing beings as beings, his thinking has in a sense left metaphysics. From the point of view of metaphysics, such thinking goes back into the ground of metaphysics. But what still appears as ground from this point of view is presumably something else, once it is experienced in its own terms—something as yet unsaid, according to which the essence of metaphysics, too, is something else and not metaphysics.

Such thinking, which recalls the truth of Being, is no longer satisfied with mere metaphysics, to be sure; but it does not oppose and think against metaphysics either. To return to our image, it does not tear up the root of philosophy. It tills the ground and plows the soil for this root. Metaphysics remains the basis of philosophy. The basis of thinking, however, it does not reach. When we think of the truth of Being, metaphysics is overcome. We can no longer accept the claim of metaphysics that it takes care of the fundamental involvement in "Being" and that it decisively determines all relations to beings as such. But this "overcoming of metaphysics" does not abolish metaphysics. As long as man remains the *animal rationale* he is also the *animal metaphysicum*. As long as man understands himself as the rational animal, metaphysics belongs, as Kant said, to the nature of man. But if our thinking should succeed in its efforts to go back into the ground of metaphysics, it might well help to bring about a change in human nature, accompanied by a transformation of metaphysics.

If, as we unfold the question concerning the truth of Being, we speak of overcoming metaphysics, this means: recalling Being itself. Such recalling goes beyond the tradition of forgetting the ground of the root of philosophy. The thinking attempted in *Being and Time* (1927) sets out on the way to prepare an overcoming of metaphysics, so understood. That, however, which prompts such thinking can only be that which is to be recalled. That Being itself and how Being itself concerns our thinking does not depend upon our thinking alone. That Being itself, and the manner in which Being itself, strikes a man's thinking, that rouses his thinking and stirs it to rise from Being itself to respond and correspond to Being as such.

Why, however, should such an overcoming of metaphysics be necessary? Is the point merely to underpin that discipline of philosophy which was the root hitherto, or to supplant it with a yet more basic discipline? Is it a question of changing the philosophic system of instruction? No. Or are we trying to go back into the ground of metaphysics in order to uncover a hitherto overlooked presupposition of philosophy, and thereby to show that philosophy does not yet stand on an unshakable foundation and therefore cannot yet be the absolute science? No.

It is something else that is at stake with the arrival of the truth of Being or its failure to arrive: it is neither the state of philosophy nor philosophy itself alone, but rather the proximity or remoteness of that from which philosophy, insofar as it means the representation of beings as such, receives its nature and its necessity. What is to be decided is nothing less than this: can Being itself, out of its own unique truth, bring about its involvement in human nature; or shall metaphysics, which turns its back to its ground, prevent further that the involvement of Being in man may generate a radiance out of the very essence of this involvement itself—a radiance which might lead man to belong to Being?

In its answers to the question concerning beings as such, metaphysics operates with a prior conception of Being. It speaks of Being necessarily and hence continually. But metaphysics does not induce Being itself to speak, for metaphysics does not recall Being in its truth, nor does it recall truth as unconcealedness, nor does it recall the nature of unconcealedness. To metaphysics the nature of truth always appears only in the derivative form of the truth of knowledge and the truth of propositions which formulate our knowledge. Unconcealedness, however, might be prior to all truth in the sense of *veritas*. 'Αλήϑεια might be the word that offers a hitherto unnoticed hint concerning the nature of *esse* which has not yet been recalled. If this should be so, then the representational thinking of metaphysics could certainly never reach this nature of truth, however zealously it might devote itself to historical studies of pre-Socratic philosophy; for what is at stake here is not some renaissance of pre-Socratic thinking: any such attempt would be vain and absurd. What is wanted is rather some regard for the arrival of the hitherto unexpressed nature of unconcealedness, for it is in this form that Being has announced itself. Meanwhile the truth of Being has remained concealed from metaphysics during its long history from Anaximander to Nietzsche. Why does metaphysics not recall it? Is the failure to recall it merely a function of some kinds of metaphysical thinking? Or is it an essential feature of the fate of metaphysics that its own ground eludes it because in the rise of unconcealedness its very core, namely concealedness, stays away in favor of the unconcealed which appears in the form of beings?

Metaphysics, however, speaks continually and in the most various ways of Being. Metaphysics gives, and seems to confirm, the appearance that it asks and answers the question concerning Being. In fact, metaphysics never answers the question concerning the truth of Being, for it never asks this question. Metaphysics does not ask this question because it thinks of Being only by representing beings as beings. It means all beings as a whole, although it speaks of Being. It refers to Being and means beings as beings. From its beginning to its completion, the propositions of metaphysics have been strangely involved in a persistent confusion of beings and Being. This confusion, to be sure, must be considered an event and not a mere mistake. It cannot by any means be charged to a mere negligence of thought or a carelessness of expression. Owing to this persistent confusion, the claim that metaphysics poses the question of Being lands us in utter error.

Due to the manner in which it thinks of beings, metaphysics almost seems to be, without knowing it, the barrier which keeps man from the original involvement of Being in human nature.

What if the absence of this involvement and the oblivion of this absence determined the entire modern age? What if the absence of Being abandoned man more and more exclusively to beings, leaving him forsaken and far from any involvement of Being in his nature, while this forsakenness itself remained veiled? What if this were the case—and had been the case for a long time now? What if there were signs that this oblivion will become still more decisive in the future?

Would there still be occasion for a thoughtful person to give himself arrogant airs in view of this fateful withdrawal with which Being presents us? Would there still be occasion, if this should be our situation, to deceive ourselves with pleasant phantasms and to indulge, of all things, in an artificially induced elation? If the oblivion of Being which has been described here should be real, would there not be occasion enough for a thinker who recalls Being to experience a genuine horror? What more can his thinking do than to endure in dread this fateful withdrawal while first of all facing up to the oblivion of Being? But how could thought achieve this as long as its fatefully granted dread seems to it no more than a mood of depression? What does such dread, which is fated by Being, have to do with psychology or psychoanalysis?

Suppose that the overcoming of metaphysics involved the endeavor to commence with a regard for the oblivion of Being—the attempt to learn to develop such a regard, in order to experience this oblivion and to absorb this experience into the involvement of Being in man, and to preserve it there: then, in the distress of the oblivion of Being, the question "What is metaphysics?" might well become the most necessary necessity for thought.

Thus everything depends on this: that our thinking should become more thoughtful in its season. This is achieved when our thinking, instead of implementing a higher degree of exertion, is directed toward a different point of origin. The thinking which is posited by beings as such, and therefore representational and illuminating in that way, must be supplanted by a different kind of thinking which is brought to pass by Being itself and, therefore, responsive to Being.

All attempts are futile which seek to make representational thinking which remains metaphysical, and only metaphysical, effective and useful for immediate action in everyday public life. The more thoughtful our thinking becomes and the more adequate it is to the involvement of Being in it, the purer our thinking will stand *eo ipso* in the one action appropriate to it: recalling what is meant for it and thus, in a sense, what is already meant.

But who still recalls what is meant? One makes inventions. To lead our thinking on the way on which it may find the involvement of the truth of Being in human nature, to open up a path for our thinking on which it may recall Being itself in its truth—to do that the thinking attempted in *Being and Time* is "on its way." On this way—that is, in the service of the question concerning the truth of Being—it becomes necessary to stop and think about human nature; for the experience of the oblivion of Being, which is not specifically mentioned because it still had to be demonstrated, involves the crucial conjecture that in view of the unconcealedness of Being the involvement of Being in human nature is an essential feature of Being. But how could this conjecture, which is experienced here, become an explicit question before every attempt had been made to liberate the determination of human nature from the concept of subjectivity and from the concept of the *animal rationale?* To characterize with a single term both the involvement of Being in human nature and the essential relation of man to the openness ("there") of Being as such, the name of "being there [*Dasein*]" was chosen for that sphere of being in which man stands as man. This term was employed, even though in metaphysics it is used interchangeably with *existentia*, actuality, reality, and objectivity, and although this metaphysical usage is further supported by the common [German] expression *"menschliches Dasein."* Any attempt, therefore, to re-think *Being and Time* is thwarted as long as one is satisfied with the observation that, in this study, the term "being there" is used in place of "consciousness." As if this were simply a matter of using different words! As if it were not the one and only thing at stake here: namely, to get men to think about the involvement of Being in human nature and thus, from our point of view, to present first of all an experience of human nature which may prove sufficient to direct our inquiry. The term "being there" neither takes the place of the term "consciousness" nor does the "object" designated as "being there" take the place of what we think of when we speak of "consciousness." "Being there" names that which should first of all be experienced, and subsequently thought of, as a place—namely, the location of the truth of Being.

What the term "being there" means throughout the treatise on *Being and Time* is indicated immediately (page 42) by its introductory key sentence: *"The 'essence' of being there lies in its existence."* [*Das "Wesen" des Daseins liegt in seiner Existenz.*]

To be sure, in the language of metaphysics the word "existence" is a synonym of "being there": both refer to the reality of anything at all that is real, from God to a grain of sand. As long, therefore, as the quoted sentence is understood only superficially, the difficulty is merely transferred from one word to another, from "being there" to "existence." In *B.&T.* the term "existence" is used exclusively for the being of man. Once "existence" is understood rightly, the "essence" of being there can be recalled: in its openness, Being itself manifests and conceals itself, yields itself and withdraws; at the same time, this truth of Being does not exhaust itself in being there, nor can it by any means simply be identified with it after the fashion of the metaphysical proposition: all objectivity is as such also subjectivity.

What does "existence" mean in *B.&T.?* The word designates a mode of Being; specifically, the Being of those beings who stand open for the openness of Being in which they stand, by standing it. This "standing it," this enduring, is experienced under the name of "care." The ecstatic essence of being there is approached by way of care, and, conversely, care is experienced adequately only in its ecstatic essence. "Standing it," experienced in this manner, is the essence of the *ekstasis* which must be grasped by thought. The ecstatic essence of existence is therefore still understood inadequately as long as one thinks of it as merely "standing out," while interpreting the "out" as meaning "away from" the inside of an immanence of consciousness and spirit. For in this manner, existence would still be understood in terms of "subjectivity" and "substance"; while, in fact, the "out" ought to be understood in terms of the openness of Being itself. The *stasis* of the ecstatic consists—strange as it may sound—in standing in the "out" and "there" of unconcealedness in which Being itself is present. What is meant by "existence" in the context of an inquiry that is prompted by, and directed toward, the truth of Being, can be most beautifully designated by the word "instancy [*Inständigkeit*]." We must think at the same time, however, of standing in the openness of Being, of enduring and outstanding this standing-in (care), and of out-braving the utmost (Being toward death); for it is only together that they constitute the full essence of existence.

The being that exists is man. Man alone exists. Rocks are, but they do not exist. Trees are, but they do not exist. Horses are, but they do not exist. Angels are, but they do not exist. God is, but he does not exist. The proposition "man alone exists" does not mean by any means that man alone is a real being while all other beings are unreal and mere appearances or human ideas. The proposition "man exists" means: man is that being whose Being is distinguished by the open-standing standing-in in the unconcealedness of Being, from Being, in Being. The existential nature of man is the reason why man can represent beings as such, and why he can be conscious of them. All consciousness presupposes ecstatically understood existence as the *essentia* of man—*essentia* meaning that as which man is present insofar as he is man. But consciousness does not itself create the openness of beings, nor is it consciousness that makes it possible for man to stand open for beings. Whither and whence and in what free dimension could the intentionality of consciousness move, if instancy were not the essence of man in the first instance? What else could be the meaning—if anybody has ever seriously thought about this—of the word *sein* in the [German] words *Bewusstsein* ["consciousness"; literally: "being conscious"] and *Selbstbewusstsein* ["self-consciousness"] if it did not designate the existential nature of that which is in the mode of existence? To be a self is admittedly one feature of the nature of that being which exists; but existence does not consist in being a self, nor can it be defined in such terms. We are faced with the fact that metaphysical thinking understands man's selfhood in terms of substance or—and at bottom this amounts to the same—in terms of the subject. It is for this reason that the first way which leads away from metaphysics to the ecstatic existential nature of man must lead through the metaphysical conception of human selfhood (*B.&T.*, §§63 and 64).

The question concerning existence, however, is always subservient to that question which is nothing less than the only question of thought. This question, yet to be unfolded, concerns the truth of Being as the concealed ground of all metaphysics. For this reason the treatise which sought to point the way back into the ground of metaphysics did not bear the title "Existence and Time," nor "Consciousness and Time," but *Being and Time*. Nor can this title be understood as if it were parallel to the customary juxtapositions of Being and Becoming, Being and Seeming, Being and Thinking, or Being and Ought. For in all these cases Being is limited, as if Becoming, Seeming, Thinking, and Ought did not belong to Being, although it is obvious that they are not nothing and thus belong to Being. In *Being and Time*, Being is not something other than Time: "Time" is called the first name of the truth of Being, and this truth is the presence of Being and thus Being itself. But why "Time" and "Being"?

By recalling the beginnings of history when Being unveiled itself in the thinking of the Greeks, it can be shown that the Greeks from the very beginning experienced the Being of beings as the presence of the present. When we translate εἶναι as "being," our translation is linguistically correct. Yet we merely substitute one set of sounds for another. As soon as we examine ourselves it becomes obvious that we neither think εἶναι, as it were, in Greek nor have in mind a correspondingly clear and univocal concept when we speak of "being." What, then, are we saying when instead of εἶναι we say "being," and instead of "being," εἶναι and *esse?* We are saying nothing. The Greek, Latin, and German word all remain equally obtuse. As long as we adhere to the customary usage we merely betray ourselves as the pacemakers of the greatest thoughtlessness which has ever gained currency in human thought and which has remained dominant until this moment. This εἶναι, however, means: to be present [*anwesen;* this verb form, in place of the idiomatic *"anwesend sein,"* is Heidegger's neology]. The true being of this being present [*das Wesen dieses Anwesens*] is deeply concealed in the earliest names of Being. But for us εἶναι and οὐσία as παρ—and ἀπουσία means this first of all: in being present there moves, unrecognized and concealed, present time and duration—in one word, Time. Being as such is thus unconcealed owing to Time. Thus Time points to unconcealedness, i. e., the truth of Being. But the Time of which we should think here is not experienced through the changeful career of beings. Time is evidently of an altogether different nature which neither has been recalled by way of the time concept of metaphysics nor ever can be recalled in this way. Thus Time becomes the first name, which is yet to be heeded, of the truth of Being, which is yet to be experienced.

A concealed hint of Time speaks not only out of the earliest metaphysical names of Being but also out of its last name, which is "the eternal recurrence of the same events." Through the entire epoch of metaphysics, Time is decisively present in the history of Being, without being recognized or thought about. To this Time, space is neither co-ordinated nor merely subordinated.

Suppose one attempts to make a transition from the representation of beings as such to recalling the truth of Being: such an attempt, which starts from this representation, must still represent, in a certain sense, the truth of Being, too; and any such representation must of necessity be heterogeneous and ultimately, insofar as it is a representation, inadequate for that which is to be thought. This relation, which comes out of metaphysics and tries to enter into the involvement of the truth of Being in human nature, is called understanding. But here understanding is viewed, at the same time, from the point of view of the unconcealedness of Being. Understanding is a pro-ject thrust forth and ecstatic, which means that it stands in the sphere of the open. The sphere which opens up as we project, in order that something (Being in this case) may prove itself as something (in this case, Being as itself in its unconcealedness), is called the sense. (Cf. *B.&T.*, p. 151) "The sense of Being" and "the truth of Being" mean the same.

Let us suppose that Time belongs to the truth of Being in a way that is still concealed: then every project that holds open the truth of Being, representing a way of understanding Being, must look out into Time as the horizon of any possible understanding of Being. (Cf. *B.&T.*, §§31-34 and 68.)

The preface to *Being and Time,* on the first page of the treatise, ends with these sentences: "To furnish a concrete elaboration of the question concerning the sense of 'Being' is the intention of the following treatise. The interpretation of Time as the horizon of every possible attempt to understand Being is its provisional goal."

All philosophy has fallen into the oblivion of Being which has, at the same time, become and remained the fateful demand on thought in *B.&T.* ; and philosophy could hardly have given a clearer demonstration of the power of this oblivion of Being than it has furnished us by the somnambulistic assurance with which it has passed by the real and only question of *B.&T.* What is at stake here is, therefore, not a series of misunderstandings of a book but our abandonment by Being.

Metaphysics states what beings are as beings. It offers a λόγος (statement) about the ὄντα (beings). The later title "ontology" characterizes its nature, provided, of course, that we understand it in accordance with its true significance and not through its narrow scholastic meaning. Metaphysics moves in the sphere of the ὄν ᾗ ὄν: it deals with beings as beings. In this manner, metaphysics always represents beings as such in their totality; it deals with the beingness of beings (the οὐσία of the ὄν). But metaphysics represents the beingness of beings [*die Seiendheit des Seienden*] in a twofold manner: in the first place, the totality of beings as such with an eye to their most universal traits (ὄν καθόλου, κοινόν;) but at the same time also the totality of beings as such in the sense of the highest and therefore divine being (ὄν καθόλου, ἀκρότατον, θεῖον). In the metaphysics of Aristotle, the unconcealedness of beings as such has specifically developed in this twofold manner. (Cf. Met. Γ, Ε, Κ.)

Because metaphysics represents beings as beings, it is, two-in-one, the truth of beings in their universality and in the highest being. According to its nature, it is at the same time ontology in the narrower sense and theology. This onto-theological nature of philosophy proper (πρώτη φιλοσοφία) is, no doubt, due to the way in which the ὄν opens up in it, namely as ὄν. Thus the theological character of ontology is not merely due to the fact that Greek metaphysics was later taken up and transformed by the ecclesiastic theology of Christianity. Rather it is due to the manner in which beings as beings have from the very beginning disconcealed themselves. It was this unconcealedness of beings that provided the possibility for Christian theology to take possession of Greek philosophy—whether for better or for worse may be decided by the theologians, on the basis of their experience of what is Christian; only they should keep in mind what is written in the First Epistle of Paul the Apostle to the Corinthians: "οὐχὶ ἐμώρανεν ὁ θεὸς τὴν σοφίαν τοῦ κόσμου; Has not God let the wisdom of this world become foolishness?" (I Cor. 1:20) The σοφία τοῦ κόσμου [wisdom of this world], however, is that which, according to 1:22, the Ἕλληνες ζητοῦσιν, the Greeks seek. Aristotle even calls the πρώτη φιλοσοφία (philosophy proper) quite specifically ζητουμένη — what is sought. Will Christian theology make up its mind one day to take seriously the word of the apostle and thus also the conception of philosophy as foolishness?

As the truth of beings as such, metaphysics has a twofold character. The reason for this twofoldness, however, let alone its origin, remains unknown to metaphysics; and this is no accident, nor due to mere neglect. Metaphysics has this twofold character because it is what it is: the representation of beings as beings. Metaphysics has no choice. Being metaphysics, it is by its very nature excluded from the experience of Being; for it always represents beings (ὄν) only with an eye to what of Being has already manifested itself as beings (ᾗ ὄν). But metaphysics never pays attention to what has concealed itself in this very ὄν insofar as it became unconcealed.

Thus the time came when it became necessary to make a fresh attempt to grasp by thought what precisely is said when we speak of ὄν or use the word "being" [seiend]. Accordingly, the question concerning the ὄν was reintroduced into human thinking. (Cf. B.&T., Preface.) But this reintroduction is no mere repetition of the Platonic-Aristotelian question; instead it asks about that which conceals itself in the ὄν.

Metaphysics is founded upon that which conceals itself here as long as metaphysics studies the ὄν ᾗ ὄν. The attempt to inquire back into what conceals itself here seeks, from the point of view of metaphysics, the fundament of ontology. Therefore this attempt is called, in Being and Time (page 13) "fundamental ontology" [Fundamentalontologie]. Yet this title, like any title, is soon seen to be inappropriate. From the point of view of metaphysics, to be sure, it says something that is correct; but precisely for that reason it is misleading, for what matters is success in the transition from metaphysics to recalling the truth of Being. As long as this thinking calls itself "fundamental ontology" it blocks and obscures its own way with this title. For what the title "fundamental ontology" suggests is, of course, that the attempt to recall the truth of Being—and not, like all ontology, the truth of beings—is itself (seeing that it is called "fundamental ontology") still a kind of ontology. In fact, the attempt to recall the truth of Being sets out on the way back into the ground of metaphysics, and with its first step it immediately leaves the realm of all ontology. On the other hand, every philosophy which revolves around an indirect or direct conception of "transcendence" remains of necessity essentially an ontology, whether it achieves a new foundation of ontology or whether it assures us that it repudiates ontology as a conceptual freezing of experience.

Coming from the ancient custom of representing beings as such, the very thinking that attempted to recall the truth of Being became entangled in these customary conceptions. Under these circumstances it would seem that both for a preliminary orientation and in order to prepare the transition from representational thinking to a new kind of thinking recalls [*das andenkende Denken*], that nothing could be more necessary than the question: What is metaphysics?

The unfolding of this question in the following lecture culminates in another question. This is called the basic question of metaphysics: Why is there any being at all and not rather Nothing? Meanwhile [since this lecture was first published in 1929], to be sure, people have talked back and forth a great deal about dread and the Nothing, both of which are spoken of in this lecture. But one has never yet deigned to ask oneself why a lecture which moves from thinking of the truth of Being to the Nothing, and then tries from there to think into the nature of metaphysics, should claim that this question is the basic question of metaphysics. How can an attentive reader help feeling on the tip of his tongue an objection which is far more weighty than all protests against dread and the Nothing? The final question provokes the objection that an inquiry which attempts to recall Being by way of the Nothing returns in the end to a question concerning beings. On top of that, the question even proceeds in the customary manner of metaphysics by beginning with a causal "Why?" To this extent, then the attempt to recall Being is repudiated in favor of representational knowledge of beings on the basis of beings. And to make matters still worse, the final question is obviously the question which the metaphysician Leibniz posed in his *Principes de la nature et de la grace: "Pourquoi il y a plutôt quelque chose que rien?"* (Opp. ed. Gerh. tom. VI, 602.n. 7).

Does the lecture, then fall short of its intention? After all, this would be quite possible in view of the difficulty of effecting a transition from metaphysics to another kind of thinking. Does the lecture end up by asking Leibniz' metaphysical question about the supreme cause of all things that have being? Why, then, is Leibniz' name not mentioned, as decency would seem to require?

Or is the question asked in an altogether different sense? If it does not concern itself with beings and inquire about their first cause among all beings, then the question must begin from that which is not a being. And this is precisely what the question names, and it capitalizes the word: the Nothing. This is the sole topic of the lecture. The demand seems obvious that the end of the lecture should be thought through, for once, in its own perspective which determines the whole lecture. What has been called the basic question of metaphysics would then have to be understood and asked in terms of fundamental ontology as the question that comes out of the ground of metaphysics and as the question about this ground.

But if we grant this lecture that in the end it thinks in the direction of its own distinctive concern, how are we to understand this question?

The question is: Why is there any being at all and not rather Nothing? Suppose that we do not remain within metaphysics to ask metaphysically in the customary manner; suppose we recall the truth of Being out of the nature and the truth of metaphysics; then this might be asked as well: How did it come about that beings take precedence everywhere and lay claim to every "is" while that which is not a being is understood as Nothing, though it is Being itself, and remains forgotten? How did it come about that with Being It really is nothing and that the Nothing really is not? Is it perhaps from this that the as yet unshaken presumption has entered into all metaphysics that "Being" may simply be taken for granted and that Nothing is therefore made more easily than beings? That is indeed the situation regarding

Being and Nothing. If it were different, then Leibniz could not have said in the same place by way of an explanation: *"Car le rien est plus simple et plus facile que quelque chose* [For the nothing is simpler and easier than any thing]."

What is more enigmatic: that beings are, or that Being is? Or does even this reflection fail to bring us close to that enigma which has occurred with the Being of beings?

Whatever the answer may be, the time should have ripened meanwhile for thinking through the lecture "What is Metaphysics?" which has been subjected to so many attacks, from its end, for once—from *its* end and not from an imaginary end.

TEN

Sartre: EXISTENTIALISM

[*Preface:* Jean-Paul Sartre was born in Paris in 1905. His short story "The Wall" is one of the classics of existentialism. It is reprinted unabridged. A brief analysis—of the following selections, too—is offered in Chapter One.

"Self-Deception" is an important chapter of Sartre's major philosophic work, *L'être et le néant.* It is also offered unabridged, in the translation of Hazel Barnes; but I have changed her translation of *mauvaise foi,* which she renders "bad faith." "Self-deception" seems much more accurate to me, and this is also how Philip Mairet has translated the same phrase in the final selection. The price I have had to pay for this change—and I think it was amply worth it—is that the contrast between "self-deception" and "good faith" is a bit less neat, and that the title of section III, "The 'Faith' of Self-Deception," no longer sounds like a play on words. That may be just as well, for Sartre's thought here does not all depend on the words. He himself is, of course, quite aware of this and soon speaks of "belief" (*croyance*) instead of "faith" (*foi*). In view of the many paradoxes he offers, it may be well to call attention to this passage, toward the end of section II: "there is a sincerity which bears on the past and which does not concern us here. . . . Here our concern is only with the sincerity which aims at itself in present immanence."

The "Portrait of the Antisemite" represents a slightly abridged version of the first part of *Réflexions sur la question Juive.*

Existentialism is a Humanism is Mairet's translation of Sartre's famous lecture, *L'existentialisme est un humanisme* (1946), unabridged. It has been published in England as *Existentialism and Humanism,* in the United States as *Existentialism,* and in Germany with the title *Ist der Existenzialismus eir Humanismus?* It has been widely mistaken for the definitive statement of existentialism, but is a brilliant lecture which bears the stamp of the moment. According to Genesis and Kierkegaard, it was not an angel that "commanded Abraham to sacrifice his son"; more important, Jaspers is not a professed Catholic; and the definition of existentialism and many of the arguments invite criticism. Plainly, this is not the alpha and omega of existentialism, but it is eminently thought-provoking, and you can almost hear Sartre talk.

"Marxism and Existentialism" is the essay with which Sartre's *Critique of Dialectical Reason* begins. *Critique de la raison dialectique (précédé de Question de méthode)* was published in 1960, and fifteen years later the only part of it that had appeared in a complete English version was *Search for a Method*, translated by Hazel Barnes. The first of the three chapters, "Marxism and Existentialism," has been abridged here; but the first sentence of this selection comes from Sartre's Preface, and the last two sentences are the beginning of the second chapter. In these pages Sartre embraces Marxism as "the one philosophy of our time which we cannot go beyond," and he tries to define the relation of his own early existentialism to Marxism.

In a way, this is the epitaph of existentialism. Jaspers and Heidegger had sought to dissociate themselves from existentialism as soon as Sartre made it world famous after World War II. This is not the place to discuss Sartre's Marxism, which is at least as eccentric as Kierkegaard's Christianity. But he no longer writes under the banner of existentialism; nor does any other major figure. In a sense, then, "Marxism and Existentialism" marks the end of existentialism. In another sense, existentialism is a timeless tendency, and the men whose writings are presented in this volume have something to say that remains worth studying and thinking about. The days of Greek tragedy are over, but reading Aeschylus, Sophocles, and Euripides is as important as ever. Jaspers, Heidegger, and Sartre do not approximate the format of these poets, but anyone who cares about humanity in the twentieth century can hardly ignore the writings collected here.]

1. The Wall

They pushed us into a big white room and I began to blink because the light hurt my eyes. Then I saw a table and

four men behind the table, civilians, looking over the papers.
They had bunched another group of prisoners in the back
and we had to cross the whole room to join them. There were
several I knew and some others who must have been
foreigners. The two in front of me were blond with round
skulls; they looked alike. I supposed they were French. The
smaller one kept hitching up his pants; nerves.

It lasted about three hours; I was dizzy and my head was
empty; but the room was well heated and I found that pleasant enough: for the past 24 hours we hadn't stopped shiv-
ering. The guards brought the prisoners up to the table,
one after the other. The four men asked each one his name
and occupation. Most of the time they didn't go any further
—or they would simply ask a question here and there: "Did
you have anything to do with the sabotage of munitions?"
Or "Where were you the morning of the 9th and what were
you doing?" They didn't listen to the answers or at least
didn't seem to. They were quiet for a moment and then looking straight in front of them began to write. They asked Tom
if it were true he was in the International Brigade; Tom
couldn't tell them otherwise because of the papers they
found in his coat. They didn't ask Juan anything but they
wrote for a long time after he told them his name.

"My brother José is the anarchist," Juan said, "you know
he isn't here any more. I don't belong to any party, I
never had anything to do with politics."

They didn't answer. Juan went on, "I haven't done anything. I don't want to pay for somebody else."

His lips trembled. A guard shut him up and took him
away. It was my turn.

"Your name is Pablo Ibbieta?"

"Yes."

The man looked at the papers and asked me, "Where's
Ramon Gris?"

"I don't know."

"You hid him in your house from the 6th to the 19th."

"No."

They wrote for a minute and then the guards took me out.
In the corridor Tom and Juan were waiting between two
guards. We started walking. Tom asked one of the guards,
"So?"

"So what?" the guard said.

"Was that the cross-examination or the sentence?"

"Sentence," the guard said.

"What are they going to do with us?"

The guard answered dryly, "Sentence will be read in your cell."

As a matter of fact, our cell was one of the hospital cellars. It was terrifically cold there because of the drafts. We shivered all night and it wasn't much better during the day. I had spent the previous five days in a cell in a monastery, a sort of hole in the wall that must have dated from the middle ages: since there were a lot of prisoners and not much room, they locked us up anywhere. I didn't miss my cell; I hadn't suffered too much from the cold but I was alone; after a long time it gets irritating. In the cellar I had company. Juan hardly ever spoke: he was afraid and he was too young to have anything to say. But Tom was a good talker and he knew Spanish well.

There was a bench in the cellar and four mats. When they took us back we sat and waited in silence. After a long moment, Tom said, "We're screwed."

"I think so too," I said, "but I don't think they'll do anything to the kid."

"They don't have a thing against him," said Tom. "He's the brother of a militiaman and that's all."

I looked at Juan: he didn't seem to hear. Tom went on, "You know what they do in Saragossa? They lay the men down on the road and run over them with trucks. A Moroccan deserter told us that. They said it was to save ammunition."

"It doesn't save gas," I said.

I was annoyed at Tom: he shouldn't have said that.

"Then there's officers walking along the road," he went on, "supervising it all. They stick their hands in their pockets and smoke cigarettes. You think they finish off the guys? Hell no. They let them scream. Sometimes for an hour. The Moroccan said he damned near puked the first time."

"I don't believe they'll do that here," I said. "Unless they're really short on ammunition."

Day was coming in through four airholes and a round opening they had made in the ceiling on the left, and you could see the sky through it. Through this hole, usually closed by a trap, they unloaded coal into the cellar. Just be-

low the hole there was a big pile of coal dust; it had been
used to heat the hospital, but since the beginning of the war
the patients were evacuated and the coal stayed there, unused; sometimes it even got rained on because they had forgotten to close the trap.

Tom began to shiver. "Good Jesus Christ, I'm cold," he
said. "Here it goes again."

He got up and began to do exercises. At each movement
his shirt opened on his chest, white and hairy. He lay on his
back, raised his legs in the air and bicycled. I saw his great
rump trembling. Tom was husky but he had too much fat. I
thought how rifle bullets or the sharp points of bayonets
would soon be sunk into this mass of tender flesh as in a
lump of butter. It wouldn't have made me feel like that if
he'd been thin.

I wasn't exactly cold, but I couldn't feel my arms and
shoulders any more. Sometimes I had the impression I was
missing something and began to look around for my coat
and then suddenly remembered they hadn't given me a coat.
It was rather uncomfortable. They took our clothes and
gave them to their soldiers leaving us only our shirts—and
those canvas pants that hospital patients wear in the middle
of summer. After a while Tom got up and sat next to me,
breathing heavily.

"Warmer?"

"Good Christ, no. But I'm out of wind."

Around eight o'clock in the evening a major came in with
two *falangistas*. He had a sheet of paper in his hand. He
asked the guard, "What are the names of those three?"

"Steinbock, Ibbieta and Mirbal," the guard said.

The major put on his eyeglasses and scanned the list:
"Steinbock . . . Steinbock . . . Oh yes . . . You are sentenced to death. You will be shot tomorrow morning." He
went on looking. "The other two as well."

"That's not possible," Juan said. "Not me."

The major looked at him amazed. "What's your name?"

"Juan Mirbal," he said.

"Well, your name is there," said the major. "You're sentenced."

"I didn't do anything," Juan said.

The major shrugged his shoulders and turned to Tom and
me.

"You're Basque?"

"Nobody is Basque."

He looked annoyed. "They told me there were three Basques. I'm not going to waste my time running after them. Then naturally you don't want a priest?"

We didn't even answer.

He said, "A Belgian doctor is coming shortly. He is authorized to spend the night with you." He made a military salute and left.

"What did I tell you," Tom said. "We get it."

"Yes," I said, "it's a rotten deal for the kid."

I said that to be decent but I didn't like the kid. His face was too thin and fear and suffering had disfigured it, twisting all his features. Three days before he was a smart sort of kid, not too bad; but now he looked like an old fairy and I thought how he'd never be young again, even if they were to let him go. It wouldn't have been too hard to have a little pity for him but pity disgusts me, or rather it horrifies me. He hadn't said anything more but he had turned grey; his face and hands were both grey. He sat down again and looked at the ground with round eyes. Tom was good hearted, he wanted to take his arm, but the kid tore himself away violently and made a face.

"Let him alone," I said in a low voice, "you can see he's going to blubber."

Tom obeyed regretfully; he would have liked to comfort the kid, it would have passed his time and he wouldn't have been tempted to think about himself. But it annoyed me: I'd never thought about death because I never had any reason to, but now the reason was here and there was nothing to do but think about it.

Tom began to talk. "So you think you've knocked guys off, do you?" he asked me. I didn't answer. He began explaining to me that he had knocked off six since the beginning of August; he didn't realize the situation and I could tell he didn't *want* to realize it. I hadn't quite realized it myself, I wondered if it hurt much, I thought of bullets, I imagined their burning hail through my body. All that was beside the real question; but I was calm: we had all night to understand. After a while Tom stopped talking and I watched him out of the corner of my eye; I saw he too had turned grey and he looked rotten; I told myself "Now it starts." It was almost dark, a dim glow filtered through the airholes and the pile of coal and made a big stain beneath the spot of sky; I could already see a star through the hole in the ceiling: the night would be pure and icy.

The door opened and two guards came in, followed by a blonde man in a tan uniform. He saluted us. "I am the doctor," he said. "I have authorization to help you in these trying hours."

He had an agreeable and distinguished voice. I said, "What do you want here?"

"I am at your disposal. I shall do all I can to make your last moments less difficult."

"What did you come here for? There are others, the hospital's full of them."

"I was sent here," he answered with a vague look. "Ah! Would you like to smoke?" he added hurriedly, "I have cigarettes and even cigars."

He offered us English cigarettes and *puros,* but we refused. I looked him in the eyes and he seemed irritated. I said to him, "You aren't here on an errand of mercy. Besides, I know you. I saw you with the fascists in the barracks yard the day I was arrested."

I was going to continue, but something surprising suddenly happened to me; the presence of this doctor no longer interested me. Generally when I'm on somebody I don't let go. But the desire to talk left me completely; I shrugged and turned my eyes away. A little later I raised my head; he was watching me curiously. The guards were sitting on a mat. Pedro, the tall thin one, was twiddling his thumbs, the other shook his head from time to time to keep from falling asleep.

"Do you want a light?" Pedro suddenly asked the doctor. The other nodded "Yes": I think he was about as smart as a log, but he surely wasn't bad. Looking in his cold blue eyes it seemed to me that his only sin was lack of imagination. Pedro went out and came back with an oil lamp which he set on the corner of the bench. It gave a bad light but it was better than nothing: they had left us in the dark the night before. For a long time I watched the circle of light the lamp made on the ceiling. I was fascinated. Then suddenly I woke up, the circle of light disappeared and I felt myself crushed under an enormous weight. It was not the thought of death, or fear; it was nameless. My cheeks burned and my head ached.

I shook myself and looked at my two friends. Tom had hidden his face in his hands. I could only see the fat white nape of his neck. Little Juan was the worst, his mouth was open and his nostrils trembled. The doctor went to him and put his hand on his shoulder to comfort him: but his eyes stayed cold. Then I saw the Belgian's hand drop stealthily along Juan's arm, down to the wrist. Juan paid no attention. The Belgian took his wrist between three fingers, distractedly, the same time drawing back a little and turning his back to me. But I leaned backward and saw him take a watch from his pocket and look at it for a moment, never letting go of the wrist. After a minute he let the hand fall inert and went and leaned his back against the wall, then, as if he suddenly remembered something very important which had to be jotted down on the spot, he took a notebook from his pocket and wrote a few lines. "Bastard," I thought angrily, "let him come and take my pulse. I'll shove my fist in his rotten face."

He didn't come but I felt him watching me. I raised my head and returned his look. Impersonally, he said to me, "Doesn't it seem cold to you here?" He looked cold, he was blue.

"I'm not cold," I told him.

He never took his hard eyes off me. Suddenly I understood and my hands went to my face: I was drenched in sweat. In this cellar, in the midst of winter, in the midst of drafts, I was sweating. I ran my hands through my hair, gummed together with perspiration; at the same time I saw my shirt was damp and sticking to my skin: I had been dripping for an hour and hadn't felt it. But that swine of a Belgian hadn't missed a thing; he had seen the drops rolling down my cheeks and thought: this is the manifestation of an almost pathological state of terror; and he had felt normal and proud of being alive because he was cold. I wanted to stand up and smash his face but no sooner had I made the slightest gesture than my rage and shame were wiped out; I fell back on the bench with indifference.

I satisfied myself by rubbing my neck with my handkerchief because now I felt the sweat dropping from my hair onto my neck and it was unpleasant. I soon gave up rubbing, it was useless; my handkerchief was already soaked and I was still sweating. My buttocks were sweating too and my damp trousers were glued to the bench.

Suddenly Juan spoke. "You're a doctor?"

"Yes," the Belgian said.

"Does it hurt . . . very long?"

"Huh? When . . . ? Oh, no," the Belgian said paternally. "Not at all. It's over quickly." He acted as though he were calming a cash customer.

"But I . . . they told me . . . sometimes they have to fire twice."

"Sometimes," the Belgian said, nodding. "It may happen that the first volley reaches no vital organs."

"Then they have to reload their rifles and aim all over again?" He thought for a moment and then added hoarsely, "That takes time!"

He had a terrible fear of suffering, it was all he thought about: it was his age. I never thought much about it and it wasn't fear of suffering that made me sweat.

I got up and walked to the pile of coal dust. Tom jumped up and threw me a hateful look: I had annoyed him because my shoes squeaked. I wondered if my face looked as frightened as his: I saw he was sweating too. The sky was superb, no light filtered into the dark corner and I had only to raise my head to see the Big Dipper. But it wasn't like it had been: the night before I could see a great piece of sky from my monastery cell and each hour of the day brought me a different memory. Morning, when the sky was a hard, light blue, I thought of beaches on the Atlantic; at noon I saw the sun and I remembered a bar in Seville where I drank manzanilla and ate olives and anchovies; afternoons I was in the shade and I thought of the deep shadow which spreads over half a bull-ring leaving the other half shimmering in sunlight; it was really hard to see the whole world reflected in the sky like that. But now I could watch the sky as much as I pleased, it no longer evoked anything in me. I liked that better. I came back and sat near Tom. A long moment passed.

Tom began speaking in a low voice. He had to talk, without that he wouldn't have been able to recognize himself in his own mind. I thought he was talking to me but he wasn't looking at me. He was undoubtedly afraid to see me as I was, grey and sweating: we were alike and worse than mirrors of each other. He watched the Belgian, the living.

"Do you understand?" he said. "I don't understand."

I began to speak in a low voice too. I watched the Belgian. "Why? What's the matter?"

"Something is going to happen to us that I can't understand."

There was a strange smell about Tom. It seemed to me I was more sensitive than usual to odors. I grinned. "You'll understand in a while."

"It isn't clear," he said obstinately. "I want to be brave but first I have to know . . . Listen, they're going to take us into the courtyard. Good. They're going to stand up in front of us. How many?"

"I don't know. Five or eight. Not more."

"All right. There'll be eight. Someone'll holler 'aim!' and I'll see eight rifles looking at me. I'll think how I'd like to get inside the wall, I'll push against it with my back . . . with every ounce of strength I have, but the wall will stay, like in a nightmare. I can imagine all that. If you only knew how well I can imagine it."

"All right, all right!" I said, "I can imagine it too."

"It must hurt like hell. You know, they aim at the eyes and the mouth to disfigure you," he added mechanically. "I can feel the wounds already; I've had pains in my head and in my neck for the past hour. Not real pains. Worse. This is what I'm going to feel tomorrow morning. And then what?"

I well understood what he meant but I didn't want to act as if I did. I had pains too, pains in my body like a crowd of tiny scars. I couldn't get used to it. But I was like him, I attached no importance to it. "After," I said, "you'll be pushing up daisies."

He began to talk to himself: he never stopped watching the Belgian. The Belgian didn't seem to be listening. I knew what he had come to do; he wasn't interested in what we thought; he came to watch our bodies, bodies dying in agony while yet alive.

"It's like a nightmare," Tom was saying. "You want to think something, you always have the impression that it's all right, that you're going to understand and then it slips, it escapes you and fades away. I tell myself there will be nothing afterwards. But I don't understand what it means. Sometimes I almost can . . . and then it fades away and I start thinking about the pains again, bullets, explosions. I'm a materialist, I swear it to you; I'm not going crazy. But something's the matter. I see my corpse; that's not hard but *I'm* the one who sees it, with *my* eyes. I've got to think . . . think that I won't see anything anymore and the world will go on for the others. We aren't made to think that, Pablo. Believe me: I've already stayed up a whole night waiting for something. But this isn't the same: this will creep up behind us, Pablo, and we won't be able to prepare for it."

"Shut up," I said, "Do you want me to call a priest?"

He didn't answer. I had already noticed he had the tendency to act like a prophet and call me Pablo, speaking in a toneless voice. I didn't like that: but it seems all the Irish are that way. I had the vague impression he smelled of urine. Fundamentally, I hadn't much sympathy for Tom and I didn't see why, under the pretext of dying together, I should have any more. It would have been different with some others. With Ramon Gris, for example. But I felt alone between Tom and Juan. I liked that better, anyhow: with Ramon I might have been more deeply moved. But I was terribly hard just then and I wanted to stay hard.

He kept on chewing his words, with something like distraction. He certainly talked to keep himself from thinking. He smelled of urine like an old prostate case. Naturally, I agreed with him, I could have said everything he said: it isn't *natural* to die. And since I was going to die, nothing seemed natural to me, not this pile of coal dust, or the bench, or Pedro's ugly face. Only it didn't please me to think the same things as Tom. And I knew that, all through the night, every five minutes, we would keep on thinking things at the same time. I looked at him sideways and for the first time he seemed strange to me: he wore death on his face. My pride was wounded: for the past 24 hours I had lived next to Tom, I had listened to him, I had spoken to him and I knew we had nothing in common. And now we looked as much alike as twin brothers, simply because we were going to die together. Tom took my hand without looking at me.

"Pablo, I wonder . . . I wonder if it's really true that everything ends."

I took my hand away and said, "Look between your feet, you pig."

There was a big puddle between his feet and drops fell from his pants-leg.

"What is it," he asked, frightened.

"You're pissing in your pants," I told him.

"It isn't true," he said furiously. "I'm not pissing. I don't feel anything."

The Belgian approached us. He asked with false solicitude, "Do you feel ill?"

Tom did not answer. The Belgian looked at the puddle and said nothing.

"I don't know what it is," Tom said ferociously. "But I'm not afraid. I swear I'm not afraid."

The Belgian did not answer. Tom got up and went to piss in a corner. He came back buttoning his fly, and sat down without a word. The Belgian was taking notes.

All three of us watched him because he was alive. He had the motions of a living human being, the cares of a living human being; he shivered in the cellar the way the living are supposed to shiver; he had an obedient, well-fed body. The rest of us hardly felt ours—not in the same way anyhow. I wanted to feel my pants between my legs but I didn't dare; I watched the Belgian, balancing on his legs, master of his muscles, someone who could think about tomorrow. There we were, three bloodless shadows; we watched him and we sucked his life like vampires.

Finally he went over to little Juan. Did he want to feel his neck for some professional motive or was he obeying an impulse of charity? If he was acting by charity it was the only time during the whole night.

He caressed Juan's head and neck. The kid let himself be handled, his eyes never leaving him, then suddenly, he seized the hand and looked at it strangely. He held the Belgian's hand between his own two hands and there was nothing pleasant about them, two grey pincers gripping this fat and reddish hand. I suspected what was going to happen and Tom must have suspected it too: but the Belgian didn't see a thing, he smiled paternally. After a moment the kid brought the fat red hand to his mouth and tried to bite it. The Belgian pulled away quickly and stumbled back against the wall. For a second he looked at us with horror, he must have suddenly understood that we were not men like him. I began to laugh and one of the guards jumped up. The other was asleep, his wide open eyes were blank.

I felt relaxed and over-excited at the same time. I didn't want to think any more about what would happen at dawn, at death. It made no sense. I only found words or emptiness. But as soon as I tried to think of anything else I saw rifle barrels pointing at me. Perhaps I lived through my execution twenty times; once I even thought it was for good: I must have slept a minute. They were dragging me to the wall and I was struggling; I was asking for mercy. I woke up with a start and looked at the Belgian: I was afraid I might have cried out in my sleep. But he was stroking his moustache, he hadn't noticed anything. If I had wanted to, I think I could have slept a while; I had been awake for 48 hours. I was at the end of my rope. But I didn't want to lose two hours of life: they would come to wake me up at dawn, I would follow them, stupefied with sleep and I would have croaked without so much as an "Oof!"; I didn't want that, I didn't want to die like an animal, I wanted to understand. Then I was afraid of having nightmares. I got up, walked back and forth, and, to change my ideas, I began to think about my past life. A crowd of memories came back to me pell-mell. There were good and bad ones—or at least I called them that *before*. There were faces and incidents. I saw the face of a little *novillero* who was gored in Valencia during the *Feria,* the face of one of my uncles, the face of Ramon Gris. I remembered my whole life: how I was out of work for three months in 1926, how I almost starved to death. I re-memberd a night I spent on a bench in Granada: I hadn't eaten for three days. I was angry, I didn't want to die. That made me smile. How madly I ran after happiness, after women, after liberty. Why? I wanted to free Spain, I ad-mired Pi y Margall, I joined the anarchist movement, I spoke in public meetings: I took everything as serious.y as if I were immortal.

At that moment I felt that I had my whole life in front of me and I thought, "It's a damned lie." It was worth nothing because it was finished. I wondered how I'd been able to walk, to laugh with the girls: I wouldn't have moved so much as my little finger if I had only imagined I would die like this. My life was in front of me, shut, closed, like a bag and yet everything inside of it was unfinished. For an instant I tried to judge it. I wanted to tell myself, this is a beautiful life. But I couldn't pass judgment on it; it was only a sketch; I had spent my time counterfeiting eternity, I had understood nothing. I missed nothing: there were so many things I could have missed, the taste of *manzanilla* or the baths I took in summer in a little creek near Cadiz; but death had disenchanted everything.

The Belgian suddenly had a bright idea. "My friends," he told us, "I will undertake—if the military administration will allow it—to send a message for you, a souvenir to those who love you . . ."

Tom mumbled, "I don't have anybody."

I said nothing. Tom waited an instant then looked at me with curiosity. "You don't have anything to say to Concha?"

"No."

I hated this tender complicity: it was my own fault, I had talked about Concha the night before, I should have controlled myself. I was with her for a year. Last night I would have given an arm to see her again for five minutes. That was why I talked about her, it was stronger than I was. Now I had no more desire to see her, I had nothing more to say to her. I would not even have wanted to hold her in my arms: my body filled me with horror because it was grey and sweating—and I wasn't sure that her body didn't fill me with horror. Concha would cry when she found out I was dead, she would have no taste for life for months afterward. But I was still the one who was going to die. I thought of her soft, beautiful eyes. When she looked at me something passed from her to me. But I knew it was over: if she looked at me *now* the look would stay in her eyes, it wouldn't reach me. I was alone.

Tom was alone too but not in the same way. Sitting cross-legged, he had begun to stare at the bench with a sort of smile, he looked amazed. He put out his hand and touched the wood cautiously as if he were afraid of breaking something, then drew back his hand quickly and shuddered. If I had been Tom I wouldn't have amused myself by touching the bench; this was some more Irish nonsense, but I too found that objects had a funny look: they were more obliterated, less dense than usual. It was enough for me to look at the bench, the lamp, the pile of coal dust, to feel that I was going to die. Naturally I couldn't think clearly about my death but I saw it everywhere, on things, in the way things fell back and kept their distance, discreetly, as people who speak quietly at the bedside of a dying man. It was *his* death which Tom had just touched on the bench.

In the state I was in, if someone had come and told me I could go home quietly, that they would leave me my life whole, it would have left me cold: several hours or several years of waiting is all the same when you have lost the illusion of being eternal. I clung to nothing, in a way I was calm. But it was a horrible calm—because of my body; my body, I saw with its eyes, I heard with its ears, but it was no longer me; it sweated and trembled by itself and I didn't recognize it any more. I had to touch it and look at it to find out what was happening, as if it were the body of someone else. At times I could still feel it, I felt sinkings, and fall- ings, as when you're in a plane taking a nosedive, or I felt my heart beating. But that didn't reassure me. Everything that came from my body was all cockeyed. Most of the time it was quiet and I felt no more than a sort of weight, a filthy presence against me; I had the impression of being tied to an enormous vermin. Once I felt my pants and I felt they were damp; I didn't know whether it was sweat or urine, but I went to piss on the coal pile as a precaution.

The Belgian took out his watch, looked at it. He said, "It is three-thirty."

Bastard! He must have done it on purpose. Tom jumped; we hadn't noticed time was running out; night surrounded us like a shapeless, somber mass, I couldn't even remember that it had begun.

Little Juan began to cry. He wrung his hands, pleaded, "I don't want to die. I don't want to die."

He ran across the whole cellar waving his arms in the air then fell sobbing on one of the mats. Tom watched him with mournful eyes, without the slightest desire to console him. Because it wasn't worth the trouble: the kid made more noise than we did, but he was less touched: he was like a sick man who defends himself against his illness by fever. It's much more serious when there isn't any fever.

He wept: I could clearly see he was pitying himself; he wasn't thinking about death. For one second, one single sec- ond, I wanted to weep myself, to weep with pity for myself. But the opposite happened: I glanced at the kid, I saw his thin sobbing shoulders and I felt inhuman: I could pity neither the others nor myself. I said to myself, "I want to die cleanly."

Tom had gotten up, he placed himself just under the round opening and began to watch for daylight. I was determined to die cleanly and I only thought of that. But ever since the doctor told us the time, I felt time flying, flowing away drop by drop.

It was still dark when I heard Tom's voice: "Do you hear them?"

Men were marching in the courtyard.

"Yes."

"What the hell are they doing? They can't shoot in the dark."

After a while we heard no more. I said to Tom, "It's day."

Pedro got up, yawning, and came to blow out the lamp. He said to his buddy, "Cold as hell."

The cellar was all grey. We heard shots in the distance.

"It's starting," I told Tom. "They must do it in the court in the rear."

Tom asked the doctor for a cigarette. I didn't want one; I didn't want cigarettes or alcohol. From that moment on they didn't stop firing.

"Do you realize what's happening," Tom said.

He wanted to add something but kept quiet, watching the door. The door opened and a lieutenant came in with four soldiers. Tom dropped his cigarette.

"Steinbock?"

Tom didn't answer. Pedro pointed him out.

"Juan Mirbal?"

"On the mat."

"Get up," the lieutenant said.

Juan did not move. Two soldiers took him under the arms and set him on his feet. But he fell as soon as they released him.

The soldiers hesitated.

"He's not the first sick one," said the lieutenant. "You two carry him; they'll fix it up down there."

He turned to Tom. "Let's go."

Tom went out between two soldiers. Two others followed, carrying the kid by the armpits. He hadn't fainted; his eyes were wide open and tears ran down his cheeks. When I wanted to go out the lieutenant stopped me.

"You Ibbieta?"

"Yes."

"You wait here; they'll come for you later."

They left. The Belgian and the two jailers left too, I was alone. I did not understand what was happening to me but I would have liked it better if they had gotten it over with right away. I heard shots at almost regular intervals; I shook with each one of them. I wanted to scream and tear out my hair. But I gritted my teeth and pushed my hands in my pockets because I wanted to stay clean.

After an hour they came to get me and led me to the first floor, to a small room that smelt of cigars and where the heat was stifling. There were two officers sitting smoking in the armchairs, papers on their knees.

"You're Ibbieta?"

"Yes."

"Where is Ramon Gris?"

"I don't know."

The one questioning me was short and fat. His eyes were hard behind his glasses. He said to me, "Come here."

I went to him. He got up and took my arms, staring at me with a look that should have pushed me into the earth. At the same time he pinched my biceps with all his might. It wasn't to hurt me, it was only a game: he wanted to dominate me. He also thought he had to blow his stinking breath square in my face. We stayed for a moment like that, and I almost felt like laughing. It takes a lot to intimidate a man who is going to die; it didn't work. He pushed me back violently and sat down again. He said, "It's his life against yours. You can have yours if you tell us where he is."

These men dolled up with their riding crops and boots were still going to die. A little later than I, but not too much. They busied themselves looking for names in their crumpled papers, they ran after other men to imprison or suppress them; they had opinions on the future of Spain and on other subjects. Their little activities seemed shocking and burlesqued to me; I couldn't put myself in their place, I thought they were insane. The little man was still looking at me, whipping his boots with the riding crop. All his gestures were calculated to give him the look of a live and ferocious beast.

"So? You understand?"

"I don't know where Gris is," I answered. "I thought he was in Madrid."

The other officer raised his pale hand indolently. This indolence was also calculated. I saw through all their little schemes and I was stupefied to find there were men who amused themselves that way.

"You have a quarter of an hour to think it over," he said slowly. "Take him to the laundry, bring him back in fifteen minutes. If he still refuses he will be executed on the spot."

They knew what they were doing: I had passed the night in waiting; then they had made me wait an hour in the cellar while they shot Tom and Juan and now they were locking me up in the laundry; they must have prepared their game the night before. They told themselves that nerves eventually wear out and they hoped to get me that way.

They were badly mistaken. In the laundry I sat on a stool because I felt very weak and I began to think. But not about their proposition. Of course I knew were Gris was; he was hiding with his cousins, four kilometers from the city. I also knew that I would not reveal his hiding place unless they tortured me (but they didn't seem to be thinking about that). All that was perfectly regulated, definite and in no way interested me. Only I would have liked to understand the reasons for my conduct. I would rather die than give up Gris. Why? I didn't like Ramon Gris any more. My friendship for him had died a little while before dawn at the same time as my love for Concha, at the same time as my desire to live. Undoubtedly I thought highly of him: he was tough. But it was not for this reason that I consented to die in his place; his life had no more value than mine; no life had value. They were going to slap a man up against a wall and shoot at him till he died, whether it was I or Gris or somebody else made no difference. I knew he was more useful than I to the cause of Spain but I thought to hell with Spain and anarchy; nothing was important. Yet I was there, I could save my skin and give up Gris and I refused to do it. I found that somehow comic; it was obstinacy. I thought, "I must be stubborn!" And a droll sort of gaiety spread over me.

They came for me and brought me back to the two officers. A rat ran out from under my feet and that amused me. I turned to one of the *falangistas* and said, "Did you see the rat?"

He didn't answer. He was very sober, he took himself seriously. I wanted to laugh but I held myself back because I was afraid that once I got started I wouldn't be able to stop. The *falangista* had a moustache. I said to him again, "You ought to shave off your moustache, idiot." I thought it funny that he would let the hairs of his living being invade his face. He kicked me without great conviction and I kept quiet.

"Well," said the fat officer, "have you thought about it?"
I looked at them with curiosity, as insects of a very rare
species. I told them, "I know where he is. He is hidden in
the cemetery. In a vault or in the gravediggers' shack."

It was a farce. I wanted to see them stand up, buckle their
belts and give orders busily.

They jumped to their feet. "Let's go. Molés, go get fifteen
men from Lieutenant Lopez. You," the fat man said, "I'll
let you off if you're telling the truth, but it'll cost you
plenty if you're making monkeys out of us."

They left in a great clatter and I waited peacefully under
the guard of *falangistas*. From time to time I smiled, thinking about the spectacle they would make. I felt stunned
and malicious. I imagined them lifting up tombstones, opening the doors of the vaults one by one. I represented this
situation to myself as if I had been someone else: this
prisoner obstinately playing the hero, these grim falangistas
with their moustaches and their men in uniform running
among the graves; it was irresistibly funny. After half an
hour the little fat man came back alone. I thought he had
come to give the orders to execute me. The others must have
stayed in the cemetery.

The officer looked at me. He didn't look at all sheepish.
"Take him into the big courtyard with the others," he said.
"After the military operations a regular court will decide
what happens to him."

"Then they're not . . . not going to shoot me? . . ."

"Not now, anyway. What happens afterwards is none of
my business."

I still didn't understand. I asked, "But why . . . ?"

He shrugged his shoulders without answering and the soldiers took me away. In the big courtyard there were about a
hundred prisoners, women, children and a few old men. I
began walking around the central grass-plot, I was stupefied.
At noon they let us eat in the mess hall. Two or three people
questioned me. I must have known them, but I didn't answer: I didn't even know where I was.

Around evening they pushed about ten new prisoners into
the court. I recognized Garcia, the baker. He said, "What
damned luck you have! I didn't think I'd see you alive."

"They sentenced me to death," I said, "and then they
changed their minds. I don't know why."

"They arrested me at two o'clock," Garcia said.

"Why?" Garcia had nothing to do with politics.

"I don't know," he said. "They arrest everybody who doesn't think the way they do. He lowered his voice. "They got Gris."

I began to tremble. "When?"

"This morning. He messed it up. He left his cousin's on Tuesday because they had an argument. There were plenty of people to hide him but he didn't want to owe anything to anybody. He said, 'I'd go and hide in Ibbieta's place, but they got him, so I'll go hide in the cemetery.'"

"In the cemetery?"

"Yes. What a fool. Of course they went by there this morning, that was sure to happen. They found him in the gravediggers' shack. He shot at them and they got him."

"In the cemetery!"

Everything began to spin and I found myself sitting on the ground: I laughed so hard I cried.

2. Self-Deception

I. SELF-DECEPTION AND FALSEHOOD

The human being is not only the being by whom négatités[1] are disclosed in the world; he is also the one who can take negative attitudes with respect to himself. In our Introduction we defined consciousness as "a being, the nature of which is to question its own being, that being implying a being other than itself." But now that we have examined the meaning of "the question," we can at present also write the formula thus: "Consciousness is a being, the nature of which is to be conscious of the nothingness of its being." In a prohibition or a veto, for example, the human being denies a future transcendence. But this negation is not verifiable. My consciousness is not restricted to considering a négatité. It constitutes itself in its own substance as the annihilation of a possibility which another human reality projects as its possibility. For that reason it must arise in the world as a *Not;* it is as a Not that the slave first apprehends the master, or that the prisoner who is trying to escape sees the guard who is watching him. There are even men (*e.g.*, caretakers, overseers, gaolers), whose social reality is uniquely that of the Not, who will live and die, having forever been only a Not upon the earth. Others, so as to make the Not a part of

their very subjectivity, establish their human personality
as a perpetual negation. This is the meaning and function of
what Scheler calls "the man of resentment"—in reality,
the Not. But there exist more subtle behaviours, the description of which will lead us further into the inwardness of
consciousness. Irony is one of these. In irony a man annihilates what he posits within one and the same act; he leads
us to believe in order not to be believed; he affirms to deny
and denies to affirm; he creates a positive object but it
has no being other than its nothingness. Thus attitudes of
negation toward the self permit us to raise a new question:
What are we to say is the nature of man who has the possibility of denying himself? But it is out of the question to discuss the attitude of "self-negation" in its universality. The
kinds of behaviour which can be ranked under this heading
are too diverse; we risk retaining only the abstract form of
them. It is best to choose and to examine one determined
attitude which is essential to human reality and which is
such that consciousness instead of directing its negation outward turns it toward itself. This attitude, it seems to me,
is self-deception (*mauvaise foi*).

Frequently this is identified with falsehood. We say indifferently of a person that he shows signs of self-deception
or that he lies to himself. We shall willingly grant that self-
deception is a lie to oneself, on condition that we distinguish
the lie to oneself from lying in general. Lying is a negative
attitude, we will agree to that. But this negation does not
bear on consciousness itself; it aims only at the transcendent. The essence of the lie implies in fact that the liar actually is in complete possession of the truth which he is
hiding. A man does not lie about what he is ignorant of; he
does not lie when he spreads an error of which he himself is
the dupe; he does not lie when he is mistaken. The ideal
description of the liar would be a cynical consciousness,
affirming truth within himself, denying it in his words, and
denying that negation as such. Now this doubly negative attitude rests on the transcendent; the fact expressed is transcendent since it does not exist, and the original negation
rests on a *truth;* that is, on a particular type of transcendence. As for the inner negation which I effect correlatively
with the affirmation for myself of the truth, this rests on
words; that is, on an event in the world. Furthermore the
inner disposition of the liar is positive; it could be the

object of an affirmative judgment. The liar intends to deceive and he does not seek to hide this intention from himself nor to disguise the translucency of consciousness; on the contrary, he has recourse to it when there is a question of deciding secondary behaviour. It explicitly exercises a regulatory control over all attitudes. As for his flaunted intention of telling the truth ("I'd never want to deceive you! This is true! I swear it!")—all this, of course, is the object of an inner negation, but also it is not recognized by the liar as *his* intention. It is played, imitated, it is the intention of the character which he plays in the eyes of his questioner, but this character, precisely because he *does not exist,* is a transcendent. Thus the lie does not put into play the inner structure of present consciousness; all the negations which constitute it bear on objects which by this fact are removed from consciousness. The lie then does not require special ontological foundation, and the explanations which the existence of negation in general requires are valid without change in the case of deceit. Of course we have described the ideal lie; doubtless it happens often enough that the liar is more or less the victim of his lie, that he half persuades himself of it. But these common, popular forms of the lie are also degenerate aspects of it; they represent intermediaries between falsehood and self-deception. The lie is a behaviour of transcendence.

The lie is also a normal phenomenon of what Heidegger calls the *"Mit-sein."* [2] It presupposes my existence, the existence of the *other,* my existence *for* the other, and the existence of the other *for* me. Thus there is no difficulty in holding that the liar must make the project of the lie in entire clarity and that he must possess a complete comprehension of the lie and of the truth which he is altering. It is sufficient that an opaqueness of principle hide his intentions from *the other,* it is sufficient that the other can take the lie for truth. By the lie consciousness affirms that it exists by nature as *hidden from the other;* it utilizes for its own profit the ontological duality of myself and myself in the eyes of others.

The situation can not be the same for self-deception if this, as we have said, is indeed a lie to oneself. To be sure, the one who practices self-deception is hiding a displeasing truth or presenting as truth a pleasing untruth. Self-deception then has in appearance the structure of falsehood. Only what changes everything is the fact that in self-deception it is from myself that I am hiding the truth. Thus the duality of the deceiver and the deceived does not exist here. Self-deception on the contrary implies in essence the unity of *a single* consciousness. This does not mean that it can not be conditioned by the *"Mit-sein"* like all other phenomena of human reality, but the *"Mit-sein"* can call forth self-deception only by presenting itself as a *situation* which self-deception permits surpassing; self-deception does not come from outside to human reality. One does not undergo his self-deception; one is not infected with it; it is not a *state.* But consciousness affects itself with self-deception. There must be an original intention and a project of self-deception; this project implies a comprehension of self-deception as such and a prereflective apprehension (of) consciousness[8] as affecting itself with self-deception. It follows first that the one to whom the lie is told and the one who lies are one and the same person, which means that I must know in my capacity as deceiver the truth which is hidden from me in my capacity as the one deceived. Better yet I must know the truth very exactly in *order* to conceal it more carefully —and this not at two different moments, which at a pinch would allow us to reestablish a semblance of duality—but in the unitary structure of a single project. How then can the lie subsist if the duality which conditions it is suppressed?

To this difficulty is added another which is derived from the total translucency of consciousness. That which affects itself with self-deception must be conscious (of) its self-deception since the being of consciousness is consciousness of being. It appears then that I must be in good faith, at least to the extent that I am conscious of my self-deception. But then this whole psychic system is annihilated. We must agree in fact that if I deliberately and cynically attempt to lie to myself, I fail completely in this undertaking; the lie falls back and collapses under my regard; it is ruined *from behind* by the very consciousness of lying to myself which pitilessly constitutes itself well within my project as its very condition. We have here an *evanescent* phenomenon which exists only in and through its own differentiation. To be sure, these phenomena are frequent and we shall see that there is in fact an "evanescence" in self-deception. It is evident that it vacillates continually between good faith and cynicism: Even though the existence of self-deception is very precarious, and though it belongs to the kind of psychic structures which we might call "metastable," [4] it presents nonetheless an autonomous and durable form. It can even be the normal aspect of life for a very great number of people. A person can *live* in self-deception, which does not mean that he does not have abrupt awakenings to cynicism or to good faith, but which implies a constant and particular style of life. Our embarrassment then appears extreme since we can neither reject nor comprehend self-deception.

To escape from these difficulties people gladly have recourse to the unconscious. In the psychoanalytical interpretation, for example, they use the hypothesis of a censor, conceived as a line of demarcation with customs, passport division, currency control, *etc.* to reestablish the duality of the deceiver and the deceived. Here instinct or, if you prefer, original drives and complexes of drives constituted by our individual history, make up *reality*. It is neither *true* nor *false* since it does not exist *for itself*. It simply *is*, exactly like this table, which is neither true nor false *in itself* but simply *real*. As for the conscious symbols of the instinct, this interpretation takes them not for appearances but for real psychic facts. Fear, forgetting, dreams exist really by virtue of concrete facts of consciousness, in the same way as the words and the attitudes of the liar are concrete, really existing patterns of behaviour. The subject has the same relation to these phenomena as the deceived to the behaviour of the deceiver. He establishes them in their reality and must interpret them. There is a *truth* in the activities of the deceiver; if the deceived could reattach them to the situation where the deceiver establishes himself and to his project of the lie, they would become integral parts of truth, by virtue of the behaviour of lying. Similarly there is a truth in the symbolic acts; it is what the psychoanalyst discovers when he reattaches them to the historical situation of the patient, to the unconscious complexes which they express, to the blocking of the censor. Thus the subject deceives himself about the *meaning* of his conduct, he apprehends it in its concrete existence but not in its *truth*, for lack of being able to derive it from an original situation and from a psychic constitution which remain alien to him.

By the distinction between the "id" and the "ego," Freud has cut the psychic whole into two. I *am* the ego but I am not the *id*. I hold no privileged position in relation to my unconscious psyche. I *am* my own psychic phenomena, in so far as I establish them in their conscious reality. For example, I am the impulse to steal this or that book from this bookstall. I am an integral part of the impulse; I bring it to light and I determine myself hand in hand with it to commit the theft. But I *am* not those psychic facts, in so far as I receive them passively and am obliged to resort to hypotheses about their origin and their true meaning, just as the scholar makes conjectures about the nature and essence of an external phenomenon. This theft, for example, which I interpret as an immediate impulse determined by the rarity, the interest, or the price of the volume which I am going to steal—it is in truth a process derived from self-punishment which is attached more or less directly to an Oedipus complex. The impulse toward the theft contains a truth which can be reached only by more or less probable hypotheses. The criterion of this truth will be the number of conscious psychic facts which it explains; from a more pragmatic point of view it will be also the success of the psychiatric cure which it allows. Finally the discovery of this truth will necessitate the cooperation of the psychoanalyst, who appears as the *mediator* between my unconscious drives and my conscious life. *The other* appears as being able to effect the synthesis between the unconscious thesis and the conscious antithesis. I can know myself only through the mediation of the other, which means that I stand in relation to *my* "id," in the position of *the other*. If I have a little knowledge of psychoanalysis, I can, under circumstances particularly favorable, try to psychoanalyze myself. But this attempt can succeed only if I distrust every kind of intuition, only if I apply to my case *from without*, abstract schemes and rules already learned. As for the results, whether they are obtained by my efforts alone or with the cooperation of a technician, they will never have the certainty which intuition confers; they will possess simply the always increasing probability of scientific hypotheses. The hypothesis of the Oedipus complex, like the atomic theory, is nothing but an "experimental idea"; as Pierce said, it is not to be distinguished from the totality of experiences which it allows to be realized and the results which it enables us to foresee. Thus psychoanalysis substitutes for the notion of self-deception, the idea of a lie without a liar; it allows me to understand how it is possible for me to be lied to without lying to myself since it places me in the same relation to myself that the other has in respect to me; it replaces the duality of the deceiver and the deceived, the essential condition of the lie, by that of the "id" and the "ego." It introduces into my subjectivity the deepest intersubjective structure of the *Mit-sein*. Can this explanation satisfy us?

Considered more closely the psychoanalytic theory is not as simple as it first appears. It is not accurate to hold that the "id" is presented as a thing in relation to the hypothesis of the psychoanalyst, for a thing is indifferent to the conjectures which we make concerning it, while the "id" on the contrary is sensitive to them when we approach the truth. Freud in fact reports resistance when at the end of the first period the doctor is approaching the truth. This resistance is objective behaviour apprehended from without: the patient shows defiance, refuses to speak, gives fantastic accounts of his dreams, sometimes even takes himself completely away from the psychoanalytic cure. It is a fair question to ask what part of himself can thus resist. It can not be the "Ego," envisaged as a psychic totality of the facts of consciousness; this could not suspect that the psychiatrist is approaching the end since its relation to the *meaning* of its own reactions is exactly like that of the psychiatrist himself. At the very most it is possible for the ego to appreciate objectively the degree of probability in the hypotheses set forth, as a witness of the psychoanalysis might be able to do, according to the number of subjective facts which they explain. Furthermore, this probability would appear to the ego to border on certainty, which he could not take offence at since most of the time it is he who by a *conscious* decision is in pursuit of the psychoanalytic therapy. Are we to say that the patient is disturbed by the daily revelations which the psychoanalyst makes to him and that he seeks to remove himself, at the same time pretending in his own eyes to wish to continue the cure? In this case it is no longer possible to resort to the unconscious to explain self-deception; it is there in full consciousness, with all its contradictions. But this resistance; for him it is secret and deep, it comes from afar; it has its roots in the very thing which the psychoanalyst is trying to make clear.

Furthermore it is equally impossible to explain the resistance as emanating from the complex which the psychoanalyst wishes to bring to light. The complex as such is rather the collaborator of the psychoanalyst since it aims at expressing itself in clear consciousness, since it plays tricks on the censor and seeks to elude it. The only level on which we can locate the refusal of the subject is that of the censor. It alone can comprehend the questions or the revelations of the psychoanalyst as approaching more or less near to the real drives which it strives to repress—it alone because it alone *knows* what it is repressing.

If we reject the language and the materialistic mythology of psychoanalysis, we perceive that the censor in order to apply its activity with discernment, must know what it is repressing. In fact if we abandon all the metaphors representing the repression as the impact of blind forces, we are compelled to admit that the censor must choose and in order to choose must be aware of so doing. How could it happen otherwise that the censor allows lawful sexual impulses to pass through, that it permits needs (hunger, thirst, sleep) to be expressed in clear consciousness? And how are we to explain that it can relax its surveillance, that it can even be *deceived* by the disguises of the instinct? But it is not sufficient that it discern the condemned drives; it must also apprehend them as *to be repressed*, which implies in it at the very least an awareness of its activity. In a word, how could the censor discern the impulses needing to be repressed without being conscious of discerning them? How can we conceive of a knowledge which is ignorant of itself? To know is to know that one knows, said Alain. Let us say rather: all knowing is consciousness of knowing. Thus the resistance of the patient implies on the level of the censor an awareness of the thing repressed as such, a comprehension of the end toward which the questions of the psychoanalyst are leading, and an act of synthetic connection by which it compares the *truth* of the repressed complex to the psychoanalytic hypothesis which aims at it. These various operations in their turn imply that the censor is conscious (of) itself. But what type of self-consciousness can the censor have? It must be the consciousness (of) being conscious of the drive to be repressed, but precisely *in order not to be conscious of it*. What does this mean if not that the censor is in self-deception?

Psychoanalysis has not gained anything for us since in order to overcome self-deception, it has established between the unconscious and consciousness an autonomous consciousness in self-deception. The effort to establish a veritable duality and even a trinity (*Es, Ich, Ueberich* expressing themselves through the censor) has resulted in a merely verbal terminology. The very essence of the reflexive idea of hiding something from oneself implies the unity of one and the same psychic mechanism and consequently a double activity in the heart of unity, tending on the one hand to maintain and locate the thing to be concealed and on the other hand to repress and disguise it. Each of the two aspects of this activity is complementary to the other; that is, it implies the other in its being. By separating consciousness from the unconscious by means of the censor, psychoanalysis has not succeeded in dissociating the two phases of the act, since the libido is a blind conatus toward conscious expression and since the conscious phenomenon is a passive, faked result. Psychoanalysis has merely localized this double activity of repulsion and attraction on the level of the censor. Furthermore the problem still remains of accounting for the unity of the total phenomenon (the repression of the drive which disguises itself and "passes" in symbolic form), to establish comprehensible connections among its different phases. How can the repressed drive "disguise itself" if it does not include (1) the consciousness of being repressed, (2) the consciousness of having been pushed back because it is what it is, (3) a project of disguise? No mechanistic theory of condensation or of transference can explain these modifications by which the drive itself is affected, for the description of the process of disguise implies a veiled appeal to finality. And similarly how are we to account for the pleasure or the anguish which accompanies the symbolic and conscious satisfaction of the drive if consciousness does not include—beyond the censor—an obscure comprehension of the end to be attained as simultaneously desired and forbidden. By rejecting the conscious unity of the psyche, Freud is obliged to imply everywhere a magic unity linking distant phenomena across obstacles, just as sympathetic magic unites the spellbound person and the wax image fashioned in his likeness. The unconscious drive (*Trieb*) through magic is endowed with the character "repressed" or "condemned," which completely pervades it, colors it, and magically provokes its symbolism. Similarly the conscious phenomenon is entirely colored by its symbolic meaning, although it can not apprehend this meaning by itself in clear consciousness.

Aside from its inferiority in principle, the explanation by magic does not avoid the coexistence—on the level of the unconscious, on that of the censor, and on that of consciousness—of two contradictory, complementary structures which reciprocally imply and destroy each other. Proponents of the theory have hypostasized and "reified" self-deception, they have not escaped it. That is what has inspired a Viennese psychiatrist, Steckel, to depart from the psychoanalytical tradition and to write in *La femme frigide:* "Every time that I have been able to carry my investigations far enough, I have established that the crux of the psychosis was conscious." [5] In addition the cases which he reports in his work bear witness to a pathological self-deception, which the Freudian doctrine can not account for. There is the question, for example, of women whom a marital infidelity has made frigid; that is, they succeed in hiding from themselves not complexes deeply sunk in half-physiological darkness, but acts of conduct which are objectively discoverable, which they can not fail to record at the moment when they perform them. Frequently in fact the husband reveals to Steckel that his wife has given objective signs of pleasure, but the woman when questioned will fiercely deny them. Here we find a pattern of detachment. Admissions which Steckel was able to draw out inform us that these pathologically frigid women apply themselves to detaching themselves in advance from the pleasure which they dread; many for example at the time of the sexual act, turn their thoughts away toward their daily occupations, make up their household accounts. Will anyone speak of an unconscious here? Yet if the frigid woman thus detaches her consciousness from the pleasure which she experiences, it is by no means cynically and in full agreement with herself; it is *in order to prove to herself* that she is frigid. We have in fact to deal with a phenomenon of self-deception since the efforts taken in order not to be present to the experienced pleasure imply the recognition that the pleasure is experienced; they imply it *in order to deny it*. But we are no longer on the ground of psychoanalysis. Thus on the one hand the explanation by means of the unconscious, due to the fact that it breaks the psychic unity, can not account for the facts which at first sight it appeared to explain. And on the other hand, there exists an infinity of types of behaviour in self-deception which explicitly reject this kind of explanation because their essence implies that they can appear only in the translucency of consciousness. We find that the problem which we had attempted to resolve is still untouched.

II. PATTERNS OF SELF-DECEPTION

If we wish to get out of this difficulty, we should examine more closely the patterns of self-deception and attempt a description of them. This description will permit us perhaps to fix more exactly the conditions for the possibility of self-deception, that is, to reply to the question we raised at the outset: "What must be the nature of man if he is to be capable of self-deception?"

Take the example of a woman who has consented to go out with a particular man for the first time. She knows very well the intentions which the man who is speaking to her cherishes regarding her. She knows also that it will be necessary sooner or later for her to make a decision. But she does not want to realize the urgency; she concerns herself only with what is respectful and discreet in the attitude of her companion. She does not apprehend this conduct as an attempt to achieve what we call "the first approach"; that is, she does not want to see the possibilities of temporal development which his conduct presents. She restricts this behaviour to what is in the present; she does not wish to read in the phrases which he addresses to her anything other than their explicit meaning. If he says to her, "I find you so attractive!" she disarms this phrase of its sexual background; she attaches to the conversation and to the behaviour of the speaker, the immediate meanings, which she imagines as objective qualities. The man who is speaking to her appears to her sincere and respectful as the table is round or square, as the wall coloring is blue or gray. The qualities thus attached to the person she is listening to are in this way fixed in a permanence like that of things, which is no other than the projection of the strict present of the qualities into the temporal flux. This is because she does not quite know what she wants. She is profoundly aware of the desire which she inspires, but the desire cruel and naked would humiliate and horrify her. Yet she would find no charm in a respect which would be only respect. In order to satisfy her, there must be a feeling which is addressed wholly to her *personality*—that is, to her full freedom—and which would be a recognition of her freedom. But at the same time this feeling must be wholly desire; that is, it must address itself to her body as object. This time then she refuses to apprehend the desire for what it is; she does not even give it a name; she recognizes it only to the extent that it transcends itself toward admiration, esteem, respect and that it is wholly absorbed in the more refined forms which it produces, to the extent of no longer figuring anymore as a sort of warmth and density. But then suppose he takes her hand. This act of her companion risks changing the situation by calling for an immediate decision. To leave the hand there is to consent in herself to flirt, to engage herself. To withdraw it is to break the troubled and unstable harmony which gives the hour its charm. The aim is to postpone the moment of decision as long as possible. We know what happens next; the young woman leaves her hand there, but she *does not notice* that she is leaving it. She does not notice because it happens by chance that she is at this moment all intellect. She draws her companion up to the most lofty regions of sentimental speculation; she speaks of life, of her life, she shows herself in her essential aspect—a personality, a consciousness. And during this time the divorce of the body from the soul is accomplished; the hand rests inert between the warm hands of her companion—neither consenting nor resisting—a thing.

We shall say that this woman is in self-deception. But we see immediately that she uses various procedures in order to maintain herself in this self-deception. She has disarmed the actions of her companion by reducing them to being only what they are; that is, to existing in the mode of the in-itself. But she permits herself to enjoy his desire, to the extent that she will apprehend it as not being what it is, will recognize its transcendence. Finally while sensing profoundly the presence of her own body—to the degree of being disturbed perhaps—she realizes herself as *not being* her own body and she contemplates it as though from above, as a passive object to which events can *happen*, but which can neither provoke them nor avoid them because all its possibilities are outside of it. What unity do we find in these various aspects of self-deception? It is a certain art of forming contradictory concepts which unite in themselves both an idea and the negation of that idea. The basic concept which is thus engendered, utilizes the double property of the human being, who is at once a *facticity* and a *transcendence*.

These two aspects of human reality are in truth and ought to be capable of a valid coordination. But self-deception does not wish either to coordinate them or to surmount them in a synthesis. Self-deception seeks to affirm their identity while preserving their differences. It must affirm facticity as *being* transcendence and transcendence as *being* facticity, in such a way that in the instant when a person apprehends the one, he can find himself abruptly faced with the other.

We can find the prototype of formulae of self-deception in certain famous expressions which have been rightly conceived to produce their whole effect in a spirit of self-deception. Take for example the title of a work by Jacques Chardonne, *Love Is Much More than Love.* We see here how unity is established between *present* love in its facticity—"the contact of two skins," sensuality, egoism, Proust's mechanism of jealousy, Adler's battle of the sexes, etc.—and love as transcendence—Mauriac's "river of fire," the longing for the infinite, Plato's *eros*, Lawrence's deep cosmic intuition, etc. Here we leave facticity to find ourselves suddenly beyond the present and the factual condition of man, beyond the psychological, in the heart of metaphysics. On the other hand, the title of a play by Sarment, *I Am Too Great for Myself*,[6] which also presents characters in self-deception, throws us first into full transcendence in order suddenly to imprison us within the narrow limits of our factual essence. We will discover this structure again in the famous phrase: "He has become what he was" or in its no less famous opposite: "Eternity at last changes each man into himself." [7] It is well understood that these various formulae have only the *appearance* of self-deception; they have been conceived in this paradoxical form explicitly to shock the mind and discountenance it by an enigma. But it is precisely this appearance which is of concern to us. What counts here is that the formulae do not constitute new, solidly structured ideas; on the contrary, they are formed so as to remain in perpetual disintegration and so that one may slide at any time from naturalistic present to transcendence and *vice versa*. We can see the use which self-deception can make of these judgments which all aim at establishing that I am not what I am. If I were not what I *am*, I could, for example, seriously consider an adverse criticism which someone makes of me, question myself scrupulously, and perhaps be compelled to recognize the truth in it. But thanks to transcendence, I am not subject to all that I am. I do not even have to discuss the justice of the reproach. As Suzanne says to Figaro, "To prove that I am right would be to recognize that I can be wrong." I am on a plane where no reproach can touch me, since what I really am is my transcendence. I flee from myself, I escape myself, I leave my tattered garment in the hands of the fault-finder. But the ambiguity necessary for self-deception comes from the fact that I affirm here that I *am* my transcendence in the mode of being of a thing. It is only thus, in fact, that I can feel that I escape all reproaches. It is in the sense that our young woman purifies the desire of anything humiliating, by being willing to consider it only as pure transcendence, which she avoids even naming. But inversely "I am too great for myself" while showing our transcendence changed into facticity, is the source of an infinity of excuses for our failures or our weaknesses. Similarly the young coquette maintains transcendence to the extent that the respect, the esteem manifested by the actions of her admirer are already on the plane of the transcendent. But she arrests this transcendence, she glues it down with all the facticity of the present; respect is nothing other than respect, it is an arrested surpassing which no longer surpasses itself toward anything.

But although this *meta-stable* concept of "transcendence-facticity" is one of the most basic instruments of self-deception, it is not the only one of its kind. We can equally well use another kind of duplicity derived from human reality which we will express roughly by saying that its being-for-itself implies complementarily a being-for-others. Upon any one of my activities it is always possible to converge two regards, mine and that of another. The activity will not present exactly the same structure in each case. But as we shall see later, as each regard perceives it, there is not between these two aspects of my being, any difference of appearance in being, as if I were to my self the truth of myself and as if the other possessed only a deformed image of me. The equal dignity of being, possessed by my being-for-another and by my being-for-myself permits a perpetually disintegrating synthesis and a perpetual game of evasion from the for-itself to the for-others and from the for-others to the for-itself. We have seen also the use which our young lady made of our being-in-the-midst-of-the-world; that is, of our inert presence as a passive object among other objects—in order to relieve herself suddenly from the functions of her being-in-the-world; that is, from the being which causes there to exist a world by projecting itself beyond the world toward its own possibilities. Let us note finally the confusing syntheses which play on the annihilating ambiguity of these temporal ek-stases, affirming at once that I am what I have been (the man who deliberately *arrests himself* at one period in his life and refuses to take into consideration the later changes) and that I am not what I have been (the man who in the face of reproaches or rancour dissociates himself from his past by insisting on his freedom and on his perpetual re-creation). In all these concepts, which have only a transitive role in the reasoning and which are eliminated from the conclusion, like hypochondriacs in the calculations of physicians, we find again the same structure. We have to deal with human reality as a being which is what it is not and which is not what it is.

But what exactly is necessary in order for these concepts of disintegration to be able to receive even a pretence of existence, in order for them to be able to appear for an instant to consciousness, even in a process of evanescence? A quick examination of the idea of sincerity, the antithesis of self-deception, will be very instructive in this connection. Actually sincerity presents itself as a demand and consequently is not a *state*. Now what is the ideal to be attained in this case? It is necessary that a man be *for himself* only what he *is*. But is this not precisely the definition of the in-itself—or if you prefer—the principle of identity? To posit as an ideal the being of things, is this not to assert by the same stroke that this being does not belong to human reality and that the principle of identity, far from being a universal axiom universally applied, is only a synthetic principle enjoying a merely regional universality? Thus in order that the concepts of self-deception can put us under illusion at least for an instant, in order that the candour of "pure hearts" (*cf.* Gide, Kessel) can have validity for human reality as an ideal, the principle of identity must not represent a constitutive principle of human reality and human reality must not be necessarily what it is but must be able to be what it is not. What does this mean?

If man is what he is, self-deception is for ever impossible and candour ceases to be his ideal and becomes instead his being. But is man what he is? And more generally, how can he *be* what he is when he exists as consciousness of being? If candour or sincerity is a universal value, it is evident that the maxim "One must be what one is" does not serve uniquely as a regulating principle for judgements and concepts by which I express what I am. It posits not merely an ideal of knowing but an ideal of *being;* it proposes for us an absolute equivalence of being with itself as a prototype of being. In this sense it is necessary that we *make ourselves* what we are. But what *are we* then if we have the constant obligation to make ourselves what we are, if our mode of being is having the obligation to be what we are?

Let us consider this waiter in the café. His movement is quick and forward, a little too precise, a little too rapid. He comes toward the patrons with a step a little too quick. He bends forward a little too eagerly; his voice, his eyes express an interest a little too solicitous for the order of the customer. Finally there he returns, trying to imitate in his walk the inflexible stiffness of some kind of automaton while carrying his tray with the recklessness of a tight-rope-walker by putting it in a perpetually unstable, perpetually broken equilibrium which he perpetually reestablishes by a light movement of the arm and hand. All his behaviour seems to us a game. He applies himself to chaining his movements as if they were mechanisms, the one regulating the other, his gestures and even his voice seem to be mechanisms, he gives himself the quickness and pitiless rapidity of things. He is playing, he is amusing himself. But what is he playing? We need not watch long before we can explain it: he is playing *at being* a waiter in a café. There is nothing there to surprise us. The game is a kind of marking out and investigation. The child plays with his body in order to explore it, to take inventory of it; the waiter in the café plays with his condition in order to *realize* it. This obligation is not different from that which is imposed on all tradesmen. Their condition is wholly one of ceremony. The public demands of them that they realize it as a ceremony; there is the dance of the grocer, of the tailor, of the auctioneer, by which they endeavour to persuade their clientele that they are nothing but a grocer, an auctioneer, a tailor. A grocer who dreams is offensive to the buyer, because such a grocer is not wholly a grocer. Politeness demands that he limit himself to his function as a grocer, just as the soldier at attention makes himself into a soldier-thing with a direct regard which does not see at all, which is no longer meant to see, since it is the rule and not the interest of the moment which determines the point he must fix his eyes on (the sight "fixed at ten paces"). There are indeed many precautions to imprison a man in what he is, as if we lived in perpetual fear that he might escape from it, that he might break away and suddenly elude his condition.

In a parallel situation, from within, the waiter in the café can not be immediately a café waiter in the sense that this inkwell *is* an inkwell, or the glass is a glass. It is by no means that he can not form reflective judgements or concepts concerning his condition. He knows well what it "means": the obligation of getting up at five o'clock, of sweeping the floor of the shop before the restaurant opens, of starting the coffee pot going, *etc*. He knows the rights which it allows: the right to the tips, the right to belong to a union, *etc*. But all these concepts, all these judgements refer to the transcendent. It is a matter of abstract possibilities, of rights and duties conferred on a "person possessing rights." And it is precisely this person *who I have to be* (if I am the waiter in question) and who I am not. It is not that I do not wish to be this person or that I want this person to be different. But rather there is no common measure between his being and mine. It is a "representation" for others and for myself, which means that I can be he only in *representation*. But if I represent myself as him, I am not he; I am separated from him as the object from the subject, separated *by nothing,* but this nothing isolates me from him. I can not be he, I can only play *at being* him; that is, to imagine to myself that I am he. And thereby I affect him with nothingness. In vain do I fulfill the functions of a café waiter. I can be he only in the neutralized mode, as the actor is Hamlet, by mechanically making the *typical gestures* of my state and by aiming at myself as an imaginary café waiter through those gestures taken as an "analogue." [8] What I attempt to realize is a being-in-itself of the café waiter, as if it were not just in my power to confer their value and their urgency upon my duties and the rights of my position, as if it were not my free choice to get up each morning at five o'clock or to remain in bed, even though it meant getting fired. As if from the very fact that I sustain this role in existence I did not transcend it on every side, as if I did not constitute myself as one *beyond* my condition. Yet there is no doubt that I *am* in a sense a café waiter—otherwise could I not just as well call myself a diplomat or a reporter? But if I am one, this can not be in the mode of being in-itself. I am a waiter in the mode *of being what I am not.*

Furthermore we are dealing with more than mere social conditions; I am never any one of my attitudes, any one of my actions. The good speaker is the one who *plays* at speaking, because he can not *be speaking.* The attentive pupil who wishes to *be* attentive, his eyes riveted on the teacher, his ears open wide, so exhausts himself in playing the attentive role that he ends up by no longer hearing anything. Perpetually absent to my body, to my acts, I am despite myself that "divine absence" of which Valéry speaks. I can not say either that I *am* here or that I *am* not here, in the sense that we say "that box of matches *is* on the table"; this would be to confuse my "being-in-the-world" with a "being-in-the-midst-of-the-world." Nor that I *am* standing, nor that I *am* seated; this would be to confuse my body with the idiosyncratic totality of which it is only one of the structures. On all sides I escape being and yet—I am.

But take a mode of being which concerns only myself: I am sad. One might think that surely I am the sadness in the mode of being what I am. What is the sadness, however, if not the intentional unity which comes to reassemble and animate the totality of my conduct? It is the meaning of this dull look with which I view the world, of my bowed shoulders, of my lowered head, of the listlessness in my whole body. But at the very moment when I adopt each of these attitudes, do I not know that I shall not be able to hold on to it? Let a stranger suddenly appear and I will lift up my head, I will assume a lively cheerfulness. What will remain of my sadness except that I obligingly promise it an appointment for later after the departure of the visitor. Moreover is not this sadness itself a *conduct?* Is it not consciousness which affects itself with sadness as a magical recourse against a situation too urgent? [9] And in this case even, should we not say that being sad means first to make oneself sad? That may be, someone will say, but after all doesn't giving oneself the being of sadness mean to *receive* this being? It makes no difference from where I receive it. The fact is that a consciousness which affects itself with sadness *is* sad precisely for this reason. But it is difficult to comprehend the nature of consciousness; the being-sad is not a ready-made being which I give myself as I can give this book to my friend. I do not possess the property of *affecting myself with being.* If I make myself sad, I must continue to make myself sad from beginning to end. I can not treat my sadness as an impulse finally achieved and put it on file without re-creating it, nor can I carry it in the manner of an inert body which continues its movement after the initial shock; there is no inertia in consciousness. If I make myself sad, it is because I *am* not sad—the being of the sadness escapes me by and in the very act by which I affect myself with it. The being-in-itself of sadness perpetually haunts my consciousness (of) being sad, but it is as a value which I can not realize, it stands as a regulative meaning of my sadness, not as its constitutive modality.

Someone may say that my consciousness at least *is,* whatever may be the object or the state of which it makes itself consciousness. But how do we distinguish my consciousness (of) being sad from sadness? Is it not all one? It is true in a way that my consciousness *is,* if one means by this that for another it is a part of the totality of being on which judgements can be brought to bear. But it should be noted, as Husserl clearly understood, that my consciousness appears originally to the other as an absence. It is the object always present as the *meaning* of all my attitudes and all my conduct—and always absent, for it gives itself to the intuition of another as a perpetual question, still better, as a perpetual freedom. When Pierre looks at me, I know of course that he is looking at me. His eyes, things in the world, are fixed on my body, a thing in the world—that is the objective fact of which I can say: it *is.* But it is also a fact *in the world.* The meaning of this look is not a fact in the world, and this is what makes me uncomfortable. Although I make smiles, promises, threats, nothing can get hold of the approbation, the free judgement which I seek; I know that it is always beyond. I sense it in my very attitude which is no longer like that of the worker toward the things he uses as instruments. My reactions, to the extent that I project myself toward the other, are no longer for myself but are rather mere *presentations;* they await being constituted as graceful or uncouth, sincere or insincere, *etc.* by an apprehension which is always beyond my efforts to provoke, an apprehension which will be provoked by my efforts only if of itself it lends them force, that is, only in so far as it causes itself to be provoked from without, *which is its own mediation with the transcendent.* Thus the objective fact of the being-in-itself of the consciousness of another is posited in order to disappear in negativity and in freedom: consciousness of another *is* as not being; its being-in-itself of "now" and of "here" is not to be.

To be conscious of another means to be conscious of what one is not.

Furthermore the being of my own consciousness does not appear to me as the consciousness of another. It exists because it makes itself, since its being is consciousness of being. But that means that making sustains being; consciousness has to be its own being, it is never sustained by being; it sustains being in the heart of subjectivity, which means once again that it is inhabited by being but that it is not being: *consciousness is not what it is.*

Under these conditions what can be the significance of the ideal of sincerity except an attempt impossible to achieve, of which the very meaning is in contradiction with the structure of my consciousness. To be sincere, we said, is to be what one is. That supposes that I am not originally what I am. But here naturally Kant's "You ought, therefore you can" is implicitly understood. I can *become* sincere; this is what my duty and my effort to achieve sincerity imply. But we definitely establish that the original structure of "not being what one is" renders impossible in advance all movement toward being in itself or "being what one is." And this impossibility is not hidden from consciousness; on the contrary, it is the very stuff of consciousness; it is the embarrassing constraint which we constantly experience; it is our very incapacity to recognize ourselves, to constitute ourselves as being what we are. It is this necessity which means that, as soon as we posit ourselves as a certain being by a legitimate judgement, based on inner experience or correctly deduced from *a priori* or empirical premises, by that very position we surpass this being—and that not toward another being but toward emptiness, toward *nothing.* How then can we blame another for not being sincere or rejoice in our own sincerity, since this sincerity appears to us at the same time to be impossible? How can we in conversation, in confession, in introspection, even attempt sincerity since the effort will by its very nature be doomed to failure and since at the very time when we announce it we have a prejudicative comprehension of its futility? In introspection I try to determine exactly what I am, to make up my mind to be my true self without delay—even though it means consequently to put myself searching for ways to change myself. But what does this mean if not that I am constituting myself as a thing? Shall I determine the ensemble of purposes and motivations which have pushed me to do this or that action? But this is already to postulate a causal determinism which constitutes the flow of my states of consciousness as a succession of physical states. Shall I uncover in myself "drives," even though it be to affirm them in shame? But is this not deliberately to forget that these drives realize themselves with my agreement, that they are not forces of nature but that I lend them their efficacy by a perpetually renewed decision concerning their value. Shall I pass judgement on my character, on my nature? Is this not to veil from myself at that moment what I know only too well, that I thus judge a past to which by definition my present is not subject? The proof of this is that the same man who in sincerity posits that he is what in actuality he was, is indignant against the reproach of another and tries to disarm it by asserting that he can no longer be what he was. We are readily astonished and upset when the penalties of the court affect a man who in his new freedom *is no longer* the guilty person he was. But at the same time we require of this man that he recognize himself as *being* this guilty one. What then is sincerity except precisely a phenomenon of self-deception? Have we not shown indeed that in self-deception human reality is constituted as a being which is what it is not and which is not what it is.

Let us take an example: A homosexual frequently has an intolerable feeling of guilt and his whole existence is determined in relation to this feeling. One will readily foresee that he is in self-deception. In fact it frequently happens that this man, while recognizing his homosexual inclination, while avowing each and every particular misdeed which he has committed, refuses with all his strength to consider himself *"a pederast."* His case is always "different," peculiar; there enters into it something of a game, of chance, of bad luck; the mistakes are all in the past; they are explained by a certain conception of the beautiful which women can not satisfy; we should see in them the results of a restless search, rather than the manifestations of a deeply rooted tendency, *etc., etc.* Here is assuredly a man in self-deception who borders on the comic since, acknowledging all the facts which are imputed to him, he refuses to draw from them the conclusion which they impose. His friend who is his most severe critic, becomes irritated with this duplicity. The critic asks only one thing—and perhaps then he will show himself indulgent: that the guilty one recognize himself as guilty, that the homosexual declare frankly—whether humbly or boastfully matters little—"*I am a pederast.*" We ask here: Who is in self-deception? The homosexual or the champion of sincerity?

The homosexual recognizes his faults, but he struggles with all his strength against the crushing view that his mistakes constitute for him *a destiny.* He does not wish to let himself be considered as a thing. He has an obscure but strong feeling that an homosexual is not an homosexual as this table is a table or as this red-haired man is red-haired. It seems to him that he has escaped from each mistake as soon as he has posited it and recognized it; he even feels that the psychic duration by itself cleanses him from each misdeed, constitutes for him an undetermined future, causes him to be born anew. Is he wrong? Does he not recognize in himself the peculiar, irreducible character of human reality? His attitude includes then an undeniable comprehension of truth. But at the same time he needs this perpetual rebirth, this constant evasion in order to live; he must constantly put himself beyond reach in order to avoid the terrible judgement of collectivity. Thus he plays on the word *being.* He would be right actually if he understood the phrase, "I am not a pederast" in the sense of "I am not what I am." That is, if he declared to himself, "To the extent that a pattern of conduct is defined as the conduct of a pederast and to the extent that I have taken on this conduct, I am a pederast. But to the extent that human reality can not be finally defined by patterns of conduct, I am not one." But instead he slides surreptitiously towards a different connotation of the word "being." He understands "not being" in the sense of "not being in itself." He lays claim to "not being a pederast" in the sense in which this table *is not* an inkwell. He is in self-deception.

But the champion of sincerity is not ignorant of the transcendence of human reality and he knows how at need to appeal to it for his own advantage. He makes use of it even and brings it up in the present argument. Does he not wish, first in the name of sincerity, then of freedom, that the homosexual reflect on himself and acknowledge himself as an homosexual? Does he not let the other understand that such a confession will win indulgence for him? What does this mean if not that the man who will acknowledge himself as an homosexual will no longer be *the same* as the homosexual whom he acknowledges being, and that he will escape into the region of freedom and of good will. The critic asks the man then to be what he is in order no longer to be what he is. It is the profound meaning of the saying, "A sin confessed is half pardoned." He demands of the guilty one that he constitute himself as a thing, precisely in order no longer to treat him as a thing. And this contradiction is constitutive of the demand of sincerity. Who can not see how offensive to the other and how reassuring for me is a statement such as, "He's just a pederast," which removes a disturbing freedom from a trait and which aims at henceforth constituting all the acts of the other as consequences following strictly from his essence. That is actually what the critic is demanding of his victim—that he constitute himself as a thing, that he should entrust his freedom to his friend as a fief, in order that the friend should return it to him subsequently—like a suzerain to his vassal. The champion of sincerity is self-deceived to the degree that in order to reassure himself, he pretends to judge, to the extent that he demands that freedom as freedom constitute itself as a thing. We have here only one episode in that battle to the death of consciousnesses which Hegel calls "the relation of the master and the slave." A person appeals to another and demands that in the name of his nature as consciousness he should radically destroy himself as consciousness, but while making this appeal he leads the other to hope for a rebirth beyond this destruction.

Very well, someone will say, but our man is abusing sincerity, playing one side against the other. We should not look for sincerity in the relations of the *"Mit-sein"* but rather where it is pure—in the relations of a person with himself. But who can not see that objective sincerity is constituted in the same way? Who can not see that the sincere man constitutes himself as a thing in order to escape the condition of a thing by the same act of sincerity? The man who confesses that he is evil has exchanged his disturbing "freedom-for-evil" for an inanimate character of evil; he *is* evil, he clings to himself, he is what he is. But by the same stroke, he escapes from that *thing*, since it is he who contemplates it, since it depends on him to maintain it under his glance or to let it collapse in an infinity of particular acts. He derives a *merit* from his sincerity, and the deserving man is not the evil man as he is evil but as he is beyond his evilness. At the same time the evil is disarmed since it is nothing, save on the plane of determinism, and since in confessing it, I posit my freedom in respect to it; my future is virgin; everything is allowed to me. Thus the essential structure of sincerity does not differ from that of self-deception since the sincere man constitutes himself as what he is *in order not to be it*. This explains the truth recognized by all, that one can fall into self-deception through being sincere. As Valéry pointed out, this is the case with Stendhal. Total, constant sincerity as a constant effort to adhere to oneself is by nature a constant effort to dissociate oneself from oneself. A person frees himself from himself by the very act by which he makes himself an object for himself. To draw up a perpetual inventory of what one is means constantly to redeny oneself and to take refuge in a sphere where one is no longer anything but a pure, free regard. The goal of self-deception, as we said, is to put oneself out of reach, it is an escape. Now we see that we must use the same terms to define sincerity. What does this mean?

In the final analysis the goal of sincerity and the goal of self-deception are not so different. To be sure, there is a sincerity which bears on the past and which does not concern us here; I am sincere if I confess *having had* this pleasure or that intention. We shall see that if this sincerity is possible, it is because in his lapse in the past, the being of man is constituted as a being-in-itself. But here our concern is only with the sincerity which aims at itself in present immanence. What is its goal? To bring me to confess to myself what I am in order that I may finally coincide with my being; in a word, to cause myself to be in the mode of the in-itself, what I am in the mode of "not being what I am." Its assumption is that fundamentally I am already in the mode of the in-itself, what I have to be. Thus we find at the base of sincerity a continual game of mirror and reflection, a perpetual passage from the being which is what it is, to the being which is not what it is and inversely from the being which is not what it is to the being which is what it is. And what is the goal of self-deception? To cause me to be what I am, in the mode of "not being what one is," or not to be what I am in the mode of "being what one is." We find here the same playing with mirrors. In fact in order for me to have an intention of sincerity, I must at the outset simultaneously be and not be what I am. Sincerity does not assign to me a mode of being or a particular quality but in relation to that quality it aims at making me pass from one mode of being to another mode of being. This second mode of being, the ideal of sincerity, I am prevented by nature from attaining, and at the very moment when I struggle to attain it, I have a vague prejudicative comprehension that I shall not attain it. But all the same, in order for me to be able to conceive an intention in self-deception, I must have such a nature that within my being I escape from my being. If I were sad or cowardly in the way in which this inkwell is an inkwell, the possibility of self-deception could not even be conceived. Not only should I be unable to escape from my being; I could not even imagine that I could escape from it. But if self-deception is possible by virtue of a simple project, it is because so far as my being is concerned, there is no difference between being and non-being if I am cut off from my project.

Self-deception is possible only because sincerity is conscious of missing its goal inevitably, due to its very nature. I can try to apprehend myself as *"not being cowardly,"* when I *am* so, only on condition that the "being cowardly" is itself "in question" at the very moment when it exists, on condition that it is itself *one* question, that at the very moment when I wish to apprehend it, it escapes me on all sides and annihilates itself. The condition under which I can attempt an effort in self-deception, is that in one sense, I *am not* this coward which I do not wish to be. But if I *were not* cowardly in the simple mode of not-being-what-one-is-not, I would be "in good faith," by declaring that I am not cowardly. Thus this inapprehensible coward is evanescent; in order for me not to be cowardly, I must in some way also be cowardly. That does not mean that I must be "a little" cowardly, in the sense that "a little" signifies "to a certain degree cowardly—and not cowardly to a certain degree." No. I must at once both be and not be totally and in all aspects a coward. Thus in this case self-deception requires that I should not be what I am; that is, that there be an imponderable difference separating being from non-being in the mode of being of human reality. But self-deception is not restricted to denying the qualities which I possess, to not seeing the being which I am. It attempts also to constitute myself as being what I am not. It apprehends me positively as courageous when I am not so. And that is possible, once again, only if I am what I am not; that is, if non-being in me does not have being even by virtue of non-being. Of course necessarily I *am not* courageous; otherwise self-deception would not be *self-deception*. But in addition my effort in self-deception must include the ontological comprehension that even in my usual being what I *am*, I am not it really and that there is no such difference between the being of "being-sad," for example—which I *am* in the mode of not being what I am—and the "non-being" of not-being-courageous which I wish to hide from myself. Moreover it is particularly requisite that the very negation of being should be itself the object of a perpetual annihilation, that the very meaning of "non-being" be perpetually in question in human reality. If I *were not* courageous in the way in which this inkwell is not a table; that is, if I were isolated in my cowardice, propped firmly against it, incapable of putting it in relation to its opposite, if I were not capable of *determining* myself as cowardly—that is, to deny courage to myself and thereby to escape my cowardice in the very moment that I posit it—if it were not on principle *impossible* for me to coincide with my *not-being-courageous* as well as with my being-courageous—then any project of self-deception would be prohibited me. Thus in order for self-deception to be possible, sincerity itself must be in self-deception. The condition of the possibility for self-deception is that human reality, in its most immediate being, in the inner structure of the prereflective *cogito*, must be what it is not and not be what it is.

III. THE "FAITH" OF SELF-DECEPTION

We have indicated for the moment only those conditions which render self-deception conceivable, the structures of being which permit us to form concepts of self-deception. We can not restrict ourselves to these considerations; we have not yet distinguished self-deception from falsehood. The two-faced concepts which we have described would without a doubt be utilized by a liar to discountenance his ques-

tioner, although their two-faced quality being established
on the being of man and not on some empirical circumstance,
can and ought to be evident to all. The true problem of self-
deception stems evidently from the fact that self-deception
is *faith*. It can not be either a cynical lie or certainty—if
certainty is the intuitive possession of the object. But if we
take belief as meaning the adherence of being to its object
when the object is not given or is given indistinctly, then
self-deception is belief; and the essential problem of self-
deception is a problem of belief. How can we believe by
self-deception in the concepts which we forge expressly to
persuade ourselves? We must note in fact that the project
of self-deception must be itself in self-deception. I am not
only in self-deception at the end of my effort, when I have
constructed my two-faced concepts and when I have persuaded myself. In truth, I have not persuaded myself; to
the extent that I could be so persuaded, I have always been
so. And at the very moment when I was disposed to put myself in self-deception, I of necessity was in self-deception
with respect to this same disposition. For me to have represented it to myself as self-deception would have been
cynicism; to believe it sincerely innocent would have been
in good faith. The decision to be in self-deception does not
dare to speak its name; it believes itself and does not believe
itself in self-deception; it believes itself and does not believe
itself in good faith. It is this which from the upsurge of self-
deception, determines the later attitude and as it were,
the *Weltanschauung* of self-deception.

Self-deception does not hold the norms and criteria of
truth as they are accepted by the critical thought of good
faith. What it decides first, in fact, is the nature of truth.
With self-deception a truth appears, a method of thinking,
a type of being which is like that of objects; the ontological
characteristic of the world of self-deception, with which the
subject suddenly surrounds himself, is that here being is what it
is not, and is not what it is. Consequently a peculiar type of
evidence appears; *non-persuasive* evidence. Self-deception apprehends evidence but it is resigned in advance to not being
fulfilled by this evidence, to not being persuaded and transformed into good faith. It makes itself humble and modest; it
is not ignorant, it says, that faith is decision and that after
each intuition, it must decide and *will what it is*. Thus self-
deception in its primitive project and in its coming into the

world decides on the exact nature of its requirements. It stands forth in the firm resolution *not to demand too much,* to count itself satisfied when it is barely persuaded, to force itself in decisions to adhere to uncertain truths. This original project of self-deception is a decision in self-deception on the nature of faith. Let us understand clearly that there is no question of a reflective, voluntary decision, but of a spontaneous determination of our being. One *puts oneself* in self-deception as one goes to sleep, and one is in self-deception as one dreams. Once this mode of being has been realized, it is as difficult to get out of it as to wake oneself up; self-deception is a type of being in the world, like waking or dreaming, which by itself tends to perpetuate itself, although its structure is of the *metastable* type. But self-deception is conscious of its structure, and it has taken precautions by deciding that the metastable structure is the structure of being and that non-persuasion is the structure of all convictions. It follows that if self-deception is faith and if it includes in its original project its own negation (it determines itself to be not quite convinced in order to convince itself that I am what I am not), then to start with, a faith which wishes itself to be not quite convinced must be possible. What are the conditions for the possibility of such a faith?

I believe that my friend Pierre feels friendship for me. I believe it *in good faith.* I believe it but I do not have for it any self-evident intuition, for the nature of the object does not lend itself to intuition. I *believe it;* that is, I allow myself to give in to all impulses to trust it; I decide to believe in it, and to maintain myself in this decision; I conduct myself, finally, as if I were certain of it, the whole in the synthetic unity of one and the same attitude. This which I define as good faith is what Hegel would call *the immediate.* It is simple faith. Hegel would demonstrate at once that the immediate calls for mediation and that belief by becoming *belief for itself,* passes to the state of non-belief. If I *believe* that my friend Pierre likes me, that means that his friendship appears to me as the meaning of all his acts. Belief is a particular consciousness *of the meaning* of Pierre's acts. But if I know that I believe, the belief appears to me as pure subjective determination without external correlative. This is what makes the very word "to believe" a term utilized indifferently to indicate the unwavering firmness of belief ("My God, I believe in you") and its character as disarmed and strictly subjective. ("Is Pierre my friend? I do not know; I believe so.") But the nature of consciousness is such that in it the mediate and the immediate are one and the same being. To believe is to know that one believes and to know that one believes is no longer to believe. Thus to believe is not to believe any longer because that is only to believe—this in the unity of one and the same non-thetic consciousness (of) self. To be sure, we have here forced the description of the phenomenon by designating it with the word *to know;* non-thetic consciousness is not to *know*. But it is in its very translucency at the origin of all knowing. Thus the non-thetic consciousness (of) believing is destructive of belief. But at the same time the very law of the prereflective *cogito* implies that the being of believing ought to be the consciousness of believing.

Thus belief is a being which questions its own being, which can realize itself only in its destruction, which can manifest itself to itself only by denying itself. It is a being for which to be is to appear and to appear is to deny itself. To believe is not to believe. We see the reason for it; the being of consciousness is to exist by itself, then to make itself be and thereby to pass beyond itself. In this sense consciousness is perpetually escaping itself, belief becomes non-belief, the immediate becomes mediation, the absolute becomes relative, and the relative becomes absolute. The ideal of good faith (to believe what one believes) is, like that of sincerity (to be what one is), an ideal of being-in-itself. Every belief is a belief that falls short; one never wholly believes what one believes. Consequently the primitive project of self-deception is only the utilization of this self-destruction through the fact of consciousness. If every belief in good faith is an impossible belief, then there is a place for every impossible belief. My inability to *believe* that I am courageous will not discourage me since every belief involves not quite believing. I shall define this impossible belief as *my* belief. To be sure, I shall not be able to hide from myself that I believe in order not to believe and that I do not believe *in order to* believe. But the subtle, total annihilation of self-deception by itself can not surprise me; it exists at the basis of all faith. What is it then? At the moment when I wish to believe myself courageous I *know* that I am a coward. And this certainly would come to destroy my belief. But *first*, I *am* not any more courageous than cowardly, if we are to understand this in the mode of being of the in-itself. In the second place, I do not *know* that I am courageous; such a view of myself can be accompanied only by *belief,* for it surpasses pure reflective certitude. In the third place, it is very true that self-deception does not succeed in believing what it wishes to believe. But it is precisely as the acceptance of not believing what it believes that it is self-deception. Good faith wishes to flee the "not-believing-what-one-believes" by finding refuge in being. Self-deception flees being by taking refuge in "not-believing-what-one-believes." It has disarmed all beliefs in advance—those which it would like to take hold of and, by the same stroke, the others, those which it wishes to flee. In *willing* this self-destruction of belief, from which science escapes by searching for evidence, it ruins the beliefs which are opposed to it, which reveal themselves as *being only belief.* Thus we can better understand the original phenomenon of self-deception.

In self-deception there is no cynical lie, nor knowing preparation for deceitful concepts. But the first act of self-deception is to flee what it can not flee, to flee what it is. The very project of flight reveals to self-deception an inner disintegration in the heart of being, and it is this disintegration which it wishes to be. In truth, the two immediate attitudes which we can take in the face of our being are conditioned by the very nature of this being and its immediate relation with the in-itself. Good faith seeks to flee the inner disintegration of my being in the direction of the in-itself which it should be and is not. Self-deception seeks to flee the in-itself by means of the inner disintegration of my being. But it denies this very disintegration as it denies that it is itself self-deception. Self-deception seeks by means of "not-being-what-one-is" to escape from the in-itself which I am not in the mode of being what one is not. It denies itself as self-deception and aims at the in-itself which I am not in the mode of "not-being-what-one-is-not." [10] If self-deception is possible, it is because it is an immediate, permanent threat to every project of the human being; it is because consciousness conceals in its being a permanent risk of self-deception. The origin of this risk is that the nature of consciousness simultaneously is to be what it is not and not to be what it is. In the light of these remarks we can now approach the ontological study of consciousness, not as the totality of the human being, but as the instantaneous nucleus of this being.

3. Portrait of the Antisemite

If a man attributes all or part of his own or the country's misfortunes to the presence of Jewish elements in the French community, if he proposes remedying this state of affairs by depriving the Jews of some of their rights or by expelling or exterminating them, he is then said to hold antisemitic *opinions*.

This word *opinion* gives us food for thought. It is the word which the mistress of the house uses to end a discussion that is becoming too embittered. It suggests that all judgments are of equal value, thus reassuming and giving an inoffensive cast to thoughts by assimilating them to tastes. There are all kinds of tastes in nature, all opinions are permissible; tastes, ideas, opinions must not be discussed. In the name of democratic institutions, in the name of freedom of opinion, the antisemite claims the right to preach his anti-Jewish crusade everywhere. At the same time, used as we are since the Revolution to seeing each object in an analytical spirit, that is as if it were a whole which can be divided into its component parts, we look at people and characters as if they were mosaics, every stone of which coexists with the others without this coexistence affecting its inherent nature. Thus an antisemitic opinion appears like a molecule which can combine with any other set of molecules without changing itself. A man can be a good father and a good husband, a zealous citizen, cultured, philanthropic and an antisemite at the same time. He may like to go fishing and he may like the pleasures of love, he may be tolerant about religion, full of generous ideas about the condition of the natives of Central Africa—and still despise the Jews. If he does not like them, people say, it is because his experience has taught him that they are bad, because statistics have taught him that they are dangerous, because certain historical factors have influenced his judgment. Thus this opinion seems to be the result of external causes and those who want to study it will neglect the antisemite himself and make much of the percentage of Jews mobilized in 1914, of the percentage of Jews who are bankers, industrialists, doctors, lawyers, of the history of the Jews in France. They will succeed in laying before us a strictly objective situation determining a certain current of likewise objective opinion which they will call antisemitism, a chart of which they can draw up or the variations of which they can establish from 1870 to 1944. In this way, antisemitism seems to be both a subjective taste which combines with other tastes to form the person, and an impersonal and social phenomenon which can be expressed by means of statistics and averages, conditioned by economic, historical and political constants.

I do not say that these two concepts are necessarily contradictory. I say that they are dangerous and false. I might, strictly speaking, admit that one might have an "opinion" about the government's wine-growing policy, that is, that one might decide for this or that reason to approve or condemn the free importation of wines from Algeria. But I refuse to call an opinion a doctrine which is expressly directed toward particular persons and which tends to suppress their rights or to exterminate them. The Jew whom the antisemite wants to reach is not a schematic being defined only by his function as in administrative law, or by his position or his acts as in the legal code. He is a Jew, son of a Jew, recognizable by his physical traits, by the color of his hair, by his clothing perhaps, and they say by his character. Antisemitism is not in the category of thoughts protected by the right to freedom of opinion.

Moreover, it is much more than an idea. It is first and foremost a *passion*. Doubtless it can present itself in the form of a theoretical proposition. The "moderate" antisemite is a polite person who gently remarks: "I don't detest Jews. I simply prefer for such and such a reason that they play a lesser part in the activity of the nation." But a moment later—if you have won his confidence—he will add the following with more abandon: "You see there must be 'something' about the Jews: physically they are irritating to me." This argument, which I have heard a hundred times, is worth examining. First of all it is the result of using logic dictated by passion. For can you imagine someone saying seriously: "There must be something about tomatoes because I can't bear them." Moreover it shows that antisemitism, even in its most moderate and evolved forms, remains a syncretic totality which is expressed by statements that appear reasonable but which can lead to corporeal modifications. Some men suddenly become impotent if they find out that the woman to whom they are making love is a

Jewess. Some people feel disgust for the Jew, just as some others feel disgust for the Chinaman or the Negro. Thus this revulsion is not based on something physical, since you could very well love a Jewess if you didn't know what race she belonged to, but it reaches the body through the mind; it is an involvement of the mind so deep, so complete, that it extends to the physiological as in cases of hysteria.

This involvement is not provoked by experience. I have questioned a hundred people about the reasons for their antisemitism. Most of them limit themselves to enumerating the faults which are traditionally attributed to the Jew. "I hate them because they are selfish, intriguing, hard to get rid of, oily, tactless, etc."—"But at least you do go with some Jews?"—"Indeed not!" A painter said to me: "I'm hostile to Jews because, with their critical habit of mind, they encourage our servants to become undisciplined." Here are some more precise experiences. A young actor without talent asserted that the Jews kept him from having a career in the theater by always giving him servile jobs. A young woman said to me: "I've had terrible rows with furriers, they've robbed me, they've burned the furs I entrusted to them. Well, they were all Jews." But why did she choose to hate Jews rather than furriers? Why Jews or furriers rather than such and such a Jew or such and such a furrier? Because she had a predisposition to antisemitism. A classmate of mine at the lycée told me that Jews "irritated" him because of the thousand injustices which "bejewed" social organizations committed in their favor. "A Jew got a scholarship the year I missed it and you're not going to try to make me believe that that fellow whose father came from Krakow or Lemberg understood one of Ronsard's poems or one of Virgil's eclogues better than I." But he admitted the next moment that he disdained the scholarship, that it was all a muddle and that he hadn't prepared for the competition. Thus he had two systems of interpretation to explain his failure, like an insane man who in his delirium pretends to be the King of Hungary but when suddenly put to the test admits that he is a shoemaker. His thinking moves on two planes without the least difficulty. Better still, he will succeed in justifying his past laziness by saying that it would have been too silly to prepare for an examination in which Jews are passed in preference to good Frenchmen. Moreover he was 27th on the final list. There were 26 before him, 12 of whom were accepted and 14 were not. Would he have gotten any further if Jews had been excluded altogether? And even if he had been the first of those who were not accepted, even if by eliminating one of the successful candidates he could have had his chance to be accepted, my classmate had to adopt in advance a certain idea of the Jew, of his nature, of his social role. And in order to be able to decide that among 26 more fortunate contestants it was the Jew who stole his place, he would apriori have to be the kind of person who runs his life on the basis of emotional reasoning.

It becomes obvious that no external factor can induce antisemitism in the antisemite. It is an attitude totally and freely self-chosen, a global attitude which is adopted not only in regard to Jews but in regard to men in general, to history and society; it is a passion and at the same time a concept of the world. No doubt certain characteristics are more pronounced in such and such an antisemite than in another. But they are always present together and they govern one another. It is this syncretic totality which we must now try to describe.

I stated a few minutes ago that antisemitism presents itself as a passion. Everyone has understood that it is a question of hate or anger. But ordinarily hate and anger are provoked: I hate the person who has made me suffer, the person who scorns or insults me. We have just seen that the antisemitic passion is not of such a nature: it precedes the facts which should arouse it, it seeks them out to feed upon, it must even interpret them in its own way in order to render them really offensive. And yet if you speak of the Jew to an antisemite, he evinces signs of lively irritation. If we remember, moreover, that we must *consent* to anger before it can manifest itself, and that we *grow* angry, to use the correct expression, we must admit that antisemitism has chosen to exist on the passionate level. It is not unusual to choose an emotional way of life rather than a reasonable one. But ordinarily one loves the *objects* of passion: women, glory, power, money. Since the antisemite has chosen hatred, we are forced to conclude that it is the emotional state that he loves. Ordinarily this kind of feeling is not pleasing: he who passionately desires a woman is passionate because of the woman and in spite of passion: one distrusts emotional reasoning which by every means aims at pointing out opinions dictated by love or jealousy or hate; one mistrusts passionate aberrations and that which has been termed monoideism. And this is what the antisemite chooses first of all. But how can one choose to reason falsely? Because one feels the nostalgia of impermeability. The rational man seeks the truth gropingly, he knows that his reasoning is only probable, that other considerations will arise to make it doubtful; he never knows too well where he's going, he is "open," he may even appear hesitant. But there are people who are attracted by the durability of stone. They want to be massive and impenetrable, they do not want to change: where would change lead them? This is an original fear of oneself and a fear of truth. And what frightens them is not the content of truth which they do not even suspect, but the very form of the true—that thing of indefinite approximation. It is as if their very existence were perpetually in suspension. They want to exist all at once and right away. They do not want acquired opinions, they want them to be innate; since they are afraid of reasoning, they want to adopt a mode of life in which reasoning and research play but a subordinate role, in which one never seeks but that which one has already found, in which one never becomes other than what one already was. Only passion can produce this. Nothing but a strong emotional bias can give instant certitude, it alone can hold reasoning within limits, it alone can remain impervious to experience and last an entire lifetime. The antisemite has chosen hate because hate is a religion: he has originally chosen to devaluate words and reasons. Since he then feels at ease, since discussions about the right of the Jew appear futile and empty to him, he has at the outset placed himself on another level. If out of courtesy he consents momentarily to defend his point of view, he lends himself without giving himself; he simply tries to project his intuitive certainty onto the field of speech.

A few moments ago I quoted some statements made by antisemites, all of them absurd: "I hate Jews because they teach indiscipline to servants, because a Jewish furrier robbed me, etc." Do not think that antisemites are completely unaware of the absurdity of these answers. They know that their statements are empty and contestable; but it amuses them to make such statements: it is their adversary whose duty it is to choose his words seriously because he believes in words. They have a *right* to play. They even like to play with speech because by putting forth ridiculous reasons, they discredit the seriousness of their interlocutor; they are enchanted with their unfairness because for them it is not a question of persuading by good argument but of intimidating or disorienting. If you insist too much they close up, they point out with one superb word that the time to argue has passed. Not that they are afraid of being convinced: their only fear is that they will look ridiculous or that their embarrassment will make a bad impression on a third party whom they want to get on their side. Thus if the antisemite is impervious, as everyone has been able to observe, to reason and experience, it is not because his conviction is so strong, but rather his conviction is strong because he has chosen to be impervious.

He has also chosen to be terrifying. One is afraid to irritate him. No one but he knows to what extremes his wayward passions will lead him: for this passion has not been provoked from the outside. He holds it well in hand, he lets himself go as much as he wants, sometimes relaxing the reins, sometimes tightening them. He is not afraid of himself: but he reads a disquieting picture in others' eyes and as he makes his statements his actions conform to this picture. This external model relieves him of the necessity of seeking his personality within himself; he has chosen to be all outside, never to examine his conscience, never to be anything but the very fear he strikes in others: he is running away from the intimate awareness that he has of himself even more than from Reason. But, you will say, what if he were only that way in regard to Jews? If he conducted himself sensibly in regard to all other matters? I answer that this is impossible: here is a fishmonger who, in 1942, irritated by the competition of two Jewish fishmongers who made a secret of their race, picked up a pen one day and denounced them. I was assured that in other respects he was kind and jovial, the best son in the world. But I don't believe it: a man who finds it natural to denounce men cannot have our concept of the humane; he does not even see those whom he aids in the same light as we do; his generosity, his kindness are not like our kindness, our generosity; one cannot localize passion.

The antisemite willingly admits that the Jew is intelligent and hard-working. He will even admit that he is inferior to him in this respect. This concession costs him little. He has put these qualities, as it were, in parentheses. Or rather, they draw their merit from the man who possesses them: the more virtues a Jew has, the more dangerous he is. As for the antisemite, he has no illusions about what he is. He considers himself an average man, modestly average, and in the last analysis a mediocre person. There is no example of an antisemite claiming individual superiority over the Jews. But do not believe for a second that this mediocrity is a cause for shame. On the contrary, he is well satisfied with it, I might even say he has chosen it. This man is afraid of any kind of solitude, that of the genius as well as that of the murderer: he is the man of the mob: no matter how short he is, he still takes the precaution of stooping for fear of standing out from the herd and of finding himself face to face with himself. If he has become an antisemite, it is because one cannot be antisemitic alone. This sentence: "I hate the Jews," is a sentence which is said in chorus; by saying it one connects oneself with a tradition and a community: that of the mediocre man. It is also well to recall that by consenting to mediocrity one is not necessarily humble, nor even modest. It is just the opposite: there is a passionate pride in being mediocre and antisemitism is an attempt to make mediocrity as such a virtue, to create an elite of the mediocre. For the antisemite, intelligence is Jewish, he can therefore disdain it in all tranquility, like all other Jewish virtues: these are all ersatz qualities which the Jews use to replace the well-balanced mediocrity which they will always lack. The true Frenchman, rooted in his province, in his country, carried along by a tradition' of twenty centuries, having the advantage of ancestral wisdom, guided by proved customs, *does not need* intelligence. The basis of his virtue is the assimilation of the qualities which the work of a hundred generations has lent to objects which surround him, i. e., property. But it goes without saying that this refers to hereditary property and not to that which one buys for oneself. The antisemite misunderstands the principle of the diverse forms of modern property: money, stocks, etc. These are abstractions, things of reason which ally themselves to the abstract intelligence of the Jew. A stock belongs to no one since it can belong to everyone and then it is a sign of wealth, not a concrete piece of property. The antisemite can conceive of but one type of primitive and landowning appropriation based on a veritable magical connection with possession, in which the object possessed and its possessor are linked by a mystical participation; he is the poet of land-holding. It transfigures the owner, endowing him with a particular and concrete sensitivity. Of course, this sensitivity is not addressed to the eternal verities, to universal values: the universal is Jewish since it has to do with the intelligence. What this subtle sense will seize upon is just what the intelligence cannot discern. In other words, the principle of antisemitism is that concrete possession of a particular object magically conveys its meaning. Maurras affirms this: a Jew will always be incapable of understanding the following line of Racine:

"Dans l'Orient desert, quel devint mon ennui." [11]

And why can I, mediocre I, understand what the most shrewd, the most cultivated intelligence cannot seize? Because I *own* Racine. Racine is my language and my soil. Perhaps the Jew speaks a purer French than I, perhaps he knows the grammar and syntax better than I, perhaps he is even a writer: it doesn't matter. He has only spoken this language for twenty years, and I have spoken it for two thousand years. The correctness of his style is abstract, acquired; the mistakes in French are in conformance with the greatness of the language. Here we recognize the reasoning which Barrès used against scholarship students. Why be surprised? Aren't these Jews scholarship students? I've done nothing to deserve my superiority and I also cannot lose rank. It is bestowed once and for all: it is a *thing*.

We begin to understand that antisemitism is not simply an "opinion" about the Jews and that it involves the entire personality of the antisemite. We are not done with him yet: for he does not limit himself to furnishing moral and political directives. He is a process of thought and a world-view all in himself. One would in fact be unable to affirm what he affirms without implicitly referring to certain intellectual principles. The Jew, he says, is entirely bad and entirely Jewish; his virtues, if any, become vices simply because they are *his* virtues, the work that comes from his hands necessarily bears his stigma: and if he builds a bridge, this bridge is bad because it is Jewish from the first span to the last. The same act committed by a Jew and by a Christian is by no means identical in the two cases. The Jew renders execrable everything he touches. The first thing the Germans did was to forbid Jews the use of swimming pools: it seemed to them that if the body of a Jew plunged into this water, it would be utterly tainted. The Jew literally sullies even the air he breathes. If we try to formulate in abstract propositions the principle referred to, this is what we would get: the whole is more than and different from the sum of all its parts; the whole determines the meaning and the true nature of the parts of which it is composed. There is not only one courageous virtue which might be indifferently a part of the Jewish or the Christian character as oxygen combines to make air either with azote or argon and combines with hydrogen to make water: but each person, with *his* courage, *his* generosity, *his* own way of thinking, of laughing, of eating and drinking, is an indivisible totality. That is to say, the antisemite has chosen to resort to the spirit of synthesis as a means of understanding the world. It is the spirit of synthesis which allows him to see himself as forming an indissoluble unity with France as a whole. It is in the name of synthesis that he denounces the purely analytical and critical intelligence of the Jew. But we must point out that for some time both the right and the left, both the traditionalists and the socialists, have brought up synthetic principles in opposition to the spirit of analysis which presided over the formation of the democratic bourgeoisie. The same principles cannot be valid for both groups. The two groups at least make different use of these principles.

Everything becomes clear if we give up expecting the Jew to behave reasonably in conformity with his interests, if we discern in him, on the contrary, a metaphysical principle which forces him *to do evil* under all circumstances, though in so doing he destroys himself. This principle, as we might expect, is magical: on the one hand it is an essence, a substantial form, and the Jew, whatever he does, cannot modify it any more than fire can keep itself from burning. And on the other hand, since the Jew must be hated and since one does not hate an earthquake or phylloxera, this virtue is also freedom. But the freedom in question is carefully limited: the Jew is free *to do evil*, not good. He has only as much free will as is necessary to bear the full responsibility of the crimes he commits, but not enough to be abe to reform.

Strange freedom which instead of preceding and constituting the essence, remains entirely subordinate to it, and which is but an irrational quality of it and yet remains freedom!

There is but one creature to my knowledge, as totally free and wedded to evil and that is the Spirit of Evil, Satan himself. Thus the Jew is assimilable to the spirit of evil. His will, contrary to the Kantian will, is one which desires to be purely, gratuitously and universally evil, it is *the will to evil*. Evil comes to the world through him; all that is bad in society (crises, wars, famines, upheavals and revolts) is directly or indirectly imputable to the Jew. The antisemite is afraid of discovering that the world is badly made: for then things would have to be invented, modified and man would find himself once more master of his fate, filled with agonizing and infinite responsibility. He localizes all the evil of the universe in the Jew. If nations wage war, it is not due to the fact that the idea of nationalism in its present form involves imperialism and conflict of interests. No, the Jew is there breathing discord—somewhere behind all governments. If there is class struggle, it is not caused by an economic organization which leaves something to be desired: it is because Jewish ringleaders, hook-nosed agitators have seduced the workers. Thus antisemitism is primarily Manicheanism; it explains the course of the world by the struggle between the principles of Good and Evil. There is no conceivable truce between these two principles: one of them must of necessity triumph and the other be destroyed. Look at Céline: his vision of the universe is catastrophic; the Jew is everywhere, the earth is lost, the Aryan must not compromise, he must never make a covenant. But he must be on guard: if he breathes, already he has lost his purity, for the very air which penetrates his bronchi is contaminated. Is this not the sermon of a Cathar? If Céline was able to uphold the socialist theses of the Nazis, it was because he was paid to do so. Deep down in his heart, he did not believe in them: as far as he is concerned, there is no solution except collective suicide, non-procreation, death. Others— Maurras or the Parti Populaire Française—are less discouraging: they foresee a long and often doubtful struggle with the final triumph of good. It is Ormuzd against Ahriman. The reader has understood that antisemitism does not have recourse to Manicheanism as to a secondary principle of explanation. But it is the original choice of Manicheanism which explains and conditions antisemitism. Therefore we must ask ourselves what this original choice can mean for a man of today.

Let us compare for a moment the revolutionary idea of the class struggle with antisemitic Manicheanism. In the eyes of the Marxist, class struggle is in no sense the struggle between good and evil: it is a conflict of intersts between human groups. The revolutionary adopts the proletariat's point of view firstly because it is *his* class and secondly because it is oppressed, because it is by far the largest class and its fate consequently tends to become fused with that of humanity, and lastly because the consequences of his victory will necessarily involve the suppression of classes. The aim of the revolutionary is to change the organization of society. And in order to do this he must of necessity destroy the old regime. But this is not enough. First and foremost a new order must be set up. If, assuming the impossible, the privileged class consented to cooperate with the socialist scheme and if one had manifest proof of its good will, there would be no valid reason to reject its co-operation. And if it remains highly improbable that the privileged class would willingly offer its assistance to the socialists, it is because its very position as a privileged class prevents it from doing so and not because of any internal demon which would force it in spite of itself to do evil. In any case, if fractions of this class detach themslves from it and become part of the oppressed class, they will be judged by their actions, not by their essence. "To hell with your eternal essence," Politzer once said to me.

The very contrary is the case with the antisemitic Manichean. His emphasis is on destruction. It is not a question of a conflict of interests but of the damage that an evil power causes to society. Behind the bitterness of the antisemite is concealed the belief that harmony will be reestablished of itself once evil has been ejected. His task therefore is purely negative: there is no question of building a society but only of purifying the one that exists. Like the Good Knight, the antisemite is sacred; but the Jew is also sacred in his own way: sacred like the untouchables, like taboo natives. Thus the battle is waged on a religious level and the end of the struggle can only be an act of sacred destruction. The advantages of this position are multiple: first of all it favors sluggishness of mind. We have seen that the antisemite understands nothing concerning modern society, and he would be incapable of inventing a constructive plan; his action cannot be put on the technical level, it remains basically emotional. He prefers an explosion of rage analogous to the running amok of the Malayans. His intellectual activity limits itself to *interpretation;* in historical events he seeks the sign of the presence of an evil power. Whence these puerile and complicated inventions which render him comparable to the real paranoiac. The antisemite, moreover, canalizes revolutionary thrusts toward the destruction of certain men, not institutions; an antisemitic mob would consider that it had done enough if it had massacred a few Jews and burned a few synagogues. It therefore represents a safety-valve for the ruling classes which encourage it . . . But, above all, this naive dualism is eminently reassuring to the antisemite himself: if it is only a matter of getting rid of Evil, it means that Good is already *assumed*. There is no reason to seek it in anguish, to invent it, to debate it patiently when one has found it, to prove it in action, to verify its consequences and finally to saddle oneself with the responsibilities of the moral choice thus made. It is not by chance that the great antisemitic uprisings hide a kind of optimism: the antisemite has decided about evil so as not to have to decide about the good. The more absorbed I become in combatting Evil, the less I am tempted to question the Good . . . When he has fulfilled his mission as the sacred destroyer, the Lost Paradise will rebuild itself. For the time being the antisemite is absorbed by so many duties that he has no time to think about it: he is forever on the verge, he fights and each of his outbursts of indignation is a pretext which distracts him from the anguished search for the good.

But there is more to it and at this point we approach the domain of psychoanalysis. Manicheanism masks a profound attraction to evil. For the antisemite, evil is his lot, his "job." Others will come later who will be concerned with good, if need be. He is at the outpost of society, he turns his back on the pure virtues which he defends; he deals only with evil, his duty is to unmask it, to denounce it, to establish its dimensions. Thus we see that he is solely worried about amassing anecdotes which reveal the lewdness of the Jew, his cupidity, his ruses and his betrayals. He washes his hands in filth. One should reread Drumont's *La France Juive:* this book "characterized by high French morality" is a collection of ignoble and obscene stories. Nothing better reflects the complex nature of the antisemite: since he did not want to *choose* his own good and, for fear of being different, allowed everyone else's concept of the good to be imposed upon him, his ethics are never based on the intuition of values or on what Plato calls Love; it manifests itself only by the strictest taboos, by the severest and most gratuitous imperatives. But the thing he contemplates constantly, the thing he understands intuitively and has a taste for is evil. He can thus minutely examine to the point of obsession the description of obscene or criminal acts which trouble him and which satisfy his perverse leanings; but since, at the same time, he attributes them to these infamous Jews whom he treats with disdain he can seek gratification without compromising himself. In Berlin I knew a Protestant whose sexual desire took the form of indignation. The sight of women in bathing suits infuriated him; he welcomed this rage, spending his time in swimming pools. The antisemite does the same thing.

One of the components of his hatred is a deep sexual attraction to Jews. First of all it is curiosity fascinated by evil. But above all, I believe, it is connected with sadism. We understand nothing about antisemitism if we do not recall that the Jew, the object of such loathing, is perfectly innocent, I might even say inoffensive. The antisemite is also careful to tell us about secret Jewish organizations, of terrifying clandestine free-masonry. But if he meets a Jew face to face he is most of the time a weak individual who, ill prepared for violence, does not even succeed in defending himself. The antisemite is not unaware of this individual weakness of the Jew which makes him the helpless victim of pogroms. In fact, this situation delights him. Hatred of the Jew is not comparable to the hatred which the Italians felt for the Austrians in 1830 or to that which the French felt for the Germans in 1942. In the last two cases it was a question of oppressors, of hard, cruel and strong men who possessed arms, money, power and who could do more harm to rebels than the latter could have dreamt of doing to them. The sadistic tendency was not an element of this hatred. But since evil for the antisemite is incarnate in these unarmed and harmless men, he never finds himself in the painful necessity of being heroic: it is *amusing* to be antisemitic. One can beat and torture the Jews without fear: the most they can do is to appeal to the laws of the Republic; but the laws are not hard. The sadistic attraction to the Jew which the antisemite feels is so strong that it is not unusual to see one of these sworn enemies of Israel surround himself with Jewish friends. Of course he calls them "exceptional Jews," he says: "They aren't like the others." In a prominent place in the studio of the painter whom I mentioned a little while ago and who in no way reproached the butchers of Lublin, there was a portrait of a Jew who was a dear friend of his and whom the Gestapo had executed. But such protestations of friendship are not sincere, for there is no idea in their conversation of sparing the "good Jews"; and while recognizing some virtues in those they know, they do not admit the fact that their interlocutors might also have met some who were equally good. In fact, it pleases them to protect these few people by a kind of inversion of their sadism; they like to keep before their eyes the living picture of these people whom they despise. Antisemitic women often feel a mixture of repugnance and sexual attraction for Jews. One whom I knew had intimate relations with a Polish Jew. She sometimes got into bed with him and let him caress her breasts and shoulders, but nothing more. She got enormous pleasure from the fact that he was respectful and submissive and also from the fact that she divined his violently frustrated and humiliated desire. She afterwards had normal sexual relations with other men. In the words "a beautiful Jewess" there is a specific sexual connotation, very different from that which is understood in the words "a beautiful Romanian," "a beautiful Greek woman" or "a beautiful American." The phrase "a beautiful Jewess" has a kind of flavor of rape and massacre. The beautiful Jewess is the woman whom the Czar's cossacks drag by the hair through the streets of a flaming village; and the special works devoted to descriptions of flagellation give Jewesses a place of honor. But we do not have to search through esoteric literature. From Rebecca in *Ivanhoe* down to the Jewess in "Gilles," not to leave out those of Ponson du Terrail, Jewesses have a well defined function in the most serious novels. Frequently raped or beaten, they sometimes succeed in escaping dishonor by death, but that is as it should be; those who keep their virtue are docile servants or humiliated women in love with indifferent Christians who marry Aryans. No more is needed to show the sexually symbolic importance of the Jewess in folklore.

With destruction his function, the antisemite—a sadist pure of heart—is in the depths of his soul a criminal. What he desires and prepares is the *death* of the Jew. Of course all the enemies of the Jew do not overtly demand his death, but the measures which they propose and which are all aimed at his debasement, his humiliation, his banishment, are the prerequisites of this murder which they are contemplating: they are symbolic murders. Only the antisemite has a clear conscience: he is a criminal with a worthy motive. It is not his fault after all if his mission is to destroy evil with evil; the *true* France has relegated to him its powers of supreme justice. Of course he does not have occasion to use them every day, but make no mistake: these sudden outbreaks of anger, these thunderous reproaches which he hurls against "kikes," are so many death sentences. Popular awareness divined this and invented the expression "Jew baiting." Thus the antisemite has chosen to be a criminal—a *pure* criminal: here again he evades responsibilities, he has censured his instinct for murder but he has found a way of satisfying it without admitting it to himself. He knows he is bad but since he is doing evil *for the sake of good;* since a whole people is awaiting deliverance at his hands, he considers himself a sort of bad sacred bull. By a kind of inversion of all values, examples of which we find in certain religions and, for instance, in India, where there is sacred prostitution, it is to anger, hate, pillage, murder and all forms of violence that the antisemite accords respect and enthusiasm; and at the very moment he is drunk with evil, he feels the lightness of heart and the peace afforded by a clear conscience and the satisfaction of duty well done.

The portrait is finished. If many people who willingly admit to hating the Jews do not recognize themselves, it is because they do not detest the Jews. They do not love them either. They would not do them the slightest harm but they would not raise their little fingers to protect them from violence. They are not antisemites, they are nothing, they are *no one;* and since in spite of everything, one must appear to be something, they murmur, without thinking of evil, without thinking at all, they go about repeating some formulas which they have learned and which give them the right to enter certain drawing rooms. Thus they know the delights of creating an ineffectual ripple, of having their heads crammed with an enormous affirmation which appears to them all the more respectable because they have borrowed it. Here antisemitism is but a justification; the futility of these people is, moreover, such that they willingly abandon this justification for any other one just as long as it be a "distinguished" one. For antisemitism is *distinguished*, like all the manifestations of an irrational collective soul tending to create a conservative and esoteric France. It seems to all these feather-brains that by repeating at will that the Jew injures the country, they are performing one of those initiation rites which allows them to feel themselves a part of the centers of warmth and social energy; in this sense antisemitism has retained something of the human sacrifice. It presents, too, a serious advantage for those people who recognize their profound instability and who are weary of it: it allows them to assume the appearance of passion and, as is the rule since the advent of Romanticism, to confuse passion with personality. These second-hand antisemites take on, without much cost to themselves, an aggressive personality. One of my friends often cites the example of an old cousin who came to dine with his family and about whom they said with a certain air: "Jules cannot abide the English." My friend cannot remember ever hearing anything else about Cousin Jules. But that was enough: there was a tacit agreement between Jules and his family. They ostensibly avoided talking about the English in front of him and this precaution gave him a semblance of existence in the eyes of his relatives and at the same time gave them an agreeable feeling of taking part in a sacred ceremony. And if someone, under certain specific circumstances, after careful deliberation and as it were inadvertently, made an allusion to Great Britan or its Dominions, Uncle Jules pretended to go into a fury and felt himself come to life for a moment. Everyone was happy. Many people are antisemites in the same way as Uncle Jules was an Anglophobe, and of course they have not the faintest idea what their attitude really implies. Simple reflections, reeds bent in the wind, they would certainly never have invented antisemitism if conscious antisemitism had not already existed. But they are the ones who, in all indifference, insure the survival of antisemitism and carry it forward through the generations.

We can now understand him. He is a man who is afraid. Not of the Jews of course, but of himself, of his conscience, his freedom, of his instincts, of his responsibilities, of solitude, of change, of society and the world; of everything except the Jews. He is a coward who does not want to admit his cowardice to himself; a murderer who represses and censures his penchant for murder without being able to restrain it and who nevertheless does not dare to kill except in effigy or in the anonymity of a mob; a malcontent who dares not revolt for fear of the consequences of his rebellion. By adhering to antisemitism, he is not only adopting an opinion, he is choosing himself as a person. He is choosing the permanence and the impenetrability of rock, the total irresponsibility of the warrior who obeys his leaders—and he has no leader. He chooses to acquire nothing, to deserve nothing but that everything be given him as his birthright—and he is not noble. He chooses finally, that good be ready-made, not in question, out of reach; he dare not look at it for fear of being forced to contest it and seek another form of it. The Jew is only a pretext: elsewhere it will be the Negro, the yellow race; the Jew's existence simply allows the antisemite to nip his anxieties in the bud by persuading himself that his place has always been cut out in the world, that it was waiting for him and that by virtue of tradition he has the right to occupy it. Antisemitism, in a word, is fear of man's fate. The antisemite is the man who wants to be pitiless stone, furious torrent, devastating lightning: in short, everything but a man.

4. Existentialism is a Humanism

My purpose here is to offer a defence of existentialism against several reproaches that have been laid against it.

First, it has been reproached as an invitation to people to dwell in quietism of despair. For if every way to a solution is barred, one would have to regard any action in this world as entirely ineffective, and one would arrive finally at a contemplative philosophy. Moreover, since contemplation is a luxury, this would be only another bourgeois philosophy. This is, especially, the reproach made by the Communists.

From another quarter we are reporached for having underlined all that is ignominious in the human situation, for depicting what is mean, sordid or base to the neglect of certain things that possess charm and beauty and belong to the brighter side of human nature: for example, according to the Catholic critic, Mlle. Mercier, we forget how an infant smiles. Both from this side and from the other we are also reproached for leaving out of account the solidarity of mankind and considering man in isolation. And this, say the Communists, is because we base our doctrine upon pure subjectivity—upon the Cartesian "I think": which is the moment in which solitary man attains to himself; a position from which it is impossible to regain solidarity with other men who exist outside of the self. The *ego* cannot reach them through the *cogito*.

From the Christian side, we are reproached as people who deny the reality and seriousness of human affairs. For since we ignore the commandments of God and all values prescribed as eternal, nothing remains but what is strictly voluntary. Everyone can do what he likes, and will be incapable, from such a point of view, of condemning either the point of view or the action of anyone else.

It is to these various reproaches that I shall endeavor to reply today; that is why I have entitled this brief exposition "Existentialism is a Humanism." Many may be surprised at the mention of humanism in this connection, but we shall try to see in what sense we understand it. In any case, we can begin by saying that existentialism, in our sense of the word, is a doctrine that does render human life possible; a doctrine, also, which affirms that every truth and every action imply both an environment and a human subjectivity. The essential charge laid against us is, of course, that of over-emphasis upon the evil side of human life. I have lately been told of a lady who, whenever she lets slip a vulgar expression in a moment of nervousness, excuses herself by exclaiming, "I believe I am becoming an existentialist." So it appears that ugliness is being identified with existentialism. That is why some people say we are "naturalistic," and if we are, it is strange to see how much we scandalize and horrify them, for no one seems to be much frightened or humiliated nowadays by what is properly called naturalism. Those who can quite well keep down a novel by Zola such as *La Terre* are sickened as soon as they read an existentialist novel. Those who appeal to the wisdom of the people—which is a sad wisdom —find ours sadder still. And yet, what could be more disillusioned than such sayings as "Charity begins at home" or "Promote a rogue and he'll sue you for damage, knock him down and he'll do you homage"? [12] We all know how many common sayings can be quoted to this effect, and they all mean much the same—that you must not oppose the powers-that-be; that you must not fight against superior force; must not meddle in matters that are above your station. Or that any action not in accordance with some tradition is mere romanticism; or that any undertaking which has not the support of proven experience is foredoomed to frustration; and that since experience has shown men to be invariably inclined to evil, there must be firm rules to restrain them, otherwise we shall have anarchy. It is, however, the people who are forever mouthing these dismal proverbs and, whenever they are told of some more or less repulsive action, say "How like human nature!"—it is these very people, always harping upon realism, who complain that existentialism is too gloomy a view of things. Indeed their excessive protests make me suspect that what is annoying them is not so much our pessimism, but, much more likely, our optimism. For at bottom, what is alarming in the doctrine that I am about to try to explain to you is—is it not?—that it confronts man with a possibility of choice. To verify this, let us review the whole question upon the strictly philosophic level. What, then, is this that we call existentialism?

Most of those who are making use of this word would be highly confused if required to explain its meaning. For since it has become fashionable, people cheerfully declare that this musician or that painter is "existentialist." A columnist in *Clartés* signs himself "The Existentialist," and, indeed, the word is now so loosely applied to so many things that it no longer means anything at all. It would appear that, for the lack of any novel doctrine such as that of surrealism, all those who are eager to join in the latest scandal or movement now seize upon this philosophy in which, however, they can find nothing to their purpose. For in truth this is of all teachings the least scandalous and the most austere: it is intended strictly for technicians and philosophers. All the same, it can easily be defined.

The question is only complicated because there are two kinds of existentialists. There are, on the one hand, the Christians, amongst whom I shall name Jaspers and Gabriel Marcel, both professed Catholics; and on the other the existential atheists, amongst whom we must place Heidegger as well as the French existentialists and myself. What they have in common is simply the fact that they believe that *existence* comes before *essence*—or, if you will, that we must begin from the subjective. What exactly do we mean by that?

If one considers an article of manufacture—as, for example, a book or a paper-knife—one sees that it has been made by an artisan who had a conception of it; and he has paid attention, equally, to the conception of a paper-knife and to the pre-existent technique of production which is a part of that conception and is, at bottom, a formula. Thus the paper-knife is at the same time an article producible in a certain manner and one which, on the other hand, serves a definite purpose, for one cannot suppose that a man would produce a paper-knife without knowing what it was for. Let us say, then, of the paper-knife that its essence—that is to say the sum of the formulae and the qualities which made its production and its definition possible—precedes its existence. The presence of such-and-such a paper-knife or book is thus determined before my eyes. Here, then, we are viewing the world from a technical standpoint, and we can say that production precedes existence.

When we think of God as the creator, we are thinking of him, most of the time, as a supernal artisan. Whatever doctrine we may be considering, whether it be a doctrine like that of Descartes, or of Leibnitz himself, we always imply that the will follows, more or less, from the understanding or at least accompanies it, so that when God creates he knows precisely what he is creating. Thus, the conception of man in the mind of God is comparable to that of the paper-knife in the mind of the artisan: God makes man according to a procedure and a conception, exactly as the artisan manufactures a paper-knife, following a definition and a formula. Thus each individual man is the realization of a certain conception which dwells in the divine understanding. In the philosophic atheism of the eighteenth century, the notion of God is suppressed, but not, for all that, the idea that essence is prior to existence; something of that idea we still find everywhere, in Diderot, in Voltaire and even in Kant. Man possesses a human nature; that "human nature," which is the conception of human being, is found in every man; which means that each man is a particular example of a universal conception, the conception of Man. In Kant, this universality goes so far that the wild man of the woods, man in the state of nature and the bourgeois are all contained in the same definition and have the same fundamental qualities. Here again, the essence of man precedes that historic existence which we confront in experience.

Atheistic existentialism, of which I am a representative, declares with greater consistency that if God does not exist there is at least one being whose existence comes before its essence, a being which exists before it can be defined by any conception of it. That being is man or, as Heidegger has it, the human reality. What do we mean by saying that existence precedes essence? We mean that man first of all exists, encounters himself, surges up in the world—and defines himself afterwards. If man as the existentialist sees him is not definable, it is because to begin with he is nothing. He will not be anything until later, and then he will be what he makes of himself. Thus, there is no human nature, because there is no God to have a conception of it. Man simply is. Not that he is simply what he conceives himself to be, but he is what he wills, and as he conceives himself after already existing—as he wills to be after that leap towards existence. Man is nothing else but that which he makes of himself. That is the first principle of existentialism. And this is what people call its "subjectivity," using the word as a reproach against us. But what do we mean to say by this, but that man is of a greater dignity than a stone or a table? For we mean to say that man primarily exists—that man is, before all else, something which propels itself towards a future and is aware that it is doing so. Man is, indeed, a project which possesses a subjective life, instead of being a kind of moss, or a fungus or a cauliflower. Before that projection of the self nothing exists; not even in the heaven of intelligence: man will only attain existence when he is what he purposes to be. Not, however, what he may wish to be. For what we usually understand by wishing or willing is a conscious decision taken—much more often than not—after we have made ourselves what we are. I may wish to join a party, to write a book or to marry—but in such a case what is usually called my will is probably a manifestation of a prior and more spontaneous decision. If, however, it is true that existence is prior to essence, man is responsible for what he is. Thus, the first effect of existentialism is that it puts every man in possession of himself as he is, and places the entire responsibility for his existence squarely upon his own shoulders. And, when we say that man is responsible for himself, we do not mean that he is responsible only for his own individuality, but that he is responsible for all men. The word "subjectivism" is to be understood in two senses, and our adversaries play upon only one of them. Subjectivism means, on the one hand, the freedom of the individual subject and, on the other, that man cannot pass beyond human subjectivity. It is the latter which is the deeper meaning of existentialism. When we say that man chooses himself, we do mean that every one of us must choose himself; but by that we also mean that in choosing for himself he chooses for all men. For in effect, of all the actions a man may take in order to create himself as he wills to be, there is not one which is not creative, at the same time, of an image of man such as he believes he ought to be. To choose between this or that is at the same time to affirm the value of that which is chosen; for we are unable ever to choose the worse. What we choose is always the better; and nothing can be better for us unless it is better for all. If, moreoever, existence precedes essence and we will to exist at the same time as we fashion our image, that image is valid for all and for the entire epoch in which we find ourselves. Our responsibility is thus much greater than we had supposed, for it concerns mankind as a whole. If I am a worker, for instance, I may choose to join a Christian rather than a Communist trade union. And if, by that membership, I choose to signify that resignation is, after all, the attitude that best becomes a man, that man's kingdom is not upon this earth, I do not commit myself alone to that view. Resignation is my will for everyone, and my action is, in consequence, a commitment on behalf of all mankind. Or if, to take a more personal case, I decide to marry and to have children, even though this decision proceeds simply from my situation, from my passion or my desire, I am thereby committing not only myself, but humanity as a whole, to the practice of monogamy. I am thus responsible for myself and for all men, and I am creating a certain image of man as I would have him to be. In fashioning myself I fashion man.

This may enable us to understand what is meant by such terms—perhaps a little grandiloquent—as anguish, abandonment and despair. As you will soon see, it is very simple. First, what do we mean by anguish? The existentialist frankly states that man is in anguish. His meaning is as follows—When a man commits himself to anything, fully realizing that he is not only choosing what he will be, but is thereby at the same time a legislator deciding for the whole of mankind—in such a moment a man cannot escape from the sense of complete and profound responsibility. There are many, indeed, who show no such anxiety. But we affirm that they are merely disguising their anguish or are in flight from it. Certainly, many people think that in what they are doing they commit no one but themselves to anything: and if you ask them, "What would happen if everyone did so?" they shrug their shoulders and reply, "Everyone does not do so." But in truth, one ought always to ask oneself what would happen if everyone did as one is doing; nor can one escape from that disturbing thought except by a kind of self-deception. The man who lies in self-excuse, by saying "Everyone will not do it" must be ill at ease in his conscience, for the act of lying implies the universal value which it denies. By its very disguise his anguish reveals itself. This is the anguish that Kierkegaard called "the anguish of Abraham." You know the story: An angel commanded Abraham to sacrifice his son: and obedience was obligatory, if it really was an angel who had appeared and said, "Thou, Abraham, shalt sacrifice thy son." But anyone in such a case would wonder, first, whether it was indeed an angel and secondly, whether I am really Abraham. Where are the proofs? A certain mad woman who suffered from hallucinations said that people were telephoning to her, and giving her orders. The doctor asked, "But who is it that speaks to you?" She replied: "He says it is God." And what, indeed, could prove to her that it was God? If an angel appears to me, what is the proof that it is an angel; or, if I hear voices, who can prove that they proceed from heaven and not from hell, or from my own subconsciousness or some pathological condition? Who can prove that they are really addressed to me?

Who, then, can prove that I am the proper person to impose, by my own choice, my conception of man upon mankind? I shall never find any proof whatever; there will be no sign to convince me of it. If a voice speaks to me, it is still I myself who must decide whether the voice is or is not that of an angel. If I regard a certain course of action as good, it is only I who choose to say that it is good and not

bad. There is nothing to show that I am Abraham: nevertheless I also am obliged at every instant to perform actions
which are examples. Everything happens to every man as
though the whole human race had its eyes fixed upon what
he is doing and regulated its conduct accordingly. So every
man ought to say, "Am I really a man who has the right to
act in such a manner that humanity regulates itself by what
I do." If a man does not say that, he is dissembling his
anguish. Clearly, the anguish with which we are concerned
here is not one that could lead to quietism or inaction. It is
anguish pure and simple, of the kind well known to all
those who have borne responsibilities. When, for instance, a
military leader takes upon himself the responsibility for an
attack and sends a number of men to their death, he chooses
to do it and at bottom he alone chooses. No doubt he acts
under a higher command, but its orders, which are more
general, require interpretation by him and upon that interpretation depends the life of ten, fourteen or twenty men.
In making the decision, he cannot but feel a certain anguish.
All leaders know that anguish. It does not prevent their
acting, on the contrary it is the very condition of their action, for the action presupposes that there is a plurality f
possibilities, and in choosing one of these, they realize that it
has value only because it is chosen. Now it is anguish of t1at
kind which existentialism describes, and moreover, as we
shall see, makes explicit through direct responsibility towards other men who are concerned. Far from being a
screen which could separate us from action, it is a condition of action itself.

And when we speak of "abandonment"—a favorite word
of Heidegger—we only mean to say that God does not exist,
and that it is necessary to draw the consequences of his
absence right to the end. The existentialist is strongly opposed to a certain type of secular moralism which seeks to
suppress God at the least possible expense. Towards 1880,
when the French professors endeavored to formulate a secular morality, they said something like this:—God is a useless
and costly hypothesis, so we will do without it. However, if
we are to have morality, a society and a law-abiding world,
it is essential that certain values should be taken seriously;
they must have an *à priori* existence ascribed to them. It
must be considered obligatory *à priori* to be honest, not to
lie, not to beat one's wife, to bring up children and so forth;

so we are going to do a little work on this subject, which will enable us to show that these values exist all the same, inscribed in an intelligible heaven although, of course, there is no God. In other words—and this is, I believe, the purport of all that we in France call radicalism—nothing will be changed if God does not exist; we shall rediscover the same norms of honesty, progress and humanity, and we shall have disposed of God as an out-of-date hypothesis which will die away quietly of itself. The existentialist, on the contrary, finds it extremely embarrassing that God does not exist, for there disappears with Him all possibility of finding values in an intelligible heaven. There can no longer be any good *à priori*, since there is no infinite and perfect consciousness to think it. It is nowhere written that "the good" exists, that one must be honest or must not lie, since we are now upon the plane where there are only men. Dostoevsky once wrote "If God did not exist, everything would be permitted"; and that, for existentialism, is the starting point. Everything is indeed permitted if God does not exist, and man is in consequence forlorn, for he cannot find anything to depend upon either within or outside himself. He discovers forthwith, that he is without excuse. For if indeed existence precedes essence, one will never be able to explain one's action by reference to a given and specific human nature; in other words, there is no determinism—man is free, man *is* freedom. Nor, on the other hand, if God does not exist, are we provided with any values or commands that could legitimize our behavior. Thus we have neither behind us, nor before us in a luminous realm of values, any means of justification or excuse. We are left alone, without excuse. That is what I mean when I say that man is condemned to be free. Condemned, because he did not create himself, yet is nevertheless at liberty, and from the moment that he is thrown into this world he is responsible for everything he does. The existentialist does not believe in the power of passion. He will never regard a grand passion as a destructive torrent upon which a man is swept into certain actions as by fate, and which, therefore, is an excuse for them. He thinks that man is responsible for his passion. Neither will an existentialist think that a man can find help through some sign being vouchsafed upon earth for his orientation: for he thinks that the man himself interprets the sign as he chooses. He thinks that every man, without any support or help whatever, is condemned at every instant to invent man. As Ponge has written in a very fine article, "Man is the future of man." That is exactly true. Only, if one took this to mean that the future is laid up in Heaven, that God knows what it is, it would be false, for then it would no longer even be a future. If, however, it means that, whatever man may now appear to be, there is a future to be fashioned, a virgin future that awaits him—then it is a true saying. But in the present one is forsaken.

As an example by which you may the better understand this state of abandonment, I will refer to the case of a pupil of mine, who sought me out in the following circumstances. His father was quarrelling with his mother and was also inclined to be a "collaborator"; his elder brother had been killed in the German offensive of 1940 and this young man, with a sentiment somewhat primitive but generous, burned to avenge him. His mother was living alone with him, deeply afflicted by the semi-treason of his father and by the death of her eldest son, and her one consolation was in this young man. But he, at this moment, had the choice between going to England to join the Free French Forces or of staying near his mother and helping her to live. He fully realized that this woman lived only for him and that his disappearance—or perhaps his death—would plunge her into despair. He also realized that, concretely and in fact, every action he performed on his mother's behalf would be sure of effect in the sense of aiding her to live, whereas anything he did in order to go and fight would be an ambiguous action which might vanish like water into sand and serve no purpose. For instance, to set out for England he would have to wait indefinitely in a Spanish camp on the way through Spain; or, on arriving in England or in Algiers he might be put into an office to fill up forms. Consequently, he found himself confronted by two very different modes of action; the one concrete, immediate, but directed towards only one individual; and the other an action addressed to an end infinitely greater, a national collectivity, but for that very reason ambiguous—and it might be frustrated on the way. At the same time, he was hesitating between two kinds of morality; on the one side the morality of sympathy, of personal devotion and, on the other side, a morality of wider scope but of more debatable validity. He had to choose between those two. What could help him to choose? Could the Christian doctrine? No. Christian doctrine says: Act with charity, love your neighbour, deny yourself for others, choose the way which is hardest, and so forth. But which is the harder road? To whom does one owe the more brotherly love, the patriot or the mother? Which is the more useful aim, the general one of fighting in and for the whole community, or the precise aim of helping one particular person to live? Who can give an answer to that *à priori?* No one. Nor is it given in any ethical scripture. The Kantian ethic says, Never regard another as a means, but always as an end. Very well; if I remain with my mother, I shall be regarding her as the end and not as a means: but by the same token I am in danger of treating as means those who are fighting on my behalf; and the converse is also true, that if I go to the aid of the combatants I shall be treating them as the end at the risk of treating my mother as a means.

If values are uncertain, if they are still too abstract to determine the particular, concrete case under consideration, nothing remains but to trust in our instincts. That is what this young man tried to do; and when I saw him he said, "In the end, it is feeling that counts; the direction in which it is really pushing me is the one I ought to choose. If I feel that I love my mother enough to sacrifice everything else for her—my will to be avenged, all my longings for action and adventure—then I stay with her. If, on the contrary, I feel that my love for her is not enough, I go." But how does one estimate the strength of a feeling? The value of his feeling for his mother was determined precisely by the fact that he was standing by her. I may say that I love a certain friend enough to sacrifice such or such a sum of money for him, but I cannot prove that unless I have done it. I may say, "I love my mother enough to remain with her," if actually I have remained with her. I can only estimate the strength of this affection if I have performed an action by which it is defined and ratified. But if I then appeal to this affection to justify my action, I find myself drawn into a vicious circle.

Moreover, as Gide has very well said, a sentiment which is play-acting and one which is vital are two things that are hardly distinguishable one from another. To decide that I love my mother by staying beside her, and to play a comedy the upshot of which is that I do so—these are nearly the same thing. In other words, feeling is formed by the deeds

that one does; therefore I cannot consult it as a guide to
action. And that is to say that I can neither seek within myself for an authentic impulse to action, nor can I expect, from
some ethic, formulae that will enable me to act. You may
say that the youth did, at least, go to a professor to ask for
advice. But if you seek counsel—from a priest, for example—
you have selected that priest; and at bottom you already
knew, more or less, what he would advise. In other words, to
choose an adviser is nevertheless to commit oneself by that
choice. If you are a Christian, you will say, Consult a priest;
but there are collaborationists, priests who are resisters and
priests who wait for the tide to turn: which will you choose?
Had this young man chosen a priest of the resistance, or one
of the collaboration, he would have decided beforehand the
kind of advice he was to receive. Similarly, in coming to me,
he knew what advice I should give him, and I had but one
reply to make. You are free, therefore choose—that is to say,
invent. No rule of general morality can show you what you
ought to do: no signs are vouchsafed in this world. The Catholics will reply, "Oh, but they are!" Very well; still, it is I
myself, in every case, who have to interpret the signs. While
I was imprisoned, I made the acquaintance of a somewhat
remarkable man, a Jesuit, who had become a member of that
order in the following manner. In his life he had suffered a
succession of rather severe setbacks. His father had died
when he was a child, leaving him in poverty, and he had
been awarded a free scholarship in a religious institution,
where he had been made continually to feel that he was accepted for charity's sake, and, in consequence, he had been
denied several of those distinctions and honours which gratify
children. Later, about the age of eighteen, he came to grief
in a sentimental affair; and finally, at twenty-two—this was a
trifle in itself, but it was the last drop that overflowed his
cup—he failed in his military examination. This young
man, then, could regard himself as a total failure: it was a
sign—but a sign of what? He might have taken refuge in
bitterness or despair. But he took it—very cleverly for him
—as a sign that he was not intended for secular successes,
and that only the attainments of religion, those of sanctity
and of faith, were accessible to him. He interpreted his record as a message from God, and became a member of the
Order. Who can doubt but that this decision as to the meaning of the sign was his, and his alone? One could have drawn

quite different conclusions from such a series of reverses—as, for example, that he had better become a carpenter or a revolutionary. For the decipherment of the sign, however, he bears the entire responsibility. That is what "abandonment" implies, that we ourselves decide our being. And with this abandonment goes anguish.

As for "despair," the meaning of this expression is extremely simple. It merely means that we limit ourselves to a reliance upon that which is within our wills, or within the sum of the probabilities which render our action feasible. Whenever one wills anything, there are always these elements of probability. If I am counting upon a visit from a friend, who may be coming by train or by tram, I presuppose that the train will arrive at the appointed time, or that the tram will not be derailed. I remain in the realm of possibilities; but one does not rely upon any possibilities beyond those that are strictly concerned in one's action. Beyond the point at which the possibilities under consideration cease to affect my action, I ought to disinterest myself. For there is no God and no prevenient design, which can adapt the world and all its possibilities to my will. When Descartes said, "Conquer yourself rather than the world," what he meant was, at bottom, the same—that we should act without hope.

Marxists, to whom I have said this, have answered: "Your action is limited, obviously, by your death; but you can rely upon the help of others. That is, you can count both upon what the others are doing to help you elsewhere, as in China and in Russia, and upon what they will do later, after your death, to take up your action and carry it forward to its final accomplishment which will be the revolution. Moreover you must rely upon this; not to do so is immoral." To this I rejoin, first, that I shall always count upon my comrades-in-arms in the struggle, in so far as they are committed, as I am, to a definite, common cause; and in the unity of a party or a group which I can more or less control—that is, in which I am enrolled as a militant and whose movements at every moment are known to me. In that respect, to rely upon the unity and the will of the party is exactly like my reckoning that the train will run to time or that the tram will not be derailed. But I cannot count upon men whom I do not know, I cannot base my confidence upon human goodness or upon man's interest in the good of society, seeing that man is free and that there is no human nature which I can take as foundational. I do not know where the Russian revolution will lead. I can admire it and take it as an example in so far as it is evident, today, that the proletariat plays a part in Russia which it has attained in no other nation. But I cannot affirm that this will necessarily lead to the triumph of the proletariat: I must confine myself to what I can see. Nor can I be sure that comrades-in-arms will take up my work after my death and carry it to the maximum perfection, seeing that those men are free agents and will freely decide, tomorrow, what man is then to be. Tomorrow, after my death, some men may decide to establish Fascism, and the others may be so cowardly or so slack as to let them do so. If so, Fascism will then be the truth of man, and so much the worse for us. In reality, things will be such as men have decided they shall be. Does that mean that I should abandon myself to quietism? No. First I ought to commit myself and then act my commitment, according to the time-honored formula that "one need not hope in order to undertake one's work." Nor does this mean that I should not belong to a party, but only that I should be without illusion and that I should do what I can. For instance, if I ask myself "Will the social ideal as such, ever become a reality?" I cannot tell, I only know that whatever may be in my power to make it so, I shall do; beyond that, I can count upon nothing.

Quietism is the attitude of people who say, "let others do what I cannot do." The doctrine I am presenting before you is precisely the opposite of this, since it declares that there is no reality except in action. It goes further, indeed, and adds, "Man is nothing else but what he purposes, he exists only in so far as he realizes himself, he is therefore. nothing else but the sum of his actions, nothing else but what his life is." Hence we can well understand why some people are horrified by our teaching. For many have but one resource to sustain them in their misery, and that is to think, "Circumstances have been against me, I was worthy to be something much better than I have been. I admit I have never had a great love or a great friendship; but that is because I never met a man or a woman who were worthy of it; if I have not written any very good books, it is because I had not the leisure to do so; or, if I have had no children to whom I could devote myself it is because I did not find the man I could have lived with. So there remains within me a wide range of abilities, inclinations and potentialities, unused but perfectly viable, which endow me with a worthiness that could never be inferred from the mere history of my actions." But in reality and for the existentialist, there is no love apart from the deeds of love; no potentiality of love other than that which is manifested in loving; there is no genius other than that which is expressed in works of art. The genius of Proust is the totality of the works of Proust; the genius of Racine is the series of his tragedies, outside of which there is nothing. Why should we attribute to Racine the capacity to write yet another tragedy when that is precisely what he did not write? In life, a man commits himself, draws his own portrait and there is nothing but that portrait. No doubt this thought may seem comfortless to one who has not made a success of his life. On the other hand, it puts everyone in a position to understand that reality alone is reliable; that dreams, expectations and hopes serve to define a man only as deceptive dreams. abortive hopes, expectations unfulfilled; that is to say, they define him negatively, not positively. Nevertheless, when one says, "You are nothing else but what you live," it does not imply that an artist is to be judged solely by his works of art, for a thousand other things contribute no less to his definition as a man. What we mean to say is that a man is no other than a series of undertakings, that he is the sum, the organization, the set of relations that constitute these undertakings.

In the light of all this, what people reproach us with is not, after all, our pessimism, but the sternness of our optimism. If people condemn our works of fiction, in which we describe characters that are base, weak, cowardly and sometimes even frankly evil, it is not only because those characters are base, weak, cowardly or evil. For suppose that, like Zola, we showed that the behavior of these characters was caused by their heredity, or by the action of their environment upon them, or by determining factors, psychic or organic. People would be reassured, they would say, "You see, that is what we are like, no one can do anything about it." But the existentialist, when he portrays a coward, shows him as responsible for his cowardice. He is not like that on account of a cowardly heart or lungs or cerebrum, he has not become like that through his physiological organism; he is like that because he has made himself into a coward by his actions. There is no such thing as a cowardly temperament. There are nervous temperaments; there is what is called im-

poverished blood, and there are also rich temperaments. But
the man whose blood is poor is not a coward for all that, for
what produces cowardice is the act of giving up or giving
way; and a temperament is not an action. A coward is defined by the deed that he has done. What people feel ob-
scurely, and with horror, is that the coward as we present him
is guilty of being a coward. What people would prefer would
be to be born either a coward or a hero. One of the charges
most often laid against the *Chemins de la Liberté* is something like this—"But, after all, these people being so base,
how can you make them into heroes?" That objection is
really rather comic, for it implies that people are born
heroes: and that is, at bottom, what such people would like
to think. If you are born cowards, you can be quite content,
you can do nothing about it and you will be cowards all
your lives whatever you do; and if you are born heroes you
can again be quite content; you will be heroes all your lives
eating and drinking heroically. Whereas the existentialist says
that the coward makes himself cowardly, the hero makes himself heroic; and that there is always a possibility for the
coward to give up cowardice and for the hero to stop being a
hero. What counts is the total commitment, and it is not by a
particular case or particular action that you are committed
altogether.

We have now, I think, dealt with a certain number of the
reproaches against existentialism. You have seen that it cannot be regarded as a philosophy of quietism since it defines
man by his action; nor as a pessimistic description of man,
for no doctrine is more optimistic, the destiny of man is
placed within himself. Nor is it an attempt to discourage man
from action since it tells him that there is no hope except in
his action, and that the one thing which permits him to have
life is the deed. Upon this level therefore, what we are considering is an ethic of action and self-commitment. However,
we are still reproached, upon these few data, for confining
man within his individual subjectivity. There again people
badly misunderstand us.

Our point of departure is, indeed, the subjectivity of the
individual, and that for strictly philosophic reasons. It is not
because we are bourgeois, but because we seek to base our
teaching upon the truth, and not upon a collection of fine
theories, full of hope but lacking real foundations. And at the
point of departure there cannot be any other truth than this,

I think, therefore I am, which is the absolute truth of consciousness as it attains to itself. Every theory which begins with man, outside of this moment of self-attainment, is a theory which thereby suppresses the truth, for outside of the Cartesian *cogito,* all objects are no more than probable, and any doctrine of probabilities which is not attached to a truth will crumble into nothing. In order to define the probable one must possess the true. Before there can be any truth whatever, then, there must be an absolute truth, and there is such a truth which is simple, easily attained and within the reach of everybody; it consists in one's immediate sense of one's self.

In the second place, this theory alone is compatible with the dignity of man, it is the only one which does not make man into an object. All kinds of materialism lead one to treat every man including oneself as an object—that is, as a set of pre-determined reactions, in no way different from the patterns of qualities and phenomena which constitute a table, or a chair or a stone. Our aim is precisely to establish the human kingdom as a pattern of values in distinction from the material world. But the subjectivity which we thus postulate as the standard of truth is no narrowly individual subjectivism, for as we have demonstrated, it is not only one's own self that one discovers in the *cogito,* but those of others too. Contrary to the philosophy of Descartes, contrary to that of Kant, when we say "I think" we are attaining to ourselves in the presence of the other, and we are just as certain of the other as we are of ourselves. Thus the man who discovers himself directly in the *cogito* also discovers all the others, and discovers them as the condition of his own existence. He recognizes that he cannot be anything (in the sense in which one says one is spiritual, or that one is wicked or jealous) unless others recognize him as such. I cannot obtain any truth whatsoever about myself, except through the mediation of another. The other is indispensable to my existence, and equally so to any knowledge I can have of myself. Under these conditions, the intimate discovery of myself is at the same time the revelation of the other as a freedom which confronts mine, and which cannot think or will without doing so either for or against me. Thus, at once, we find ourselves in a world which is, let us say, that of "inter-subjectivity." It is in this world that man has to decide what he is and what others are.

Furthermore, although it is impossible to find in each and

every man a universal essence that can be called human nature, there is nevertheless a human universality of *condition*. It is not by chance that the thinkers of today are so much more ready to speak of the condition than of the nature of man. By his condition they understand, with more or less clarity, all the *limitations* which à *priori* define man's fundamental situation in the universe. His historical situations are variable: man may be born a slave in a pagan society, or may be a feudal baron, or a proletarian. But what never vary are the necessities of being in the world, of having to labor and to die there. These limitations are neither subjective nor objective, or rather there is both a subjective and an objective aspect of them. Objective, because we meet with them everywhere and they are everywhere recognizable: and subjective because they are *lived* and are nothing if man does not live them—if, that is to say, he does not freely determine himself and his existence in relation to them. And, diverse though man's purposes may be, at least none of them is wholly foreign to me, since every human purpose presents itself as an attempt either to surpass these limitations, or to widen them, or else to deny or to accommodate oneself to them. Consequently every purpose, however individual it may be, is of universal value. Every purpose, even that of a Chinese, an Indian or a Negro, can be understood by a European. To say it can be understood, means that the European of 1945 may be striving out of a certain situation towards the same limitations in the same way, and that he may reconceive in himself the purpose of the Chinese, of the Indian or the African. In every purpose there is universality, in this sense that every purpose is comprehensible to every man. Not that this or that purpose defines man for ever, but that it may be entertained again and again. There is always some way of understanding an idiot, a child, a primitive man or a foreigner if one has sufficient information. In this sense we may say that there is a human universality, but it is not something given; it is being perpetually made. I make this universality in choosing myself; I also make it by understanding the purpose of any other man, of whatever epoch. This absoluteness of the act of choice does not alter the relativity of each epoch.

What is at the very heart and center of existentialism, is the absolute character of the free commitment, by which every man realizes himself in realizing a type of humanity

—a commitment always understandable, to no matter whom in no matter what epoch—and its bearing upon the relativity of the cultural pattern which may result from such absolute commitment. One must observe equally the relativity of Cartesianism and the absolute character of the Cartesian commitment. In this sense you may say, if you like, that every one of us makes the absolute by breathing, by eating, by sleeping or by behaving in any fashion whatsoever. There is no difference between free being—being as self-committal, as existence choosing its essence—and absolute being. And there is no difference whatever between being as an absolute, temporarily localized—that is, localized in history—and universally intelligible being.

This does not completely refute the charge of subjectivism. Indeed that objection appears in several other forms, of which the first is as follows. People say to us, "Then it does not matter what you do," and they say this in various ways. First they tax us with anarchy; then they say, "You cannot judge others, for there is no reason for preferring one purpose to another"; finally, they may say, "Everything being merely voluntary in this choice of yours, you give away with one hand what you pretend to gain with the other." These three are not very serious objections. As to the first, to say that it does not matter what you choose is not correct. In one sense choice is possible, but what is not possible is not to choose. I can always choose, but I must know that if I do not choose, that is still a choice. This, although it may appear merely formal, is of great importance as a limit to fantasy and caprice. For, when I confront a real situation—for example, that I am a sexual being, able to have relations with a being of the other sex and able to have children—I am obliged to choose my attitude to it, and in every respect I bear the responsibility of the choice which, in committing myself, also commits the whole of humanity. Even if my choice is determined by no *à priori* value whatever, it can have nothing to do with caprice: and if anyone thinks that this is only Gide's theory of the *acte gratuit* over again, he has failed to see the enormous difference between this theory and that of Gide. Gide does not know what a situation is, his "act" is one of pure caprice. In our view, on the contrary, man finds himself in an organized situation in which he is himself involved: his choice involves mankind in its entirety, and he cannot avoid choosing. Either he must remain single, or he must marry without having children, or he must marry and have children. In any case, and whichever he may choose, it is impossible for him, in respect of this situation, not to take complete responsibility. Doubtless he chooses without reference to any pre-established values, but it is unjust to tax him with caprice. Rather let us say that the moral choice is comparable to the construction of a work of art.

But here I must at once digress to make it quite clear that we are not propounding an aesthetic morality, for our adversaries are disingenuous enough to reproach us even with that. I mention the work of art only by way of comparison. That being understood, does anyone reproach an artist, when he paints a picture, for not following rules established à priori? Does one ever ask what is the picture that he ought to paint? As everyone knows, there is no pre-defined picture for him to make; the artist applies himself to the composition of a picture, and the picture that ought to be made is precisely that which he will have made. As everyone knows, there are no aesthetic values à priori, but there are values which will appear in due course in the coherence of the picture, in the relation between the will to create and the finished work. No one can tell what the painting of tomorrow will be like; one cannot judge a painting until it is done. What has that to do with morality? We are in the same creative situation. We never speak of a work of art as irresponsible; when we are discussing a canvas by Picasso, we understand very well that the composition became what it is at the time when he was painting it, and that his works are part and parcel of his entire life.

It is the same upon the plane of morality. There is this in common between art and morality, that in both we have to do with creation and invention. We cannot decide à priori what it is that should be done. I think it was made sufficiently clear to you in the case of that student who came to see me, that to whatever ethical system he might appeal, the Kantian or any other, he could find no sort of guidance whatever; he was obliged to invent the law for himself. Certainly we cannot say that this man, in choosing to remain with his mother —that is, in taking sentiment, personal devotion and concrete charity as his moral foundations—would be making an irresponsible choice, nor could we do so if he preferred the sacrifice of going away to England. Man makes himself; he is not found ready-made; he makes himself by the choice of his morality, and he cannot but choose a morality, such is the pressure of circumstances upon him. We define man only in relation to his commitments; it is therefore absurd to reproach us for irresponsibility in our choice.

In the second place, people say to us, "You are unable to judge others." This is true in one sense and false in another. It is true in this sense, that whenever a man chooses his purpose and his commitment in all clearness and in all sincerity, whatever that purpose may be, it is impossible for him to prefer another. It is true in the sense that we do not believe in progress. Progress implies amelioration; but man is always the same, facing a situation which is always changing, and choice remains always a choice in the situation. The moral problem has not changed since the time when it was a choice between slavery and anti-slavery—from the time of the war of Secession, for example, until the present moment when one chooses between the M.R.P. [*Mouvement Républicain Populaire*] and the Communists.

We can judge, nevertheless, for, as I have said, one chooses in view of others, and in view of others one chooses himself. One can judge, first—and perhaps this is not a judgment of value, but it is a logical judgment—that in certain cases choice is founded upon an error, and in others upon the truth. One can judge a man by saying that he deceives himself. Since we have defined the situation of man as one of free choice, without excuse and without help, any man who takes refuge behind the excuse of his passions, or by inventing some deterministic doctrine, is a self-deceiver. One may object: "But why should he not choose to deceive himself?" I reply that it is not for me to judge him morally, but I define his self-deception as an error. Here one cannot avoid pronouncing a judgment of truth. The self-deception is evidently a falsehood, because it is a dissimulation of man's complete liberty of commitment. Upon this same level, I say that it is also a self-deception if I choose to declare that certain values are incumbent upon me; I am in contradiction with myself if I will these values and at the same time say that they impose themselves upon me. If anyone says to me, "And what if I wish to deceive myself?" I answer, "There is no reason why you should not, but I declare that you are doing so, and that the attitude of strict consistency alone is that of good faith." Furthermore, I can pronounce a moral judgment. For I declare that freedom, in respect of concrete circumstances, can have no other end and aim but itself; and when once a man has seen that values depend upon himself, in that state of forsakenness he can will only one thing, and that is freedom as the foundation of all values. That does not mean that he wills it in the abstract: it simply means that the actions of men of good faith have, as their ultimate significance, the quest of freedom itself as such. A man who belongs to some communist or revolutionary society wills certain concrete ends, which imply the will to freedom, but that freedom is willed in community. We will freedom for freedom's sake, in and through particular circumstances. And in thus willing freedom, we discover that it depends entirely upon the freedom of others and that the freedom of others depends upon our own. Obviously, freedom as the definition of a man does not depend upon others, but as soon as there is a commitment, I am obliged to will the liberty of others at the same time as my own. I cannot make liberty my aim unless I make that of others equally my aim. Consequently, when I recognize, as entirely authentic, that man is a being whose existence precedes his essence, and that he is a free being who cannot, in any circumstances, but will his freedom, at the same time I realize that I cannot not will the freedom of others. Thus, in the name of that will to freedom which is implied in freedom itself, I can form judgments upon those who seek to hide from themselves the wholly voluntary nature of their existence and its complete freedom. Those who hide from this total freedom, in a guise of solemnity or with deterministic excuses, I shall call cowards. Others, who try to show that their existence is necessary, when it is merely an accident of the appearance of the human race on earth—I shall call scum. But neither cowards nor scum can be identified except upon the plane of strict authenticity. Thus, although the content of morality is variable, a certain form of this morality is universal. Kant declared that freedom is a will both to itself and to the freedom of others. Agreed: but he thinks that the formal and the universal suffice for the constitution of a morality. We think, on the contrary, that principles that are too abstract break down when we come to defining action. To take once again the case of that student; by what authority, in the name of what golden rule of morality, do you think he could have decided, in perfect peace of mind, either to abandon his mother or to remain with her? There are no means of judging. The content is always concrete, and therefore unpredictable; it has always to be invented. The one thing that counts, is to know whether the invention is made in the name of freedom.

Let us, for example, examine the two following cases, and you will see how far they are similar in spite of their difference. Let us take *The Mill on the Floss*. We find here a certain young woman, Maggie Tulliver, who is an incarnation of the value of passion and is aware of it. She is in love with a young man, Stephen, who is engaged to another, an insignificant young woman. This Maggie Tulliver, instead of heedlessly seeking her own happiness, chooses in the name of human solidarity to sacrifice herself and to give up the man she loves. On the other hand, La Sanseverina in Stendhal's *Chartreuse de Parme*, believing that it is passion which endows man with his real value, would have declared that a grand passion justifies its sacrifices, and must be preferred to the banality of such conjugal love as would unite Stephen to the little goose he was engaged to marry. It is the latter that she would have chosen to sacrifice in realizing her own happiness, and, as Stendhal shows, she would also sacrifice herself upon the plane of passion if life made that demand upon her. Here we are facing two clearly opposed moralities; but I claim that they are equivalent, seeing that in both cases the overruling aim is freedom. You can imagine two attitudes exactly similar in effect, in that one girl might prefer, in resignation, to give up her lover while the other preferred, in fulfillment of sexual desire, to ignore the prior engagement of the man she loved; and, externally, these two cases might appear the same as the two we have just cited, while being in fact entirely different. The attitude of La Sanseverina is much nearer to that of Maggie Tulliver than to one of careless greed. Thus, you see, the second objection is at once true and false. One can choose anything, but only if it is upon the plane of free commitment.

The third objection, stated by saying, "You take with one hand what you give with the other," means, at bottom, "your values are not serious, since you choose them yourselves." To that I can only say that I am very sorry that it should be so; but if I have excluded God the Father, there must be somebody to invent values. We have to take things as they are. And moreover, to say that we invent values means neither more nor less than this; that there is no sense in life *à priori*. Life is nothing until it is lived; but it is yours to make sense of, and the value of it is nothing else but the sense that you choose. Therefore, you can see that there is a possibility of creating a human community. I have been reproached for suggesting that existentialism is a form of humanism: people have said to me, "But you have written in your *Nausée* that the humanists are wrong, you have even ridiculed a certain type of humanism, why do you now go back upon that?" In reality, the word humanism has two very different meanings. One may understand by humanism a theory which upholds man as the end-in-itself and as the supreme value. Humanism in this sense appears, for instance, in Cocteau's story *Round the World in 80 Hours*, in which one of the characters declares, because he is flying over mountains in an airplane, "Man is magnificent!" This signifies that although I, personally, have not built airplanes I have the benefit of those particular inventions and that I personally, being a man, can consider myself responsible for, and honored by, achievements that are peculiar to some men. It is to assume that we can ascribe value to man according to the most distinguished deeds of certain men. That kind of humanism is absurd, for only the dog or the horse would be in a position to pronounce a general judgment upon man and declare that he is magnificent, which they have never been such fools as to do —at least, not as far as I know. But neither is it admissible that a man should pronounce judgment upon Man. Existentialism dispenses with any judgment of this sort: an existentialist will never take man as the end, since man is still to be determined. And we have no right to believe that humanity is something to which we could set up a cult, after the manner of Auguste Comte. The cult of humanity ends in Comtian humanism, shut-in upon itself, and—this must be said—in Fascism. We do not want a humanism like that.

But there is another sense of the word, of which the fundamental meaning is this: Man is all the time outside of himself: it is in projecting and losing himself beyond himself that he makes man to exist; and, on the other hand, it is by pursuing transcendent aims that he himself is able to exist. Since man is thus self-surpassing, and can grasp objects only in relation to his self-surpassing, he is himself the heart and center of his transcendence. There is no other universe except the human universe, the universe of human subjectivity. This relation of transcendence as constitutive of man (not in the sense that God is transcendent, but in the sense of self-surpassing) with subjectivity (in such a sense that man is not shut up in himself but forever present in a human universe)—it is this that we call existential humanism. This is humanism, because we remind man that there is no legislator but himself; that he himself, thus abandoned, must decide for himself; also because we show that it is not by turning back upon himself, but always by seeking, beyond himself, an aim which is one of liberation or of some particular realization, that man can realize himself as truly human.

You can see from these few reflections that nothing could be more unjust than the objections people raise against us. Existentialism is nothing else but an attempt to draw the full conclusions from a consistently atheistic position. Its intention is not in the least that of plunging men into despair. And if by despair one means—as the Christians do—any attitude of unbelief, the despair of the existentialists is something different. Existentialism is not atheist in the sense that it would exhaust itself in demonstrations of the non-existence of God. It declares, rather, that even if God existed that would make no difference from its point of view. Not that we believe God does exist, but we think that the real problem is not that of His existence; what man needs is to find himself again and to understand that nothing can save him from himself, not even a valid proof of the existence of God. In this sense existentialism is optimistic. It is a doctrine of action, and it is only by self-deception, by confusing their own despair with ours that Christians can describe us as without hope.

5. Marxism and Existentialism

. . . I consider Marxism the one philosophy of our time which we cannot go beyond and . . . I hold the ideology of existence and its "comprehensive" method to be an enclave inside Marxism, which simultaneously engenders it and rejects it. . . .

If philosophy is to be simultaneously a totalization of knowledge, a method, a regulative Idea, an offensive weapon, and a community of language, if this "vision of the world" is also an instrument which ferments rotten societies, if this particular conception of a man or of a group of men becomes the culture and sometimes the nature of a whole class—then it is very clear that the periods of philosophical creation are rare. Between the seventeenth century and the twentieth, I see three such periods, which I would designate by the names of the men who dominated them: there is the "moment" of Descartes and Locke, that of Kant and Hegel, finally that of Marx. These three philosophies become, each in its turn, the humus of every particular thought and the horizon of all culture; there is no going beyond them so long as man has not gone beyond the historical moment which they express. I have often remarked on the fact that an "anti-Marxist" argument is only the apparent rejuvenation of a pre-Marxist idea. A so-called "going beyond" Marxism will be at worst only a return to pre-Marxism; at best, only the rediscovery of a thought already contained in the philosophy which one believes he has gone beyond. . . .

Those intellectuals who come after the great flowering and who undertake to set the systems in order or to use the new methods to conquer territory not yet fully explored, those who provide practical applications for the theory and employ it as a tool to destroy and to construct—they should not be called philosophers. They cultivate the domain, they take an inventory, they erect certain structures there, they may even bring about certain internal changes; but they still get their nourishment from the living thought of the great dead. They are borne along by the crowd on the march, and it is the crowd which constitutes their cultural milieu and their future, which determines the field of their investigations, and even of their "creation." These *relative* men I propose to call "ideologists." And since I am to speak of existentialism, let it be understood that I take it to be an "ideology." It is a parasitical system living on the margin of Knowledge, which at first it opposed but into which today it seeks to be integrated. If we are to understand its present ambitions and its function we must go back to the time of Kierkegaard. . . .

Compared with Hegel, Kierkegaard scarcely seems to count. He is certainly not a philosopher; moreover, he himself refused this title. In fact, he is a Christian who is not willing to let himself be enclosed in the system and who, against Hegel's "intellectualism," asserts unrelentingly the irreducibility and the specificity of what is lived. There is no doubt, as Jean Wahl has remarked, that a Hegelian would have assimilated this romantic and obstinate consciousness to the "unhappy consciousness," a moment which had already been surpassed and known in its essential characteristics. But it is precisely this objective knowledge which Kierkegaard challenges. For him the surpassing of the unhappy consciousness remains purely verbal. The *existing* man cannot be assimilated by a system of ideas. . . .

We see that Kierkegaard is inseparable from Hegel, and that this vehement negation of every system can arise only within a cultural field entirely dominated by Hegelianism. The Dane feels himself hemmed in by concepts, by History, he fights for his life; it is the reaction of Christian romanticism against the rationalist humanization of faith. It would be too easy to reject this work as simply subjectivism; what we ought rather to point out, in placing it back within the framework of its period, is that Kierkegaard has as much right on his side as Hegel has on his. Hegel is right: unlike the Danish ideologist, who obstinately fixed his stand on poor, frozen paradoxes ultimately referring to an empty subjectivity, the philosopher of Jena aims through his concepts at the veritable concrete; for him, mediation is always presented as an enrichment. Kierkegaard is right: grief, need, passion, the pain of men, are brute realities which can be neither surpassed nor changed by knowledge. To be sure, Kierkegaard's religious subjectivism can with good reason be taken as the very peak of idealism; but in relation to Hegel, he marks a progress toward realism, since he insists above all on the *primacy* of the specifically real over thought, that the real cannot be reduced to thought. There are today some psychologists and psychiatrists who consider certain evolutions of our inward life to be the result of a work which it performs upon itself. In this sense Kierkegaardian *existence* is the *work* of our inner life—resistances overcome and perpetually reborn, efforts perpetually renewed, despairs surmounted, provisional failures and precarious victories—and this work is directly opposed to intellectual knowing. Kierkegaard was perhaps the first to point out, against Hegel and thanks to him, the incommensurability of the real and knowledge. . . .

Now, in the present phase of our history, productive forces have entered into conflict with relations of production. Creative work is alienated; man does not recognize himself in his own product, and his exhausting labor appears to him as a hostile force. Since alienation comes about as the result of this conflict, it is a historical reality and completely irreducible to an idea. If men are to free themselves from it, and if their work is to become the pure objectification of themselves, it is not enough that "consciousness think itself"; there must be *material* work and revolutionary *praxis*. When Marx writes: "Just as we do not judge an individual by his own idea of himself, so we cannot judge a . . . period of revolutionary upheaval by its own self-consciousness," he is indicating the priority of action (work and social *praxis*) over *knowledge* as well as their heterogeneity. He too asserts that the human fact is irreducible to knowing, that it must *be lived* and *produced*; but he is not going to confuse it with the empty subjectivity of a puritanical and mystified petite bourgeoisie. He makes of it the immediate theme of the philosophical totalization, and it is the concrete man whom he puts at the center of his research, that man who is defined simultaneously by his needs, by the material conditions of his existence, and by the nature of his work—that is, by his struggle against things and against men.

Thus Marx, rather than Kierkegaard or Hegel, is right, since he asserts with Kierkegaard the specificity of human *existence* and, along with Hegel, takes the concrete man in his objective reality. Under these circumstances, it would seem natural if existentialism, this idealist protest against idealism, had lost all usefulness and had not survived the decline of Hegelianism. . . .

Between the two World Wars the appearance of a German existentialism certainly corresponds—at least in the work of Jaspers[9]—to a surreptitious wish to resuscitate the transcendent. Already—as Jean Wahl has pointed out—one could wonder if Kierkegaard did not lure his readers into the depths of subjectivity for the sole purpose of making them discover there the unhappiness of man without God. This trap would be quite in keeping with the "great solitary" who denied communication between human beings and who saw no way to influence his fellow man except by "indirect action."

Jaspers himself put his cards on the table. He has done nothing except to comment upon his master; his originality consists especially in putting certain themes into relief and in hiding others. The transcendent, for example, appears at first to be absent from his thought, which in fact is haunted by it. We are taught to catch a presentiment of the transcendent in our failures; it is their profound meaning. . . .

Kierkegaard was unwilling to play the role of a concept in the Hegelian system; Jaspers refuses to cooperate *as an individual* with the history which Marxists are making. . . .

It is one more existentialism which has developed at the margin of Marxism and not against it. It is Marx with whom we claim kinship, and Marx of whom I wish to speak now. . . . It was at about this time [1925] that I read *Capital* and *German Ideology*. I found everything perfectly clear, and I really understood absolutely nothing. To understand is to change, to go beyond oneself. This reading did not change me. By contrast, what did begin to change me was the *reality* of Marxism, the heavy presence on my horizon of the masses of workers, an enormous, somber body which *lived* Marxism, which *practiced* it, and which at a distance exercised an irresistible attraction on petit bourgeois intellectuals. . . .

Why then has "existentialism" preserved its autonomy? Why has it not simply dissolved in Marxism?

Lukacs believed that he had answered this question in a small book called *Existentialism and Marxism*. . . . Lukacs fails absolutely to account for the principal fact: we were convinced *at one and the same time* that historical materialism furnished the only valid interpretation of history and that existentialism remained the only concrete approach to reality. I do not pretend to deny the contradictions in this attitude. I simply assert that Lukacs does not even suspect it. Many intellectuals, many students, have lived and still live with the tension of this double demand. How does this come about? It is due to a circumstance which Lukacs knew perfectly well but which he could not at that time even mention: Marxism, after drawing us to it as the moon draws the tides, after transforming all our ideas, after liquidating the categories of our bourgeois thought, abruptly left us stranded. It did not satisfy our need to understand. In the particular situation in which we were placed, it no longer had anything new to teach us, because it had come to a stop.

Marxism stopped. . . .

Existentialism has been able to return and to maintain itself because it reaffirmed the reality of men as Kierkegaard asserted his own reality against Hegel. However, the Dane rejected the Hegelian conception of man and of the real. Existentialism and Marxism, on the contrary, aim at the same object. . . .

Far from being exhausted, Marxism is still very young, almost in its infancy; it has scarcely begun to develop. It remains, therefore, the philosophy of our time. We cannot go beyond it because we have not gone beyond the circumstances which engendered it. . . .

Let us go further. We agree with Garaudy when he writes (*Humanité*, May 17, 1955): "Marxism forms today the system of coordinates which alone permits it to situate and to define a thought in any domain whatsoever—from political economy to physics, from history to ethics." . . .

As soon as there will exist *for everyone* a margin of *real* freedom beyond the production of life, Marxism will have lived out its span; a philosophy of freedom will take its place. But we have no means, no intellectual instrument, no concrete experience which allows us to conceive of this freedom or of this philosophy. . . .

Why, then, are we not simply Marxists? It is because we take the statements of Engels and Garaudy as guiding principles, as indications of jobs to be done, as problems—not as concrete truths.

ELEVEN

Camus: THE MYTH OF SISYPHUS

[*Preface:* Albert Camus was born in Algeria in 1913 and died in France in 1960. He published plays as well as two notable novels, *The Stranger* and *The Plague,* and two volumes of reflections, *The Myth of Sisyphus* and *The Rebel.* He was close to Sartre at one time, but the two men broke after Sartre decided to make common cause with the Communist Party in France. Partly owing to his association with Sartre, he was often called an existentialist, though many critics insist that this was an invidious error. Be that as it may, even as Dostoevsky's *Notes from Underground* furnish the best overture, Camus' "Myth of Sisyphus," the concluding chapter of his book by that name, is an excellent finale.]

The gods had condemned Sisyphus to ceaselessly rolling a rock to the top of a mountain, whence the stone would fall back of its own weight. They had thought with some reason that there is no more dreadful punishment than futile and hopeless labor.

If one believes Homer, Sisyphus was the wisest and most prudent of mortals. According to another tradition, however, he was disposed to practice the profession of highwayman. I see no contradiction in this. Opinions differ as to the reasons why he became the futile laborer of the underworld. To begin with, he is accused of a certain levity in regard to the gods. He stole their secrets. Aegina, the daughter of Aesopus,

375

was carried off by Jupiter. The father was shocked by that disappearance and complained to Sisyphus. He, who knew of the abduction, offered to tell about it on condition that Aesopus would give water to the citadel of Corinth. To the celestial thunderbolts he preferred the benediction of water. He was punished for this in the underworld. Homer tells us also that Sisyphus had put Death in chains. Pluto could not endure the sight of his deserted, silent empire. He dispatched the god of war, who liberated Death from the hands of her conqueror.

It is said also that Sisyphus, being near to death, rashly wanted to test his wife's love. He ordered her to cast his un-buried body into the middle of the public square. Sisyphus woke up in the underworld. And there, annoyed by an obedi-ence so contrary to human love, he obtained from Pluto per-mission to return to earth in order to chastise his wife. But when he had seen again the face of this world, enjoyed water and sun, warm stones and the sea, he no longer wanted to go back to the infernal darkness. Recalls, signs of anger, warn-ings were of no avail. Many years more he lived facing the curve of the gulf, the sparkling sea, and the smiles of earth. A decree of the gods was necessary. Mercury came and seized the impudent man by the collar and, snatching him from his joys, led him forcibly back to the underworld, where his rock was ready for him.

You have already grasped that Sisyphus is the absurd hero. He *is*, as much through his passions as through his torture. His scorn of the gods, his hatred of death, and his passion for life won him that unspeakable penalty in which the whole being is exerted toward accomplishing nothing. This is the price that must be paid for the passions of this earth. Noth-ing is told us about Sisyphus in the underworld. Myths are made for the imagination to breathe life into them. As for this myth, one sees merely the whole effort of a body strain-ing to raise the huge stone, to roll it and push it up a slope a hundred times over; one sees the face screwed up, the cheek tight against the stone, the shoulder bracing the clay-covered mass, the foot wedging it, the fresh start with arms outstretched, the wholly human security of two earth-clotted hands. At the very end of his long effort measured by skyless space and time without depth, the purpose is achieved. Then Sisyphus watches the stone rush down in a few moments to-ward that lower world whence he will have to push it up again toward the summit. He goes back down to the plain.

It is during that return, that pause, that Sisyphus interests me. A face that toils so close to stones is already stone itself! I see that man going back down with a heavy yet measured step toward the torment of which he will never know the end. That hour like a breathing-space which returns as surely as his suffering, that is the hour of consciousness. At each of those moments when he leaves the heights and gradually sinks toward the lairs of the gods, he is superior to his fate. He is stronger than his rock.

If this myth is tragic, that is because its hero is conscious. Where would his torture be, indeed, if at every step the hope of succeeding upheld him? The workman of today works every day in his life at the same tasks, and this fate is no less absurd. But it is tragic only at the rare moments when it becomes conscious. Sisyphus, proletarian of the gods, powerless and rebellious, knows the whole extent of his wretched condition: it is what he thinks of during his descent. The lucidity that was to constitute his torture at the same time crowns his victory. There is no fate that cannot be surmounted by scorn.

* * *

If the descent is thus sometimes performed in sorrow, it can also take place in joy. This word is not too much. Again I fancy Sisyphus returning toward his rock, and the sorrow was in the beginning. When the images of earth cling too tightly to memory, when the call of happiness becomes too insistent, it happens that melancholy rises in man's heart: this is the rock's victory, this is the rock itself. The boundless grief is too heavy to bear. These are our nights of Gethsemane. But crushing truths perish from being acknowledged. Thus, Oedipus at the outset obeys fate without knowing it. But from the moment he knows, his tragedy begins. Yet at the same moment, blind and desperate, he realizes that the only bond linking him to the world is the cool hand of a girl. Then a tremendous remark rings out: "Despite so many ordeals, my advanced age and the nobility of my soul make me conclude that all is well." Sophocles' Oedipus, like Dostoevsky's Kirilov, thus gives the recipe for the absurd victory. Ancient wisdom confirms modern heroism.

One does not discover the absurd without being tempted to write a manual of happiness. "What! by such narrow ways—?" There is but one world, however. Happiness and the absurd are two sons of the same earth. They are inseparable. It would be a mistake to say that happiness necessarily springs from the absurd discovery. It happens as well that the feeling of the absurd springs from happiness. "I conclude that all is well," says Oedipus, and that remark is sacred. It echoes in the wild and limited universe of man. It teaches that all is not, has not been, exhausted. It drives out of this world a god who had come into it with dissatisfaction and a preference for futile sufferings. It makes of fate a human matter, which must be settled among men.

All Sisyphus' silent joy is contained therein. His fate belongs to him. His rock is his thing. Likewise, the absurd man, when he contemplates his torment, silences all the idols. In the universe suddenly restored to its silence, the myriad wondering little voices of the earth rise up. Unconscious, secret calls, invitations from all the faces, they are the necessary reverse and price of victory. There is no sun without shadow, and it is essential to know the night. The absurd man says yes and his effort will henceforth be unceasing. If there is a personal fate, there is no higher destiny, or at least there is but one which he concludes is inevitable and despicable. For the rest, he knows himself to be the master of his days. At that subtle moment when man glances backward over his life, Sisyphus returning toward his rock, in that slight pivoting he contemplates that series of unrelated actions which becomes his fate, created by him, combined under his memory's eye and soon sealed by his death. Thus, convinced of the wholly human origin of all that is human, a blind man eager to see who knows that the night has no end, he is still on the go. The rock is still rolling.

I leave Sisyphus at the foot of the mountain! One always finds one's burden again. But Sisyphus teaches the higher fidelity that negates the gods and raises rocks. He too concludes that all is well. This universe henceforth without a master seems to him neither sterile nor futile. Each atom of that stone, each mineral flake of that night-filled mountain, in itself forms a world. The struggle itself toward the heights is enough to fill a man's heart. One must imagine Sisyphus happy.

NOTES

DOSTOEVSKY: NOTES FROM UNDERGROUND

[1] The author of the diary and the diary itself are, of course, imaginary. Nevertheless it is clear that such persons as the writer of these notes not only may, but positively must, exist in our society, when we consider the circumstances in the midst of which our society is formed. I have tried to expose to the view of the public more distinctly than is commonly done, one of the characters of the recent past. He is one of the representatives of a generation still living. In this fragment, entitled "Underground," this person introduces himself and his views, and, as it were, tries to explain the causes owing to which he has made his appearance and was bound to make his appearance in our midst.

KIERKEGAARD: THE FIRST EXISTENTIALIST

[1] It was for the same reason that at the moment when the whole of *Either/Or* was ready to be transcribed into a fair copy, I printed a little article in the *Fatherland* over my own signature, in which I gratuitously disclaimed that I was the author of a good many interesting articles which had appeared anonymously in various newspapers, acknowledging and admitting my idleness, and making one petition, that henceforth no one would ever regard me as the author of anything beneath which my name was not signed.

[2] Perhaps it may be well to note here once for all a thing that goes without saying and which I never have denied, that in relation to all temporal, earthly, worldly matters the crowd may have competency, and even decisive competency as a court of last resort.

But it is not of such matters I am speaking, nor have I ever concerned myself with such things. I am speaking about the ethical, about the ethico-religious, about "the truth," and I am affirming the untruth of the crowd, ethico-religiously regarded, when it is treated as a criterion for what "truth" is.

3 Perhaps it may be well to note here, although it seems to me almost superfluous, that it naturally could not occur to me to object to the fact, for example, that preaching is done or that the truth is proclaimed, even though it were to an assemblage of hundreds of thousands. Not at all; but if there were an assemblage even of only ten—and if they should put the truth to the ballot, that is to say, if the assemblage should be regarded as the authority, if it is the crowd which turns the scale—then there *is* untruth.

4 The reader will also remember that here the word "crowd" is understood in a purely formal sense, not in the sense one commonly attaches to "the crowd" when it is meant as an invidious qualification, the distinction which human selfishness irreligiously erects between 'the crowd' and superior persons, etc. Good God! How could a religious man hit upon such an inhuman equality! No, "crowd" stands for number, the numerical, a number of noblemen, millionaires, high dignitaries, etc.—as soon as the numerical is involved it is "crowd," "the crowd."

5 The reader will remember that this was written in 1847. The world-upheaval of 1848 has brought understanding considerably nearer.

6 And every one who has even a little dialectic will perceive that it is impossible to attack the System from a point within the System. But outside of it there is only one point, truly a spermatic point, the individual, ethically and religiously conceived and existentially accentuated.

7 And how much less now, in 1848!

8 With regard to this one may consult *Either/Or* (Copenhagen 1843), noting especially that Part I represents melancholy and egoism characterized by the sympathy of dread, which in Part II is explained.

ORTEGA: "MAN HAS NO NATURE"

1 *Vide* my *Goethe desde dentro*, 1932.

2 Vide *Meditaciones del Quijote*, 1914. In this early book of mine it is already suggested that *I* am no more than one ingredient in that radical reality "my life," whose other ingredient is circumstance.

3 Be it recalled that the Stoics spoke of an "imagining of oneself." φαντασία ἑαυτοῦ.

HEIDEGGER: THE QUEST FOR BEING

[1] *ist es einem unheimlich.* Literally, "it is uncanny to one."

[2] *Nichtung.* The word "nihilation" has been coined in the hope of conveying Heidegger's meaning. His thought, which is also expressed in the verb *nichten* at the end of this paragraph and elsewhere, is very difficult to reproduce in the negative terms of its German formulation. *Nichtung* is a causative process, and *nichten* a causative and intransitive verb. Ordinarily we would express the process in positive terms and would speak, for instance, of the "becoming" of Nothing or the "de-becoming" of something, as would be clear in a term like *Nichtswerdung* or the *Entwerdung* of Meister Eckhart.

[3] Cf. "Tao Te Ching" XL: for though all creatures under heaven are the products of Being, Being itself is the product of Not-being. Trans.

[4] *Geworfenheit.* Literally "thrownness." M. Corbin, in his French version of this essay, renders the term by *déréliction*. The underlying thought would appear to be that in *Da-sein* we are "thrown there" and left derelict, like a thing cast up by the waves on the seashore.

[5] Here *Seiendes* has been translated by "being," with the proviso that it be understood as "being" in simple contrast to "not-being." Heidegger's *Sein* is always rendered as "Being" with a capital B.

[6] See note 5.

[7] Hölderlin, "Patmos."

SARTRE: EXISTENTIALISM

[1] *Négatités:* Sartre's word for kinds of human experience which blend negative and positive—such as absence, change, otherness, repulsion, regret, *etc.* [Translator]

[2] A "being-with" others in the world. [Translator]

[3] Sartre has explained earlier in *Being and Nothingness* that he will put the *of* in parentheses in such expressions as "consciousness of something" so as to show the lack of any real separation between consciousness and that which it is conscious of being. Consciousness is never, he reminds us, the same as knowledge. [Translator]

[4] Sartre's own word, meaning subject to sudden changes or transitions. [Translator]

[5] Nouvelle Revue Française.

6 *Je suis trop grand pour moi.*

7 *Il est devenu ce qu'il était.*
Tel qu'en lui-même enfin l'éternité le change.

8 *Cf. L'Imaginaire.* (Nouvelle Revue Française, 1939) Conclusion.

9 *Esquisse d'une théorie des émotions.* Hermann Paul. English: *The Emotions. Outline of a Theory.* Philosophical Library. 1948.

0 If it is indifferent whether one is in good faith or in self-deception, because self-deception reapprehends good faith and slides to the very origin of the project of good faith, that does not mean that we can not radically escape self-deception. But that supposes a self-recovery of being which was previously corrupted. This self-recovery we shall call authenticity, the description of which has no place here.

11 Racine's *Berenice.*

12 *Oignez vilain il vous plaindra, poignez vilain il vous oindra.*

SOURCES AND ACKNOWLEDGMENTS

DOSTOEVSKY: *Notes from Underground,* translated by Constance Garnett. Macmillan: Part One.

KIERKEGAARD: *Concluding Unscientific Postscript,* translated by David F. Swenson, completed after his death and provided with an Introduction and Notes by Walter Lowrie. Princeton University Press: pp. 164 ff. (for "On His Mission"); pp. 18-20, 25, 27, 29-31, 178-192 (for "Truth is Subjectivity").

————: *The Point of View,* etc., translated with Introduction and Notes by Walter Lowrie. Oxford University Press: pp. 42-53, 112-121, 130-132.

————: *The Concept of Dread,* translated by Walter Lowrie. Princeton University Press: pp. 37-41, 44, 45, 55.

————: *On Authority and Revelation: The Book on Adler, Or a Cycle of Ethico-Religious Essays,* translated by Walter Lowrie. Princeton University Press: pp. xviii, 105, 108-110, 116-118, 163, 168, 169.

NIETZSCHE: *The Portable Nietzsche,* selected and translated, with an Introduction, Prefaces, and Notes by Walter Kaufmann. The Viking Press: pp. 82, 95-99, 183-186.

————: Selections 1, 4, and 5, translated by Walter Kaufmann, appeared here for the first time.

RILKE: These selections, translated by Walter Kaufmann, appeared here for the first time.

KAFKA: "The Imperial Message" and "Couriers" are from *Parables.* "The Imperial Message" was translated by Willa and Edwin Muir and "Couriers" was translated by Clement Greenberg. Both are copyright 1946, 1947 by Schocken Books, Inc. *The Trial,* translated by Willa and Edwin Muir, Alfred A. Knopf, Inc.: pp. 268-278.

ORTEGA: *History as a System and Other Essays Toward a Philosophy of History* (1961), translated by Helene Weyl. W. W. Norton & Company, Inc.: pp. 111-113, 201-203, 215-217.

JASPERS: *Reason and Existenz*, translated by William Earle. Copyright 1955 by The Noonday Press: Chapters I and II. The first selection, "On My Philosophy," translated by Felix Kaufmann, appeared here for the first time. The original text is found in *Rechenschaft und Ausblick: Reden und Aufsätze*, R. Piper & Co., München.

HEIDEGGER: *On Time and Being*, translated by Joan Stambaugh. Harper & Row, Publishers, Inc.: pp. 74-82 ("My Way to Phenomenology").

————: *Existence and Being*, translated by R. F. C. Hull and Alan Crick. Henry Regnery Company (and Vision Press): pp. 325-361.

————: "The Way Back into the Ground of Metaphysics," translated by Walter Kaufmann, appeared here for the first time in English. The original text of *Was ist Metaphysik?* is published by Vittorio Klostermann, Frankfurt a. M.

SARTRE: *The Wall*, translated by Lloyd Alexander. Copyright 1948 by New Directions.

————: The second selection is from *Existential Psychoanalysis*, translated by Hazel Barnes and published by The Philosophical Library.

————: "Portrait of the Anti-Semite" was translated by Mary Guggenheim and published in *Partisan Review*, Spring, 1946. It is reprinted here by permission of Schocken Books, Inc. Copyright 1946.

————: The fourth selection, translated by Philip Mairet, first appeared in *Existentialism and Humanism*, Methuen & Co., Ltd., London.

————: *Search for a Method*, translated by Hazel Barnes. Alfred A. Knopf, Inc., (and Methuen & Co., Ltd.): pp. xxxiv, 6-35.

CAMUS: This selection, translated by Justin O'Brien, is reprinted from *The Myth of Sisyphus*, Copyright 1955 by Alfred A. Knopf, Inc.